The Rule of Law in Nascent Democracies

The Rule of Law in Nascent Democracies

Judicial Politics in Argentina

REBECCA BILL CHAVEZ

Stanford University Press
Stanford, California
2004

Stanford University Press
Stanford, California
www.sup.org

Library of Congress Cataloging-in-Publication Data

Chavez, Rebecca Bill.
The rule of law in nascent democracies : judicial politics in Argentina / Rebecca Bill Chavez.
p. cm.
ISBN 0-8047-4812-8 (alk. paper)
1. Rule of law. 2. Democracy. 3. Rule of law—Agentina—Mendoza (Province) 4. Mendoza (Argentina : Province)—Politics and government—Case studies. 5. Rule of law—Argentina—San Luis (Province) 6. San Luis (Argentina : Province)—Politics and government—Case studies. I. Title.
K3171.C49 2004
340'.11—dc22 2004001040

Printed in the United States of America on acid-free, archival-quality paper.

Original Printing 2004

Last figure below indicates year of this printing:
13 12 11 10 09 08 07 06 05 04

Designed and typeset at Stanford University Press in 10.5 / 12 Bembo.

To my parents Ann Marie and James Alban Bill
and my husband Pablo Lizárraga Chavez

Contents

List of Illustrations and Tables ix

Acknowledgments xi

Introduction 1

1. Constructing the Rule of Law 9

2. Argentina's Shifting Executive-Judicial Balance of Power 28

3. Monolithic Party Control and Critical Junctures: The Erosion of the Rule of Law under Perón and Menem 53

4. A Tale of Two Provinces: Judicial Autonomy in San Luis and Mendoza 80

5. Monolithic Party Control and Executive Dominance in San Luis 99

6. Party Competition and the Rule of Law in Mendoza 116

7. The Politics of Reform Coalitions 134

Conclusion: Competitive Politics and the Rule of Law in Presidential Systems 157

Appendix: A Spatial Model of Supreme Court Independence 167

Notes 171

Bibliography 217

List of Interviews 237

Index 243

Illustrations and Tables

Map of Argentina xvi

Figures

4.1 Changes in Supreme Court size in San Luis and Mendoza, 1983–2000 91
A.1 Spatial models of unified and divided government 168
A.2 The sequential game 169

Tables

1.1 Indicators of Executive Subordination of the Judiciary 26
2.1 Argentine Supreme Court Appointees, 1983–99 37
2.2 History of Informal Practices in Argentina, 1862–1999 50
3.1 Divided Government in Argentina, 1916–46 57
3.2 Monolithic Party Control in Argentina, 1946–83 60
3.3 Distribution of Senate Seats under Alfonsín, 1983–89 61
3.4 Distribution of House Seats under Alfonsín, 1983–89 61
3.5 Distribution of Senate Seats under Menem, 1989–98 62
3.6 Distribution of House Seats under Menem, 1989–99 63
3.7 Composition of the Impeachment Jury 74
4.1 Indicators of Executive Subordination of the Judiciary in San Luis and Mendoza 82
4.2 Compliance with Formal Rules: San Luis versus Mendoza 95
5.1 San Luis General Election Results, 1973–91 101
5.2 Unified Government in San Luis, 1983–2003 103
6.1 Divided Government in Mendoza, 1983–2003 119
6.2 The Judicial Council: San Luis versus Mendoza 128

Acknowledgments

I wish I could acknowledge by name everyone who has lent me a helping hand since I embarked on this project, but the list would be far too long. I have been blessed with extraordinary support networks in Argentina, at Stanford University, at the U.S. Naval Academy, and at home.

My fieldwork would have been fruitless without the help of a large and diverse group of Argentine activists, lawyers, politicians, judges, and scholars. In addition to the formal interviews, those who shared their personal stories over an *asado* or *mate* taught me much about the realities of the rule of law in Argentina. I am forever indebted to Luis Moreno Ocampo and Horacio Lynch, both of whom opened their offices, files, and minds to me. I also thank Carlos and Cristina Badano, Teresa Bittleston, Martín Coria, Josefina Dibilio, Ana Giordano, Graciela Groppa, Mariana Guisarri, Guillermo Jorge, Eduardo and Ana Lanari, Felipe Lanari, Valeria Palanza, Marcela Rizzo, Adrián Ventura, and Carolina Vidal Hahn. I am deeply appreciative of the generous assistance and friendship of Guillermo Molinelli who passed away before I completed this book. In San Luis, I learned much about the rule of law both as an abstract concept and as a political and social force. I am especially grateful to Gachi Rosso, Juanjo Laborda Ibarra, and Adriana Gallo. My sincere thanks also go to Alfredo Rehren and his family for opening their home to me in Santiago, Chile.

I owe much to a number of outstanding Stanford professors. I am especially indebted to Larry Diamond who encouraged me and gave me incisive feedback at each stage of this project. My interaction with Larry and with Terry Karl allowed me to learn from academics who produce scholarship without divorcing its meaning for real people across the globe. I thank Barry Weingast for introducing me to a new set of methodological tools and for being a constant source of intellectual support. David Abernethy, John Ferejohn, Seymour Martin Lipset, Robert Packenham, Philippe Schmitter, and Abraham Sofaer provided me with valuable and insightful input along the way. Stanford was also the source of lasting friendships. I would like to express my gratitude to Norma Alvarez, Liz Beaumont, Jennie Belissent, Brandice Canes-Wrone, Kathleen Collins, Erica Gould, Erin Jenne, Jeanette Lee-Oderman, Dave Lewis, Raul Madrid, Heather McCallum, Gretchen Sims, Harukata Takenaka, Sean Theriault, Shawn Treier, and the many other wonderful people who enriched my life at Stanford.

I owe a special debt to two leading scholars of Latin American politics, Forrest Colburn and Jorge Castañeda, who left permanent imprints on my heart and on my mind while I was an undergraduate at Princeton University. My gratitude also goes to my colleagues and friends at the United States Naval Academy for their encouragement, especially my colleagues in the Political Science Department. Special thanks go to Tom Bendel, Kurt Beyer, Chuck Cochran, Yong Deng, Linda Hull, Ellie Malone, Gale Mattox, William Miller, Arthur Rachwald, Perla Sasson-Henry, and Pam Schmitt. I deeply appreciate the unwavering support provided by my friends Carolyn Casey, Rachel Davidson, Melissa Hale, Charisse Kiino, Martha Moon, Thea Robertson, and Virginia Goss Tusher. I also want to thank the editors at Stanford University Press, especially Amanda Moran and Tony Hicks.

A number of institutions provided generous financial support for my endeavor. The Fulbright Foundation funded my first year-long trip to Argentina in 1994, which sparked my interest in the relationship between the rule of law and democratization. Grants from the Stanford University Department of Political Science, the Stanford Institute for International Studies, the Earhart Foundation, the Tinker Foundation, and the U.S. Naval Academy were also vital for various stages of this project. I am grateful to Alex Chafuen, Leonard Liggio, and Antony Sullivan who selflessly helped guide me through the competitive thickets of research support.

My greatest source of inspiration has been family. It was my parents and my brother Tim who taught me to think both critically and compassionately. Since my childhood, my parents have shared their love of other countries through stories of travel in the Middle East and life in Iran. They awoke in me the desire to learn about and from other cultures and societies. Special thanks go to my father, James Alban Bill, who is also a political scientist. Over the course of my life, my father's role has shifted from teacher to mentor to colleague. Writing this book gave me the opportunity to exchange ideas with him as a colleague—something I will cherish for the rest of my life.

Most importantly, I would like to thank my husband Pablo who has been an integral part of this book since its inception. He cheered me on every step of the way, and his warmth and sense of humor kept me on track. Without Pablo's love and unwavering support, I could never have completed this project.

The Rule of Law in Nascent Democracies

BOLIVIA
JUJUY
PARAGUAY
SALTA
FORMOSA
BRAZIL
CHILE
TUCUMÁN
CHACO
CATAMARCA
SANTIAGO
DEL
ESTERO
MISIONES
CORRIENTES
LA RIOJA
SANTA
FE
SAN JUAN
CÓRDOBA
ENTRE
RÍOS
PACIFIC
OCEAN
SAN
LUIS
URUGUAY
MENDOZA
Buenos Aires
BUENOS AIRES
LA PAMPA
NEUQUÉN
RÍO NEGRO
CHUBUT
ATLANTIC
OCEAN
SANTA CRUZ
Falkland Islands
(Islas Malvinas)
0
200
400 mi
0
300
600 km
TIERRA DEL FUEGO
N

Argentina

Introduction

DEMOCRACY IS under siege across much of Latin America. Economies have collapsed, political systems are floundering, and social structures are crumbling. Meanwhile, crime, corruption, and cynicism exacerbate the challenges facing democracy in the region. One need only turn to the constitutional crisis in Venezuela, the civil war in Colombia, the upheaval in Bolivia, and the economic and political uncertainty in Argentina to see that the much-lauded democratic transitions of the 1980s are at risk of reversal. In Latin America today, reversal means the gradual erosion of democratic rules, procedures, restraints, and norms.

The myopic focus on elections is partly to blame for the fragility of Latin America's democratic scaffolding. Competitive elections have masked the fact that other essential components of democracy have not taken root. For instance, weak political institutions and the remnants of authoritarianism have impeded the development of the rule of law in much of Latin America, resulting in "illiberal" or "delegative" democracies.[1] An effective rule of law constitutes an important bulwark against executive dominance and ensures that state actors comply with the constitution. Without the rule of law, democratic consolidation in Latin America and in nascent democracies elsewhere may never occur. This book seeks to explain how the rule of law emerges, how it survives, and ultimately how it shapes the democratic process over time.

The Rule of Law and Democracy

In a rule of law system, powerful state and private actors are subject to legality and are bound by the formal rules of the game. In theory, the rule of law and democracy go together. In practice, however, many new democracies have yet to construct the rule of law. The democratization pattern of most third wave nations has been very different from that of advanced industrialized countries.[2] In mature democracies such as the United States and those in Western Europe, the rule of law preceded or developed in tandem with democracy. The rule of law began to take shape in Europe between the fifteenth and eighteenth centuries when there were some small self-governing communes, limited republicanism, and a few representative institutions, but no democracy as we know it today. In Germany, the rule of law, *Rechtsstaat*, took root long before democracy. Notions of *Rechtsstaat* emerged in the seventeenth century, and by the end of the eighteenth century, Germany had established legal codes. In England, the rule of law developed during the early eighteenth century with Blackstone's legal codification.[3] In many emerging democracies, the sequence has been reversed. Countries such as Argentina, Russia, and Brazil instituted open electoral competition before developing autonomous judicial institutions that hold state actors accountable to the constitution. As a result, these nations confront the problem of whether democratic rules and procedures can be used to establish the rule of law.

This book examines the relationship between open elections and the rule of law, a nonelectoral dimension of democracy. It seeks to uncover the conditions under which fair and free elections yield judicial autonomy. Proponents of the Schumpeterian, minimalist conception of democracy, with its focus on procedure, classify countries as democratic based on the presence of free and competitive elections. Huntington, for instance, treats democracy as a dichotomous variable that depends on "the selection of leaders through competitive elections by the people they govern."[4] Such definitions do not consider important nonelectoral components of liberal democracy such as the rule of law and freedom of expression.[5] They are subject to what Karl calls the "fallacy of electoralism" or "the faith that merely holding elections will channel political action into peaceful contests among elites and accord public legitimacy to winners."[6]

In contrast to electoral democracy, the rule of law is a central requisite of liberal democracy. Liberal democracy demands rights that transcend elections and requires constraints on rulers. The rule of law constrains rulers by holding them accountable to those they govern. As Linz declares, "No *Rechtsstaat*, No democracy."[7] The rule of law helps ensure the supremacy of constitutions and the predictable, consistent application of law to all sectors of society, including the state. Despite the presence of elections, executive subordination of the judiciary persists in many Latin American nations where presidents are not subject to the law. Ultrapresidentialism stands in the way of the rule of law.

The rule of law enhances the quality and sustainability of democracy. According to Linz and Stepan, democratic consolidation requires an attitudinal component, meaning an enduring faith in democracy as the best form of government, and a constitutional component, defined as resolution of conflict according to the rule of law.[8] The rule of law is a necessary condition for the attitudinal as well as the constitutional component. Where rules are not applied consistently and predictably to all sectors of society including state actors, citizens' enduring commitment to democracy is unlikely. For instance, without a rule of law, government corruption and impunity can thrive, which undermines citizen faith in democracy.[9] Moreover, the rule of law has important normative implications for the quality of democracy. Diamond considers a rule of law under which all citizens are equal to be a cornerstone of liberal democracy. His ingredients of liberal democracy include the protection of civil liberties and protection from "unjustified detention, exile, terror, torture, and undue interference in the personal lives not only by the state but also by organized nonstate or antistate forces."[10] Without a rule of law to protect human rights, citizens are unlikely to value democracy, and its survival is at risk.

In the ultrapresidential systems of Latin America, the separation of powers, a requisite component of the rule of law, remains largely a fiction. Montesquieu's *The Spirit of the Laws* is the classic formulation of what is at stake in the separation of powers. In presidential systems, when the same person or body exercises executive, legislative, and judicial functions, tyranny is the outcome. Liberty is impossible if the judiciary is not autonomous:

> Nor is there liberty if the power of judging is not separate from legislative power and from executive power. If it were joined to legislative power, the power over the life and liberty of the citizens would be arbitrary, for the judge would be the legislator. If it were joined to the executive power, the judge could have the force of an oppressor.[11]

Hamilton echoes Montesquieu: "The accumulation of all powers, legislative, executive, and judiciary, in the same hands, whether of one, a few, or many, and whether hereditary, self-appointed, or elective, may justly be pronounced the very definition of tyranny."[12] In most of Latin America, democratic transitions have occurred, yet the judicial branch remains unable to place real constraints on the executive branch. Leaders have not taken advantage of the democratic opportunity to change the incentive structures that have encouraged the subordination of the courts. A politically malleable judiciary is one of the most entrenched obstacles in the way of the rule of law in Latin America.

This book considers patterns of power in the political, economic, and societal realms to explain how the rule of law emerges. It argues that the dispersal of political power among competing actors of comparable strength is a necessary condition for the rule of law. In other words, competitive politics fosters the rule of law. The dispersal of economic resources among members of a divided elite is one route to the requisite fragmentation of political power. In cases of convergent institutional and economic power, a reform coalition of nonstate actors can activate societal power, which fractures monopolies in the political realm.

Methodology and Case Selection

This book employs the comparative case study method to develop and refine hypotheses about how nascent democracies construct the rule of law. The research design couples a diachronic study of Argentina at the federal level with a synchronic comparison of two Argentine provinces, San Luis and Mendoza. By comparing across space, across time, and across regime type, this book explores the validity of the theory in three different ways. Argentina experienced varying levels of judicial independence during different phases in history, each of which is treated as a separate case. The comparative method over time generates theoretical propositions at the national level, which are subsequently tested and refined at the provincial level. After illustrating the mechanisms of executive control in Argentina, this study considers the presence or absence of these mechanisms in San Luis and Mendoza. The variations internal to Argentina demonstrate that the strength of the rule of law can vary within presidential systems, depending upon the level of party competition.

The in-depth case study is ideally suited to formulate and refine hypotheses on the construction of the rule of law because it is an area where remarkably little theorizing exists. Heuristic case studies permit the consideration of all possible variables, not only those with quantitative indicators. Eckstein writes, "The track record of case studies as stimulants to the theoretical imagination is good . . . Case studies permit intensive analysis that does not commit the researcher to a highly limited set of variables, and thus increases the possibility that critical variables and relations will be found."[13] Empirical data on particular political systems, in this case on Argentina at the federal level and the provinces of San Luis and Mendoza, constitute a critical building block for theory construction. Area-based knowledge can advance our understanding of the complex process of constructing the rule of law. The in-depth study of cases is central to "descriptive inference" that leads to an understanding of specific events and of their larger systematic patterns.[14] Detailed empirical data on Argentina, San Luis, and Mendoza complement the formulation of causal hypotheses.

Remaining within the Argentine context allows for a high degree of control. A focus on comparable cases using Mill's Method of Difference involves comparing cases that are similar in ways that are treated as parameters but dissimilar with regard to the dependent variable. This method allows one to locate explanatory variables.[15] Intraregional comparison mitigates the problem of comparing phenomena across diverse sociocultural contexts and therefore lends itself to the comparable case methodology.[16] Argentina at the national level, and San Luis and Mendoza at the provincial level, all share the legacy of Spanish colonialism, a tradition of civil law, and a history of executive dominance. In addition, San Luis and Mendoza are neighboring provinces in the Cuyo region of Argentina. Although the two provinces have many characteristics in common, they vary on the dependent variable, the rule of law.

This book synthesizes the inductive and the deductive modes of explanation. King, Keohane, and Verba advocate the interplay between induction and deduction: "[W]e need not have a complete theory before collecting data nor must our theory remain fixed throughout. Theory and data interact. As with the chicken and the egg, some theory is always necessary before data collection and some data are required before any theorizing."[17] In this book, the relationship between induction and deduction is interactive and takes the form of induction, followed by deduction, and then by induction. Empirical observations generate hypotheses that in turn are refined through deductive reasoning and tested on other cases. The comparative method demands data that come from observation and experience. The development of hypotheses does not take place in an empirical vacuum. Even Bueno de Mesquita, an ardent advocate of the deductive method of inquiry, recognizes that "theory construction always follows from our previous experience and observation."[18]

Argentina, a country ruled largely by individuals rather than by laws, is the theory-generating case. Argentina serves as the first case because it is representative of the ultrapresidentialism that is widespread throughout Latin America and in other nascent democracies such as Russia. Most third wave democracies were born with weak judiciaries. Argentina is a classic example of a country where democratic procedures were established prior to the creation of autonomous judicial institutions. The frequent inability of the Argentine judiciary to constrain the executive illuminates the challenges that confront other nations.

Argentina's experience with the rule of law since its independence from Spain indicates that executive subordination of the judiciary is not immutable and permits process tracing.[19] An understanding of the particular historical and social aspects of the Argentine case aids in the development of generalizable theory. Mann criticizes "static" theories of comparative sociologists: "[C]omparative analysis should also be *historical*. Each case develops temporally, and this dynamic itself must be part of our explanation of its structure."[20] Comparative history facilitates the formulation of causal inferences by allowing the researcher to develop an understanding of the uniqueness of each case and how the unique features impact the rule of law.[21]

The study of Argentina permits a diachronic comparison. Extending the analysis longitudinally increases the number of cases and allows comparison across time and across regime type. The relationship between Argentina's executive and judicial branches experienced four phases that are treated as separate cases: 1862 through Juan Domingo Perón's assumption of power in 1946, 1946 through the 1983 democratic transition, the post-transition administration of Raúl Alfonsín (1983–89), and the presidency of Carlos Menem (1989–99).

The shifting executive-judicial balance of power across the four phases illustrates that the construction of the rule of law is not a linear process. An analysis of the Argentine case over time shows that there are moments of regression away from as well as progress toward the rule of law. For instance, the years 1946 and 1989 were key moments of regression. Moreover, from 1983 through 1999, two presidents governed Argentina, one who used the democratic opportunity to begin constructing autonomous judicial institutions and the other who dismantled them. Under Alfonsín, signs that Argentina was moving toward an independent judiciary appeared for the first time since 1946. In contrast, when Menem assumed power in 1989, he retreated from the steps taken by his predecessor and fundamentally weakened the courts.

After developing hypotheses on the national level, this book turns to the provincial level. In contrast to statistical methods that are susceptible to the "whole-nation bias," the comparative method demands careful selection of cases that fit a specific research problem. Such selection is conducive to the analysis of subnational cases.[22] Argentina's federal structure provides a multitude of cases for analysis. Each of Argentina's twenty-four provinces has its own judicial branch that can be treated as a discrete system. Moreover, each of the twenty-four judiciaries reflects a different degree of autonomy.

The Argentine provinces of San Luis and Mendoza serve as contrasting cases. They lie at different ends of the judicial autonomy continuum. Comparison facilitates the identification of the explanatory variables behind the province of Mendoza's relative success in constructing the rule of law. The two provinces demonstrate that systems of horizontal accountability governed by similar constitutional rules can function very differently. Competitive politics is as important at the provincial level as it is at the national level. Patterns of executive dominance that have existed at the national level in Argentina have been replicated in San Luis but have broken down in Mendoza.

Fieldwork was central to this study. The dearth of secondary resources demanded four research trips to Argentina beginning in 1998. While living first in Buenos Aires and then in San Luis and Mendoza, I established the requisite network of contacts for personal interviews and primary source material. I ultimately gained access to opposition and ruling parties at both the federal and provincial levels. I conducted over two hundred interviews. On the federal level and in both provinces, I interviewed current and former Supreme Court justices and lower court judges, members of the legislative and the executive branches, journalists, academics, lawyers, and civil society actors who focus their efforts on judicial reform. This diverse group of actors provided the rare access that is indispensable for the success of such a project. The ruling party in San Luis was the most difficult to penetrate, but the governor's coterie eventually spoke candidly with me. My primary sources included newspaper archives, congressional records, court rulings, personal archives of key actors, and reports of civil society actors.

Overview of the Book

This book proceeds as follows. Chapter 1 defines the rule of law and relates it to judicial autonomy. Next, the chapter traces the roots of executive subordination of the courts in Latin America to Spanish colonialism and the civil law tradition. It then delves into how patterns of power in the political, economic, and societal realms impact the rule of law. It lays out the theory of competitive politics as a necessary condition for the rule of law. In particular, it shows how political party competition fosters the rule of law. Finally, Chapter 1 delineates five indicators that determine a country's level of judicial autonomy and demonstrates how informal practices that permit executive subordination of the courts can overshadow formal rules that call for judicial independence.

Chapters 2 and 3 focus on Argentina at the national level. By tracing Argentina's history of judicial autonomy, Chapter 2 shows that the construction of the rule of law has not been a linear process. Chapter 3 analyzes two critical junctures in Argentine history: the years 1946 and 1989. It demonstrates how unified government coupled with party discipline allowed first Perón and later Menem to strip countervailing power centers including the judiciary of their autonomy and therefore of the capacity to check executive power.

Chapter 4 turns from the federal to the provincial level. It first demonstrates how the fragmentation of economic resources in Mendoza fostered judicial autonomy early in the province's history, whereas the concentration of economic power in the hands of a unified elite contributed to executive subordination of the courts in San Luis. Next, the chapter uses the five indicators of executive subordination of the courts delineated in Chapter 1 to show that San Luis and Mendoza lie at opposite ends of the judicial independence continuum.

Chapter 5 illustrates how the combination of unified government and strict party discipline in San Luis undermined the ability of not only the legislature and the judiciary but of all potential agencies of horizontal accountability to check the governor. Chapter 6 shifts to Mendoza where competition among three relevant political parties fostered the emergence of an effective system of horizontal accountability that includes an autonomous judiciary.

Chapter 7 explores the role of reform coalitions in Menem's Argentina and in the two provinces. It focuses on how the push from below and outside helped fracture Menem's monopoly on power in Argentina and how it has begun to disperse power in San Luis. The concluding chapter reviews the major hypotheses and empirical findings before demonstrating that the theory put forth in this study has the potential to travel to other Latin America countries and beyond. It applies the theory to other Argentine provinces, to Chile and the United States at the federal level, and to the state of Louisiana in the hope of encouraging future research on these cases as well as on other regions of the world.

CHAPTER 1

Constructing the Rule of Law

A COMPLETE STORY about how emerging democracies construct the rule of law must address patterns of power in the political, economic, and societal realms. The balanced dispersal of political power is a necessary condition for the rule of law. The distribution of economic resources among members of a divided elite is one path to the requisite political fragmentation. Countries that are characterized by a concentration of both political and economic power are not, however, necessarily trapped without a rule of law. A reform coalition of nonstate actors can activate societal power, which fractures monopolies in the political realm.

This chapter begins with a definition of the rule of law. Although the rule of law cannot be reduced to judicial independence, judicial autonomy serves as an indicator of the rule of law in ultrapresidential systems. Section II traces the roots of the weak rule of law in Latin America to Iberian colonialism and the region's civil law tradition. Section III lays out the theoretical framework of this book, explaining how the balanced dispersal of power among competing institutional actors contributes to the construction of the rule of law. In particular, the section shows how competition among political parties fosters the rule of law. After explaining the importance of competitive politics, it demonstrates how patterns of power in the economic and societal realms impact the rule of law. Section IV explores how to determine the degree of judicial autonomy in a given country. It demonstrates how informal practices can allow presidents to control the courts, overshadowing formal guarantees of judicial independence. These informal practices serve as indicators of a subordinate judiciary.

Judicial Autonomy as an Indicator of the Rule of Law

The rule of law is a broad concept that encompasses many areas including judicial autonomy, access to justice, human rights, and property rights. It entails the equality of all citizens under the law and predictability in the application of laws, rules, and regulations. Although political scientists increasingly list the rule of a law as a critical element of liberal democracy, they seldom define, seriously examine, or empirically research the concept. Merryman's definition provides a starting point: the rule of law is "a system of government in which the acts of agencies and officials of all kinds are subject to the principle of legality, and in which procedures are available to interested persons to test the legality of governmental action and to have an appropriate remedy when the act in question fails to pass the test."[1] Scholars often limit their definition of the rule of law to constraints on state actors.[2] A complete definition must go a step further. The rule of law requires that not only state agents but that any individual or sector that exercises significant power be subject to legality. Otherwise, these actors can use their economic or political power to violate the formal rules of the game.

Threats to the rule of law can come from a diverse group of powerful actors that includes executive functionaries, legislators, military officials, wealthy businesspeople, religious leaders, and labor union representatives. Any actor who wields political, economic, or military power must submit to the law: "[The rule of law] meant that the respective heads of each body would be bound by the law which they themselves had enacted; they could change it lawfully, but until they did so they must obey it—they must rule *under* law."[3] In cases of concentration of power in a single person or group, however, there is no way to ensure that those who wield power will act within the law. Instead, the individual or group can make, change, and enforce laws but is not bound by those laws.[4]

The rule of law requires an effective system of horizontal accountability that is composed of government institutions that hold one another accountable to the law and to the public. Such a system is necessary to check arbitrary government actions and to ensure that state actors comply with the constitution. As O'Donnell argues, horizontal accountability is a critical ingredient of democracy:

> In institutionalized democracies, accountability runs not only vertically, making elected officials answerable to the ballot box, but also horizontally, across a network of relatively autonomous powers (i.e., other institutions) that can call into question, and eventually punish, improper ways of discharging the responsibility of a given official.[5]

State agencies with the autonomy, the authority, and the will to act as controls on other government agencies and on the private sector are a necessary condition for horizontal accountability. Where power is dispersed and embedded in multiple institutions that act as horizontal accountability agencies, the rule of law is possible. Without these agencies, dominant actors have little or no incentive to relinquish power but rather have incentives to ignore or eliminate these institutions. An independent judicial branch is part of a larger system of overlapping and mutually reinforcing agencies of horizontal accountability.

An independent judiciary on its own is not enough to ensure the rule of law, but it can help in the construction by binding powerful actors. In addition to being efficient, accessible, well-funded, and well-staffed, the courts must be independent from all actors that tend to monopolize power. In order to function as a horizontal accountability agency, the judiciary cannot be subordinate to the other branches of government, to the military, or to powerful elements of the private sector. An independent judiciary can help build the rule of law by guaranteeing that those who wield power submit to the rules. Only a judiciary that is independent of pressure, inducement, and manipulation can check abuses of power. Judicial independence requires impartiality and "political insularity."[6] Judges must not be biased in favor of or fear to challenge the powers that be. In the context of Latin American ultrapresidentialism, judges must have the capacity to act as controls on the executive branch.

Without effective constraints such as an independent judiciary, countries are trapped in what Weingast calls "asymmetric equilibrium." Here, the sovereign, or the executive branch in the Latin American context, has incentives to transgress formal limits on its power.[7] Williamson argues that ex ante arrangements ensuring compliance with formal limits can prevent costly ex post opportunistic behavior or shirking. In his discussion of transaction cost economics, he writes, "Rather than reply to opportunism in kind, therefore, the wise prince [i.e., the governing regime] is one who seeks both to give and receive 'credible commitments.' Incentives may be realigned, and/or superior governance structures within which to organize transactions may be devised."[8] An autonomous judicial branch is one institutional means of organizing transactions to achieve credible commitments and to prevent transgressions. By placing costs on ex post opportunism, an independent judiciary creates incentives that discourage abuses of power.

England prior to the Glorious Revolution and Old Regime France illustrate the negative consequences of the failure to develop independent judicial institutions. These historical cases are predecessors of today's nascent democracies that have yet to construct the rule of law. North and Weingast use the case of England prior to 1689 to demonstrate the disastrous effects of failing to limit the Crown's authority. Until the Revolution Settlement, an elite pact that served as a coordinating device, sovereign transgressions were common. The Revolution Settlement introduced parliamentary supremacy, abolished many royal powers, and established the rule of law. The development of a constitution that established the supremacy of common law effectively tied the king's hands.[9] Root shows that only with the creation of institutions capable of checking the king's power was France able to establish the conditions necessary for economic and political stability.[10] As seventeenth century England and Old Regime France illustrate, institutions condition the behavior of governments. In particular, autonomous judicial institutions can compel powerful state actors to govern according to law.

The threats to the rule of law vary across and within regions. Different countries face different dangers depending on where economic and political power is concentrated. In the England described by North and Weingast and the France described by Root, the Crown represented the principal danger. In Russia and in much of Latin America, a major challenge is the presidency, which may be elected democratically but is thereafter subject to few constraints.[11] In contrast, in Iran, the elected president does not have authority over the judiciary. Instead, the *faqih*, the leader of the clerics who control the judiciary, represents the real threat to the rule of law. In Pakistan, the military and extremist religious groups represent a challenge.[12] In many developing countries, members of the private sector with a monopoly on the means of production are a major threat.

Variation also exists within regions. For most of Latin America, the major challenge to the rule of law is no longer a military coup, yet in Venezuela the armed forces remain a potential hazard alongside the executive. In Colombia, drug lords and guerilla and paramilitary groups present a danger. Across Latin America as a region, however, the concentration of power in the president is a principal challenge to the rule of law. As a result of executive supremacy, other state actors lack effective checks on the president.

The Peculiar Pattern of Latin America

In Latin America, the executive branch, dominated by the presidency, represents a principal threat to the rule of law. Judicial subordination to executive interests is a major obstacle to fair and predictable application of the law. Across most of the region, the executive overshadows both the legislative and judicial branches. The roots of this ultrapresidentialism can be found in the colonial era.[13] The dependent judiciaries of Latin America reflect political engineering whereby the informal processes of power remained in place with the formal-legal organization existing as political camouflage.

The concentration of power is a legacy of European colonialism. Spanish, Portuguese, French, and Dutch colonial patterns of power set nations on a trajectory that discouraged political pluralism in favor of control by a dominant group.[14] In contrast to the British in North America, the Spanish did not install a system of checks and balances. Instead, power relations encouraged the king's arbitrary dominance. Because the Spanish did not establish representative institutions, the colonies lacked countervailing power centers to offset the monarch's absolute power. The Crown built an elaborate bureaucracy to control colonial administrators. In order to stifle opposition, the Crown used the *residencia*, a review of administrators' conduct, and the *visita*, a secret judicial inquiry into officials who challenged the Crown. In 1524, Spain established the Council of Indies that served as the colonies' administrative board, legislative body, and appeals court. The Council was subordinate to the king and combined executive, legislative, and judicial powers as well as military and religious authority; there was no separation of powers.[15]

Viceroys loyal to the Crown carried out the Council's policies. The viceroy was a single official who exercised executive, legislative, and judicial powers. The viceroy had broad authority to collect taxes, maintain public order, set fiscal policy, and defend against military attacks. As head of the Real Audiencia, the highest court, the viceroy could order punishments and administer sentences. Moreover, the Crown used its discretion over who served in the *audiencias*, the lower courts, to appoint judges who protected its interests. In addition, judicial decisions lacked transparency; they were secret because the monarch was considered to be infallible.[16]

The constitutions that replaced the Spanish system reflect Spain's monarchical tradition in that they contain provisions for dominant executives. Although the framers of Latin America borrowed heavily from the U.S. Constitution, most Latin American constitutions privilege the executive over Congress.[17] In the Spanish system, the Crown silenced opposition from the elected members of parliament.[18] Latin American presidents continued this pattern of stifling congressional opposition. Executive supremacy, an extension of *caudillismo*, hindered the development of an autonomous legislature with the power to check the president. In addition, although the constitutions of Latin America provide for civil liberties, they permit the executive to suspend individual and group rights in times of national emergency.[19] Indeed, Latin American presidents have often resorted to emergency powers and have frequently bypassed Congress altogether.

The civil law tradition has further undermined the judiciary's power relative to the executive. Civil law in Latin America privileges the executive over the courts. Law is supposed to be written with enough clarity to render judicial interpretation unnecessary. Unlike common law countries where judges participate in policymaking, civil law judges are perceived as functionaries who apply laws made by others.[20] The French civil law tradition had a deep impact in Latin America beginning in the late eighteenth century. At the time of the French Revolution, scandal plagued France's judiciary and the demand for judicial reform was high. The French model was a reaction to widespread distrust of judges who were associated with the landed aristocracy and who had opposed progressive legislation. Reformers sought to prevent judicial interference in executive and legislative functions.[21]

Civil law has a long tradition in Latin America. It has become embedded in society and culture:

> [I]t is a set of deeply rooted, historically conditioned attitudes about the nature of law, about the role of law in the society and the polity, about the proper organization and operation of a legal system, and about the way law is or should be made, applied, studied, perfected, and taught. The legal tradition relates the legal system to the culture of which it is a partial expression.[22]

Edelmann explains, "It was as much a part of the Iberian culture in the New World as was the use of the Spanish and Portuguese languages . . . The civil law was as firmly rooted there by the time of independence as was the English common law in the 13 colonies that formed the United States."[23] Civil law continues to influence the views and behavior of Latin American judges today. Latin American legal education reinforces the civil law tradition by promoting a restricted idea of judicial functions. Law students learn to memorize codes rather than to interpret laws. The belief that judges merely apply law has proved resilient.

The combination of the colonial legacy and the civil law tradition has undercut the rule of law in Latin America. Iberian colonialism set the stage for ultrapresidentialism; civil law contributed to executive dominance. In much of the region, the judiciary lacks the status and authority to constrain the president's abuse of power. Thus, the fortification of old or the creation of effective new controls on presidential power is necessary to clear the way for the rule of law.

The Balanced Dispersal of Power and the Rule of Law

How is the rule of law constructed where it has not previously existed? Fundamentally, this is a question of power. This book employs three models of dispersed power to explain how the rule of law emerges. It addresses patterns of power in the political, economic, and societal realms. The first model specifies a necessary condition for the rule of law: the balanced dispersal of institutional power. In Latin America, political party competition can be the catalyst for competing institutional power centers. Competitive politics fosters the rule of law. The second and third models specify the mechanisms to reach the requisite fragmentation of power in the political realm. In the second model, the historical dispersal of economic resources and interests sets the stage for competitive politics. Differences in economic development and the resulting elite competition or collusion impact the level of political competition. The third model requires a reform coalition of nonstate actors that employs societal power to fracture institutional power. The three models are not mutually exclusive and can interact in a sequence. Either a dispersal of economic power or the formation of a reform coalition can lead to a balanced dispersal of institutional power.

THE BALANCED DISPERSAL OF INSTITUTIONAL POWER: PARTY COMPETITION AND THE RULE OF LAW

The initial construction of the rule of law requires the balanced dispersal of institutional power, defined as a balance of power between at least two political actors of comparable strength with competing interests. Due to the plurality of strong interests, the emergence of state institutions that check and balance one another is likely. For instance, in a competitive environment, the judiciary can emerge as an arbiter among political actors rather than as a tool held exclusively by a single dominant actor. In Latin America where the executive is the primary threat to the rule of law, the creation of competing rather than converging institutional power centers can draw power away from the president, thereby creating the conditions for the rule of law.

Party competition can be the key mechanism for the fragmentation of political power. The rule of law is in part a product of a balance of power between at least two political parties, neither of which sustains monolithic control, meaning that no highly disciplined party sustains control of both the legislative and executive branches. Party balance and a low level of discipline create a climate in which horizontal accountability agencies emerge. The executive is unable to prevent their emergence and may even see advantages in creating agencies with the autonomy and resources necessary to act as controls.

A competitive party system encourages frequent rotation of the party in power and divided government, both of which permit the legislature to check the president. Divided government makes it difficult for an executive to subvert horizontal accountability agencies. Without a majority in Congress, a president cannot push through legislation that undermines the ability of control organs to serve as checks.[24] Electoral laws and the number of parties play a role in determining whether there is divided government. For instance, when there are more than two relevant parties, divided government is likely. Moreover, when three or more parties of comparable strength have representation in the legislature, coalition government is likely and the executive finds it especially difficult to dismantle countervailing power centers. Electoral rules that call for nonsimultaneous legislative and executive elections or that call for partial reelection of the legislative branch also foster divided government.[25]

Whereas divided government means that the executive *cannot* eliminate agencies that check its power, rotation of the party in power means that the executive *does not want to* eliminate these agencies. A ruling party that foresees that it will be displaced in the future has incentives to fortify countervailing power centers, including the judiciary. Such displacement is always possible under what Przeworski calls the "institutionalized uncertainty" of democracy.[26] When there is real party competition, the ruling party knows that it could find itself in the opposition and therefore needs the protection of an autonomous judiciary and other countervailing power centers. The agencies that protect the opposition today may protect the ruling party tomorrow when it becomes the opposition.

In contrast to party competition, monolithic party control, defined as a prolonged period of unified government under a highly disciplined party, stands in the way of the rule of law. A single, highly disciplined party that controls both the legislative and executive branches can strip horizontal accountability agencies of their autonomy and therefore of their ability to check the executive. Monolithic party control increases the president's ability to pass laws that permit executive subordination of organs of control, including the courts. Strict party discipline exacerbates the effects of unified government by increasing the executive's partisan powers.[27] Without party discipline, copartisanship is insufficient to ensure legislative acquiescence to the executive's will. Unified government occurs at times in virtually all presidential democracies but does not necessarily undermine the system of checks and balances. Legislators and the executive of the same party may have countervailing ambitions. By compelling legislators to respond to the executive rather than to their constituents, strict discipline eliminates competing executive-legislative preferences.

Discipline is in part a function of nomination and election procedures. Closed party lists, for instance, encourage discipline because of party leaders' influence over a candidate's chances at reelection. Presidents who are also party leaders can use their discretion over placement on the ballot to punish or reward legislators. Other potential resources at the president's disposal include control over access to party financing and influence over congressional committee assignments.

Together, unified government and party discipline permit the executive to dismantle an effective system of horizontal accountability. With the help of his or her party, the president can manipulate the institutional design of horizontal accountability agencies to prevent them from acting as checks. For instance, by changing the appointment and removal process for agency members, the president can eliminate opposition representation. Congress can pass legislation that permits the president to appoint pliant individuals to the agencies. In contrast, party competition contributes to the agencies' effectiveness by encouraging transparency and depoliticization in appointments and insulation from subsequent government interference. When horizontal accountability agencies are the seat of significant power resources and are controlled by the opposition, or at least not by loyalists of the ruling party, they can act as controls on the executive.

In Latin America, along with legislative and judicial branches, potential countervailing power centers that help ensure the rule of law include the Consejo de la Magistratura (Judicial Council), Jurado de Enjuiciamiento (Impeachment Jury), Fiscalía de Estado (Office of the State Prosecutor), Tribunal de Cuentas (Accounting Tribunal), and Ministerio Público (Attorney General's Office). Many Latin American countries recently created a Judicial Council and an Impeachment Jury that intervene in the appointment and removal of judges with the goal of reducing executive control over court composition.[28] The State Prosecutor has the power to challenge the constitutionality of any government act. The Accounting Tribunal has the authority to audit government accounts. The public prosecutors of the Attorney General's Office initiate proceedings against public officials and agencies suspected of illegal practices, an especially important function in the many Latin American countries with high levels of government corruption and traditions of executive impunity. In theory, each of these agencies has the power to serve as a countervailing power center. However, like the judiciary, in order to fulfill their constitutional roles as control organs, these five agencies must be independent of the executive branch.

FRAGMENTATION OF ECONOMIC POWER: ONE PATH TO COMPETITIVE POLITICS

What are the historical roots of the rule of law? Socioeconomic complexity increases the likelihood of disputes that pave the way for the emergence of countervailing power centers. The historical dispersal of economic resources among a divided elite contributes to competitive politics. When there is a plurality of strong economic actors in competition with one another, they require a secure way to protect property rights, to enforce contracts, and to mediate economic disputes. Competing economic groups that vie for power push for a mechanism of adjudication. For instance, when certain groups base their livelihood upon agriculture, others on industry, and others on mineral extraction, an autonomous judiciary is likely to emerge. Balanced competition within sectors also fosters the rule of law.

Competing economic power centers facilitate the emergence of the rule of law. Climate and geography help determine the concentration of land ownership and the likelihood of disputes. Because they require a referee to produce peaceful adjudication, property disputes create pressure for the rule of law. Schubert contrasts the nomadic Cheyenne Indians of the nineteenth century and the pre-World War II Barotse farmers of Northern Rhodesia. Unlike the roving Indians whose need for an arbiter was minimal, disputes over property rights were common among the Barotse farmers and led to demand for a legal system.[29] Sociologists Schwartz and Miller found that societies with the least developed legal institutions were the "simplest" with the lowest degree of economic specialization. The "mediationless" societies had no need to institutionalize mechanisms of dispute settlement. The authors attribute the absence of mediation to a lack of substantial property: "There is much evidence to support the hypothesis that property provides something to quarrel about."[30] In Europe, the introduction of powerful new economic actors set the stage for the rule of law. Tocqueville reflects on how democracy advanced as asset ownership expanded from a small group of landholders to include the clergy and eventually the "commoners." Tocqueville points to the "general leveling" as land distribution patterns shifted away from a feudal structure. He also highlights the equalizing effects of the wars that "decimated the nobles and divided their possessions."[31]

In contrast, the concentration of assets stands in the way of the rule of law; there is no need for a body to adjudicate. In countries where a dominant elite is coherent and unified, concentrated ownership of the means of production obstructs the emergence of a neutral referee. Tocqueville recalls the concentration of assets in the hands of the oligarchy that characterized France before the establishment of the rule of law:

> I look back for a moment on the situation of France seven hundred years ago when the territory was divided among a small number of families, who were the owners of the soil and the rulers of the inhabitants; the right of governing descended with the family inheritance from generation to generation; force was the only means by which man could act on man; and landed property was the sole source of power.[32]

Like the France that Tocqueville describes, a unified group with a monopoly on economic power and a coherent set of interests characterized the early history of many third wave democracies.

The monopoly on economic resources early in Latin American history exacerbated the monopoly on political power. Plantation- and resource-based development characterized most Iberian colonies. In predatory resource-based economies like Venezuela and in plantation-based economies like Mexico, the concentration of economic power shaped political institutions; politics became the province of the rich. With the exception of Costa Rica and Uruguay, ownership of enormous tracts of land was the norm. Latin American sugar, cotton, and tobacco producers benefited from economies of scale.[33] In addition, Latin America inherited the Spanish system of primogeniture, which further encouraged asset concentration. Tocqueville explains that primogeniture linked family and power in a system that "unites, draws together, and vests property and power in a few hands; it causes an aristocracy, so to speak, to spring out of the ground." In contrast, Tocqueville observes that the abolition of primogeniture in the United States helped to "divide, distribute, and disperse both property and power."[34]

Although concentration of economic and political power continued to characterize most of Latin America after independence from Spain, there has been variation within the region. In Costa Rica, Uruguay, and Chile, economic power was dispersed among a divided elite, which set the stage for a deconcentration of political power and for the establishment of the rule of law. The economic development of Costa Rica and Uruguay was not plantation-based but rather featured small yeoman farmers and ranchers. In contrast to most of Latin America where a small number of actors controlled vast tracts of land, in Costa Rica and Uruguay, land was divided among a larger number of actors. Because both countries lacked a landless labor force to exploit, subsistence farming was the norm. In Costa Rica, the dearth of slaves and the decimation of the indigenous population precluded the development of a landed elite with large haciendas.[35]

In Chile's diversified economy, competing economic actors of comparable strength had to bargain with one another. Like its neighbors in Latin America, Chile had a landed elite. However, the landed elite in Chile did not have a monopoly on power. Instead, it competed with a strong manufacturing-based elite and the nascent mineral-based elite. These three sectors with distinct bases of economic power demanded secure contracts and enforceable laws, and they secured equal access to a paternalistic state. This fragmentation of economic power helped set the stage for pluralism in political institutions. Today Costa Rica, Uruguay, and Chile have the strongest non-presidential political institutions in Latin America.

Colonial patterns of economic power in the United States and Asia were very different from those in most of Latin America. The fragmentation of economic power that paved the way for the rule of law was a consequence of colonialism in the U.S. and in parts of Asia. As in Costa Rica and Uruguay, climate and geography did not provide a basis for a landed elite in the United States. According to Tocqueville,

> [T]he soil of America was opposed to a territorial aristocracy. It was realized that in order to clear this land, nothing less than the constant and self-interested efforts of the owner himself were essential; the ground prepared, it became evident that its produce was not sufficient to enrich at the same time both an owner and a farmer. The land was then naturally broken up into small portions, which the proprietor cultivated for himself.[36]

In order to control their Asian colonies, Japanese colonists broke up large landholdings. Furthermore, after the Japanese occupation, the United States promoted extensive land reform in much of Asia, which further dispersed economic power. In stark contrast to the Spanish in Latin America, colonists in countries such as Taiwan and Korea made a concerted effort to fracture the link between land and power.

The challenges to the rule of law are greatest where both economic and political power are concentrated in the hands of a single, unified group. When the economic elite overlaps with the political elite, it is easy for that overlapping elite to ignore formal rules. Where the executive has a monopoly on both political and economic power, as is the case in much of Latin America, the executive can use its resources to stifle opposition. For instance, the government can use its economic power to finance political campaigns, to control the press by purchasing newspapers, and to practice clientelism. Under these conditions, the challenge is to break the nexus of economic and political power.

REFORM COALITIONS: THE MOBILIZATION OF SOCIETAL POWER

Another path to dispersed political power lies outside of the state apparatus. The mobilization of a reform coalition draws from societal power to disperse resources away from the executive. A network of nonstate actors that pressures for institutional reform can serve as the catalyst for the fragmentation of political power. The coalition can incorporate a diverse set of actors that includes domestic civil society groups, international organizations, and the mass media. The push from below and outside can fracture the monopoly on power.

The formation of a reform coalition is a dynamic process. In Keck and Sikkink's model, members coalesce around a shared value and focus on issues that involve "principled ideas" about what is right and wrong. The transnational network attributes the wrong to an intentional act of an identifiable actor.[37] The success of a coalition with the goal of bolstering the rule of law depends in part on its ability to demonstrate that the executive took deliberate steps to weaken the courts. In order to expand coalition membership, coalition members must show that a pliant judiciary undermines shared values such as human rights and economic development. For instance, the coalition could attract business groups by highlighting the importance of judicial autonomy for property rights. Other actors that value an independent judicial branch include lawyers, prosecutors, judges, and members of human rights organizations.

Dense, well-organized coalitions with strong leadership, access to information, and the ability to disseminate that information are most effective. Individual activists including representatives from within the judiciary itself, from academic institutions, and from civil society can provide the leadership. These leaders formulate coalition strategy and provide technical proposals to help implement reform. Their power comes from their knowledge and expertise and from their deep commitment to the rule of law.[38] They play a central role in recruiting members and in coordinating the activity of the coalition's diverse components.

A strong, well-organized domestic civil society is an essential foundation for a reform coalition. Civil society consists of organized groups that seek to influence government policy and are autonomous from the state and from political parties. The individuals who comprise civil society act "collectively in the public sphere to express their interests, passions, and ideas, exchange information, achieve mutual goals, make demands on the state, and hold officials accountable."[39] A variety of local civil society groups that represent different sectors can mobilize broad societal demand for reform. Civil society organizations can contribute to the rule of law in a number of ways. They can act as watchdogs that expose executive subordination of the judiciary. They can lobby legislators, call strikes, and stage protests. Domestic civil society groups can also disseminate information to international organizations, thereby encouraging foreign actors to join the coalition. Consciousness about violations of the rule of law typically enters domestic civil society before the network expands to include international actors. The involvement of local activists legitimizes the participation of foreign groups.[40]

Coalitions are most effective when they transcend national borders. Foreign government agencies and international organizations raise awareness about challenges to the rule of law and pressure countries to strengthen the judiciary relative to the executive branch. When local groups acting on their own are unable to influence the state, they can forge linkages to powerful international organizations. In order to recruit outside support, domestic groups must demonstrate the absence of the rule of law by documenting and condemning abuses. Access to advanced technology can overcome the obstacles of geographic distance, facilitating the exchange of information across national borders. In addition, the issue must resonate in order to spur foreign actors to participate. Keck and Sikkink argue that this scenario sets the stage for the "boomerang pattern" in which domestic groups turn to their international contacts to exert pressure on their government. Foreign pressure counters the government's unresponsiveness to domestic groups.[41]

When the target is vulnerable to material pressure, external actors can use leverage to pressure for change. Material leverage is a means of imposing a reform agenda when the target country requires outside economic assistance.[42] International organizations can employ aid conditionality or impose sanctions on countries that do not implement desired reforms. International actors can also provide valuable financial or technical aid to strengthen judicial institutions. External assistance can also take the form of bolstering domestic civil society groups that in turn push for judicial autonomy from within the country.[43]

International influence, however, can have positive, negative, or negligible effects, depending on the nature of the intervention and on the domestic context. Successful intervention requires long-term, low profile implementation and the support and collaboration of domestic groups. Moreover, external actors' ability to play a meaningful role in the reform coalition is greatest when their policies are pursued consistently. When multiple foreign actors seek to influence policy in a given country, their efforts are most fruitful if there is coordination and agreement among them. When the organizations share an immediate interest or an overriding objective, coordination is likely.[44]

This book expands upon the notion of a transnational network by showing the potential for an intranational advocacy network. It applies Keck and Sikkink's framework within the borders of a single nation. When the target is a subnational unit, national civil society groups and the federal government of the nation in which the target is embedded can be central elements in the coalition. Civil society groups based in other provinces and the federal government can play the role of external actors in a coalition that pushes for reform at the provincial level. They function like foreign actors in the boomerang pattern scenario. When the unit of analysis is a province or state, the province can be treated as a discrete system with boundaries.

The national government can use leverage to exert pressure on a state or province. It can instigate change on the provincial level through economic pressure or through direct federal intervention. Several factors determine whether the federal government will exercise this role. For instance, if the president and the governor are of the same party, the national executive is unlikely to intervene. On the other hand, if opposing parties control the national and provincial governments, the federal government is more likely to pressure for change. In addition, the federal government's capacity to exert economic pressure on local government depends on the province's level of financial dependence on the central government.

The collection and dissemination of information are essential building blocks of an effective reform strategy. A free and pluralistic press can raise awareness of the challenges to the rule of law and draw civil society into the coalition. Tocqueville highlights the relationship between newspapers and civil society. He argues that more newspapers lead to more civic associations.[45] In his study of Italy, Putnam finds that citizens who read newspapers are more likely to participate in civil society units.[46] When the reform coalition seeks to strengthen the rule of law, independent newspapers, television programs, and radio programs can expose abuses that undermine judicial autonomy.[47] By raising awareness of abuses, the press fosters the formation of civil society groups committed to the struggle for the rule of law.

The government can impede the media's role as a watchdog if it threatens journalists with violence, arrest, or defamation suits. If the government owns newspapers or television stations, it can act as a censor. In addition, favoritism in government advertising affects the role of the press. By withholding advertising, the government can make it difficult for independent papers to survive. The international media as well as the local press can pressure for reform. By focusing attention on subordination of the judiciary and its consequences, the local media encourages the participation of domestic civil society actors, whereas the international media alerts foreign actors.

Five Indicators of Executive Subordination of the Judiciary

A counterargument to the claim that competitive politics is a necessary condition for the rule of law is that constitutional guarantees of judicial autonomy are a sufficient condition. As a result of the concentration of power, however, informal institutions and practices that allow Latin American presidents to control the courts are often stronger than the formal constitutional guarantees of judicial independence.[48] Although a system of checks and balances exists in theory as part of the formal constitutional structure, informal practices have persisted since the colonial era, undermining the potential for sustainable democracy. In much of Latin America, the power relationships embodied in informal practices diverge from formal rules: "A basic difference between effective democracies and the oligarchic quasi-democracies might be expressed this way: the administration of justice in the former is frequently better than the written rule on which it operates; in the quasi-democratic oligarchies, the practice is nearly always worse than the rule."[49]

The gap between rules and practices highlights the need to focus on informal patterns of power. The size of the gap varies across Latin America. In most of Central America and in countries such as Argentina and Venezuela, multiple constitutional guarantees indicate a high degree of judicial independence, yet in reality, the judiciary often acts as a rubber stamp of the executive. In contrast, in Chile, Uruguay, and Costa Rica, the gap is much smaller; informal practices uphold many of the formal rules.

In order to determine the degree of judicial autonomy in a given country, a consideration of informal practices must accompany the analysis of the formal rules outlined in national constitutions—what Madison calls "parchment barriers."[50] An understanding of informal practices that shape behavior and incentives is essential where actual behavior is inconsistent with constitutional provisions. Many scholars mistakenly limit their analysis to formal guarantees of judicial autonomy.[51] Actual practices may illustrate that the formal institutions are mere façades that hide subordination of the courts. Sociologists refer to the divergence between the formal and the informal as "decoupling." Actors pay lip service to the formal rules, or "scripts," which are frequently invoked but rarely practiced.[52] An accurate assessment of judicial independence requires moving beyond an analysis of scripts.

Practices that allow the executive to subordinate the judiciary suggest a weak rule of law. Informal practices can shape the incentive structure in such a way that judges are unlikely to challenge the executive. Where presidents have had the unfettered right to remove judges, for instance, judicial figures have accepted their subordinate and passive roles. Compliance with the formal rules is unlikely and irrational where judges are punished for attempting to limit the prerogatives of the executive. In such a context, the executive easily exerts control over the judiciary. This book delineates five practices that indicate a politically malleable judiciary.

Violation of a transparent and merit-based appointment process is the first indicator of executive subordination of the courts. Highly politicized, secretive selection based on cronyism and political contacts helps ensure the appointment of pliant judges, thereby undermining their impartiality. Presidents who seek to dominate the courts attempt to fill them with subservient judges. In his discussion of Eastern European constitutional courts, Schwartz writes, "Strongmen do not like to have checks on their power, and often take steps to eliminate them in advance. Choosing judges who will not be overly independent is one such step."[53] In determining whether a president violates the formal appointment process in order to select docile judges, factors to consider include the speed of the selection process, the level of transparency, and the nature of congressional debate. For instance, rushing an appointment through the Senate is one way to avoid public input, facilitating the appointment of judges with questionable merits. However, the appointment of judges who are expected to support the president is insufficient on its own to indicate subordination of the judiciary. United States presidents, for instance, make an effort to select justices who are likely to support presidential ambitions.[54] Thus, a consideration of other practices such as whether presidents respect judges' tenure protection must accompany an analysis of the appointment process. Life tenure mitigates appointments based on political considerations.[55]

Violation of judges' tenure protection is the second indicator of a subordinate judiciary. Hamilton stresses the importance of tenure protection for judicial autonomy: "In a monarchy it [tenure protection] is an excellent barrier to the despotism of the prince; in a republic it is a no less excellent barrier to the encroachments and oppressions of the representative body. And it is the best expedient which can be devised in any government, to secure a steady, upright, and impartial administration of the laws."[56] Although all

Latin American constitutions grant judges tenure protection, presidents have often circumvented the formal rules. When the executive bypasses the constitutional channels for removal, judges have incentives to support the president's wishes. The violation of tenure protection subjects justices to greater political pressure than would be the case if these guarantees were respected: "The judge who must consider what the effect of his decision will be on his chances for reappointment may too frequently find a conflict between his self-interest and his duty to impartiality."[57] Court purges, a high turnover rate, and low average tenure suggest a violation of tenure protection. For instance, where judicial terms are coterminous with presidential terms, it is likely that the executive has violated the formal rule.

A third indicator of executive manipulation of the courts is violation of judges' salary protection. Hamilton stresses the importance of insulating judges from wage reduction: "[A] power over a man's subsistence amounts to a power over his will."[58] A decline in judges' real wages is an obvious sign that the executive or Congress has violated salary protection. A refusal to adjust judges' wages to reflect increases in the cost of living during inflationary periods suggests noncompliance with the formal rule.[59]

Variation in Supreme Court size is a fourth indicator of a pliant judicial branch. By increasing the number of justices, a president can pack the court with politically loyal judges and increase executive influence over rulings. In order to assess whether court expansion undermines Supreme Court independence, however, one must consider the merits of the individuals appointed to fill the new posts. A study of judges' backgrounds helps determine whether they were appointed for their professional skills or for their partisan stances. Variables to consider include judges' career paths, their reputations within the legal, academic, and political worlds, their performance in law school, their publication record, their partisan affiliation, and their past political activity.

Rulings in favor of the government that contradict the law are the fifth indicator of subordinate courts. Although not enough on its own, an analysis of court decisions is central to the assessment of judicial autonomy.[60] In particular, rulings that declare government acts unconstitutional suggest that the judiciary is an effective check: "Judicial review is not simply the most visible and dramatic example of judicial independence; it is related to (a function of) the force of judicial independence. If the judicial independence is a paper independence, then the judicial review, if provided for at all, can be only a sham review. Thus, the former is an indispensable, though not significant, precondition for any existence of the latter."[61] Executive subjugation of the judiciary can preclude the exercise of judicial review. Where the executive has the authority to punish judges, judges are unlikely to endure the costs of challenging executive ambitions. In addition, court decisions

TABLE 1.1

Indicators of Executive Subordination of the Judiciary

Practice	Indicators
The executive uses an opaque process to appoint pliant judges	• Opaque, politicized Senate debate over judicial nominees • Unqualified appointees (little prior experience in the judiciary, weak publication record, poor reputation) • Appointees with strong ties to the political party that controls the executive branch (militant partisanship) or personal ties to the administration (cronyism)
The executive violates judges' tenure protection	• Opaque, politicized removal proces • Noncompliance with formal impeachment rules • Short average tenure of judges • High number of judges dismissed during president's term
The executive violates judges' salary protection	• Reduction in judges' real salaries
The executive packs the Supreme Court	• Frequent changes in the number of Supreme Court justices
Judges are unwilling to endure the costs of ruling against executive interests	• Rulings that uphold government acts of dubious constitutionality • Rulings in favor of executive officials suspected of corruption

against government functionaries suspected of corruption suggest judicial autonomy. When the government is a party to a suit, judicial independence permits the judge to rule against the government organization or to prosecute the official. The primary criterion for considering cases in this book is the presence of a political interest; it excludes the many rulings that have no political significance for the executive.[62] Moreover, because examining all decisions in which the government is a party is beyond the scope of this book, high profile cases that received coverage in major newspapers have priority; it does not include the many cases that only marginally impacted the government.

Table 1.1 summarizes the five indicators that together suggest executive subordination of the courts.

This study considers each indicator in Table 1 in conjunction with the assessments of outside observers and inside actors to determine the level of judicial independence in a given country or province. The outside observers include journalists, academics, civil society groups, foreign governments, and international nongovernmental organizations. The inside actors include judges, lawyers, public prosecutors, and members of the executive and legislative branches. Moreover, this study treats judicial autonomy as a continuous rather than a dichotomous variable. Nations vary in their level of judicial independence, resting at different points along a spectrum: "Each country's political-judicial accommodation must be located along a spectrum that only in theory ranges from a completely unfettered judiciary to one that is completely subservient. The actual situation in all countries lies somewhere in between."[63] In addition, a country can move along the continuum at different points in time, reflecting an increase or decrease in judicial autonomy.

This book now turns to the cases of Argentina at the national level and the provinces of San Luis and Mendoza. Performance on the five indicators coupled with the assessments of outside observers and inside actors determines placement on the judicial autonomy continuum for each of the three cases. After showing where each case lies on the spectrum, the book demonstrates how different patterns of power explain the varying degrees of progress toward the rule of law.

CHAPTER 2

Argentina's Shifting Executive-Judicial Balance of Power

THE CHANGING relationship between Argentina's president and the judicial branch shows that the establishment of the rule of law is not a linear process. There have been key moments of regression away from as well as progress toward the rule of law. The size of the gap between constitutional guarantees of judicial autonomy and actual practice has varied over the course of Argentine history. Although the executive-judicial balance of power has always favored the executive in the ultrapresidential system of Argentina, the balance has nonetheless shifted over time.

Between 1862 and 1999, the relationship between Argentina's executive and judicial branches went through four phases: 1862 through Juan Domingo Perón's 1946 assumption of power, 1946 through the 1983 democratic transition, the administration of Raúl Alfonsín (1983–89), and the Carlos Menem presidency (1989–99). Although judicial autonomy began to decline with the 1930 coup that installed a military government, from 1862 until 1946, the courts enjoyed a relatively high degree of independence from the executive.[1] In 1943, Argentine constitutional law scholar Amadeo characterized the Supreme Court as the political institution "which has established itself most profoundly in the public conscience and most perfected itself in actual practice."[2] Under Perón, however, Amadeo's assessment no longer reflected reality. Despite constitutional guarantees of judicial autonomy, executive subordination of the courts characterized the 1946–83 period. Perón's 1946 assumption of the presidency marked a rapid increase in presidential power and an equally rapid deterioration of judicial independence.

As a result of the 1946–83 regression, post-transition Argentina faced the challenge of constructing the rule of law from scratch rather than restoring independent judicial institutions. Reflecting on his tenure as the first president after the 1983 transition to democracy, Alfonsín recalls:

> In our society, the building of democracy could not be viewed simply as a process of restoration; it was essentially a process of creating new institutions and implementing new routines, new habits, and new ways for people to live together. It was not a matter of reconstructing a system that was functioning well until it was interrupted by authoritarianism, but of establishing new foundations for an authentic democratic system.[3]

Alfonsín lacked a recent tradition of an autonomous judiciary on which to draw. He took hesitant steps to bring informal practices in line with the formal rules that call for judicial independence, but in 1989, Menem reversed Alfonsín's progress.

Menem reinforced the traditional patterns of power that had compromised the rule of law during the 1946–83 era and built upon Perón's foundation for executive dominance. Menem's 1989 assumption of the presidency was the first constitutional succession in almost forty years. The institutional continuity had the potential to foster the lengthy process of accommodation to formal constitutional rules, but Menem did not use the continuity to promote judicial autonomy. Instead, he revived the tradition of executive subordination of the courts.

This chapter first lays out Argentina's formal constitutional rules that, on their own, suggest a high degree of judicial autonomy. The chapter then traces in detail the history of five practices that indicate executive subordination of the courts: an opaque appointment process; violation of judges' tenure protection; court-packing; courts' unwillingness to challenge the executive branch; and courts' acceptance of laws passed by military regimes that came to power by force rather than election, known as the de facto doctrine.[4] Although the gap between formal rules and informal practices has always been present, an analysis of actual practices demonstrates that the gap has fluctuated in nature and in size across the four phases. The final section uses the assessments of outside observers and inside actors to support the argument that formal guarantees of judicial independence did not guide behavior in Menem's Argentina.

Constitutional Guarantees of Judicial Autonomy

Argentina's constitutional guarantees are misleading because on their own they indicate a high degree of judicial autonomy. Since Argentina's independence from Spain in 1810, formal rules have emphasized the separation of powers. The early constitutional experiments, the 1853 constitution, and the 1994 constitutional reform provided for an independent judicial branch capable of checking presidential power.

The constitutional experiments of 1811–52 contained explicit provisions for the separation of powers. The 1811 Organic Regulations forbade the executive from assuming judicial powers. An independent judiciary had the authority to apply laws and to try persons accused of crimes. The constitutions of 1819 and of 1826 vested judicial power in a high court appointed by the president with Senate approval. In order to bolster judges' independence, the constitutions granted them life tenure during good conduct and salary protection.[5]

The 1853 constitution reflected the early emphasis on the separation of powers.[6] Montesquieu, Hamilton, and United States constitutional principles influenced the Argentine framers. A delegate at Argentina's 1853 constitutional convention declared, "[The Argentine Constitution] is modeled on that of the United States, the only federation in the world which is worthy of being copied."[7] Like the early constitutional experiments, the 1853 constitution granted judges life tenure and salary protection.[8]

In 1994, Argentina underwent a constitutional reform that bolstered the formal guarantees of judicial autonomy. Menem introduced the reform as part of his strategy to gain reelection for a second consecutive term, which was prohibited by the 1853 constitution. In the 1993 Olivos Pact between Menem's Peronist Party, known as the Partido Justicialista (PJ), and Alfonsín's Unión Cívica Radical (UCR), Alfonsín agreed to support a reform permitting reelection in exchange for new controls on executive power. Because UCR support was necessary for the PJ president to obtain the requisite two-thirds of both houses of Congress for a constitutional reform, Menem accepted provisions with the potential to deconcentrate power. In theory, the 1994 constitution reduced presidential dominance and bolstered judicial autonomy. For instance, it raised the Senate approval requirement for the president's Supreme Court nominees from a majority to two-thirds. It also called for the creation of a Judicial Council and an Impeachment Jury to reduce executive discretion over judicial appointments and dismissals.[9] Despite the new guarantees of judicial autonomy, however, the informal practices that had permitted Menem to subordinate the courts endured.

Performance on the Five Indicators of Judicial Autonomy across Argentina's History

The formal rules call for the separation of powers, yet executive subordination of the judiciary has a long history in Argentina. The informal practices embraced by Perón in 1946 and reintroduced by Menem in 1989 have bolstered the traditional executive supremacy and allowed Argentine presidents to control the courts. The resilient informal patterns of power have obstructed the development of judicial autonomy, often overshadowing formal guarantees of judicial independence. In addition, the frequent alternation between civilian and military rule since 1930 further weakened the judiciary by destroying the opportunity for developmental continuity. Political instability contributed to the divergence between formal rules and informal practices. This section uses the five informal practices to trace the changing relationship between Argentina's executive and judicial branches across the four phases.

RESPECT FOR THE FORMAL APPOINTMENT PROCESS

From 1862 until 1946, most Argentine presidents abided by a transparent, merit-based process to appoint judges whose past activity indicated they would maintain their independence from the executive branch. A majority of judges were opposition members from prestigious judicial careers. From 1862 through 1943, 71 percent of Supreme Court appointees had prior experience as jurists.[10] Argentina's first president, Bartolomé Mitre, made a concerted effort to appoint opposition members to the Court. He declared, "In order to increase citizens' faith in the Court's ability to protect their rights, I sought impartial justices from opposition parties who would be independent of the political branches of government."[11] Mitre appointed five justices to whom he had no personal or political ties. In fact, a majority of Mitre's appointees had supported his opponent, Justo José de Urquiza. Appointees Francisco de las Carreras, José Barros Pazos, Salvador María del Carríl, Francisco Delgado, and Valentín Alsina were among Mitre's main rivals. When Alsina did not accept a seat on the Court, Mitre appointed José Benjamín Gorostiaga, who had been an advisor to Urquiza.[12]

Judicial Appointments: The Predominance of Informal Practice during the 1946–83 Period

The informal practice of using a secretive process to appoint acquiescent judges became commonplace after 1946. The unified government and frequent coups that characterized the 1946–83 period contributed to executive discretion over judicial appointments. Following each military coup and subsequent return to civilian rule, the executive had the opportunity to select new judges. In 1947, Perón replaced four of the five Supreme Court justices with his political allies. In fact, all of his appointees had declared their loyalty to Perón and his wife Eva. Perón rushed the approval of his nominees through the Peronist-dominated Senate.[13] Following Perón, the de facto military regimes of 1955–58 and 1966–73 did not submit their pro-military candidates to the Senate for approval.

Ironically, a rupture in the practice of appointing unqualified justices occurred during the 1976–83 government of the military junta, a period of massive assaults against the rule of law. The majority of the junta appointees to the Supreme Court were individuals with extensive experience in the judiciary. In fact, 84 percent had prior experience as jurists, and another 8 percent had been attorneys.[14] Andrés D'Alessio, who later helped prosecute the military government for human rights abuses, and Argentine constitutional law expert María Angélica Gelli acknowledge the high quality of the justices. Adolfo Gabrielli, the Chief Justice of the junta Court, and Roberto Durrieu, the military's Undersecretary of Justice, emphasize the professional merits of appointees to the lower courts as well as to the Supreme Court. During Durrieu's three-year tenure in the Justice Ministry (1978–81), 95 percent of lower court appointees had experience in the judiciary. Only six appointees did not come from judicial careers, and those six appointees were distinguished legal scholars.[15]

The military's respect for the formal appointment process did not, however, signal respect for the rule of law. The junta had no reason to abuse appointment power when it had other ways to ensure that the Supreme Court would support its policies. Despite their professional experience, the justices refrained from challenging the military regime. As discussed below, in order to regularize relations with the new military government, the Court upheld the junta's seizure of emergency powers, accepted the de facto doctrine, and did little to prevent the regime's rampant human rights violations. The fact that this first indicator suggests a strong rule of law from 1976–83 illustrates the importance of considering all five indicators. An analysis based on a single indicator is incomplete and can even be misleading.[16] As this chapter demonstrates, the other indicators reveal the military government's subordination of the courts and disregard for the rule of law.

The Appointment Process under Alfonsín: Respect for the Formal Rules

Alfonsín complied with the formal rules governing judicial appointments. Furthermore, as discussed in Chapter 3, divided government compelled him to nominate opposition members. One of Alfonsín's first moves as president was to appoint prestigious individuals with diverse political viewpoints to the Supreme Court. In fact, he initially nominated Italo Luder, the defeated PJ presidential candidate, as Chief Justice. Although Luder did not accept the position, Alfonsín's willingness to nominate an opposition figure suggests selection based on merit rather than partisanship. Only two of Alfonsín's five appointees were members of his UCR: José Severo Caballero and Augusto Belluscio. Enrique Petracchi was a staunch Peronist, and Carlos Fayt was a former socialist. In addition, all members of the Alfonsín Court had been judges or academics before assuming their seats on the highest court.

Alfonsín's appointment of opposition members to the lower courts and to the Attorney General's Office also suggests compliance with the constitutional appointment process. In 1983, he appointed PJ member León Carlos Arslanian as an appellate court judge. When Arslanian revealed his PJ affiliation, Alfonsín's Justice Minister responded, "Look, we are looking for the best, and we know that you are one of them."[17] Ricardo Gil Lavedra recalls the diverse ideological and partisan backgrounds of appellate court judges during the Alfonsín administration. He reports that he and his colleagues in the appellate courts acted with "total independence."[18] In addition, Alfonsín's Attorney General, Andrés D'Alessio, asserts that Alfonsín made a conscious effort to appoint autonomous public prosecutors such as Aníbal Ibarra. Alfonsín appointed D'Alessio as Attorney General despite his mistaken belief that D'Alessio was a Peronist.[19]

The Menem Years: Violations of the Formal Appointment Process

In contrast to Alfonsín, Menem embraced an opaque appointment process as a means to enhance executive dominance over the courts. The majority of Menem's Supreme Court appointees had weak qualifications and had demonstrated loyalty to the PJ before joining the Court. Menem used his appointment power to create a pro-government majority on the Court, known in Argentina as the "*mayoría automática menemista*," the automatic Menemist majority, because of its propensity for ruling in favor of Menem on important cases. Members of the Menem Court acknowledge the existence of the "automatic majority." According to one justice, Menem created the majority to ensure that the Court would uphold laws of dubious constitutionality.[20] Menem's Justice Minister, Raúl Granillo Ocampo, articulated the Menem administration's view: "An administration . . . cannot govern with a judiciary whose views are antagonistic to those of the government. If the Court were to have a vision completely different from ours and to declare our laws unconstitutional, we could not implement our political and economic plans."[21] Another Menem functionary declared: "We need justices who share the government's policy preferences."[22]

Like Perón's 1946 appointees, each of Menem's 1989–90 appointees had strong personal or political ties to the president. The resignations of two Alfonsín appointees who protested Menem's court-packing, Jorge Bacqué and Caballero, along with the expansion of the Court from five to nine justices allowed Menem to appoint six justices early in his term. Menem replaced Bacqué and Caballero with his longtime friend Julio Oyhanarte and with Eduardo Moliné O'Connor. Moliné O'Connor's background suggests selection based on personal ties to the administration rather than professional qualifications. At the time of his appointment, Moliné O'Connor's most recent legal publication had appeared in 1968 and his most recent professional post was president of the Argentine Tennis Association. His sisters were married to two of Menem's closest political operators, the Anzorreguy brothers. Hugo Anzorreguy was at the helm of the Argentine intelligence agency, the

Secretaría de Inteligencia del Estado (SIDE). His brother Jorge Anzorreguy advised Menem on the appointment of dozens of federal judges considered loyal to Menem.[23]

In order to ensure Senate approval of his nominees, Menem did not abide by a transparent selection process when he appointed four justices following his 1990 expansion of the Court. The speed of congressional proceedings impeded a thorough evaluation of the candidates. On April 18, 1990, only one day after announcing the expansion, Menem submitted his list of nominees to the PJ-controlled Senate. The two UCR representatives on the Senate Appointment Committee were absent from the hearing during which the PJ Committee members unanimously approved Menem's candidates. When the Committee's approval reached the floor, the Senate approved the list in a secret session only seven minutes long with no UCR senators in attendance. The new justices took their seats only eight days after Menem had nominated them.[24]

Menem appointed his allies Rodolfo Barra, Mariano Augusto Cavagna Martínez, Julio Salvador Nazareno, and Ricardo Eugenio Gabriel Levene to fill the four new seats. Barra had strong ties to the PJ and to Menem. He had a close friendship with executive functionaries Eduardo Bauzá and Carlos Corach and had been Menem's Undersecretary of the Interior.[25] Menem declared that when faced with legal challenges, Barra would "fix the problem."[26] In addition, Barra made a public admission of his deference to Menem: "My only bosses are Perón and Menem."[27] In a 1993 radio interview, Barra declared, "I cannot dictate a ruling that is against the government. I only issue rulings that are favorable to administration officials."[28] After resigning from the Court in 1993, Barra returned to a political post that required ties to Menem. Menem appointed him Justice Minister in 1994.

Like Barra, Cavagna Martínez had been a staunch Peronist. In 1974, he was Undersecretary of Justice in the province of Buenos Aires under PJ Governor Victorio Calabró. In addition, Cavagna Martínez had personal ties to the government. He often attended social gatherings of Menem functionaries.[29] Like Barra, he returned to politics after his 1993 resignation from the Court. Menem appointed Cavagna Martínez ambassador to Italy in 1994. In 1997, he became a high level Menem advisor.[30] In 2001, when Menem was under house arrest for illegal arms sales to Ecuador and Croatia that occurred during his administration, Cavagna Martínez served as Menem's personal attorney. Unlike most Menem appointees, however, Cavagna Martínez was a prestigious legal scholar who advocated important judicial reforms. In 1991, for instance, he spearheaded efforts to improve Supreme Court efficiency.

Nazareno and Levene also had connections to Menem and to his party before joining the Court. Nazareno had lived in La Rioja, Menem's home province, where he was close to Menem's family. He worked in a law firm with the president's brother, who dated Nazareno's sister. In 1986, Menem, who was governor of La Rioja at the time, appointed Nazareno to the provincial Attorney General's Office and then to the La Rioja Supreme Court. Levene also had a long history of ties to the PJ. In 1975, he served on the Supreme Court of the PJ administration. In addition, he had been an advisor to Menem's Undersecretary of Justice.[31]

Menem continued to select loyal judges later in his term. When Oyhanarte resigned in 1991, Menem appointed Antonio Boggiano, a friend of Barra and a member of Opus Dei, the conservative Catholic group with strong links to the Menem administration. Despite Boggiano's extensive publication record and prior experience in the academic and legal worlds, he was considered to be part of the "automatic majority." According to a prominent Buenos Aires attorney, Menem moved Boggiano "by remote control."[32]

As a result of the 1993 Olivos Pact, Menem had another opportunity to appoint pliant judges. As part of the PJ-UCR agreement, Menem pledged to replace three justices with individuals acceptable to the UCR. The UCR and PJ agreed on three replacements: Gustavo Bossert, Guillermo López, and Héctor Masnatta. López was a friend of Menem's Labor Minister, and Masnatta had been a Supreme Court justice during the 1973–76 PJ administration. Only Bossert was free of links to Menem and his party. Ultimately, however, the PJ reneged on its promise when only Barra and Cavagna Martínez resigned. Levene did not fulfill his pledge to resign until November 1995. Thus, only Bossert and López joined the Court in February 1994.[33]

When Levene finally resigned, Adolfo Vázquez rather than Masnatta filled the vacancy. In contrast to Masnatta who was a prestigious judge with links to the UCR, Vázquez had little experience in the judiciary and had a close personal relationship with Menem. In response to accusations that the appointment violated the Olivos Pact, Barra, who was Justice Minister at the time, declared that Menem had first offered the post to Masnatta. To support his claim, Barra distributed a facsimile in which Masnatta declined the offer. According to the fax, however, the government offered the position to Masnatta on November 28. By that date, Menem had already extended an offer to Vázquez. Menem announced the Vázquez nomination on November 27.[34]

In order to ensure the appointment of Vázquez, the Senate approval process was replete with irregularities. By the time of the appointment, the 1994 constitution was in effect, which increased the Senate approval requirement for Supreme Court justices from a majority to two-thirds. The Menem administration foresaw difficulties in getting the necessary two-thirds after December 10 when new UCR senators would take their seats. Thus, the PJ attempted to delay the entrance of UCR senators. When that strategy failed, the PJ violated Article 23 of the Senate Rules, which stipulates that judicial nominations must be open for citizen consideration for seven days. The PJ violated this rule in order to hold the Senate vote before December 10.[35]

Vázquez's background and his public statements demonstrate his loyalty to Menem. Vázquez admitted that his friendship with the president was the criterion for his appointment. At the time of his nomination, Vázquez declared that he would support Menem's policy agenda.[36] He admitted that Menem told him, "I selected you for your career, your rulings, and especially for your position regarding cases against the state. Never let the state lose a case."[37] In a 1997 public appearance, Vázquez declared, "When there is a case against the government, I do not rule against the administration."[38] In response to his admission, Argentina's Ombudsman sought to recuse Vázquez from cases involving a state interest.[39]

Selection on the basis of personal or partisan loyalty led to an enormous number of impeachment suits against Menem appointees. In fact, the House Impeachment Committee received more impeachment suits between 1990 and 1998 than the total number between 1860 and 1990.[40] Opposition legislators advocated impeaching Menem's appointees because of their subordination to the executive: "A majority in the Supreme Court is more concerned with pleasing Menem and his friends than with protecting constitutional rights."[41] In 1998, the opposition announced its intent to impeach Menem's automatic majority. Two hundred legislators and prominent legal figures signed a declaration that the five justices "worked as a Menemist bench within the highest court."[42]

Table 2.1 contains information about the Alfonsín and Menem Supreme Court appointees. The data on tenure, partisan affiliation, qualifications, and reasons for leaving the Court permit a comparison of Alfonsín's justices with those of Menem.

RESPECT FOR JUDGES' TENURE PROTECTION

The framers of the Argentine Constitution included a provision for judges' tenure protection with the intent of advancing judicial independence. From 1862 through 1946, Argentine presidents respected formal rules regarding life tenure during good conduct. Not a single justice was impeached or removed for political reasons. Supreme Court composition changed only as a result of the death, retirement, or resignation of a member. Of the 38 justices who left the Court between 1862 and 1945, 53 percent died while on the Court, 31 percent reached the legal retirement age, and 16 percent resigned. Even the military governments following the 1930 and 1943 coups respected the life tenure of justices. Between 1862 and 1946,

TABLE 2.1

Argentine Supreme Court Appointees, 1983–99

	Appointed by	Term	Partisan Affiliation	Qualification	Reason for Leaving
Petracchi	Alfonsín	1983–	PJ	Merit	—
Carrió	Alfonsín	1983–86	Independent	Merit	Resignation
Caballero	Alfonsín	1983–90	UCR	Merit, ties to UCR	Protest court expansion
Belluscio	Alfonsín	1983–	UCR	Merit, ties to UCR	—
Fayt	Alfonsín	1983–	Socialist	Merit	—
Bacqué	Alfonsín	1986–90	Independent	Merit	Protest court expansion
Oyhanarte	Menem	1990–91	PJ	Ties to Menem; merit	Resignation
Barra	Menem	1990–94	PJ	Ties to Menem, PJ	Olivos Pact (inducement)
Cavagna Martínez	Menem	1990–94	PJ	Ties to PJ; merit	Olivos Pact (inducement)
Nazareno	Menem	1990–2003	PJ	Ties to Menem, PJ	Resignation (imminent impeachment)
Levene	Menem	1990–95	PJ	Ties to PJ; merit	Olivos Pact (inducement)
Moliné O'Connor	Menem	1990–	PJ	Ties to Menem administration	—
Boggiano	Menem	1991–	PJ	Links to Barra; merit	—
Bossert	Menem	1994–2002	Independent	Merit	Resignation
López	Menem	1994–	PJ	Ties to Menem administration	—
Vázquez	Menem	1995–	PJ	Ties to Menem	—

the average tenure of justices was ten years.[43] As a result of this respect for tenure protection, presidents often encountered Courts that had been appointed by the opposition.

The careers of Chief Justices illustrate the respect for life tenure during this early phase of Argentine history. Only ten justices presided over the Court from 1862 until 1946. The first Chief Justice, Francisco de las Carreras, served for seven years until his death. His successor, Salvador María del Carril, also served for seven years. The third Chief Justice, José Barros Plazos, had been a member of the Court since its inception. When Barros Plazos died after only a few months as Chief Justice, José Benjamin Gorostiaga, also from the Mitre Court, succeeded him and served until 1887. Benjamín Victorica was Chief Justice from 1887 until 1892 when he retired to become Minister of Defense. Benjamín Paz was Chief Justice for ten years until his death. His successor, Abel Bazán, also served until his death in 1905 when Antonio Bermejo assumed the post. Bermejo was Chief Justice for twenty-four years during seven administrations. After Bermejo died, José Figueroa Alcorta became Chief Justice until his death. In 1931, Roberto Repetto became Chief Justice and served for fifteen years. He resigned in 1946 when his impeachment by Perón was imminent.[44]

Violations of Tenure Protection during the 1946–83 Period

From 1946 through 1983, actual practice did not uphold the formal rule that prohibits the removal of justices for political reasons. Supreme Court terms tended to be coterminous with presidential terms, subjecting the justices to political pressure. The average tenure of justices fell from ten years to four years. In contrast to the early stability, the Court experienced purges in 1946, 1955, 1966, 1973, and 1976. Unlike the 1862–1946 period when not a single judge was removed for political reasons, 33 percent of the justices who left the Court between 1946 and 1983 faced irregular removal and 6 percent were impeached.[45]

Perón embraced the practice of dismissing judges. In response to unfavorable rulings, the PJ-controlled Senate impeached four of the five justices and the Attorney General in 1947. The only justice who retained his seat, Tomás Casares, was a militant supporter of Perón. The other four had ties to the opposition. The 1947 impeachments aroused a wave of opposition from members of civil society, including Argentine bar associations.[46] After the 1955 coup that deposed Perón, the de facto government of General Pedro Eugenio Aramburu bypassed constitutional channels when it dismissed the Court and appointed five anti-Peronist justices. After the 1966 coup, Juan Carlos Onganía purged the Court and appointed individuals favorable to the military. In 1973, the PJ government of Héctor Cámpora dismissed the entire Court. On the day that it seized power in 1976, the military junta issued a decree removing all justices and the Attorney General.[47]

Comparison of the length of judicial terms and of the appointment rate in Argentina to those of other nations demonstrates Argentina's relatively high Supreme Court turnover. In his comparative study of Argentina, the United States, and Mexico, Biles provides the mean tenure on each nation's Court between 1953 and 1972, which serves as a measure of stability. Mean tenure was 4.1 years in Argentina, 9.8 years in the U.S., and 7.0 years in Mexico. Median tenure was 4.0 years in Argentina, 8.0 years in the United States, and 5.0 years in Mexico. Moreover, between 1953 and 1972, the appointment rate in Argentina was 10.4 months. In contrast, a new member assumed a seat on the nine-member U.S. Court every 22.8 months, and Mexico's appointment rate for its 21-member Court was 5.6 months.[48]

Purges also became frequent in Argentina's lower courts. The practice of dismissing lower court judges began in 1930, even earlier than it did for the Supreme Court. General José Uriburu removed first instance and appellate court judges in the wake of the 1930 coup. In 1949, Perón removed lower court judges considered unfriendly to his party. He submitted all members of the federal judiciary to the Senate for reconfirmation, and the PJ-controlled Senate removed over seventy federal judges.[49] In 1955, General Aramburu removed lower court judges who were not sympathetic to the military administration. In 1958, President Arturo Frondizi subjected the entire federal judiciary to reconfirmation, which enabled him to dismiss judges that he considered to be a threat. In response, a Supreme Court justice declared, "There were many who felt that Frondizi's behavior [in dismissing the judges] was exorbitant and lacking in respect [to the judiciary]. A sort of abuse of the law."[50] The 1966 Onganía administration created a "Jury" that removed unsympathetic lower court justices; the "Jury" permitted Onganía to maintain a façade of legality while violating tenure protection.[51] The military junta of 1976–83 suspended all federal judges and subjected them to reconfirmation. During the first two weeks after the coup, the junta dismissed twenty-four judges. Between 1976 and 1983, the de facto government dismissed 32 percent of federal judges in Buenos Aires and 42 percent of federal judges in the other twenty-three provinces.[52]

The Removal Process under Alfonsín

The practice of purging the Supreme Court continued after the 1983 restoration of democracy. Alfonsín rejected the formal impeachment process when he announced his intention to dismiss the entire Court by decree. The five justices resigned upon learning of Alfonsín's plan. Although both Alfonsín and Menem undermined the constitutional guarantee of life tenure during good conduct, they did so under very different circumstances. Alfonsín inherited a Court from a military government that came to power by unconstitutional means. In contrast, Menem inherited a Court from a civilian administration.

Despite the very different circumstances, any unconstitutional purge threatens the development of judicial autonomy. Like Frondizi and Cámpora who also inherited Courts from military governments, Alfonsín's rejection of formal impeachment proceedings reinforced an informal practice that had undermined judicial autonomy since Perón's first term. Alfonsín could have used the impeachment process.[53] Compliance with the constitution would have been an important step toward restoring a formal rule that Argentine presidents had violated since 1947.

Menem's Use of Inducements to Create Vacancies

Menem tried to bypass the requirements of formal impeachment proceedings. Upon assuming power, he attempted to induce Alfonsín's appointees to resign. He offered Caballero a post as Argentina's representative on the United Nations Human Rights Commission in Geneva, and he offered Fayt the ambassadorship to Colombia.[54] When the inducement strategies failed, Menem resorted to another informal mechanism of control: he expanded the Court.

The effort to remove judges continued later in Menem's first term. Fulfillment of the 1993 Olivos Pact required the resignation of three justices. Menem had a difficult time compelling three members of the Court to resign. Belluscio, Petracchi, and Fayt, the three justices who remained from Alfonsín's Court, refused to step down. Boggiano rejected a 1993 offer to become Argentina's ambassador to the Vatican. The president's brother, Eduardo Menem, used his seat in the Senate to lead a failed attempt to pass legislation requiring justices to retire at age 75, which would have secured the removals of Levene and Fayt.[55]

Menem finally secured two vacancies when Barra and Cavagna Martínez yielded to pressure and inducements. Both attribute their resignations to their desire to help Menem fulfill the Olivos Pact.[56] Furthermore, their career paths suggest that inducements influenced their decisions. Barra assumed the post of Justice Minister shortly after he resigned from the Court. Cavagna Martínez became Argentina's ambassador in Rome. With the resignations of Barra and Cavagna Martínez, Menem secured two of the three vacancies. For the third, Levene had agreed to retire in February 1994. When Levene did not resign in February, the Menem administration offered him an ambassadorship. In addition, because Levene had conditioned his resignation on his absolution in an impeachment suit, Menem pressured the PJ bloc in Congress to dismiss the charges against Levene. The impeachment case was not resolved until June 1995, finally opening the way for Levene to resign in November 1995.[57]

THE PRESIDENT'S USE OF COURT-PACKING

By increasing the number of justices, a president can pack the Court with pliant judges and thus increase executive influence over rulings. As in the United States, the Argentine Constitution does not specify the number of judges. Before 1946, Argentine presidents did not use their discretion over the number of Supreme Court justices as a means of subordinating the judiciary. The size of the Court changed only once between 1862 and 1946. Five members comprised Argentina's first Court. In 1869, the number rose to eight where it remained until 1950.

Court-Packing during the 1946–83 Period

The size of the Court has varied frequently since Perón's first term as president. In 1950, Perón reduced the number of justices from eight to five. In 1958, Frondizi raised the number from five to seven. In response, Chief Justice Alfredo Orgaz resigned and attributed his resignation to "moral exhaustion" stemming from the attempts to manipulate the Court through court-packing.[58] After the 1966 coup, Onganía reduced the size once again to five.

Despite their similar formal rules, in contrast to Argentina, court-packing did not become a practice in the United States. The U.S. started with six justices but has remained fixed at nine since 1869. Franklin Roosevelt's 1937 court-packing scheme failed due to opposition from Congress, the American Bar Association, and the general populace. Even Roosevelt's supporters and the expansion's intended beneficiaries opposed the plan.[59] Perón did not confront opposition in Congress or such broad-based public outcry, which helped permit the evolution of an informal practice that has enabled Argentine presidents to change the number of justices.

Court-Packing during the Alfonsín and Menem Administrations

Both Alfonsín and Menem attempted to expand the size of the Court, but only Menem succeeded. In 1987, Alfonsín sent a proposal to Congress that called for an increase in the size of the Court from five to seven. He argued that a Court of five judges was too small to address the large number of cases. He invoked technical reasons, but critics argue that his motivation was to form an acquiescent Court.[60] As a result of divided government, however, expansion in 1987 would not have been as detrimental to judicial autonomy as was Menem's 1990 expansion. In 1987, the PJ held a majority in the Senate. Thus, Alfonsín's UCR would have had to share the appointments with the PJ.

In one of Menem's first moves as president, he almost doubled the size of the Court when he expanded it from five to nine. Interior Minister Bauzá admitted that Menem intended to use the expansion to form a docile Court.[61] The expansion confronted opposition from the Supreme Court itself. Justices Belluscio, Bacqué, Petracchi, and Fayt signed Acordada 44, which denounced the proposal and argued that it would compromise judicial autonomy and increase backlogs.[62] In the words of one Supreme Court justice, the additional four justices were an obstacle to efficiency; the expansion converted the Court into a "rheumatic elephant."[63] Opposition legislators also resisted expansion, arguing that it would violate the spirit of the Argentine Constitution and politicize the Court.[64]

In order to overcome the opposition, the PJ used unconstitutional, secretive means to ensure passage of the law in the House of Representatives. The PJ ensured that the vote took place before dawn with impostors attending the session to fulfill quorum requirements. In response to the irregularities, UCR legislators pointed to "the presence of impostors on the benches, a bogus quorum, and the abrupt adjournment of the session that prevented the representatives from exercising their prerogatives."[65] The House approval permitted Menem to appoint four loyal justices in 1990: Barra, Cavagna Martínez, Nazareno, and Levene.

In a move similar to his Supreme Court expansion, in 1992, Menem doubled the number of first instance criminal court judges from six to twelve and filled the new seats with pliant judges.[66] Menem used the new appointments to ensure the impunity of executive officials. Criminal verdicts were particularly important in light of the large number of corruption scandals that plagued Menem's presidency. Federal criminal judges ruled on the many corruption cases that involved government functionaries. According to a federal prosecutor, Menem selected criminal judges who would not conduct thorough investigations and who would absolve functionaries.[67] Menem's appointments led to Arslanian's resignation as Justice Minister in 1992. Arslanian explains that he opted to resign rather than serve in an administration that appointed unfit judges.[68]

JUDICIAL RULINGS THAT CHALLENGE EXECUTIVE INTERESTS

In theory, Argentine judges have the authority to declare any executive or legislative act unconstitutional. Although the Argentine Constitution contains no explicit provision for judicial review, the framers of the constitution accepted the power. Judicial review was not subject to debate at the Constitutional Convention. Amadeo and Miller argue that because the Argentine framers modeled their constitution after the U.S. system where judicial review was already established, they accepted judicial review as a given.[69]

The Argentine Constitution provides the basis for judicial review: "This Constitution, the laws dictated by Congress, and the treaties with other nations are the supreme law of the Nation."[70] The constitution establishes the courts' authority to address all issues regulated by the constitution: "To the Supreme Court and lower courts belong the trial and decision of all cases arising under the Constitution."[71] According to Law 27 of 1862, the judiciary's duties include ensuring that no branch of government violates the constitution. Law 48 of 1868 stipulates that judges apply the constitution as the supreme law of the nation, giving the courts the power to examine the constitutionality of laws and decrees.[72] Argentina has a decentralized system of judicial review in which lower court judges as well as Supreme Court justices have the power to rule on the constitutionality of laws and decrees. In the 1927 *Chiaparrone* decision, the Court ruled that a justice of the peace could rule on constitutional questions.[73]

There are, however, limits on the formal power of judicial review. Only those individuals affected by alleged unconstitutional acts have the standing to challenge their constitutionality. Judges can only exercise judicial review when a specific case reaches them; they cannot exercise this control on their own initiative. In addition, judges cannot question the constitutionality of bills before they become law. Finally, rather than revoke unconstitutional statutes, judges can only refuse to apply the statutes to particular claimants.[74] Despite the limits, judicial review has the potential to serve as a powerful check on the executive and legislative branches.

Early in Argentina's history, the Court asserted its authority to exercise judicial review. The stability of the Court between 1862 and 1946 set the stage for judges to act as guardians of the constitution. In the 1863 *Ríos* decision, the Court declared an executive decree unconstitutional on the basis that the president does not possess judicial powers. In the 1864 *Calvete* ruling, the Court asserted its power to review the constitutionality of all lower court decisions. In 1869, the Court defended property rights when it declared a provincial statute that would have deprived the plaintiff of property to be unconstitutional. In 1871, the Court protected contractual rights when it overruled a governor's decree to dissolve a charitable society.[75] In its 1888 *Municipalidad de la Capital* decision, the Court ruled that the judiciary has the power to:

> examine the laws in the concrete cases which are brought to their decision, compare them with the text of the Constitution . . . and abstain from applying them if they oppose the Constitution. This moderating attribution is one of the fundamental ends of the federal judiciary and one of the greatest guarantees with which constitutional rights are deemed to be secured against possible and involuntary abuses of power.[76]

In the Court's 1887 *Sojo* decision, the Court ruled on the constitutionality of a federal statute. The Court asserted that Congress cannot alter the Supreme Court's constitutional jurisdiction.[77]

The Supreme Court also asserted its role as protector of individual liberties from government abuse. Miller demonstrates that from 1862 through the 1930 coup, the Supreme Court prevented the government from repressing political opponents. For instance, the Court upheld the right of citizens arrested for rebellion to be released on bail, and it refused to grant military courts the authority to try civilians. The role of safeguarding individual rights was especially significant due to the high level of political unrest and the frequency of revolts during this early phase of Argentine history.[78]

In addition, from 1862 through 1932, the Supreme Court defended freedom of the press. Miller uses case law to demonstrate that the Court played an important role in upholding Article 32 of the Argentine Constitution, which prohibited Congress from restricting press freedom. He cites a dozen cases in which the Court ruled that the federal judiciary could not exercise criminal jurisdiction over the press, even when the government had a strong interest in a particular case. For instance, the Court denied the federal courts jurisdiction over cases involving the defamation of public officials. With the help of the Court, Argentina developed a free press that represented a wide variety of political viewpoints.[79]

Although the Court began to show restraint in the areas of press freedom and the protection of individual liberties in the wake of the 1930 military coup, the Court continued to exercise judicial review after the 1943 coup. Between 1943 and 1945, the Court tried to limit the military government's power. These attempts ultimately led to the assaults on the Court's autonomy under Perón. In 1945, the Court declared that the military government in which Perón was a cabinet minister could not create new courts by decree. The Court also declared the removal of a federal judge unconstitutional. In addition, it ruled that a series of transfers of judges from one district to another violated the constitutional guarantee of salary protection. Because federal judges' salaries varied across regions, some transfers were tantamount to a salary reduction. In reaction to unfavorable rulings, Perón impeached four of the five Supreme Court justices when he assumed the presidency.[80]

Judicial Rulings: The 1946 Turning Point

In contrast to early judges who asserted their role as guardians of the Argentine Constitution, the Court showed great restraint from 1946 through 1983. As presidents began to assert the power to remove justices, the Court became reluctant to declare laws and decrees unconstitutional. Perón's 1947 impeachment of four justices sent a clear message: the government removes judges who challenge its interests. Indeed, after 1947, the Perón Court supported acts of dubious constitutionality. For instance, in the 1950 *Balbín* decision, the Court upheld the 1949 law that forbade *desacato*, offending the dignity of or showing contempt for a public official. The Court accepted the administration's use of the law to dismiss UCR Congressman Ricardo Balbín from his seat in Congress on the basis that he had harmed Perón's dignity. In effect, the Court permitted the administration to silence opposition legislators.[81]

Limits on judicial review continued under the military government of 1976–83. Although the judiciary challenged the government on a number of high profile cases such as the *Timerman* ruling, restrictions on judicial review remained. The Court failed to stop the rampant violation of constitutional rights, and it validated unconstitutional legislation. In the wake of the Dirty War, the Argentine Truth Commission asserted that, "the judicial route became an almost non-operational recourse."[82] Between 1977 and 1979, the Argentine courts rejected over 20,000 writs of habeas corpus.[83] Prominent Argentine legal scholar Eugenio Zaffaroni argues that the military junta's subordination of the Court was unprecedented. For instance, the Court upheld decrees that submitted civilians to military tribunals, that prohibited the sale and ownership of certain books, and that prohibited the practice of homeopathic medicine.[84] Only after its domestic popularity plummeted and it found itself under increasing international scrutiny did the Court free Jacobo Timerman, the political prisoner who was the subject of the well-known *Timerman* case, and accept habeas corpus pleas for individuals who had been in prison, often for five or more years.[85]

Alfonsín Court Rulings: Challenges to the Executive

The Argentine judiciary demonstrated a renewed ability to challenge the executive under Alfonsín. Although the Alfonsín Court supported a number of controversial executive policies, Court rulings reflected a growing independence from the executive.[86] In the *Rolón Zappa* ruling, the Court rejected Alfonsín's economic emergency justification for seizing the assets of retired persons. In *Sejean*, the Court declared the law that prohibited divorce unconstitutional, a law that Alfonsín supported. In the *La Prensa* ruling, the Court prohibited the Alfonsín administration's price controls on newspapers. In addition, the Alfonsín Court entered an era of unprecedented activism in protecting constitutional rights. Court rulings supported free expression, the right to information, and the protection of privacy. The Court also ruled that evidence illegally obtained during a police investigation is inadmissible in court. The Court annulled the military self-amnesty and asserted its power to rule on cases that involved political issues.[87] Alfonsín Supreme Court justices Bacqué, Belluscio, and Petracchi recall the Court's ability to exercise judicial review. They report that the Alfonsín administration never pressured the justices to support its preferences.[88]

The Menem Court's Unwillingness to Challenge the President

In contrast to the Alfonsín Court, the Menem Court refrained from challenging the executive branch in cases of political significance. Only when the government had no interest in a case were judges free to exercise judicial review. A member of the Menem Court refers to the Court's unwillingness to challenge the president as the "Menem Doctrine." As part of the Doctrine, the Court believed that one of its primary duties was to help Menem govern.[89] Bacqué observes that the Menem Court used weak legal reasoning to uphold the constitutionality of decrees and laws.[90] For instance, the Court allowed Menem to remove officials from administrative oversight agencies without congressional approval as required by law. The Court's decision to uphold Menem's 1991 decree dismissing Ricardo Molinas, the Federal Prosecutor of Administrative Investigations, or the head of the Fiscalía Nacional de Investigaciones Administrativas (FNIA), is representative of the Court's stance toward Menem. Menem's decree violated the federal prosecutor's tenure protection and the constitutional right to a defense. According to Argentine law, impeachment is the only means of removing the head of the FNIA. Both first instance and appellate courts had ruled in favor of Molinas. In 1991, the Supreme Court overturned the lower court decisions and upheld Menem's decree. Menem's six appointees, the "automatic majority," supported the president. The three dissenters, all of whom remained from the Alfonsín Court, argued that the decree was unconstitutional.[91]

In the 1990 *Peralta* ruling, the Court aligned itself with the president when it upheld Menem's Plan Bonex decree. In contrast to the Alfonsín Court's *Rolón Zappa* ruling, the Menem Court accepted the president's economic emergency justification for the seizure of extraordinary powers. By permitting banks to honor deposits with bonds that had a weak market value, the Plan Bonex decree freed banks of the obligation to return deposits in cash. The Supreme Court overturned lower court rulings that were in favor of individuals who were harmed by the decree. By upholding Menem's decree, the Court gave the executive tremendous discretion over bank deposits, violating Article 17 of the Argentine Constitution, which declares that property is inviolable. In effect, the ruling permitted the government to use economic emergency as a pretext to infringe on property rights. Moreover, *Peralta* sanctioned the use of decrees of necessity and urgency, a tool that permitted Menem to bypass Congress when formulating legislation.[92]

Like *Peralta*, the 1990 *Aerolineas Argentinas* ruling upheld a controversial Menem policy. The privatization of the state-owned airline occurred at a critical moment in the implementation of Menem's economic reform plan.

Congressman Moisés Fontela (UCR) had opposed the airline sale on the basis of irregularities. In response to a ruling that suspended the sale, Menem's Minister of Public Works, Roberto Dromi, circumvented the appellate courts and appealed directly to the Supreme Court. In order to remove obstacles to the airline privatization, the Court obtained jurisdiction over the case by claiming that the sale was a "serious institutional matter." The Court applied "per saltum," a means for a higher court to bypass lower courts, arguing that the matter required quick resolution to avoid "irreparable harm." The *Aerolineas Argentinas* decision was the first time in Argentina's history that the Court used per saltum to bypass lower courts. The ruling set a dangerous precedent that the Supreme Court could use per saltum to intervene in any case involving a "serious institutional matter," regardless of whether the case had first reached a lower court. The Buenos Aires Bar Association argued that the decision violated Article 101 of the Argentine Constitution, which "is clear in requirement that, except in cases of original jurisdiction, the Court will follow the appeal process according to rules dictated by Congress."[93]

The scandal surrounding the disappearance of a ruling against the Central Bank also cast doubt on the Menem Court's autonomy. On June 8, 1993, Justices Levene, Petracchi, Belluscio, Barra, and Fayt had signed a ruling in favor of an attorney who was trying to collect fees from Argentina's Central Bank. The June 8 ruling disappeared from Court records. A new ruling in favor of the Bank reached Petracchi's desk on June 16 with the signatures of Boggiano, Barra, Moliné O'Connor, and Nazareno, the four justices who had voted against the original ruling. The Supreme Court Auditing Committee held that Chief Justice Boggiano was responsible for the disappearance. Executive officials had pressured Boggiano to replace the June 8 decision with a ruling favorable to the Menem administration. The executive interference in the Court was the source of widespread criticism and led to a barrage of impeachment suits against Supreme Court justices. Petracchi and Belluscio denounced the executive interference, and bar associations across Argentina, including the Buenos Aires, La Roca, and Santa Fe associations, voiced opposition.[94]

The Supreme Court also intervened in local elections to ensure the victory of pro-Menem candidates. In 1992, the Court intervened in the province of Corrientes's gubernatorial election. The provincial Supreme Court had upheld the Corrientes Electoral College's decision that the Pacto Autonomista Liberal (PAL) candidate had defeated the PJ candidate. The Corrientes PJ appealed the Electoral College's decision to the federal Supreme Court, and the Menem Court nullified the election on the very day of the appeal. By declaring null the decision of the Corrientes Electoral College, the Court violated Article 105 of the Argentine Constitution, which declares that provinces elect their officials without federal intervention. By disregarding the guarantee of provincial autonomy, the Court satisfied the national government. Constitutional law scholar Jorge Vanossi argues that the PJ used the judicial branch to obtain what it could not achieve through the electoral process.[95] The Court also intervened in local elections in the 1991 *Avellaneda* case. Although the elections for the mayor of Avellaneda were replete with irregularities, the Court ruled that the Menemist candidate could assume the mayorship. The UCR candidate declared that the ruling was proof of the Court's subordination to the executive: "We all know that there were voters from outside the district and that the irregularities included voting twice . . . If the Court had taken into account the fraud verified by the Electoral Tribunal, the PJ candidate would not be mayor."[96]

THE DE FACTO DOCTRINE

In order to regularize relations with the de facto military governments that have been commonplace since 1930, the Argentine Supreme Court has given the same validity to laws passed by military governments as to those passed by civilian administrations. The Court has a long history of accepting the legitimacy of laws passed by governments that came to power by force rather than by election. In 1930, the Supreme Court recognized the military government of General Uriburu: "The provisional government, which has just been established in the country, is, then, a de facto government the title of which cannot be judicially disputed with success by persons in so far as it carries out the administrative and political function derived from the possession of force as an instrument of order and security."[97] In 1935, the Court reiterated the de facto principle in two cases, *Administración de Impuestos Internos* and *Avellaneda Huergo*. In the former, the Court ruled that the provisional president had the same powers granted to elected presidents by Article 86 of the Argentine Constitution. Moreover, the Court ruled that in the absence of Congress, the de facto government could exercise legislative authority by issuing decrees. In *Avellaneda Huergo*, the Court rejected a suit filed by a judge who had been dismissed by the military government. The Court ruled that de facto governments could remove judges, the president, the vice-president, and legislators. In the wake of the 1943 coup, the Court declared all military government acts legal until repealed by a constitutional government.[98]

The De Facto Doctrine during the 1946–83 Period

Beginning in 1946, the Court broadened its legitimization of de facto governments. The Perón Court ruled in *Arlandini* that legislation passed by a de facto government is exempt from judicial review. In the 1947 *Egidio Ziella* ruling, the Court declared that the only way to repeal de facto decrees is through the passage of new laws: "[T]he decree-laws enacted by de facto governments are valid on the basis of their origin, and because they have the value of laws, they are valid even when not ratified by Congress; once Congress is re-established, they may only be abrogated by other legislative commitments."[99] The Court continued to validate the de facto doctrine through the 1970s. In 1970, the Court recognized the military government that deposed Onganía.[100] In the 1977 *Lockman* decision, the Court legitimized the junta that seized power in 1976: "[T]he Institutional Acts and the Statute of the Process for National Reorganization are part of the constitution so long as the causes which conferred legitimacy to those norms remain in existence, those norms being grounded on the state of necessity which prompted the adoption of exceptional measures."[101]

Alfonsín's Rejection and Menem's Reinstatement of the De Facto Doctrine

Alfonsín abandoned the de facto doctrine that had legitimized past military regimes. Under Alfonsín, Argentine judges repealed de facto laws. Congress unanimously approved Alfonsín's proposal to nullify the junta's self-amnesty law on the basis that de facto laws do not possess the same validity as laws passed by civilian governments. The Alfonsín Court upheld the new law in its *Aramayo* and *Dufourq* rulings. In its 1987 *Budano* ruling, the Court ruled that constitutional governments could reject de facto laws due to their unconstitutional origin.[102]

In 1990, the Menem Court reinstated the de facto doctrine. In *Godoy*, the Menem Court overturned the Alfonsín Court ruling that had rejected the validity of de facto laws. The Menem Court argued that because of Argentina's short history of democracy, refusal to accept de facto laws would create legal uncertainty.[103] Although the ruling provided a degree of continuity to counter the instability created by coups, it undermined the legitimacy of the courts. By validating the de facto doctrine, Menem retreated from an important step taken by his predecessor toward the establishment of judicial autonomy.

Table 2.2 summarizes the history of the gap between informal and formal rules in Argentina. It demonstrates that most constitutional guarantees of judicial autonomy prevailed from 1862 through Perón's 1946 assumption of the presidency, although a decline in judicial independence began as early 1930. By 1946, it was clear that a set of informal practices had emerged. These practices that allowed presidents to control the courts continued through the 1976–83 military dictatorship. The 1983–89 era marked a tentative return to Argentina's pre-Perón history when practice upheld the formal rules. Menem's 1989 assumption of power, however, brought about an abrupt end to Alfonsín's compliance with the formal rules of the game.

TABLE 2.2

History of Informal Practices in Argentina, 1862–1999

	1862–1946	1946–83	Alfonsín (1983–89)	Menem (1989–99)
The executive uses an opaque process to appoint pliant justices	No	Yes—except the 1976–1983 military government	No	Yes
The executive violates judges' tenure protection	No—except the 1930 de facto government's dismissal of lower court judges	Yes	Yes	Yes
The executive packs the Supreme Court	No—except the 1869 Court expansion	Yes	No	Yes
Judges are unwilling to endure the costs of ruling against executive interests	No—although the Court began to show some restraint after the 1930 coup	Yes	No	Yes
Judges uphold the de facto doctrine	Yes	Yes	No	Yes
Number of practices that indicate executive subordination of the judiciary	1 out of 5: High degree of judicial autonomy (although decline began in 1930)	5 out of 5: Executive subordination of the courts	1 out of 5: High degree of judicial autonomy	5 out of 5: Executive subordination of the courts

Menem appeared to have modeled his treatment of the courts after that of the founder of his party, Perón himself.

Assessments of Judicial Autonomy during the Menem Presidency

Menem's treatment of the judiciary demonstrates that he embraced the informal practices that had allowed past presidents to control the courts. In addition, outside observers and inside actors report that Menem restored the traditional executive subordination of the judiciary. The U.S. State Department, the U.S. press, and Freedom House assert that Menem influenced and sought to control judges.[104] According to a survey of business executives from 4,022 firms operating in fifty-nine countries, Argentina ranked a low fifty-fourth for judicial independence.[105] Horacio Lynch, the founder of the Argentine civil society group Foro de Estudios para la Justicia (FORES), argues that the Menem Court acted as a tool of rather than as a check on the president. Many Argentine academics concur with the FORES conclusion. According to political scientists Ana María Mustapic and Catalina Smulovitz, Menem subverted the Argentine Supreme Court. María Angélica Gelli, a prominent constitutional law expert, asserts that Menem manipulated the judiciary to further his political goals.[106]

Political actors also report that Menem subordinated the courts. Domingo Cavallo, Menem's Minister of Economy, criticized Menem's control of the courts. According to Cavallo, the subordination of the courts was an obstacle to economic growth. In addition, Cavallo accused Menem's Interior Minister Carlos Corach of pressuring federal judges to dismiss corruption charges against administration officials.[107] UCR Congresswoman Elisa Carrió, a 2003 presidential candidate, characterizes the "Menemist regime" as a system in which the president undermined judicial autonomy in order to guarantee the impunity of executive officials and to ensure that judges did not challenge his policies. According to UCR Congressman Melchor Cruchaga and former UCR Congressman Vanossi, Menem took deliberate steps to gain control of the judiciary.[108]

The Argentine public also believed that Menem dominated the federal courts. According to a 1992 public opinion poll, only 11 percent of Argentines believed that the Menem judiciary performed "well" or "very well." Respondents attributed their negative assessment to the assaults on judicial autonomy from administration officials seeking impunity.[109] In 1994, only 8 percent of Argentines believed that the Supreme Court was independent of Menem; 78 percent of respondents characterized the Court as subordinate to the president.[110] In 1995, 49 percent described the judiciary as "bad" or "very bad," and 40 percent described it as only mediocre.[111] In addition, opinion polls demonstrate that the image of the federal judiciary declined over the course of the Menem administration. In 1990, 20 percent of respondents had a positive image and 29 percent had a negative image. In 1996, only 11 percent had a positive image and 48 percent had a negative image of the courts.[112] According to a 1984 Gallup poll, 57 percent of the population had faith in the judiciary. A 1996 Gallup poll revealed that the percentage had plummeted to 11 percent.[113]

Inside actors including lawyers, public prosecutors, and judges shared the negative assessment. In a 1992 survey, 93 percent of Buenos Aires attorneys characterized the judiciary as "not independent" or only "marginally independent."[114] According to a federal prosecutor, judicial autonomy declined under Menem. Due to personal ties to Menem, most federal criminal judges and Supreme Court justices were vulnerable to executive pressure. A federal judge reports that the Menem administration pressured judges who ruled on cases in which the president had an interest; the judge's colleagues received direct pressure in the form of phone calls. Members of the Menem Supreme Court also criticize Menem's subordination of the judiciary.[115]

The next chapter explains why judicial autonomy has grown and receded at key moments in Argentine history. It explores the factors behind the concentration of power in the hands of particular presidents. Specifically, it assesses how dominant one-party configurations and strict party discipline can render horizontal accountability agencies including the judiciary unable to check the executive branch.

CHAPTER 3

Monolithic Party Control and Critical Junctures

The Erosion of the Rule of Law under Perón and Menem

THE CHANGING LEVEL of party competition has been a principal factor behind Argentina's nonlinear experience with the rule of law. The monolithic party control that emerged in 1946 under Perón and in 1989 under Menem was the reason for Argentina's two key moments of regression away from the rule of law. Both 1946 and 1989 constituted critical junctures in Argentina's political development.[1] Unified Partido Justicialista (PJ) government coupled with a high level of party discipline provided the Peronist presidents with the congressional support necessary to subordinate organs of control, including the courts. In contrast, competitive politics in pre-Perón Argentina and during the Alfonsín era fostered the rule of law. The progress toward the rule of law during these periods was in part a product of a balance of power between at least two political parties, neither of which sustained monolithic control, meaning that no highly disciplined party controlled both the legislative and executive branches. Party competition and a low level of discipline created a climate in which horizontal accountability agencies could emerge.

This chapter explores the relationship between party competition and the rule of law in Argentina. It begins by tracing the history of competitive politics across the four phases delineated in Chapter 2 to demonstrate that both elements of monolithic party control, unified government and party discipline, were present during periods of executive subordination of the courts. In contrast, competitive politics characterized the eras of judicial independence. Section I demonstrates that party competition fostered divided government during Argentina's pre-Perón history, a period characterized by a high degree of judicial autonomy. Section II turns to Argentina's first prolonged period of regression away from the rule of law, the 1946–83 phase, when monolithic party control prevailed. Section III explores the post-transition era and contrasts the divided government of the Alfonsín presidency (1983–89) and of the final two years of Menem's term (1997–99) with the monolithic PJ control that characterized Menem's first eight years in office (1989–97). Section IV explores the sources of monolithic party control in Argentina. It shows how the party system has encouraged unified government since 1946 and how the rules that govern elections and nominations have produced party discipline.

The rule of law requires a system of institutions that constrain arbitrary government action. Along with the judiciary, a legislative branch that checks executive power is a critical component of the rule of law. Section V examines how monolithic party control enabled Perón and Menem to seize informal powers not granted by the Argentine Constitution to bypass Congress. Unified government and party discipline rendered the legislature as well as the judiciary unable to check the executive branch. The remainder of the chapter focuses on the post-transition years to illustrate the importance of party competition for the rule of law. In contrast to Alfonsín who faced divided government throughout his term, the opposition was not a relevant force in Congress until the final two years of Menem's decade-long presidency. Until the opposition's defeat of the PJ in the 1997 midterm elections, monolithic PJ control enabled Menem to manipulate not only the judiciary and Congress, but also to subordinate five other horizontal accountability agencies: the Judicial Council, the Impeachment Jury, the Attorney General's Office, the Accounting Tribunal, and the Office of the Federal Prosecutor in charge of Administrative Investigations. However, the return of divided government in 1997 created a climate propitious for the development of an effective system of horizontal accountability. For the first time since 1989, countervailing power centers began to check executive power.

Party Competition and the Rule of Law in Pre-Perón Argentina (1862–1946)

From 1862 through the 1943 coup, competitive politics permitted progress toward a system that compelled presidents to submit to the law. As Chapter 2 demonstrates, actual practice upheld formal guarantees of judicial autonomy during this early period of Argentine history. Party balance fostered divided government, making it difficult for presidents to subvert the courts. From 1862 through 1880, competition among three relevant parties encouraged divided government. The Nationalist Party, the Autonomist Party, and the National Party vied for power. Argentina's first two presidents, Bartolomé Mitre and Domingo Sarmiento, faced strong opposition in Congress. In addition, the three-party balance fostered coalition government, which made it especially difficult for presidents to push through legislation that would strip control organs of their power. For instance, in order to win the 1874 presidential election, Nicolás Avellaneda of the Nationalist Party entered an alliance with the Autonomist Party. Because of the constantly shifting alliances, the three parties functioned like loosely composed groups rather than as stable political parties.[2]

The years 1880–1906 marked a period of unified government, but the second element of monolithic party control, party discipline, was absent during this period. The party that held the executive and legislative branches was a loose coalition rather than a unified party. Upon assuming power in 1880, President Julio Roca united the disparate groups that brought him to power into a single bloc, the Partido Autonomista Nacional (PAN). Because of its loose organization, lack of party identity, and low discipline, however, PAN dominance was short-lived. Between 1880 and 1906, the coalition unraveled as internal factions emerged. After Roca's first term (1880–86), PAN presidents were unable to maintain the coalition's unity. By the time José Figueroa Alcorta assumed the presidency in 1906, the PAN had broken down. Because of the shift away from PAN dominance and the low level of discipline during this era, Congress was able to check executive power.[3]

The 1891 emergence of the Unión Cívica Radical (UCR) contributed to the demise of the PAN and to competitive politics. The UCR became an increasingly relevant force in Congress beginning in the 1890s. In 1894, the UCR won twelve of the eighty-six seats in the House, and the number rose to sixteen in 1895. In addition, the UCR bloc became increasingly active in Congress. In 1894, the UCR bloc in the House introduced 9 percent of all bills. Just one year later, the UCR bloc introduced 21 percent.[4] In 1916, the UCR captured the presidency.

Competitive politics continued to characterize Argentina from 1916 through the 1943 coup. The UCR administrations of 1916–30 faced a hostile Senate dominated by a strong conservative alliance. When Hipólito Yrigoyen assumed the presidency in 1916, his UCR had only one seat in the Senate and held a minority in the House.[5] Moreover, UCR discipline was low. In fact, UCR leaders such as Senator Bernardo de Irigoyen eschewed strict discipline:

> I do not believe that those who sit in the National Congress, even though their candidacies had been raised by the political parties, should behave as members of those groups. I sustain that, once the scrutiny of the elections is over, the citizens whose candidacies have been sponsored by the parties have no right to favor the interests of these parties.[6]

In 1924, internal feuding led to a split in the UCR, making it even more difficult for the UCR to hold a legislative majority.[7]

The 1930 coup brought the conservative parties back to power and introduced two years of monolithic party control under General José Uriburu, but it did not end the era of party competition. With the restoration of civilian rule in 1932, competitive politics reemerged. With the exception of Agustín Justo's first four years in the presidency, the conservative Concordancia administrations faced a UCR-dominated Congress. Moreover, only the first element of monolithic party control characterized the Justo administration. Justo's Concordancia had a majority in Congress from 1932 until 1936, but discipline was low. Like the PAN, the Concordancia was a loose alliance of conservative parties rather than a unified party.[8] Table 3.1 shows that competitive politics was the norm from 1916 through 1946 and that there were only two cases of monolithic party control, both of which occurred in the wake of military coups.[9]

Monolithic Party Control and the First Period of Regression (1946–83)

The year 1946 was a critical juncture that marked the beginning of a prolonged period of unified government and strict party discipline. Monolithic party control coupled with frequent military coups was behind Argentina's first period of regression away from the rule of law. As Chapter 2 illustrates, executive subordination of the courts characterized the 1946–83 period.

From 1946 through 1983, Argentina had only three years of divided government. The president's party had majorities in both houses from 1946 through 1955, 1958 through 1963, and again from 1973 through 1976. Moreover, the de facto military regimes that governed from 1955 through 1958, 1966 through 1973, and 1976 through 1983 had a monopoly on political power that was tantamount to monolithic party control. Along with unified government, a high level of party discipline contributed to the erosion of the rule of law beginning in 1946. Presidents used their control over their parties to subordinate horizontal accountability agencies, including the judiciary.

Monolithic PJ control allowed Perón to dominate the legislative process and provided him with the congressional support necessary to subordinate checks on his power. For instance, the Peronist majority in the Senate supported his 1947 Supreme Court purge. Perón enjoyed unified PJ government throughout his 1946–55 term in office. He captured the presidency with 54 percent of the vote, and his party held two-thirds of the House and all but two seats in the Senate. Perón engaged in gerrymandering and intimidation to ensure that his party gained congressional seats in the midterm elections. Indeed, in 1948, the Peronists gained total control of the Senate and fourteen additional seats in the House. Unanimous Senate votes became common.[10]

Strict party discipline also characterized the Perón administration. Perón

TABLE 3.1

Divided Government in Argentina, 1916–46

	President	Party of President	Percentage of Senate Seats	Percentage of House Seats	Character of Government
1916–18	Hipólito Yrigoyen	UCR	< 50	37	Divided government
1918*–20	Yrigoyen	UCR	< 50	46	Divided government
1920*–22	Yrigoyen	UCR	< 50	53	Divided government
1922–24	Marcelo T. de Alvear	UCR	46	57	Divided government
1924*–26	Alvear	UCR	30	46	Divided government
1926*–28	Alvear	UCR	23	38	Divided government
1928–30	Yrigoyen	UCR	33	58	Divided government
1930–32	José Uriburu	Military government			Monolithic party control
1932–34	Agustín Pedro Justo	Concordancia (loose alliance)	72	53	Unified government, but low party discipline
1934*–36	Justo	Concordancia	72	52	Unified government, but low party discipline
1936*–38	Justo	Concordancia	76	43	Divided government
1938–40	Roberto M. Ortiz	Concordancia	60	40	Divided government
1940*–42	Ortiz	Concordancia	60	48	Divided government
1942*–43	Ramón S. Castillo	Concordancia	63	42	Divided government
1943–46	Arturo Rawson/ Pedro Ramírez/ Edelmiro Farrell	Military government			Monolithic party control

* Midterm election year.

came to power as the head of a heterogeneous coalition comprised of three parties, but he had eliminated all internal factions by 1950. Shortly after the 1946 election, Perón announced a merger of the three parties and the formation of the hierarchical Partido Único de la Revolución Argentina (renamed the Peronist Party in 1947). Cipriano Reyes, the leader of the strongest of the three parties, the Partido Laborista, voiced opposition to the merger from his seat in Congress. Perón used his authority as president of the Peronist Party to sanction and expel his opponents, including Reyes, from the party. In 1947, Perón visited Congress where he warned that he would punish those who threatened party unity: "If we have to use a knife, we will use it."[11] In 1948, Perón outlawed the Partido Laborista and ordered the arrest of Reyes. Perón based the PJ structure on the vertical organization of the army and even used military terminology. For instance, Perón assumed the title "Supreme Commander" of the PJ.[12]

Monolithic party control also characterized the administration of Unión Cívica Radical Intransigente (UCRI) President Arturo Frondizi (1958–62), permitting him to violate judges' tenure protection and to increase the size of the Supreme Court, as documented in Chapter 2. Like Perón, Frondizi had a two-thirds majority in the House and absolute control of the Senate. In addition, like Perón, Frondizi was at the reins of a highly disciplined party. In fact, 90 percent of UCRI legislators supported Frondizi's bills. Frondizi suspended or expelled party members who dissented. For instance, in order to get the necessary support for a controversial 1960 bill, Frondizi threatened to expel UCRI members who voted against the legislation. After the law's passage, he expelled three and suspended six UCRI legislators who had dissented. When Frondizi pursued policies that contradicted his party's nationalistic platform, UCRI legislators changed the official party platform to reflect Frondizi's policies rather than voice dissent.[13]

In contrast to Frondizi and Perón, Arturo Illia of the Unión Cívica Radical del Pueblo (UCRP) faced divided government from 1963 through 1966, which prevented him from manipulating the courts. Illia won the 1963 presidential elections with only 26 percent of the vote. Moreover, he had a plurality but not a majority in Congress and was unable to form a coalition that would support his bills. Because of the strong legislative opposition, Illia's 1963 attempt to expand the Supreme Court to eleven failed, and he was unable to tamper with Court composition.[14] Illia's three years in the presidency were the exception to the monolithic control that resumed in 1966 and remained until 1983.

As is true in virtually any military regime, the military administrations that governed during the 1946–83 phase had a monopoly on political power that enabled them to subordinate countervailing power centers. After each coup, the dissolution of Congress led to the concentration of power in the ruling junta. This "unified" military government permitted further erosion of the rule of law. As discussed in Chapter 2, in the wake of the coups of 1955, 1966, and 1976, the de facto governments bypassed constitutional channels to purge the Court. Table 3.2 shows that, with the exception of a three-year period, monolithic party control characterized the 1946–83 era.

Competitive Politics in the Post-Transition Era: The Alfonsín and Menem Years

Competitive politics fostered progress toward the rule of law during the Alfonsín administration. In contrast, monolithic PJ control from 1989 until 1997 allowed Menem to return to the executive dominance that had compromised the rule of law during the 1946–83 era. With the opposition's defeat of Menem's PJ in the 1997 midterm elections, however, the courts and other horizontal accountability agencies began to assert their autonomy from the president.

DIVIDED GOVERNMENT OF THE ALFONSÍN YEARS (1983–89)

During Alfonsín's presidency, divided government helped drain power away from the executive. The presence of a strong opposition in Congress from 1983 through 1989 provided the opportunity to develop mechanisms of accountability within the law. As Chapter 2 demonstrates, the judiciary was more autonomous of the executive under Alfonsín than it was under Menem. Divided government compelled Alfonsín's UCR to cooperate with the PJ in Congress. Alfonsín did not have the support necessary to push bills through the legislature. For instance, in contrast to Menem, Alfonsín was unable to expand the size of the Supreme Court.

Alfonsín faced strong opposition in both the Senate and the House. As Table 3.3 shows, Alfonsín's UCR never had a majority in the Senate. In the 1983 elections, the UCR obtained only 39 percent of Senate seats. The PJ and its allies won 46 percent. In order to form a majority necessary to pass legislation, UCR senators compromised with opposition members. UCR-PJ agreements were frequent. For instance, senators engaged in intense interparty bargaining over judicial appointments. Divided government prevented Alfonsín from filling the courts with UCR judges. The strength of the PJ led to the Senate's frequent rejection of Alfonsín nominees.[15] PJ member Vicente Saadi presided over the Senate Appointment Committee. Renowned as a tough negotiator, Saadi used his skills to ensure that there was a PJ appointee for each UCR appointee. Journalist Horacio Verbitsky recalls the frequency of tacit agreements between the two parties. For instance, when the UCR appointed a judge, the PJ often selected a public prosecutor and vice versa.[16]

TABLE 3.2

Monolithic Party Control in Argentina, 1946–83

	President	Party of President	Percentage of Senate Seats	Percentage of House Seats	Character of Government
1946–48	Juan Domingo Perón	PJ	93	67	Monolithic party control
1948*–52	Perón	PJ	100	69	Monolithic party control
1952–54	Perón	PJ	100	64	Monolithic party control
1954*–55	Perón	PJ	100	90	Monolithic party control
1955–58	Eduardo Lonardi/ Pedro E. Aramburu	Military government			Monolithic party control
1958–60	Frondizi	UCRI	100	70	Monolithic party control
1960*–62	Frondizi	UCRI	100	57	Monolithic party control
1962–63	José María Guido	Military government			Monolithic party control
1963–65	Arturo Illia	UCRP	54	37	Divided government
1965*–66	Illia	UCRP	54	35	Divided government
1966–73	Juan Carlos Onganía/ Roberto M. Levingston/ Alejandro Lanusse	Military government			Monolithic party control
1973–76	Hector Cámpora/ Raúl Lastiri/ Perón	PJ	65	53	Monolithic party control
1976–83	Jorge Videla/ Roberto Viola/ Leopoldo Galtieri/ Reynaldo Bignone	Military government			Monolithic party control

* Midterm election year.

TABLE 3.3

Distribution of Senate Seats under Alfonsín, 1983–89

Political Party	Number of Seats	Percentage
UCR	18	39.1
PJ	21	45.7
Other	7	15.2
TOTAL	46	100

SOURCE: N. Guillermo Molinelli, M. Valeria Palanza, and Gisela Sin, *Congreso, presidencia y justicia en Argentina: Materiales por su estudio* (Buenos Aires: Temas Grupo Editorial, 1999), 242–43.

TABLE 3.4

Distribution of House Seats under Alfonsín, 1983–89

Party	1983–85		1985–87		1987–89	
	Seats	Percentage	Seats	Percentage	Seats	Percentage
UCR	129	50.8	129	50.8	114	44.9
PJ	111	43.7	85	33.5	97	38.2
Other	14	5.5	40	15.7	43	16.9
TOTAL	254	100	254	100	254	100

SOURCE: Molinelli, Palanza, and Sin, *Congreso, presidencia y justicia*, 242–43.

Alfonsín's UCR did not dominate the House. As Table 3.4 shows, during his first four years in office, the UCR had a narrow majority with just over 50 percent of the seats. When the UCR lost its majority in the 1987 legislative elections, Alfonsín's party no longer had a sufficient percentage of seats for a quorum. UCR House members had to cooperate with the PJ to pass legislation.[17]

MONOLITHIC PARTY CONTROL OF THE MENEM YEARS (1989–97)

Menem's 1989 assumption of power ushered in a return to the monolithic party control that had enabled Perón and Frondizi to subordinate the judiciary. In contrast to the competitive politics that reduced Alfonsín's partisan powers, unified PJ government and party discipline under Menem permitted the reemergence of Argentina's traditional ultrapresidentialism

TABLE 3.5

Distribution of Senate Seats under Menem, 1989–98

Party	1989–92		1992–95		1995–98	
	Seats	Percentage	Seats	Percentage	Seats	Percentage
PJ	26	54.2	29	60.5	37	52.8
UCR	14	29.2	10	20.8	18	25.7
Other	8	16.6	9	18.7	15	21.5
TOTAL	48	100	48	100	70	100

SOURCE: Molinelli, Palanza, and Sin, *Congreso, presidencia y justicia*, 242–43. The number of senators rose from 46 to 48 in 1991 when Tierra del Fuego became a province. In 1995, the number rose to 72 when each province began to elect three rather than two senators. From 1995 through 1998, the province of Catamarca sent only one senator, leaving two seats vacant.

and of practices such as court-packing. As Table 3.5 illustrates, the PJ had an absolute majority in the Senate throughout Menem's ten years in the presidency, which contributed to Menem's discretion over judicial appointments. During Menem's two terms, the Senate never rejected a Supreme Court candidate nominated by the president.

The PJ and its allies held a majority in the House from 1989 until 1997. Table 3.6 shows that during Menem's first term (1989–95), the PJ and its ally, the conservative Unión del Centro Democrático (UCeDé), held a majority. In 1995, Menem's PJ gained an absolute majority with 51 percent.[18]

Party discipline enhanced Menem's partisan powers, exacerbating the effects of unified government. PJ legislators practiced a relatively high level of discipline during the Menem administration, enabling the president to pass legislation with relative ease. From 1955 until Menem's 1989 assumption of the presidency, the PJ experienced a decline in the level of discipline. After the 1955 coup that overthrew Perón, a decentralized, informal organization emerged that overshadowed the formal hierarchy.[19] After Perón's death in 1974, internal struggle over his successor led to further collapse of the party's vertical structure. The PJ emerged from the 1976–83 military dictatorship in disarray. Conflict between the orthodox PJ trade unions and reformers split the party through the late 1980s. Internal divisions persisted as late as the July 1988 PJ primaries when Menem defeated Antonio Cafiero by a narrow margin. By the time Menem became president, however, the reformers had defeated the orthodox Peronists.[20]

Under Menem, PJ voting behavior reflected a high degree of discipline. During the weekly PJ bloc meetings, party leaders informed legislators of

TABLE 3.6

Distribution of House Seats under Menem, 1989–99

Party	1989–91		1991–93		1993–95		1995–97		1997–99	
	Seats	%	Seats	%	Seats	%	Seats	%	Seats	%
PJ	120	47.2	116	45.1	127	49.4	131	51	119	46.3
UCR	90	35.4	84	32.7	84	32.7	68	26.5	—	—
UCeDé	11	4.4	10	3.9	4	1.6	2	0.7	1	.4
Frepaso	—	—	—	—	—	—	22	8.6	—	—
Alianza	—	—	—	—	—	—	—	—	111	43.2
Other	33	13	47	18.3	42	16.3	34	13.2	26	10.1
TOTAL	254	100	257	100	257	100	257	100	257	100

SOURCE: The 1989–1997 data are from Molinelli, Palanza, and Sin, *Congreso, presidencia y justicia*, 277–78.

the official party stance in upcoming votes. In his analysis of 1989–91 roll call votes in the House of Representatives, Jones finds that PJ members rarely voted against their party. PJ legislators who opposed the official stance usually missed the session rather than register an abstention or vote against the PJ. Of the PJ House members who cast a vote during the 1989–97 legislative sessions, 97 percent voted with the party majority. Moreover, the infrequency of roll call votes suggests that Menem did not have to resort to these votes to produce discipline. In addition, the PJ voted as a unified bloc in the congressional committees that produce *dictamenes*, the majority and minority reports on proposed legislation. PJ committee members voted for the same *dictamen* in 496 out of 507 House votes, or 98 percent, and 519 out of 525 Senate votes, or 99 percent.[21] Furthermore, Argentine legislators report a high level of party discipline. According to Congresswoman Elisa Carrió, due to strict party discipline, a president who has a majority in both houses is "hegemonic." Former Congressman Jorge Vanossi attributes executive dominance to Menem's control of the party apparatus.[22]

As de facto PJ president, Menem had a set of tools to produce discipline. Due to PJ decentralization, leaders must produce discipline; it does not arise naturally.[23] Although the PJ charter prohibits the Argentine president from serving as PJ president, Menem acted as the party leader. In order to maintain a façade of respect for the formal rules, the PJ designated Menem as party president and then placed him on sabbatical. In reality, however, he acted as PJ president. Menem's dual role as PJ leader and national president allowed him to create incentives for PJ legislators to support his policy preferences. He used his discretion over access to PJ electoral lists, to economic resources, and to party leadership posts to counter the decentralized nature of the party. Like Perón, he used these resources to reward PJ legislators who voted according to his orders and to punish those who strayed.[24]

THE 1997 RETURN OF DIVIDED GOVERNMENT

In the 1997 midterm elections, divided government reemerged. The PJ lost its majority in the House, and the UCeDé was no longer a relevant force in Congress. Senator Juan Aguirre Lanari recalls that for the first time Menem had difficulty imposing his agenda on the House.[25] In addition, divided government permitted the Court and other horizontal accountability agencies to begin to act as checks on the president. The return of divided government set the stage for the Supreme Court to oppose Menem's reelection for a third consecutive term, which Menem ultimately chose not to seek. A change in the Court's composition was not necessary for the Court to assert its autonomy from Menem. Competitive politics was sufficient to provide judges with the opportunity to rule against executive interests. Before the PJ defeat in the 1997 midterm elections, it appeared likely that the Court would permit Menem to run for a third term despite the constitutional ban on more than two consecutive terms. The growing strength of the opposition in Congress, however, permitted the Menem Court to resist executive pressure. Justices, including members of the "automatic Menemist majority," signaled that they would declare a third consecutive term unconstitutional if the case were to reach the Supreme Court.[26]

The growing strength of opposition parties also allowed the Court to reverse its stance on the Menem administration's illegal arms sales to Croatia and Ecuador. The 1991 arms shipments to Croatia violated a United Nations arms embargo, and the 1995 sale of weapons to Ecuador violated official Argentine policy. At the time, Argentina was a moderator in the conflict between Ecuador and Peru. Until 1997, the Court had supported Menem's efforts to stop investigations into executive functionaries' role in the arms sales. After the 1997 midterm congressional election, however, the Court no longer shielded the Menem administration from investigation. When public prosecutor Carlos Stornelli attempted to convict government officials in the first instance courts, the Menem administration appealed directly to the Supreme Court. In contrast to the Court's 1990 *Aerolineas Argentinas* ruling that applied per saltum, in 1998, the Court refused to bypass appellate courts and seize jurisdiction.[27]

Explaining Monolithic Party Control in Argentina: The Sources of Unified Government and Party Discipline

This section explores the sources of the monolithic party control that permitted assaults against the rule of law from 1946 through 1983 and during Menem's first eight years as president. The predominance of two parties contributed to unified government in Argentina. Electoral rules, the procedures governing nominations, and the power of party presidents explain the high level of party discipline.

ARGENTINA'S TWO-PARTY SYSTEM AND UNIFIED GOVERNMENT

The number of political parties plays a role in determining whether there is unified government, the first element of monolithic party control. When there are more than two relevant parties, divided government is likely. Moreover, the likelihood of coalition government increases with the number of parties. Indeed, in pre-Perón Argentina, competition among at least three relevant parties fostered divided government and the formation of coalitions.

In contrast to the three-party competition and coalition governments of the 1862–1946 period, the dominance of two parties increased the likelihood of unified government after the 1946 emergence of the Peronist Party (PJ). Throughout the latter half of the twentieth century, the PJ and UCR dominated the political arena. As of 1993, 31 percent of Argentines were affiliates of either the PJ or the UCR. With 3.85 million members, or 18 percent of the electorate, the PJ was one of the world's largest democratic parties.[28] Despite a decrease in the UCR-PJ share of seats after the 1983 transition, no relevant third party competed at the national level until 1994. As of 1991, affiliation in a third party did not surpass 1 percent. Most third parties competed in only one province. Until 1994, no party other than the PJ or UCR received over 6 percent of the vote in national legislative elections.[29] The two strongest third parties at the national level, the Partido Instransigente (PI) and the UCeDé, played only a marginal role. In 1983, of the eight third parties with representation in the House, the PI was the strongest with only three of the 254 House seats. In 1991, of the twenty-five third parties that held a total of fifty-seven House seats, the UCeDé had the most with nine. The PI disappeared in 1987, and the UCeDé had disappeared by 1993.[30]

Only once in contemporary Argentine history has a third party appeared in a position to topple the two-party system. From 1994 to 1997, the Frente por un País Solidario (Frepaso), a leftist party led by dissident PJ members, won a significant number of congressional seats and presidential votes, and the UCR share of the vote fell. The UCR share of House seats dropped from 51 percent in 1985 to 27 percent in 1995. In the 1995 presidential election, the Frepaso candidate received 29 percent of the vote, whereas the UCR candidate received only 17 percent.[31] Although the rise of Frepaso appeared to signal a shift toward a three party system, Frepaso's 1997 alignment with the UCR brought about a return to two blocs. Despite tensions between Frepaso and UCR, they formed a coalition, the Alianza para el Trabajo, la Justicia y la Educación (Alianza).

ELECTORAL RULES AND PARTY DISCIPLINE

Argentina's electoral rules and nomination procedures have encouraged party discipline, the second element of monolithic party control. In Argentina, party affiliation is necessary to run for office, and victory requires a good relationship with the party. In fact, political campaigns emphasize party affiliation rather than candidates' qualifications.[32] As a result of Argentina's d'Hondt system of proportional representation (PR) and closed party lists, legislators owe their political careers to the national party.

In Argentina's closed-list PR system, the party's discretion over legislators' chances of reelection provides an incentive for legislators to respond to the party president rather than to voters. Although reelection motivates members of Congress in both Argentina and the United States, legislators from the two countries work within different electoral systems, which lead to very different incentive structures. In the U.S. system of single member districts and direct primaries, legislators have incentives to maximize their electoral support in their district.[33] In contrast, Argentine voters select a party rather than a candidate, which motivates legislators to build a good relationship with their party. The party determines the order of candidates on the party list, and voters cannot eliminate or change the order of names on the list. Legislators who vote against their party risk losing access to electoral lists.[34] As a result, a national president who is also party president wields tremendous power over fellow party members in Congress. Macdonald explains,

> Because the president is the head of the nation and the leader of his party, he is able to wield a large measure of authority not contemplated by the constitution but resulting from the party system. He frequently determines party policies, and enforces his will not only upon his lieutenants, but also upon the rank and file of the party workers. Party candidates, especially for national deputy or senator, are generally chosen after conferences between the president and the governors of the provinces directly concerned . . . it is almost impossible for any member of the president's party to be elected to Congress without presidential consent. Under such circumstances, it is no great feat to subordinate the legislative branch to the executive.[35]

Even Argentine legislators who do not seek reelection face incentives to vote with their party. Their career prospects after leaving Congress continue to demand a good relationship with their party. Jones demonstrates that most legislators hold party-related posts after their congressional terms. Of the 108 Argentine House members who left Congress following their 1991–95 term, 82 occupied party-related posts after leaving the legislature.[36]

Argentine party leaders also use their discretion over the distribution of congressional committee seats and party leadership posts to achieve discipline. In Argentina, a seniority system does not determine committee assignments. Although Senate and House presidents have the formal power to allocate leadership posts such as committee chair, in practice, party leaders exercise this power. For instance, during the Menem administration, House President Alberto Pierri (PJ) honored party leaders' requests regarding committee leadership positions.[37]

Leadership posts increase legislators' access to valuable financial and personnel resources. As a result of the shortage of legislative assistants to help research and draft bills, staff is an important resource. House members receive only $5,000 per month to pay staffers. The party leader can increase this sum by appointing a legislator to serve as a committee chair or as a member of the party directorate. Committee chairs receive 50 percent more money for staff than do other legislators. Committee secretaries and party directorate members receive 25 percent over the base for staff. In addition, committee members have access to their committee's four-member permanent staff.[38]

The national party organization's power to expel members also promotes discipline. Both the PJ and UCR have expelled members who vote against the official party line. Expulsion from the party effectively ends a legislator's political career and carries high personal costs. Partisan affiliation is central to the identity of both PJ and UCR legislators. Many legislators have been active in their party since their youth. They tend to socialize exclusively with fellow party members; interparty friendship is rare.[39] According to Mustapic, the PJ and UCR behave like "families," which discourages internal ruptures. Party members are unlikely to abandon or betray their family.[40] Levitsky points to a strong PJ subculture that includes common traditions, symbols, and beliefs.[41]

Monolithic PJ Control and the Demise of Congress as a Check on Executive Power

The year 1946 represented a turning point not only for the courts, but also for the Argentine Congress. Like the judiciary, Congress is an essential check on executive power in a rule of law system. Monolithic Peronist control, however, enabled both Perón and Menem to seize legislative powers not granted by the Argentine Constitution. Mainwaring and Shugart focus on two types of executive authority: partisan and formal or constitutional powers.[42] Unified government coupled with party discipline permitted the two Peronist presidents to exercise a third type, informal power, which hindered the ability of Congress to act as a control on the executive. Like the informal practices that allowed Perón and Menem to subordinate the courts, the informal powers that allowed them to bypass Congress violated the constitution. In particular, the line-item veto and decrees of necessity and urgency permitted the passage of new legislation that altered the status quo without congressional consent.

THE LINE-ITEM VETO: AN INFORMAL POWER

Since Perón's first term, the line-item veto, an informal proactive power, has undermined the legislature's role as a check on the president's power.[43] The 1853 constitution stipulated that the executive could object to a bill in whole or in part but must then return the entire bill to Congress for reconsideration. Nevertheless, since 1946, presidents have ratified portions of bills that they supported and returned the vetoed parts to Congress. As with other informal practices that violate the constitution, the line-item veto became a frequent practice under Perón and reached an unprecedented level under Menem. Until 1946, line-item vetoes were rare and limited for the most part to budgetary law. From 1862 through 1946, Argentine presidents resorted to the line-item veto on only ten occasions. Moreover, throughout the 1862–1946 period, Congress and leading constitutional scholars shared the view that the line-item veto violated the constitution. In 1932, for instance, the House issued a resolution declaring the line-item veto unconstitutional.[44]

Beginning in 1946, however, a Congress dominated by the president's party and the pliant Supreme Court accepted the line-item veto as a valid executive power. Unlike their predecessors, Perón and Frondizi resorted frequently to the line-item veto. Perón issued ten line-item vetoes, and he did not limit these vetoes to budgetary law. Perón's short-lived 1949 constitution gave the line-item veto constitutional status, which encouraged tacit congressional acceptance of the informal practice after the 1956 reinstatement of the 1853 constitution. Indeed, after 1956, Congress did not oppose the practice. Frondizi used the line-item veto seven times during his four years in office from 1958 until 1962. In the 1967 *Colella* decision, the Court implicitly sanctioned the line-item veto by ruling that the president could veto portions of a bill if the change did not affect the "unity" or "spirit" of the bill. As Molinelli argues, even with the unity restriction, the line-item veto undermines congressional will. A law is a delicate equilibrium of its parts. Legislators' agreement to sanction one part of a bill is often contingent on the inclusion of another part. The line-item veto violates complex transactions between party blocs, between the two houses, and between the legislative and executive branches.[45]

Use of this proactive power continued after the 1983 democratic transition and increased under Menem. Although Alfonsín did resort to the line-item veto, his use of the informal power did not approach that of Menem. Alfonsín issued twelve line-item vetoes. Menem resorted to the line-item veto sixty-one times between 1989 and 1995.[46]

Argentina's 1994 constitutional reform transformed the line-item veto from an informal to a formal executive power. Although the 1994 constitution grants line-item veto authority to the president, constitutional limitations on its use have the potential to prevent future abuse of the proactive power. According to Article 82, the executive can no longer use the argument that Congress tacitly approved a line-item veto: "The will of each House shall be expressly stated; tacit or fictitious approval is forbidden."[47] Moreover, Article 80 states: "When a bill is partially rejected, the remaining part shall not be approved. Non-vetoed parts may be promulgated only if they have normative autonomy and if their partial approval does not alter the spirit or the unity of the bill approved by Congress."[48] In addition to incorporating the unity limitation, the 1994 constitution stipulates:

> Within ten days, the Chief of Cabinet shall personally submit the [line-item veto] decision to the consideration of the Joint Standing Committee of Congress, which shall be composed to reflect the proportion of seats held by each party in both houses. Within ten days, this standing committee shall submit its report to the plenary meeting of both houses for their immediate consideration. A special law enacted by the absolute majority of all members of both houses shall regulate the procedure and scope of congressional participation.[49]

In theory, the intervention of a Joint Standing Committee increases Congress's ability to intervene and prevent executive abuse of the line-item veto. The new limitations on the line-item veto have the potential to check the executive, especially under divided government.

DECREES OF NECESSITY AND URGENCY: AN INFORMAL POWER

Like the line-item veto, the informal power to issue decrees of necessity and urgency (DNUs) shifted the balance of power from the legislative to the executive branch. Like most Latin American presidents, the Argentine executive has had the constitutional power to issue regulatory and administrative decrees but not to issue new legislation without having been delegated that power by Congress. Argentine presidents, however, have seized the informal power to issue decrees without prior congressional delegation in times of necessity or urgency. This proactive power has usurped congressional authority and contributed to executive dominance in Argentina. As Mainwaring and Shugart explain, decrees are potent executive instruments. Decrees become law before Congress or the judiciary can react. In addition, when a president issues multiple decrees in a short period, Congress does not have sufficient time to repeal them before they make an impact.[50] Jones demonstrates how decree power can serve as a tool to pressure Congress to sanction a particular law. Menem warned legislators that if they did not pass a particular bill, he would implement it by DNU, thereby eliminating congressional ability to influence the bill's content.[51]

Until Menem assumed power, DNUs were rare. From 1862 until 1983, presidents issued a total of twenty-five DNUs. The use of DNUs increased under Alfonsín, who issued ten of these decrees. However, Menem's reliance on the DNU dwarfed that of Alfonsín. The majority of Alfonsín's DNUs addressed the national economic crisis, arguably a true emergency. In addition, the Alfonsín Court placed restraints on DNUs. In the *Rolón Zappa* ruling, the Court rejected Alfonsín's economic emergency justification for a DNU that permitted the state to seize the assets of retired persons. Menem faced no such restrictions on his decree power. Between 1989 and the 1994 constitutional reform, Menem issued 336 DNUs. In his attempt to justify the decrees, he argued that they treated urgent matters requiring immediate attention. In reality, his DNUs addressed issues such as donating cement to Bolivia, televising soccer games, and taxing movies. Furthermore, although Menem claimed that Congress was in recess when he issued the DNUs, he issued 38 percent of his DNUs when Congress was in ordinary session and 62 percent during extraordinary sessions.[52]

Despite the dubious constitutionality of the DNUs, neither the PJ-dominated Congress nor the Menem Court challenged the decrees. Most DNUs were brought to congressional attention, yet Congress met 91 percent with silence, ratified 8 percent, and repealed only 1 percent.[53] Moreover, the PJ majority in the House rejected UCR Congressman Vanossi's 1992 bill to limit DNUs.[54] UCR Congresswoman Carrió traces Menem's accumulation of power to congressional inaction in the face of DNUs and line-item vetoes.[55] Like Congress, the Menem Court did not restrict DNUs. As discussed in Chapter 2, in contrast to the Alfonsín Court's *Rolón Zappa* ruling, the Menem Court's *Peralta* ruling sanctioned DNUs.

The 1990 *Peralta* decision set the stage for the 1994 reform that gave DNUs constitutional status. Although the 1994 constitution transformed the informal practice into a formal power, as with the line-item veto, new constitutional limits on DNUs have the potential to prevent abuse. Article 99 forbids DNUs in matters involving crime, taxation, elections, and political parties and requires presidents to use the same procedure for DNUs that they use for line-item vetoes. Thus, the executive must submit the DNU to the Joint Standing Committee, which has ten days to submit its report to the plenary sessions of both houses for immediate consideration.[56] As with the line-item veto, under divided government, Congress could prevent future presidents from abusing DNUs. On the other hand, monolithic party control could render meaningless the constitutional restrictions on DNUs.

Monolithic Party Control and the Erosion of Argentina's Horizontal Accountability System

The monolithic PJ control of 1989–97 neutralized not only the judiciary and Congress, but the entire system of horizontal accountability that should uphold the rule of law. In the absence of competitive politics, Menem was able to strip horizontal accountability agencies of their power to act as controls. In theory, the 1994 constitutional reform created new agencies with the authority to check the president. However, unified government and party discipline allowed Menem to delay the creation of a Judicial Council and an Impeachment Jury with the autonomy necessary to reduce executive discretion over judicial appointments and removals. The challenge facing Menem's Argentina was not a dearth of potential countervailing power centers but rather the PJ dominance that allowed Menem to subordinate the Attorney General's Office, the Accounting Tribunal, and the Federal Prosecutor in charge of Administrative Investigations, all of which had existed long before Menem assumed power. It was not until the 1997 reemergence of divided government that these agencies along with the Judicial Council and the Impeachment Jury began to check executive power.

PARTY COMPETITION AND THE JUDICIAL COUNCIL

Monolithic PJ control gave Menem tremendous discretion over judicial appointments. As Chapter 2 demonstrates, Menem used an opaque, highly politicized process to appoint pliant judges. Before the 1994 constitutional reform, the Senate confirmed the president's Supreme Court appointees by a majority vote. As part of the Olivos Pact that allowed Menem to run for reelection, the 1994 constitution raised the Senate approval requirement for Supreme Court justices from a majority to two-thirds. The 1994 reform also created a Judicial Council to intervene in the selection of lower court judges. For each vacancy, the Council proposes a *terna*, a three-person rank order list, from which the president selects one member with Senate approval. Like many of its neighbors in Latin America, Argentina created a Judicial Council with the goal of reducing executive appointment power.[57] Monolithic PJ control, however, prevented the Council from reaching its potential as a countervailing power center until the Alianza defeated the PJ in the 1997 legislative elections.

The 1994 constitution dictated the Judicial Council's general guidelines and left it up to the legislature to determine how the new organ would function. Article 114 stipulated that the Judicial Council's composition must reflect a balance among four groups: representatives of the elected branches of government, federal judges, attorneys, and academics. Congress had the important task of determining the exact meaning of balanced membership. Due to intense debate over composition, Congress did not sanction a Judicial Council law until December 1997, and the Council did not begin to function until November 1998.[58]

In its attempt to control the body, the PJ-dominated Senate proposed legislation for a 23-member Judicial Council subordinate to Menem. The Senate bill called for a Council composed of eight legislators, two executive representatives, two Supreme Court justices, three academics, four lawyers, and four federal judges. Before 1997, the PJ majority in both houses meant that a majority of the eight legislators would be members of Menem's party. Menem could handpick the two executive representatives. Furthermore, because of executive subordination of the Court, the two justices would most likely answer to the president. The Senate bill even gave the PJ discretion over the selection of the three academics. The PJ-dominated Constitutional Affairs Committee would choose the academics. Only the lawyers and judges had any real potential to be autonomous of the executive. Menem's Justice Minister, Raúl Granillo Ocampo, acknowledged that the Senate version was "unbalanced," and the opposition declared it unacceptable.[59]

The reemergence of divided government in 1997 permitted the defeat of the Senate proposal and the creation of a Judicial Council capable of acting as an agency of horizontal accountability. The 1997 PJ loss to the Alianza sounded the death knell for the Senate bill. In December 1997, Congress passed Law 24,937 that calls for a twenty-member Judicial Council composed of four senators, four House members, one executive representative, the Chief Justice, two academics, four attorneys, and four federal judges. The 1997 law calls for a much more balanced Council than did the PJ proposal. The law dictates that of the four Senate representatives, two would be from the majority party, one from the minority party, and one from the second minority. The same rule applies to the four House members. Even under unified government, only four of the eight legislators represent the president's party. This balance mitigates the high number of representatives from the elected branches. In addition, in contrast to the Senate proposal, the 1997 law stipulates that the academics be selected by their colleagues.[60] Moreover, the law requires that two-thirds of Council members support a recommendation before the Council passes it on to the president. This high requirement impedes the executive from pushing through its preferred candidates.[61]

In addition, the 1997 Judicial Council law calls for transparency and objectivity. The law requires that the selection process be open to the public and that the Council establish the evaluation standards for candidates before the process begins. At the time of a lower court vacancy, the Judicial Council publishes exam dates and the list of jurors who will evaluate candidates' records. All contestants take the same exam. After the Council announces the vacancy, it selects by lot one judge, one attorney, and one law professor to form the committee that assesses candidates and compiles a rank order list. The committee members are from different jurisdictions than the vacancy to be filled. The Judicial Council then uses the committee's ranking along with the results of personal interviews and written exams to recommend a threesome to the president. The names of candidates are publicized, which permits the public to raise objections.[62] In addition, the Council proposes *ternas vinculantes*, binding threesomes, which means that the president must select one of the three candidates. The executive cannot propose anyone who is not part of the threesome. Observers and Council members report the Judicial Council has reached its potential for neutrality, objectivity, and transparency and that it has reduced the role of cronyism in the appointment process.[63]

MONOLITHIC PARTY CONTROL AND THE IMPEACHMENT JURY

Monolithic party control gave Menem authority over the removal as well as the appointment of judges. Before the creation of the Impeachment Jury, Congress was responsible for dismissing judges. During the Menem administration, the composition of the congressional Impeachment Committee reflected the PJ majority in the legislature. Under the direction of Menem ally César Arias, the Committee did not pursue charges against Menemist judges suspected of corruption.[64] The 1994 constitution called for the creation an Impeachment Jury to replace Congress in the removal of lower court judges. In theory, the Jury reduces the president's ability to remove judges for political reasons.

With the help of the PJ-controlled Congress, Menem delayed the creation of an effective Impeachment Jury until 1997. Article 115 of the 1994 constitution stipulated that the Jury must include legislators, judges, and lawyers but did not specify the distribution of seats among the three sectors. As with the Judicial Council, composition was a major point of contention during congressional debate. Table 3.7 outlines the PJ and UCR proposals regarding the make-up of the Jury. In its attempt to dominate the new organ, the PJ proposed that a majority be legislators. The UCR advocated greater balance among the three sectors.[65]

The Alianza's victory in the 1997 midterm election permitted the defeat of the PJ bill and provided the opportunity to create a balanced Impeachment Jury of three legislators, three judges, and three lawyers. In addition to equilibrium among sectors, the law calls for a balance within the legislative sector: one senator from the majority party, one senator from the first minority, and one House member from the majority. Moreover, it stipulates

TABLE 3.7
Composition of the Impeachment Jury

	Legislators	Judges	Attorneys
PJ proposal	6	3	2
UCR proposal	2	3	2
Law 24,937	3	3	3

that the judges and lawyers be selected by their colleagues. The equilibrium has reduced the political influence that had been prevalent in the congressional Impeachment Committee. The law also requires a two-thirds majority of Jury members to remove a judge and calls for oral and public proceedings.[66]

COMPETITIVE POLITICS AND THE ATTORNEY GENERAL'S OFFICE

Monolithic PJ control also prevented the Office of the Attorney General from acting as a horizontal accountability agency until the reemergence of divided government in 1997. In theory, the Attorney General's Office is independent of the executive and has the authority to initiate proceedings against government functionaries. Menem's violation of the Attorney General's autonomy is consistent with and indicative of the executive dominance and assaults against the rule of law that characterize periods of monolithic party control. Executive subordination of public prosecutors was central to Menem's impunity and to his ability to manipulate the courts.

The role of the Attorney General's Office as a check was particularly critical due to the high level of government corruption during the Menem administration: "Deeds of corruption by governmental officials are reported almost daily. Yet judicial procedures have not been helpful in investigating them. Indeed, despite persistent rumors of corruption by the highest officials in the Menem government, few, if any, serious judicial investigations have taken place against these officials."[67] Autonomy from the executive branch is a necessary condition when investigating and prosecuting government officials for the abuse of power.

In order to boost the independence of the Office, Argentine law stipulated that the Attorney General was part of the Supreme Court. Thus, like Supreme Court justices, the Attorney General had tenure protection, and Senate approval was necessary for appointment.[68] Menem, however, violated tenure protection and bypassed the Senate when appointing his Attorneys General. Menem handpicked pliant individuals who in turn issued directives, or *instrucciones*, to lower level prosecutors about how and when to pursue investigations.[69] Until 1997, Menem's subordination of the Attorney General enabled him to prevent the entire Office from acting as a horizontal accountability agency.

Menem was the first Argentine president since Perón to violate the Attorney General's tenure protection. Menem demanded the resignation of Alfonsín's Attorney General, Andrés D'Alessio, who recalls: "Menem thought I would pose a threat."[70] After just five weeks as president, Menem tried to induce D'Alessio to resign by offering him a judgeship in his choice of appellate court. Although D'Alessio ultimately resigned, he initially resisted and condemned the pressure. In response to the scandal surrounding D'Alessio's resignation, the PJ-controlled Congress changed the formal removal process to permit Menem to dismiss future Attorneys General. The 1990 law that expanded the Court from five to nine, Law 24,774, removed the Attorney General from the Supreme Court. The 1990 law stipulates that the Court is composed of nine judges and that the Attorney General acts alongside the Court. Because the law excluded the Attorney General from the Court, the Attorney General no longer enjoys the tenure protection of justices.[71]

In addition, Menem violated the formal appointment process when he bypassed the Senate and appointed Attorneys General by decree. D'Alessio's final act as Attorney General was to urge Menem to resist becoming Argentina's first civilian president to select the Attorney General by decree.[72] Menem did not heed D'Alessio's advice when he appointed his friend Oscar Eduardo Roger without Senate consent. He also bypassed the Senate when he appointed Attorneys General Aldo Montesano Rebón, Oscar Luján Fappiano, and Ángel Agüero Iturbe, all of whom stopped investigations into government functionaries. Agüero Iturbe, the most loyal of Menem's Attorneys General, was from Menem's home province of La Rioja and was an administration official during Menem's term as governor of La Rioja.[73]

Menem's control over the Attorney General's Office extended to lower level prosecutors. He used transfers and disciplinary proceedings to silence lower level prosecutors that challenged his interests. In order to halt the high profile investigations of government officials conducted by Norberto Quantín and his team of prosecutors known as "Los Centauros," Attorney General Agüero Iturbe transferred the Centauros from under Quantín's direction. Agüero Iturbe also removed all cases involving functionaries from Quantín's jurisdiction, a violation of Article 196 of Argentina's Procedural Code. Article 196 states that a prosecutor who begins an investigation must continue the investigation until its completion.[74] When public prosecutor Aníbal Ibarra disobeyed the Attorney General's order not to challenge Menem's pardon of a former cabinet member, the administration initiated disobedience proceedings against him. Ibarra eventually resigned in response to government pressure.[75] Prosecutors report that they received direct pressure from the Menem administration. One prosecutor recalls his resentment when he received phone calls from executive representatives regarding specific cases.[76]

The threat of physical violence was a last resort for stopping independent prosecutors. Because of insufficient police protection, public prosecutors often lacked security. During Menem's presidency, aggression against prosecutors and their families increased, yet the number of police officers protecting prosecutors fell from one officer for each prosecutor to one officer for every twelve prosecutors. During Pablo Lanusse's 1997 investigation of Menem administration involvement in a gold contraband case, Lanusse and his sister faced violent attacks. An assailant used a knife to cut the letters ORO, which means gold, into the face of Lanusse's sister. Menem's former Minister of Economy Domingo Cavallo alleged that the administration was behind the brutal assault. The aggression ultimately led to Lanusse's resignation, effectively ending the investigation of government involvement in the contraband case.[77]

Menem's ability to impose his will on prosecutors decreased as the opposition's strength in Congress increased. The 1997 emergence of divided government presented an opportunity for the Attorney General's Office to begin to fulfill its constitutional role as a horizontal accountability agency. For the first time, Menem did not appoint the Attorney General by decree. In 1997, he submitted his candidate, Nicolás Becerra, to the Senate for approval. Unlike his predecessors, Becerra asserted his autonomy by issuing decisions that challenged government interests. Moreover, by 1998, Menem could no longer simply dismiss independent prosecutors or use sanctions to silence them. He no longer had the tools that he had used to halt Ibarra's investigations. For instance, Menem could not stop Carlos Stornelli's investigation of the administration's illegal arms sales to Ecuador and Croatia. In an attempt to silence Stornelli, the Menem administration accused him of leaking privileged information to journalists. Attorney General Becerra, however, refused to sanction Stornelli. In a show of support for Stornelli, Becerra called a meeting of three hundred public prosecutors.[78]

The PJ loss in the 1997 legislative elections permitted the passage of legislation that has the potential to bolster the Attorney General's Office. As with the Judicial Council and the Impeachment Jury, until 1997, the PJ-controlled Congress was able to delay the passage of a law to enact the 1994 constitution's call for a reform of the Attorney General's Office. Article 120 of the 1994 constitution stipulates that the Attorney General's Office is "an independent organ with functional and financial autonomy" and that its members "enjoy salary protection."[79] The constitution, however, left it up to Congress to pass the legislation that would implement the reform. The PJ-controlled Senate initially proposed a bill that would have permitted Attorney General Agüero Iturbe to retain his post while submitting all lower level prosecutors to the Senate for reconfirmation. The reconfirmation process would have permitted the PJ-controlled Senate to dismiss prosecutors who had investigated members of the Menem administration. The opposition in Congress resisted the proposal and argued that because Menem had appointed him by decree, only Agüero Iturbe should be subject to the Senate approval process.[80]

The Alianza victory in 1997 led to the defeat of the PJ proposal and to the passage of the 1998 law that characterizes the Attorney General's Office as *extrapoder*, a fourth branch of government that is independent of the judicial and executive branches.[81] In addition, the law prohibits presidents from handpicking the Attorney General. It stipulates that two-thirds of the Senate is necessary to confirm the president's nominee. Moreover, only Congress can remove the Attorney General through formal impeachment proceedings. The law also calls for a transparent selection process and competitive exams for lower level prosecutors. The new legislation maintains the hierarchical structure of the Office, but it prohibits the Attorney General from issuing specific directives to prosecutors, thus increasing the autonomy of lower level prosecutors. This new clause hinders the president's ability to intervene in investigations of government functionaries.[82]

PJ CONTROL OF THE ACCOUNTING TRIBUNAL

Menem also violated the formal rules that protect the autonomy of the Accounting Tribunal. In theory, the Accounting Tribunal has the authority to review government spending. According to the 1956 decree that created the Tribunal, the president appoints the five Tribunal members with Senate approval, and Tribunal members enjoy tenure protection.[83] Alfonsín respected the tenure protection of Tribunal members. In fact, when Menem assumed power in 1989, four of the five members had been on the Tribunal since before Alfonsín's 1983 assumption of the presidency.[84]

In contrast to Alfonsín, Menem violated the tenure protection of Tribunal members. In response to the Tribunal's challenges to administration spending, Menem replaced four Tribunal members. Between September 1989 and March 1990, the Tribunal that Menem had inherited from Alfonsín questioned the legality of fifty-one Menem administration policies. For Menem, the last straw was the Tribunal's 1990 denunciation of a $3 million government contract for public school uniforms, the infamous *guardapolvos* case. After documenting multiple irregularities including fraudulent bookkeeping and contract violations, the Tribunal compelled Menem to rescind the contract.[85]

Menem's reaction to the challenges was swift. In 1990, he requested the resignation of all five members of the Alfonsín Tribunal. When they refused to step down, the president issued a decree that replaced four of the five members with individuals who had demonstrated their loyalty to him: two members of his administration, an advisor to his brother, and a longtime friend from La Rioja. Menem further reduced the Tribunal's potential as a check by replacing it with the Controladuría y Auditoría de la Nación (National Comptroller and Auditor). Unlike its predecessor, the new organ cannot prevent government acts before they take effect. Instead, it only reviews the legality of government spending after the fact.[86]

COMPETITIVE POLITICS AND THE FEDERAL PROSECUTOR IN CHARGE OF ADMINISTRATIVE INVESTIGATIONS

Until the 1997 return of divided government, monolithic party control also hindered the ability of the Office of the Federal Prosecutor in charge of Administrative Investigations, known as the Fiscalía Nacional de Investigaciones Administrativas (FNIA), to check the president. Menem's treatment of the FNIA exemplified his strategy of dismissing oversight agency members who challenged his interests. According to the formal rules, the FNIA has the authority to investigate and denounce criminal acts of government functionaries. The 1962 law that created the organ granted the head of the FNIA tenure protection and stipulated that presidents appoint the FNIA head with Senate approval. Nevertheless, monolithic party control prevented the important agency from fulfilling its mission. As with other oversight agencies, military regimes and dominant presidents dismissed FNIA members who challenged government interests.[87]

The 1983 emergence of divided government under Alfonsín permitted the FNIA to assert its independence. In 1983, Alfonsín appointed an opposition member, Ricardo Molinas, who remained as head of the FNIA until 1991. Although Molinas challenged the Alfonsín administration, the president did not infringe on the FNIA's autonomy. In just six years under Molinas's leadership, the FNIA initiated ten thousand investigations, three times the number initiated from 1962 through 1982. Molinas's investigations reached high-level officials including the vice president of the state-owned Bank of Iguazú, José Figueroa, and Alfonsín's Economy Minister, José Alfredo Martínez de Hoz.[88]

Upon assuming office, Menem took steps to dismantle the FNIA's autonomy. He halted proceedings against Figueroa when Figueroa became a national PJ senator. In response to Molinas's investigations of high-level Menem functionaries including María Julia Alsogaray, Roberto Dromi, and Raúl Granillo Ocampo, Menem dismissed Molinas by decree. As discussed in Chapter 2, the "automatic majority" in the Court upheld the Menem decree that violated Molinas's tenure protection.[89]

Menem's next move was to appoint a pliant replacement for Molinas. He selected Jorge Néstor Pinzón whose son was an advisor to Menem's Minister of Interior. Under Pinzón's leadership, the FNIA did not act as a control on executive power. In contrast to Molinas, Pinzón did not challenge the administration. In fact, throughout his ten-year tenure in the FNIA, he initiated only one investigation of the Menem administration.[90]

After the 1997 legislative elections, the strength of the Alianza in the House presented an opportunity for the FNIA to reclaim its autonomy. The 1998 law that increased the independence of the Attorney General's Office also bolstered the FNIA. Because it incorporated the FNIA into the Office of the Attorney General, the 1998 law has the potential to increase the autonomy of the FNIA. The FNIA is now part of the fourth branch of government that is independent of the executive, the legislative, and the judicial branches. The law also prohibits the president from appointing and removing the head of the FNIA by decree.[91]

Monolithic control provided both Perón and Menem with the partisan powers necessary to subordinate potential horizontal accountability agencies, including the judiciary and Congress. The two Peronist presidents dismantled the elements of the rule of law that had emerged during the divided government of their predecessors. The recurrence of unified government coupled with party discipline trapped Argentina in a vicious cycle in which converging power centers exacerbated executive dominance to the detriment of the rule of law.

A prolonged period of competitive politics could help convert the vicious circle into a virtuous cycle by encouraging future presidents to develop an independent judiciary as part of a meaningful system of checks and balances. Although the return of divided government in 1997 led to a series of reforms meant to strengthen the rule of law, these reforms have not yet been embedded either institutionally or culturally. Such a process requires time. A new president with a monolithic majority could reverse the progress made since the resurgence of competitive politics. Because most of the post-1997 reforms are in law rather than in the Argentine Constitution, Congress can easily overturn them. The following three chapters turn from the diachronic study of Argentina at the federal level to a synchronic comparison of two Argentine provinces, San Luis and Mendoza. The case of Mendoza shows that a long history of interparty competition indeed creates a virtuous cycle that fortifies the rule of law.

CHAPTER 4

A Tale of Two Provinces

Judicial Autonomy in San Luis and Mendoza

THE PROVINCES of San Luis and Mendoza are side by side in the Cuyo region of northwestern Argentina, yet their experiences with the rule of law are worlds apart. San Luis faces the task of constructing the rule of law from scratch, whereas the Mendoza executive branch is bound by law. Although the neighboring provinces share the Spanish colonial legacy and the civil law tradition, they lie at opposite ends of the judicial autonomy continuum. In San Luis, Governor Adolfo Rodríguez Saá and his party, the Partido Justicialista (PJ), dominated politics from Argentina's 1983 transition through 2003.[1] The governor's accumulation of power over five consecutive terms permitted him to subvert potential organs of control, including the judiciary. The PJ-controlled Congress sanctioned a series of laws that subordinate the courts to the whims of the governor. In contrast to the monolithic party control of San Luis, competitive politics in Mendoza has led to considerable progress toward judicial autonomy. Since Argentina's 1983 democratic transition, judicial independence in Mendoza has become increasingly entrenched.

The constitutions of both provinces provide the formal guarantees of judicial independence, yet informal practices that erode the separation of powers have prevailed in San Luis. Both constitutions prohibit the reduction of judges' salaries and grant judges life tenure during good conduct. Indeed, standing on their own, the San Luis Constitution and the Mendoza Constitution indicate a high degree of judicial autonomy.[2] Governor Rodríguez Saá's supporters, including members of the San Luis Supreme Court, pointed to the constitutional guarantees of judicial independence when faced with allegations that the governor controlled the courts.[3] An analysis of provincial legislation and actual practice, however, demonstrates that the San Luis executive has not respected the formal guarantees. In Mendoza, on the other hand, practices uphold the formal rules that protect judicial autonomy.

This chapter contrasts the extreme executive subordination of the courts in San Luis with the high level of judicial independence in Mendoza. Section I explores the origins of the different patterns of power in the two provinces. In particular, it shows how the historical fragmentation of economic resources in Mendoza fostered judicial autonomy, whereas the concentration of economic power and the resulting elite collusion in San Luis led to subservient courts. The remainder of the chapter analyzes to what extent actual practice has upheld constitutional guarantees of judicial autonomy in the two provinces. It uses the five practices that indicate executive subordination of the courts delineated in Chapter 1 to compare and contrast the level of judicial independence in San Luis and Mendoza. Section II contrasts the highly politicized judicial appointment process in San Luis with Mendoza's transparent, merit-based selection process. Section III demonstrates that, in contrast to the Mendoza executive, the San Luis governor has violated judges' tenure protection. Section IV contrasts the violation of salary protection in San Luis with the defense of this protection in Mendoza. Section V discusses Rodríguez Saá's use of court-packing to subordinate the provincial Supreme Court, a practice that Mendoza governors have not exercised. Section VI shows that, in contrast to San Luis, the Mendoza judiciary has been willing to issue decisions that challenge the executive. Table 4.1 summarizes the practices used to compare the levels of judicial autonomy in San Luis and Mendoza. Section VII considers the assessments of outside observers and inside actors regarding the judiciary's ability to check the governor in each province. These assessments support the conclusion that the two provinces lie at opposite ends of the judicial independence spectrum.[4]

The Historical Roots of the Rule of Law: San Luis versus Mendoza

Comparative historical analysis of San Luis and Mendoza suggests that the dispersal of economic resources among members of a divided elite is one path to the competitive politics that is a necessary condition for the rule of law. The different patterns of economic power help explain why the two provinces had different starting points at the time of Argentina's 1983 democratic transition. The dispersal of economic power among competing actors set the stage for judicial autonomy in Mendoza, whereas in San Luis, the concentration of economic resources has stood in the way of independent courts. In Mendoza, competing economic actors required a secure way to protect property rights, to enforce contracts, and to mediate economic con-

TABLE 4.1

Indicators of Executive Subordination of the Judiciary in San Luis and Mendoza

Practice	Indicators
The governor uses an opaque process to appoint pliant judges	• Opaque, politicized appointment process • Unqualified appointees (little prior experience in the judiciary, weak publication record, poor reputation) • Appointees with strong ties to the governor's political party (militant partisanship) or personal ties to the administration (cronyism)
The governor violates judges' tenure protection	• Opaque, politicized removal process • Noncompliance with formal impeachment rules • Short average tenure of judges • High number of judges dismissed during governor's term • Supreme Court purges
The governor violates judges' salary protection	• Reduction in judges' real salaries
The governor packs the Supreme Court	• Frequent changes in the number of Supreme Court justices
Judges are unwilling to endure the costs of ruling against the governor's interests	• Rulings that uphold government acts of dubious constitutionality • Rulings in favor of administration officials suspected of corruption

flicts. Socioeconomic complexity led to economic disputes that paved the way for an effective horizontal accountability system, including an autonomous judiciary.

THE HISTORICAL DISPERSAL OF ECONOMIC POWER IN MENDOZA

Competition both within and among economic sectors paved the way for countervailing power centers in Mendoza. The plurality of strong economic actors in competition with one another early in Mendoza's history facilitated the emergence of the rule of law and shaped the political institutions that have endured. Since the nineteenth century, Mendoza has had a diversified economy in which actors of comparable strength have had to bargain with one another. Competition among the agricultural, livestock, and wine sectors along with intense competition within the viticultural sector led to the fragmentation of economic power.

Mendoza's climate and geography discouraged the concentration of land ownership and increased the likelihood of economic disputes. Like most of nineteenth-century Argentina, Mendoza had a sector that based its livelihood on agriculture and livestock. In contrast to most of the country, however, this sector failed to gain a monopoly on economic power in Mendoza. Like other provinces at the base of the Andes mountain range in northwestern Argentina, an arid climate shaped Mendoza's development. With an average annual rainfall of less than ten inches, Mendocinos focused production around three small oases formed by Andean streams. In contrast to the favorable conditions of Argentina's fertile pampa, the *pampa húmeda*, where the export-based cattle and agricultural sectors grew rapidly during the latter half of the nineteenth century, these sectors remained small in Mendoza's dry climate where producers did not benefit from economies of scale. Indeed, like Costa Rica, which also has a high degree of judicial autonomy, Mendoza has a long history of small and medium-sized ranches and farms.[5] As sociologist Carlos la Rosa explains, Mendoza's hostile climate led to small landholdings, or *minifundios*, whereas fertile natural conditions encouraged large-scale estates, or *latifundios*, in most of Argentina.[6]

Mendoza used its comparative advantage in grape cultivation to become Argentina's principal wine producer. In contrast to the temperate *pampa húmeda* where average landholdings were several thousand hectares, five hectares were sufficient for a winery in Mendoza.[7] Mendoza's viticultural industry experienced rapid growth during the latter half of the nineteenth century. The predominance of inexpensive, small units of land fostered social mobility and enabled newcomers to take part in the viticultural boom. The wine industry expanded rapidly during the final decades of the nineteenth century. In 1884, for instance, the Mendoza government granted 333 new licenses for wineries. In 1893, the number of acres devoted to grape cultivation tripled. The introduction of new economic actors encouraged the expansion of asset ownership and the further dispersal of economic resources. Economic assets were fragmented among multiple families with vineyards.[8] The Mendoza economy remains diversified and has continued to foster the rule of law in the province. The economic arena is still shaped by multiple actors of comparable strength.[9]

THE CONCENTRATION OF ECONOMIC AND POLITICAL POWER IN SAN LUIS

The concentration of economic resources has obstructed and continues to thwart the rule of law in San Luis. Throughout the history of San Luis, a small group with a coherent set of interests has had a monopoly on economic power. Moreover, this economic elite has overlapped with the political elite. Both economic and political power have been highly concentrated in the executive branch. In contrast to Argentina at the national level where the economic and political elite have often acted as partners, in San Luis they have been one and the same. In San Luis, there is little differentiation between those with a monopoly on political power and those who control economic resources.

The concentration of economic power has shaped political institutions in San Luis. Since the nineteenth century, the rich have controlled politics. As in Argentina's other "provincial oligarchies," a unified elite has dominated provincial economic and political life.[10] In contrast to Mendoza where economic resources were divided among a large number of families, a single family controlled the economy and politics of San Luis from 1870 until 1904. The Mendoza family controlled the province in an authoritarian style under the succession of three brothers, Torbirio, Gerónimo, and Eriberto.[11] This concentration of power continues today, although in the hands of a different family: the Rodríguez Saá family. In 2003, Alberto Rodríguez Saá, Adolfo's brother, became governor, marking the sixth consecutive term that the Rodríguez Saá family has held the governorship. The Rodríguez Saá brothers have used their family's monopoly on political and economic resources to stifle opposition. For instance, they used their economic assets to finance their political campaigns and to purchase all local newspapers, which has given them control of the provincial press.[12]

The San Luis economy has not diversified as it has in Mendoza. Since the 1974 implementation of the federal Industrial Promotion program (IP) in San Luis, economic assets have been concentrated in the industrial sector, which in turn has been controlled by the governor. IP provides tax exemptions and tax deferrals to industries that operate in San Luis. The San Luis economy has depended upon IP, and IP has depended on the governor. Beginning in 1983, Rodríguez Saá used his discretion over which companies benefit from IP tax exemptions to accumulate economic power. He amassed a personal fortune through corrupt implementation of the program. He sold the IP contracts at high prices to his friends and relatives who comprise the elite of San Luis, which fortified their monopoly on economic power.[13] The sale of IP contracts excluded small enterprises with scarce resources from benefiting from the program, which, in the words of Sawers, "fortified oligopolistic power."[14] Without competing economic actors, the economic and political elite had no incentive to construct an autonomous judiciary. Only the introduction of powerful new economic actors can fracture the monopoly on economic resources. This seems unlikely in light of the Rodríguez Saá brothers' unwillingness to promote policies that would foster the development of small and medium-sized business. However, as discussed in Chapter 7, the introduction of international companies on the San Luis economic scene could encourage the fragmentation of economic power.

The remainder of this chapter turns to the consequences of the different patterns of power. In particular, it contrasts the high degree of judicial autonomy in Mendoza with the San Luis governor's subordination of the courts. Indeed, Mendoza has an independent judiciary that provides a predictable environment for contracts and commerce. In contrast, the concentration of assets has obstructed judicial autonomy in San Luis.

Governors' Respect for the Formal Judicial Appointment Process

San Luis and Mendoza share the same formal rules for selecting judges, but only Mendoza governors have abided by a transparent, merit-based appointment process. Rodríguez Saá's discretion over judicial appointments permitted him to fill the courts with pliant judges. Until the creation of a Judicial Council, both provincial constitutions stipulated that the governor appoints all judges with congressional approval. In 1987, both San Luis and Mendoza created a Judicial Council, which serves as a preselection mechanism that intervenes in the selection of lower court judges. In theory, the congressional approval requirement and intervention of the Judicial Council should moderate executive appointment power in both provinces. In reality, however, as Chapters 5 and 6 explain, these checks on the governor's appointment power have functioned only in Mendoza with its competitive party system.

The composition of the provincial Supreme Courts illustrates the effects of the different selection procedures. In contrast to Mendoza where justices enjoy national recognition for their knowledge and skill, monolithic party control in San Luis allowed the governor to fill the Court with judges with weak credentials. Rodríguez Saá was able to rush the approval process through the PJ-controlled Senate, which never rejected one of his nominees. A majority of Mendoza justices are opposition members, whereas all San Luis justices have been militant members of the governor's PJ. The primary criterion for appointment in San Luis has been a link to Rodríguez Saá and his party. All seven members of the 1993 San Luis Court had demonstrated loyalty to the governor before assuming their seats. Only two, Carlos Maqueda and Cruz Ortiz, had previous experience as judges. Ortiz had served as Rodríguez Saá's Minister of Education, and Maqueda had been director of the newspaper owned by the governor's family, the *Diario de la República*. Julio Cesar Niño had been a local PJ leader. Luis Escudero Gauna had served as the governor's attorney. Luis Amitrano had been Minister of Industry and Tourism and president of the state-owned provincial bank. Carlos Nellar had been the governor's advisor.[15] As discussed below, when Rodríguez Saá appointed a new Court in 1997, each of the new justices had close ties to the governor.

Rodríguez Saá also used a politicized process to appoint pliant *conjueces* who serve as temporary replacements for judges that cannot be impartial due to a personal interest in a particular case. Until 1996, *conjueces* were selected by lottery from a list of all San Luis Bar Association members, giving each practicing attorney an equal chance of selection. Before the 1996 law that changed the appointment system for *conjueces*, *conjueces* had helped the San Luis judiciary maintain a modicum of independence from the executive. In 1995, for instance, *conjueces* ruled that the reduction of judges' salaries was unconstitutional. In recognition that appointing loyal *conjueces* would prevent such rulings against executive interests, in 1996, the PJ-controlled Congress passed legislation that gave Rodríguez Saá discretion over the selection of *conjueces*. Law 5070 of 1996 abolished the lottery system and gave the governor the power to appoint *conjueces* with Senate approval. In addition, the law removed all *conjueces* who had assumed their positions before February 1996.[16]

In contrast to San Luis, Mendoza governors have abided by a transparent, merit-based appointment process. Unified UCR government permitted Mendoza's first governor after the 1983 transition, Santiago Felipe Llaver, to select only individuals linked to his UCR. Llaver's Minister of Government León Victor Chade explains, however, that the transparency of the process compelled the governor to select justices based on their professional qualifications as well as on partisanship. For instance, Llaver appointee Aída Kemelmajer de Carlucci is a well-known legal scholar throughout Argentina with an extensive publication record.[17]

Nevertheless, the members of Llaver's Court were not merely UCR affiliates; they had been UCR functionaries. Elías Baglini, the first Chief Justice of Llaver's Supreme Court, served as a Unión Cívica Radical Intransigente (UCRI) senator during the 1950s. Baglini's son was a provincial UCR Congressman during the 1990s. During the final three months of his term in 1987, Llaver appointed three more UCR justices, Jorge Nanclares, Carlos Eduardo Moyano, and Pedro Llorente, thereby consolidating UCR control of the Court. Llorente had served as vice president of the UCR bloc in the provincial Senate in 1983 and 1984. Moyano had been director of the state-run Mendoza Housing Institute and was a local UCR leader. As Llaver's advisor on legal issues, Nanclares had worked under Chade in the Ministry of Government.[18]

As the case of San Luis illustrates, the practice of appointing judges with similar political views has the potential to undermine judicial autonomy. As a result of the actions of later administrations, however, Mendoza was spared this potential consequence of unified government. With time, Llaver's partisan-based appointments actually strengthened the Supreme Court's independence. The respect for the life tenure of Llaver's UCR justices during subsequent PJ administrations was an important step toward the consolidation of judicial autonomy. According to PJ Governor Arturo Lafalla (1995–99), in order to begin the process of building an autonomous judiciary, PJ administrations had to resist the Argentine tradition of purging the Court.[19] A key to judicial autonomy in Mendoza since 1987 has been governors' respect for judicial tenure. As Chapter 6 demonstrates, competitive politics in Mendoza fostered respect for the formal guarantees of judicial autonomy, including tenure protection.

Executive Compliance with Judges' Tenure Protection

San Luis and Mendoza have performed differently on the second indicator of executive subordination of the courts: violation of judges' tenure protection.[20] Rodríguez Saá embraced the informal practice of dismissing justices, whereas Mendoza governors have rejected it. In fact, Rodríguez Saá exercised the practice with even greater zeal than have Argentine presidents. In Argentina at the national level, Supreme Court terms have tended to be coterminous with presidential terms, whereas in San Luis, three purges occurred under a single governor.

Rodríguez Saá began clearing the way for the most recent purge when he requested the resignations of Supreme Court members in 1995. When his request failed, Rodríguez Saá used his control of the principal San Luis newspaper, the *Diario de la República*, to pressure the justices to resign. During the climax of the press campaign to discredit the Court in 1996, the newspaper published a front-page photograph of the five justices in their underwear each day over a three-month period. The newspaper also attacked the judges individually. In addition, the governor used his control of the press to mobilize PJ members to participate in public demonstrations against the Court.[21]

By December 1996, the governor had secured the resignation of three justices. Appellate Court judges Osvaldo Suriani and Carlos Cacace temporarily replaced two of the three; the third seat remained vacant. After December 1996, the Court functioned with only four judges, a violation of the San Luis Constitution and of a 1991 provincial law, both of which stipulate that the Court requires at least five members to function.[22] The effort to secure another resignation increased in response to the 1997 San Luis Supreme Court resolution condemning the governor's subordination of the judiciary. In June 1997, a third justice had resigned, and Rodríguez Saá removed Cacace and Suriani from their temporary posts.[23]

In June 1997, Governor Rodríguez Saá filled the vacancies with justices who had demonstrated loyalty to his party before assuming their seats. Only Eduardo Gatica remained from the 1995 Court, and he had retracted his support for the resolution that condemned executive subordination of the judiciary. In fact, the new Court voted unanimously to annul the 1997 resolution. After the 1997 purge, the governor's control of the highest court was absolute. In contrast to the federal Supreme Court where the Menem administration had a narrow majority of five to four, all San Luis Supreme Court justices supported the governor.

In selecting the new justices, the primary criterion was a close relationship with the Rodríguez Saá administration. Former Chief Justice Carlos Sergnese illustrates this criterion. Before joining the Court, Sergnese had occupied various posts that required close ties to the governor. He had served as Rodríguez Saá's Minister of Government, Undersecretary of Housing, and as the governor's personal attorney. In addition, the governor violated formal rules in order to extend Sergnese's tenure as Chief Justice. The PJ-controlled legislature approved legislation that changed the method of selecting the Chief Justice, a violation of the constitutional requirement that the post rotate each year among members. The new law called for election of the Chief Justice with the possibility of reelection. As a result, Sergnese served as Chief Justice from 1997 through 1999 when he resigned to become a national PJ Senator. In 1999, José Guillermo Catalfamo, another former government official close to Rodríguez Saá, replaced Sergnese as Chief Justice.[24]

In addition, the San Luis governor used his party's control of the legislature to pass laws that violate the life tenure of lower court judges and other judicial actors. The PJ-controlled Congress approved of Law 5141 that created the Aptitude Evaluation Tribunal that administers exams to lower court judges and has the authority to dismiss those who fail. These subjective tests lack transparency and have been used to remove judges who challenge the governor. Furthermore, the 1998 Judicial Emergency Law gave the Supreme Court the power to remove *secretarios* without a formal hearing. *Secretarios* are judicial functionaries who are second in importance only to judges. The *secretarios* help dictate sentences and manage judicial personnel. A few days after the law's passage, the Court called for the removal of eleven *secretarios*, all of whom had protested an unconstitutional reduction of judges' salaries.[25] On the same day as the dismissals, the Court filled the eleven vacancies with government allies who lacked experience in the judiciary. The replacements included former executive functionaries, former PJ legislators, relatives of government officials, and members of the Partido Unión y Libertad (PUL), a party allied with the PJ and led by the governor's brother. José Ramón Cerato and Nancy Arimondi, for instance, were close to the governor and had no background in the judiciary prior to becoming *secretarios*. Cerato had served as a congressman for the Movimiento de Integración y Desarrollo (MID), a party allied with Rodríguez Saá's PJ. Arimondi had been a PJ advisor.[26]

In contrast to Rodríguez Saá, Mendoza governors have respected the life tenure of judges. Of Mendoza's five governors between 1983 and 2003, Llaver (UCR), José Octavio Bordón (PJ), Rodolfo Gabrielli (PJ), Lafalla (PJ), and Roberto Iglesias (UCR), only Llaver violated tenure protection. Like President Raúl Alfonsín at the national level, Llaver faced the dilemma of how to treat the judges that he had inherited from the 1976–83 military government. Llaver's strategy was similar to that of Alfonsín. Llaver allowed the majority of lower court judges to remain in their posts but replaced the entire Supreme Court. The governor sent the lower court judges to the Mendoza Senate for approval. The UCR-dominated Senate voted to approve 86 percent of lower court judges who had served under the military government. In contrast to the treatment of lower court judges, the Llaver administration did not comply with the formal impeachment process when it removed all seven of the military government's Supreme Court justices. Llaver argued that because the justices took their oath before the de facto government's proclamation rather than before the 1916 Mendoza Constitution, their oath was invalid under the 1983 constitutional government.[27] By bypassing constitutional channels for removal, the Llaver administration threatened the development of an autonomous judiciary.

Since the end of Llaver's term in 1987, Mendoza governors have respected formal impeachment proceedings. Although the subsequent three governors were PJ members, they respected the life tenure of Llaver's appointees. They did not tamper with the Court's composition despite the sitting justices' strong ties to the UCR. In 1997 during the PJ administration of Lafalla, five of the seven justices had been appointed by a UCR governor and approved by a UCR-dominated Senate.[28] Kemelmajer and Hernán Amilton Salvini remained from the 1983 Court, and Nanclares, Llorente, and Moyano remained from Llaver's 1987 appointments. Based on her experience, Kemelmajer reports, "It is easier for a judge to be independent when the current governor is a member of a different party than the governor who appointed that judge."[29]

Executive Adherence to the Rules Governing Judges' Salary Protection

Both provincial constitutions prohibit the reduction of judges' wages, but only Mendoza governors have complied with the formal rules that call for salary protection.[30] The Mendoza Supreme Court prevented the 1984 attempts by Llaver and the UCR majority in Congress to lower judges' salaries. The Mendoza Court declared the salary reduction unconstitutional.[31]

In contrast to Mendoza, monolithic PJ control in San Luis permitted the passage of a 1995 law that reduced judges' wages. In opposition to the law,

90 percent of judicial employees sued the government. In response to the legal challenges, the province's first instance and appellate courts ruled in favor of the judicial functionaries and declared the salary reduction unconstitutional. The governor, however, used his control of Congress and of the Supreme Court to prevent the rulings from taking effect. The PJ-dominated Congress sanctioned the Economic Emergency Law that declared a state of economic emergency in San Luis and suspended all judicial decisions against the state, including the ruling that declared the salary reduction unconstitutional. The docile San Luis Supreme Court upheld the emergency law.[32]

Governors' Use of Court-Packing

The use of court-packing to subordinate the judiciary has also distinguished the two provinces from one another. Neither the San Luis nor the Mendoza Constitution specifies the size of the Supreme Court above a minimum number. According to Article 191 of the San Luis Constitution, the Court is composed of "five or more members."[33] Article 143 of the Mendoza Constitution stipulates, "The Supreme Court will be composed of at least seven members."[34] Despite their similar constitutional clauses, in contrast to Rodríguez Saá, Mendoza governors have not used their discretion over the size of the Court to fill it with pliant judges. The number of justices on the Mendoza Court has remained constant at seven since 1983.

Rodríguez Saá changed the size of the Court in order to increase his control over rulings. Until 1990, five members sat on the Court. In a move similar to President Carlos Menem's expansion of the federal Supreme Court from five to nine, Rodríguez Saá expanded the provincial Court to nine members in 1990. Each of the four new appointees had ties to the governor. The number fell to seven in 1993 and to four in 1996.[35] Moreover, the PJ-controlled Congress sanctioned two laws that have facilitated frequent change in Court size. According to a 1991 law, the Court can have up to nine members, but it requires only five to function. Although it violates the San Luis Constitution, a 1998 law reduced the maximum size of the Court from nine to five and the minimum from five to three.[36] Figure 4.1 contrasts the variation in the San Luis Court's size with Mendoza where the number of justices has remained stable at seven since 1983.

Judicial Rulings against Executive Interests

Judicial decisions also suggest that San Luis and Mendoza lie at different ends of the judicial autonomy continuum. Mendoza courts have declared important government acts unconstitutional and prosecuted administration officials, thereby acting as a check on the executive. Governors in Mendoza

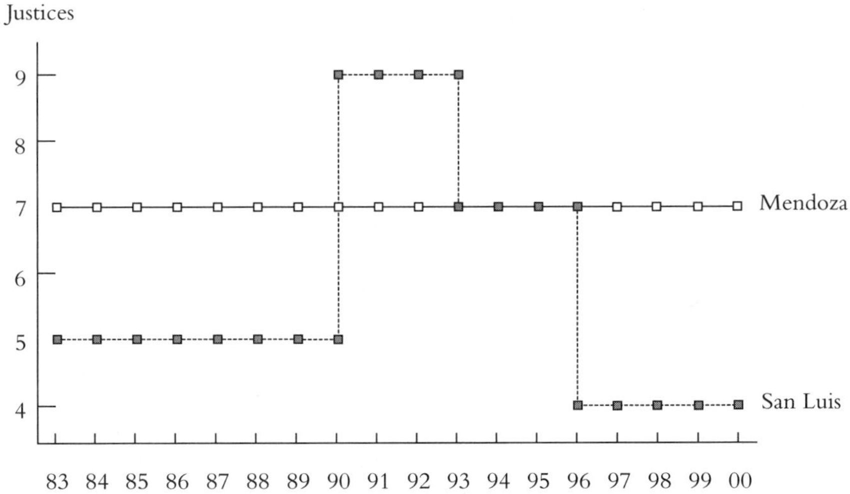

FIGURE 4.1 Changes in Supreme Court size in San Luis and Mendoza, 1983–2000.

have accepted these rulings. Former governor Bordón (1989–93) reports that he respected the many Supreme Court decisions that were against his interests.[37] Justice Nanclares points to this respect for Court decisions as a factor that has strengthened judicial independence in Mendoza.[38] In contrast to Mendoza judges, San Luis judges have demonstrated an unwillingness to endure the costs of challenging the executive. Rodríguez Saá punished judges who challenged his policies or who prosecuted executive officials.

By punishing independent judges, Rodríguez Saá created a disincentive for those judges who considered challenging his administration. Judges who challenged the governor either faced attack in the local press or removal by the Impeachment Jury. The severity of the punishment encouraged judges to accept their subordinate and passive roles. When intense press campaigns against independent judges failed to silence them, the governor removed them from office. When ruling on a corruption charge against a government official, judges had a choice: either absolve the official or face attack and ridicule from the government-controlled media. In the rare case when a judge decided to investigate despite persecution by the press, a second disincentive operated: the prospect of removal by the Impeachment Jury. As discussed in Chapter 5, the PJ-controlled Impeachment Jury removed judges who issued decisions against the administration's interests.

The punishment of independent judges set an example of the dire consequences of challenging the governor. For instance, the government targeted judges Ruth Relly de Closa, Adriana Gallo, and Ana María Careaga after they protested the 1995 salary reduction. In an effort to remove Relly, the governor attacked her in the *Diario de la República*. The newspaper published daily articles criticizing Relly on both a professional and personal level, damaging her reputation in the small community. Because of the intense media pressure, Relly resigned. When Gallo and Careaga did not respond to the media pressure, Rodríguez Saá used the Impeachment Jury to remove them from office.[39]

The provincial Supreme Courts' contrasting treatment of emergency laws illustrates their different performance on the fifth indicator of executive subordination of the courts: unwillingness to rule against the governor. Unlike the Mendoza Court, the San Luis Court has accepted emergency laws. The San Luis Court did not challenge either the Economic Emergency Law or the Judicial Emergency Law, both of which suspended judgments against the state. The Judicial Emergency Law declared the judiciary in a state of emergency for a one-year period that the Supreme Court could extend for another 180 working days. During this period, provincial courts could abstain from hearing new cases. The law released courts from their obligation to rule on suits against the state and on suits regarding the constitutionality of laws and decrees. The Court exercised its power to extend the state of emergency, effectively paralyzing the administration of justice for over five hundred days.[40]

In contrast, the Mendoza courts rejected the governor's emergency justifications for the suspension of constitutional guarantees. For instance, in the 1994 *Merga* ruling, the Mendoza Court ruled that economic emergency did not justify application of a law that would have released the state from its obligation to pay damages resulting from a public transit accident. In the 1994 *Campoy* decision, the Mendoza Court rejected the state-owned Bank of Mendoza's attempt to use the economic emergency justification to avoid paying attorneys' fees. In addition to reiterating the arguments put forth in *Merga*, the Court declared that no bank, regardless of whether it is state-owned, could shirk obligations generated in the normal course of business.[41]

In addition, the provincial courts have had different stances toward per saltum, an extraordinary remedy that allows the highest court to bypass lower courts. Per saltum has permitted the San Luis Supreme Court to intervene in any case regardless of whether the case first reached a lower court. Unlike the Mendoza Supreme Court, the San Luis Court has accepted per saltum in cases that involve a "serious institutional matter." In fact, San Luis is the only Argentine province in which per saltum has become an accepted practice. Like the Menem Court at the national level as discussed in Chapter 2, the pro-Rodríguez Saá San Luis Court used per saltum to avoid rulings that conflict with executive interests.[42]

The two provincial Supreme Courts have also responded differently to governors' attempts to reform provincial constitutions to permit their reelection. Both the San Luis and the Mendoza constitutions contained clauses that prohibited the governor's reelection for a second consecutive term. The Mendoza Court did not permit a constitutional reform that would have permitted reelection. In contrast, the San Luis Court did not challenge the 1987 PJ-driven constitutional reform initiative that permitted Rodríguez Saá's indefinite reelection.[43]

The Mendoza Court declared a reform of the constitution that would have permitted the governor's reelection for a second consecutive term to be unconstitutional. In Mendoza, ratification by a popular plebiscite is a requirement for constitutional reform. In a 1987 referendum, the majority of those who voted supported a constitutional reform that would permit reelection, yet the Mendoza Court ruled in 1989 that the majority was insufficient to ratify the reform. The Court argued that Bordón's decree calling for a Constitutional Convention violated Article 221 of the constitution, which required "a majority of the electorate" to approve a reform.[44] The Court's 1989 interpretation of "majority of the electorate" was unprecedented in Mendoza. Throughout the province's history, the "majority" had been based on the total votes submitted in a referendum. In 1989, the Court declared that approval required the support of the majority of citizens who were eligible to vote, not of those who actually voted. Due to the low voter turnout in the 1987 referendum, the Court concluded that the majority of Mendocinos did not support a reform.[45] With the 1989 ruling, the Court demonstrated its power to check the executive by entering a political realm that previous Mendoza Courts had not entered. Moreover, Bordón respected the decision and aborted the reform effort.[46]

Like the San Luis Supreme Court, the San Luis criminal courts have been unwilling to challenge the executive. In San Luis where the large number of corruption scandals has increased the importance of criminal courts, the governor used the subordinate court system as a tool to ensure the impunity of functionaries. Judge Néstor Ochoa, for instance, refused to rule on corruption allegations against Rodríguez Saá. At one point, Ochoa had twelve different corruption charges against the governor. Ochoa investigated only one of the twelve, and he absolved the governor of that charge after a cursory investigation.[47] Furthermore, Ochoa followed the governor's orders. In a 1991 case involving the disappearance of a young woman, Rodríguez Saá instructed the judge to jail suspects with or without proof. Ochoa obeyed.[48]

Rodríguez Saá's control over the judiciary encompassed federal judges who work in San Luis as well as provincial judges. Before appointing federal judges in a particular province, the Argentine president consults with governors who are members of his party. During the PJ administration of

Menem, the president appointed only allies of fellow PJ member Rodríguez Saá. Indeed, federal judges in San Luis answered to Rodríguez Saá. While serving as defense counsel in a federal case in which the governor was the plaintiff, Eugenio Raúl Zaffaroni, a prominent legal scholar, experienced the governor's control of federal judges firsthand. The federal judge demonstrated a clear bias in favor of the governor and even violated legal procedure. He cited the defendant twice for the same crime.[49]

In contrast to San Luis, federal judges in Mendoza have demonstrated autonomy in their rulings. They have issued high profile rulings that challenge the provincial government. For example, in 1996 during the PJ administration of Lafalla, Federal Judge Luis Leiva prosecuted twenty-six former Bank of Mendoza officials for irregularities during their tenure with the state-owned bank. Many of the former bank officials had been part of the PJ administrations of Bordón and Gabrielli. For instance, Leiva prosecuted Gabrielli's Undersecretary of Government, a former PJ Housing Minister, and a former PJ Minister of Interior. The prosecutions cast the PJ administrations in a negative light and represented a blow to Governor Lafalla who had been vice-governor under Bordón. Although the ruling damaged Lafalla's party, the governor respected the decision. In fact, he asked all government officials involved in the case, including his vice-governor Jorge Antonio López who headed the bank from 1992 until 1994, to resign and appear before Leiva.[50] According to a 1996 survey, 84 percent of Mendocinos supported Leiva's ruling and 61 percent reported that Lafalla's respect for Leiva's decision was a sign of judicial independence.[51]

The Mendoza courts have demonstrated their autonomy in many other cases. For instance, Leiva detained former Banco Multicrédito officials and questioned high-ranking air force officials during his investigation of the safety of El Plumerillo airport. The ruling against former directors of the Banco de Previsión Social also challenged the interests of the executive branch. Many former directors were PJ leaders. For example, two former bank presidents were undersecretaries during Gabrielli's administration.[52] Table 4.2 contains a summary comparison of the compliance with the formal rules in San Luis with compliance in Mendoza.

Assessments of Judicial Autonomy in San Luis and Mendoza

Along with the comparative analysis of compliance with the formal rules, the assessments of outside observers and inside political and judicial actors suggest very different levels of judicial autonomy in the two provinces. Independent observers assert that San Luis has one of the lowest levels of judicial autonomy of Argentina's twenty-four provinces and that Mendoza has one of the highest levels. A 1998 in-depth study of provincial judiciaries co-

TABLE 4.2

Compliance with Formal Rules: San Luis versus Mendoza

Informal Practice	Indicators in San Luis	Indicators in Mendoza
Governor uses an opaque process to appoint pliant judges	Yes • Politicized appointment process • Unqualified appointees with weak publication records and little experience in the judiciary • Appointees with strong links to Rodríguez Saá and his party • Weak, ineffective Judicial Council	No • Transparent, merit-based process • Highly qualified appointees with extensive publication records, strong reputations, and long careers in the judicial branch • Effective, autonomous Judicial Council
Governor violates judges' tenure protection	Yes • Short average tenure of judges • High number of judges dismissed during governor's term • Three Supreme Court purges during the Rodríguez Saá governorship	No • Long average tenure of judges • Governors' respect for the life tenure of judges appointed by members of the opposition • Not a single Supreme Court purge
Governor violates judges' salary protection	Yes • 1995 law that reduced judges' salaries (not challenged by the San Luis Supreme Court)	No • 1984 Supreme Court decision prohibiting judges' salary reduction
Governor packs the Supreme Court	Yes • Frequent changes in Court size	No • Constant Court size since the 1983 transition
Judges are unwilling to rule against the governor's interests	Yes • Rulings that uphold laws of dubious constitutionality • Rulings permitting emergency justification for the governor's seizure of extraordinary powers • Rulings in favor of executive officials suspected of corruption	No • Ruling prohibiting governor's reelection • Rulings against economic emergency justification for the governor's seizure of extraordinary powers • Rulings against administration officials
Number of practices that indicate the governor's subordination of the judiciary	5 out of 5 • Executive subordination of the courts	0 out of 5 • High degree of judicial autonomy

produced by the Consejo Empresario Argentino (CEA), an association of Argentine business leaders, and the Argentine civil society group Foro de Estudios para la Justicia (FORES) concludes that the San Luis judiciary is the least independent of the twenty-four provinces. In contrast, the study asserts that a high degree of judicial autonomy characterizes Mendoza.[53]

National judges' organizations and bar associations have reached similar conclusions. Argentina's largest organization of judges, the Federación Argentina de la Magistratura (FAM), denounced the assaults against the rule of law in San Luis.[54] The Buenos Aires-based judges' associations Justicia Democrática and Asociación de Mujeres Jueces (Argentine Association of Women Judges) also condemned Rodríguez Saá's subordination of the courts.[55] The national umbrella organization for Argentina's provincial bar associations, the Federación Argentina de Colegios de Abogados (FACA), concluded that the San Luis governor violated the separation of powers.[56] Provincial bar associations across Argentina denounced Rodríguez Saá's treatment of the judiciary. For instance, the bar associations of Mendoza, Corrientes, and Córdoba asserted that the lack of judicial autonomy stands in the way of the rule of law in San Luis. In contrast, they argued that executive subordination of the courts does not present a challenge to the rule of law in Mendoza.[57] According to FAM, an independent judicial branch differentiates Mendoza from the rest of Argentina; FAM characterizes Mendoza as an "oasis" of judicial autonomy within Argentina.[58]

Lawyers in Buenos Aires, Mendoza, and San Luis concur that the executive's advance on judicial autonomy has been even more devastating in San Luis than on the federal level. According to one San Luis lawyer, 90 percent of San Luis judges answered to Rodríguez Saá.[59] Christian Courtis, an attorney for the Buenos Aires-based civil society group Centro de Estudios Legales y Sociales (CELS), asserts that violations of judicial independence have been much more serious in San Luis than in other provinces. He declares that San Luis has been under the "rule of discretion rather than the rule of law."[60] According to Martín Abregú, director of CELS, the degree of executive dominance differentiates San Luis from the national level. In San Luis, Rodríguez Saá had absolute power. Such absolutism is impossible at the national level due to the greater quantity of institutional and nonstate actors, including political parties and civil society. In addition, clientelism has facilitated executive dominance in San Luis.[61] As discussed in Chapter 7, many citizens of San Luis depend on the provincial government for jobs and housing.

The decision of prestigious Buenos Aires law firms to open offices in Mendoza and to avoid business in San Luis also suggests different levels of judicial autonomy. After the 1983 transition to democracy, the number of corporate law firms in Argentina grew along with the national economy.

With the growth in investment, Buenos Aires-based firms began to expand their practices to other provinces. An independent judicial branch has been a major factor in a firm's decision to expand to a particular province. Without judicial independence, firms cannot count on predictability and their practices risk failure because they are subject to the whims of local government.[62]

Many corporate firms have moved into Mendoza. For instance, Pérez Alati, Grondona, Benites, Arntsen & Martínez de Hoz opened a Mendoza office in 1998. Before selecting Mendoza, the partners considered other provinces. Their decision-making process centered on the amount of investment in a given province and the independence and efficiency of the provincial judiciary. The partners first narrowed down the number of potential provinces to those that were attracting major companies and banks. The partners concluded that three cities other than Buenos Aires had attracted the most business: Rosario, Province of Santa Fe; Córdoba, Province of Córdoba; and Mendoza, Province of Mendoza. Although more investment had entered Rosario and Córdoba, the partners chose Mendoza as the site of their first branch office. They concluded that Mendoza had greater judicial autonomy and transparency than either Córdoba or Santa Fe. In contrast, firms have avoided opening offices in San Luis. Because Pérez Alati has had legal problems in San Luis due to the lack of judicial autonomy, the partners have steered clear of cases that involve work in that province.[63]

San Luis judges report that the governor has obstructed their autonomy. According to a former San Luis Supreme Court justice, the judiciary has been in a state of "total submission."[64] The governor removed or imposed limits on the few judges who were willing to challenge the governor. Rodríguez Saá made sure that cases that affected his interests did not reach the few independent judges that retained their seats. For instance, Judges Cacace and Suriani have not been involved in a case with political consequences since 1995.[65]

Legislators from the San Luis PJ as well as from the opposition concur with judges regarding the lack of judicial autonomy in the province. PJ Congressman José Samper and UCR Congressman Walter Ceballos assert that judges have answered to the executive. According to Samper, the courts have been independent only when resolving conflicts between private citizens that do not affect the government. When ruling on disputes with political consequences, the judiciary has not been independent of the governor. Journalists and academics also emphasize Rodríguez Saá's subordination of the courts. For instance, journalists Eduardo Olivares, Mario Otero, and Miguel Wiñazki drew attention to the governor's use of pressure to subordinate judges.[67] As a high-ranking administrator at the San Luis National

University explains, Rodríguez Saá gained control of the courts in order to ensure impunity for himself and for administration officials.[68]

Mendoza judges, lawyers, legislators, and journalists, on the other hand, assert that the Mendoza judiciary is independent. Criticism of Mendoza's judiciary focuses on inefficiency rather than a lack of autonomy. Judge Leiva asserts that the judiciary in Mendoza has maintained its independence despite a deficient infrastructure.[69] Mendoza Supreme Court justices also report that the judicial branch is autonomous. Kemelmajer and Llorente have served during five different administrations. During that time, the executive never pressured them to rule in its favor.[70]

Lawyers, legislators, scholars, and journalists agree with the judges regarding the Mendoza judiciary. According to Oscar Portabella, a prominent Mendoza attorney, judges work without pressure from the executive. Another prestigious lawyer, Alejandro Pérez Hualde, attributes judicial independence to the governor's willingness to respect judges' rulings.[71] National Congressman Carlos Balter (PD) and national PJ Congresswoman Ana María Mosso de Mortarotti assert that neither the lower courts nor the Supreme Court are subservient or "*adicta*" to the governor's party.[72] Sociologist Carlos la Rosa claims that the judiciary is autonomous in Mendoza because power is not concentrated in the executive. Journalist Andrés Gabrielli argues that Mendoza's judiciary has been independent. Moreover, he asserts that autonomy has increased over time, especially after Lafalla's 1995 assumption of the governorship.[73]

A system of horizontal accountability that protects the rule of law has constitutional status in both San Luis and Mendoza, yet the neighboring provinces lie at opposite ends of the judicial autonomy spectrum. The next two chapters explain why systems of checks and balances have functioned so differently despite similar constitutional structures. Chapter 5 explores how monolithic party control enabled Rodríguez Saá to violate not only the constitutional guarantees of judicial autonomy but to subordinate all potential organs of control that should protect the rule of law. Chapter 6 focuses on how competitive politics in Mendoza has fostered the development of an effective system of horizontal accountability that includes an independent judiciary.

CHAPTER 5

Monolithic Party Control and Executive Dominance in San Luis

MONOLITHIC party control in San Luis provided Governor Adolfo Rodríguez Saá with the partisan powers necessary to eliminate the independence of all potential agencies of horizontal accountability that are essential to the rule of law, including the judiciary. Rodríguez Saá controlled the Partido Justicialista (PJ), and the PJ held a majority in the legislature. As a result, the governor found it easy to strip countervailing power centers of their autonomy and therefore of the capacity to check his power. The PJ-controlled San Luis Congress passed a series of laws that altered the institutional design of control organs and rendered them subordinate to the executive branch.

The extreme concentration of power in the governor has stood in the way of the rule of law in San Luis. During five consecutive four-year terms as governor, Rodríguez Saá came to embody Bodin's sovereign who wields absolute power.[1] Indeed, like Bodin's sovereign, Rodríguez Saá eliminated enforceable restraints on his authority.[2] In the words of one observer: "Power is concentrated in Adolfo. His staff and the rest of the government cannot make decisions or formulate policy independent of him."[3] Rodríguez Saá's dominance was evident in his nickname, "the last emperor," and in references to San Luis as *Adolfolandia*.

This chapter analyzes the monolithic PJ control that permitted Rodríguez Saá to accumulate tremendous partisan powers and to dismantle the system of checks and balances. Section I traces the mounting strength of Rodríguez Saá's PJ in San Luis, which led to unified PJ government. Section II turns to the second component of monolithic party control, party discipline, and shows how PJ discipline increased after the 1983 transition. The remainder of the chapter demonstrates how monolithic PJ control allowed the governor to seize informal powers not granted by the San Luis

Constitution and to systematically subordinate all potential checks on his power, including the Judicial Council, the Impeachment Jury, the Office of the State Prosecutor, the Accounting Tribunal, and the Attorney General's Office.

The Party System and Unified Government in San Luis

As a result of sustained unified PJ government and strict party discipline, executive dominance was more pronounced in Rodríguez Saá's San Luis than in Menem's Argentina. The structure of the San Luis party system has been a major factor behind unified government, the first component of monolithic party control. San Luis was under unified PJ government from 1987 through 2003.

THE DEMISE OF THIRD PARTIES IN SAN LUIS

The demise of third parties after 1983 contributed to unified PJ government in San Luis. In contrast to Mendoza, third parties in San Luis have not helped disperse power away from the governor. Since Rodríguez Saá assumed the governorship, no relevant third party has had representation in Congress. San Luis conservative parties underwent a rapid decline beginning in 1983. Until the 1983 transition to democracy, conservative parties represented a significant political force in San Luis. San Luis is one of three provinces along with Mendoza and Corrientes that had strong conservative parties through the 1970s. In 1973, the San Luis conservative bloc received 27 percent of the vote, outperforming the UCR. Just ten years later, conservative parties received only 7 percent of the vote, and their share had dwindled to 3 percent by 1991. PJ efforts to coopt conservative party leaders contributed to the decline. For instance, the renowned conservative leader and critic of PJ corruption, Amalia Esequilla, joined the Rodríguez Saá administration.[4] Leftist third parties in San Luis have also been weak. The strongest leftist party, Nuestro Compromiso, had only one seat in Congress during the Rodríguez Saá administration. As a result, Rodríguez Saá's PJ had no need to bargain with third parties and instead had only one opposition party to battle and defeat, the UCR.

THE MOVE TOWARD SINGLE PARTY DOMINANCE

With third parties either eliminated or coopted, the San Luis PJ gradually consolidated power, leading to unified government. Since 1983, only two parties, the PJ and the UCR, have had significant representation in the legislature, and the PJ maintained a majority in both houses from 1987 through 2003. Unlike the party competition that has characterized Mendoza, UCR opposition in the San Luis Congress has been weak.[5] The PJ lost control of

TABLE 5.1
San Luis General Election Results, 1973–91

	1973 Percentage	1983 Percentage	1985 Percentage	1987 Percentage	1991 Percentage
PJ	41	40	45	52	51
UCR	10	38	48	33	37
Conservative parties	27	7	4	7	3
Other	22	15	3	8	9
TOTAL	100	100	100	100	100

SOURCE: José Samper, *San Luis: La (in)dependencia de los poderes* (San Luis: Alta Editorial, 1993), 58–59.

Congress only once while Rodríguez Saá was in office. The only period in post-transition history during which the San Luis UCR threatened the PJ was between 1983 and 1987 when the UCR temporarily captured the support of members of conservative parties. Rodríguez Saá's 1983 victory over the UCR candidate for the governorship was slim. Rodríguez Saá won by a narrow margin of 2 percent. In the 1985 legislative elections, the UCR defeated the PJ, and the thirty-member unicameral Congress was divided evenly with fifteen UCR and fifteen PJ legislators.[6] The UCR's brief success, however, was an aberration. Table 5.1 shows the demise of conservative parties since 1973 and the short-lived rise in electoral support for the UCR in 1985.

The UCR's inability to maintain its new status after 1987 was due in part to deliberate PJ strategies. Rodríguez Saá sabotaged UCR mayors in the province's two largest cities by withholding funds from those communities. In addition, during his first term, the governor tempted UCR leaders to collaborate with the PJ in exchange for posts in his administration. For instance, Arturo Negri, former president of the San Luis UCR and a former national UCR congressman, accepted a post in Rodríguez Saá's cabinet.[7] The cooptation strategy paralleled the PJ absorption of conservative leaders between 1983 and 1987.

Internal divisions over whether to cooperate with the PJ contributed to the fall of the UCR. In the wake of the 1985 UCR victory, Governor Rodríguez Saá resorted to strong-arm tactics in an attempt to prevent divided government. He ordered the local police to prevent the newly elected UCR legislators from entering Congress. PJ legislators then voted to annul the 1985 elections. The UCR legislators denounced the governor's strategy. Despite the initial UCR opposition, however, the UCR ultimately struck a deal with the PJ. In the UCR-PJ Acta Institucional, Rodríguez Saá agreed to permit the new UCR legislators to assume their seats in exchange for UCR support for a constitutional reform. By agreeing to the reform, the UCR unwittingly gave Rodríguez Saá a tool to increase his power. As discussed below, the reform permitted the governor to restructure the legislature to avoid divided government in the future, and it permitted his unlimited reelection. UCR members Roberto Pagano and Graciela Rosso fault their party for cooperating with rather than attacking the governor when the UCR was in a position of strength.[8]

THE 1987 CONSTITUTIONAL CONVENTION AND UNIFIED GOVERNMENT

Contrary to UCR expectations, the PJ dominated the 1987 Constitutional Convention. UCR leaders had agreed to support constitutional reform because they interpreted their party's victory in the 1985 legislative election as an indicator that their party would win a majority of seats at the Convention. In addition, the UCR expected internal PJ divisions to weaken the PJ's position at the Convention. The UCR was wrong on both counts. The PJ won thirty-three of the sixty seats. The UCR won twenty-five, and conservative parties won two seats. In addition, the PJ overcame internal conflict and maintained party discipline throughout the reform process. As president of the PJ bloc at the Convention, José Samper succeeded in the difficult task of keeping his party unified.[9]

The PJ used its majority at the Convention to achieve its goal of preventing future recurrences of divided government. The PJ sought unified government to eliminate the opposition's use of the legislature as a check on the governor's power. From 1985 through 1987, Rodríguez Saá had faced strong opposition in the evenly divided Congress. The fifteen PJ versus fifteen UCR split had prevented him from pushing bills through the legislature. In addition, due to the strong UCR presence in Congress during his first term, Rodríguez Saá faced limits on his ability to appoint allegiant judges. For instance, the appointments of opposition members Carlos Cacace, Rosales Arnaldo, and Osvaldo Suriani were a result of UCR strength at the time. Unified PJ government would permit the governor to push through legislation, to appoint pliant judges, and to avoid congressional investigations of executive officials.[10]

The PJ majority restructured Congress and changed electoral rules to secure unified PJ government in the future. The UCR had no representation on the constitutional committee that dealt with the reform of Congress. Thus, the UCR had no input regarding the future bicameral legislature before the PJ proposal reached the floor. UCR representatives at the Conven-

TABLE 5.2

Unified Government in San Luis, 1983–2003

	Party of Governor	Percentage of House Seats	Percentage of Senate Seats	Unified Government
1983–85	PJ	56.7	Unicameral until 1987	Yes
1985–87	PJ	50.0	—	No
1987–89	PJ	55.8	100	Yes
1989–91	PJ	51.2	100	Yes
1991–93	PJ	54.6	100	Yes
1993–95	PJ	56.8	100	Yes
1995–97	PJ	57.8	100	Yes
1997–99	PJ	53.4	100	Yes
1999–2001	PJ	55.5	77.8	Yes
2001–3	PJ	67.4	77.8	Yes

SOURCE: Data from Juan José Laborda Ibarra and Centro de Estudios para el Desarrollo Institucional (CEDI).

tion could only raise their hands to vote in opposition during the plenary session.[11] The PJ majority replaced the unicameral legislature with a bicameral Congress that was controlled by the PJ throughout Rodríguez Saá's tenure as governor. The nine-member Senate contains one elected representative from each district. Because each district elects a single senator, the PJ needed just over 50 percent of the vote in each district to acquire 100 percent of Senate seats. Indeed, as Table 5.2 illustrates, the PJ held all nine Senate seats from 1987 through 1999 and had a majority from 1999 through 2003. The PJ maintained a majority in the House from 1987 through 2003.

THE CONSTITUTIONAL CONVENTION AND EXECUTIVE DOMINANCE

PJ dominance at the Convention also paved the way for Rodríguez Saá's indefinite reelection and provided him with a proactive power that permits the passage of laws without congressional consent. Article 138 of the 1987 San Luis Constitution allows the governor to bypass Congress by classifying bills as "urgent" or "very urgent." Each house has thirty days to vote on urgent issues and fifteen days for very urgent issues. If Congress fails to meet the time constraint, the proposal automatically becomes law. The constitution does not define what constitutes an urgent or very urgent issue, giving the governor discretion over the classification of bills. Moreover, two-thirds of each house is necessary to remove the urgency classification. PJ control of both houses from 1987 through 2003 prevented the opposition in Congress from removing the time constraint. For instance, when Rodríguez Saá designated three bills as "very urgent" in December 1991, the PJ bloc rejected the UCR request to extend the fifteen-day time limit.[12]

The disciplined PJ majority at the Convention overcame UCR opposition to the governor's indefinite reelection. The 1987 reelection clause is more detrimental to the separation of powers than its counterpart in Argentina's national constitution. The 1994 reform of the Argentine Constitution permitted Menem's reelection for a second consecutive term but forbade a third term. Limits on reelection hinder Argentine presidents' ability to control the courts. Menem took steps that undermined judicial autonomy, but he faced the constraint of two terms. In contrast, the San Luis Constitution allowed Rodríguez Saá to serve an uninterrupted five terms in office, accumulating more power with each four-year term. Indefinite reelection permitted Rodríguez Saá to implement a long-term strategy of executive subordination of the courts. Experience at the provincial level demonstrates that extending a governor's term beyond two terms undermines democratic institutions that are essential to the rule of law and weakens controls on the executive. Executive subordination of the courts has characterized the three other Argentine provinces with unlimited reelection, Catamarca since 1988, La Rioja since 1986, and Santa Cruz since 1998.[13]

In addition, in contrast to Mendoza where family members cannot succeed one another in the governorship, the San Luis Constitution's reelection clause permits the concentration of power in a single family.[14] Indeed, in May 2003, Rodríguez Saá passed power on to his brother Alberto, his closest political ally. With the 1987 constitution, San Luis returned to the "provincial oligarchy" that it had been at end of the nineteenth century. In provincial oligarchies, a single family dominates the political arena and family members succeed one another indefinitely.[15] In San Luis, a single clan controlled the province in an authoritarian style from 1870 until 1904 under the succession of three brothers. In 1904, Rodríguez Saá's grandfather overthrew the brothers with the help of the federal government. In order to avoid future recurrences of provincial oligarchy in San Luis, the first Adolfo Rodríguez Saá campaigned successfully to include an article in the 1905 San Luis Constitution that prohibited passing the governorship from one family member to another. PJ representatives at the 1987 Convention erased this institutional inheritance of Rodríguez Saá's grandfather.[16]

Electoral Rules and Party Discipline in San Luis

In contrast to Mendoza where the PJ has become less hierarchical since 1983, PJ discipline has increased in San Luis, enhancing the governor's partisan powers and exacerbating the effects of unified government. Over time, Rodríguez Saá gained absolute control of his party. During his first term (1983–87), internal divisions and a low level of discipline plagued the PJ. The San Luis PJ emerged weak and unorganized from the 1976–83 military dictatorship. It lacked the leadership necessary to unite its two internal factions, the Orange List and the Blue and White List. In 1983, Rodríguez Saá's Blue and White List won the PJ primaries by fraud. Even with the help of fraud, his list defeated the Orange List by a narrow margin of 52 percent to 48 percent. In recognition of his precarious victory, Rodríguez Saá granted concessions to the losing faction. For instance, he gave two of the four cabinet posts to members of the opposition list. Divisions remained strong through 1987. In the 1985 PJ elections, Rodríguez Saá's faction again won by a narrow margin with 52 percent.[17] During the 1987 Constitutional Convention, Samper's primary duty as leader of the PJ bloc was to keep his party unified. He reports that his task was difficult in 1987, whereas the task would have been easy two years later because Rodríguez Saá had gained absolute control of the party by 1989.[18]

After realizing that negotiation and compromise could not ensure party discipline, Rodríguez Saá took deliberate steps to take control of the PJ. In 1985, he became PJ president and his brother Alberto assumed the second highest post, president of the PJ Congress. After the governor assumed the PJ presidency, he expelled his opponents from the party. By 1989, the governor had eliminated internal divisions and had total control of the hierarchical PJ. In the words of a San Luis judge, Rodríguez Saá had become the "owner of the party."[19]

Rodríguez Saá used his dual role as governor and PJ president to secure party discipline. His discretion over the closed electoral lists and over the distribution of party resources created incentives for PJ legislators to support his policy preferences. His authority over placement on the closed PJ lists translated into control over legislators' chances at reelection. In order to secure a spot on the PJ list, legislators had to vote with the party line. On important bills, PJ legislators who opposed the official party stance tended to miss a session rather than incur the costs of voting against the PJ. Indeed, Rodríguez Saá used his power over the political career of PJ members to secure discipline. For instance, he punished Ángel Rafael Ruiz (PJ) who planned to run for reelection to the national Congress in 1993. Shortly before the 1993 elections, Ruiz voted against the governor's orders. As a result,

Rodríguez Saá eliminated him from the PJ electoral list. The fate of Ruiz sent a clear message to PJ legislators: Rodríguez Saá would terminate the political careers of those who dared to disobey his orders.[20]

Monolithic Party Control and Informal Executive Power

Unified PJ government and party discipline permitted Rodríguez Saá to exercise informal powers that violated the formal rules delineated in the San Luis Constitution. Along with the governor's partisan powers, this informal authority contributed to the legislature's inability to act as a countervailing power center that checks the executive. Like Menem, Rodríguez Saá's informal authority supplemented his partisan and formal or constitutional powers.[21] Informal prerogatives were part of the constellation of powers that permitted Rodríguez Saá to dominate the legislative process and to totally dismantle the rule of law.

In order to avoid open congressional debate and to prevent opposition to his proposals, Rodríguez Saá instructed the disciplined PJ majority in the House of Representatives to support an unconstitutional modification of House Rules. The modification weakened the capacity of the House, the only political institution with opposition representation, to check the governor. In response to opposition legislators' use of the House as a forum to criticize Rodríguez Saá, the new House rule permitted the PJ majority to silence opposition members such as Roberto Pagano and Juan José Laborda Ibarra. When Pagano (UCR) opposed the 1995 reduction of judges' salaries, PJ legislators initiated proceedings to suspend him. At the time, however, the PJ was one vote short of the two-thirds necessary to sanction Pagano. The PJ also sought to silence Laborda Ibarra, who had accused Rodríguez Saá of corruption.[22]

The new House rule has weakened opposition voices by stipulating that a simple majority is sufficient to sanction a House member, a violation of the provincial and national constitutions.[23] According to the San Luis Constitution, two-thirds of the total members are necessary to sanction a legislator. The Argentine Constitution stipulates: "No member of Congress may be accused, questioned, or harassed for opinions or speeches pronounced during his legislative term"[24] PJ legislators used the new standard to silence members of opposition parties. For instance, after a Congressman from the leftist party Nuestro Compromiso criticized PJ legislators, the PJ majority in the House prohibited him from speaking during three sessions.[25]

Monolithic Party Control and the Erosion of Horizontal Accountability in San Luis

Due to the sustained monolithic PJ control, San Luis has had fewer points of independent opposition than either the province of Mendoza or Argentina at the national level. Rodríguez Saá's partisan, formal, and informal powers permitted him to dismantle all remnants of a system of horizontal accountability that are part of the rule of law. As discussed in Chapter 4, the PJ-controlled Congress passed a series of laws that subordinated the judicial branch to the governor. In addition, by changing their institutional design, Governor Rodríguez Saá and his PJ stripped the Judicial Council, the Impeachment Jury, the State Prosecutor, the Accounting Tribunal, and the Attorney General's Office of the capacity to act as countervailing power centers.

PJ DOMINANCE AND THE SUBORDINATION OF THE JUDICIAL COUNCIL

The 1987 San Luis Constitution created a Judicial Council that participates in selection of first instance and appellate court judges. In a deal similar to the 1993 Olivos Pact between Menem and Alfonsín, Rodríguez Saá accepted the creation of a Judicial Council in exchange for the possibility of indefinite reelection. In theory, the Council serves as a preselection mechanism that reduces executive discretion over judicial appointments. In reality, however, monolithic PJ control permitted the San Luis governor to handpick judges despite the creation of a Judicial Council. Unified government coupled with PJ discipline rendered the Council unable to reduce executive appointment power. With the help of his party, Rodríguez Saá prevented the Council from fulfilling its constitutional role.

The PJ majority at the 1987 Constitutional Convention created a Judicial Council that is weaker than its counterpart in Mendoza and at the national level. Article 196 of the San Luis Constitution permits the governor to disregard the Council's input. For each vacant post, the Judicial Council proposes a *terna*, a three-person rank order list, from which the governor selects one member with Senate approval. In contrast to Argentina at the federal level and the province of Mendoza, the first *terna* is not binding, or *vinculante*, in San Luis. If either the governor or the Senate rejects the proposed *terna*, the Council must submit a second threesome. Moreover, if the Senate rejects the candidate from the first *terna*, the second *terna* cannot include anyone from the original threesome.[26]

The PJ-controlled San Luis legislature sanctioned laws that further constrain the Judicial Council's capacity to serve as a horizontal accountability agency. In 1990, the disciplined PJ majority in Congress weakened the

Council by modifying the *terna* system. Before 1990, if the governor rejected the first threesome, the Council could include members of the original threesome in the second threesome. The San Luis Constitution stipulates that only a candidate rejected by the Senate cannot form part of the second *terna*.[27] According to the 1990 law, however, if the governor does not submit a member of the *terna* for Senate approval within thirty days, the Council must propose three new candidates; no member of the original *terna* can be part of the second threesome. This law permits the governor to tacitly reject all three individuals in the Council's first recommendation. The law gives the governor a power that the provincial constitution reserves for the Senate.[28] Former Judicial Council member Miriam Agundez recalls that Rodríguez Saá took advantage of the law. He frequently rejected the entire first *terna* by allowing the thirty-day limit to lapse.[29]

In 1996, Rodríguez Saá used his decree power to further undermine the Judicial Council. His 1996 decree stipulates that the Council has only ten days to present a *terna*. The decree violates multiple constitutional provisions. The ten-day limit precludes thorough examination of candidates, violating the constitutional requirement that the Council offer exams and conduct a comprehensive assessment of potential judicial nominees. In addition, the decree violates the constitutional provision that gives the Judicial Council sixty days to submit a *terna*.[30]

With the help of his party, Rodríguez Saá eliminated opposition representation on the Judicial Council. The San Luis Council has eight members: a Supreme Court justice, a representative from the executive branch, two judges, two provincial legislators, and two San Luis Bar Association members.[31] All eight members answered to Rodríguez Saá. Because of the governor's control over the composition of the judiciary, the Supreme Court justice and the two lower court judges who served on the Council answered to the governor. The governor handpicked the executive representative. Furthermore, as a result of PJ control of Congress, both legislators on the Council were members of the PJ. Rodríguez Saá's 1996 dissolution of San Luis's independent bar association gave him control over the lawyers on the Council. Law 5123 of 1996 replaced the independent bar association with Asociaciones de Abogados, which were controlled by Rodríguez Saá's allies.[32]

MONOLITHIC PARTY CONTROL AND THE SUBORDINATION OF THE IMPEACHMENT JURY

Monolithic PJ control prevented the Impeachment Jury from reducing the governor's discretion over the removal of judges. According to the 1987 constitution, the Impeachment Jury is the organ with the authority to remove judges.[33] Rodríguez Saá used his control of Congress to convert the Jury into another tool to subordinate the judicial branch. The governor utilized the Jury to dismiss judges who challenged his interests. In 1996, the disciplined PJ bloc in the legislature approved laws that obstruct the Jury's capacity to serve as an agency of horizontal accountability. By altering the Jury's institutional design, PJ legislators subordinated it to the governor. The legislation modified the Jury's composition, allowing the governor to determine who serves on the important organ.

Before the 1996 legislation, the Impeachment Jury was independent of the executive branch. According to the San Luis Constitution, the nine-member Jury is composed of three judges, three lawyers, and three legislators. Based on his experience as a Jury member, Pagano asserts that until 1996, the method of selecting Jury members protected the autonomy of the organ. The three attorneys and the three judges were selected by lottery from among their colleagues. Two of the three House members were PJ affiliates, and one was from the minority party. The balanced composition enabled the Jury to resist the governor's pressure to dismiss Judge Ana María Careaga in 1993 and Judge Adriana Gallo in 1996, both of whom were later removed from their judicial posts by the governor's handpicked Jury. Eugenio Raúl Zaffaroni, a prominent Argentine criminal law expert, concurs with Pagano's assessment. Based on his experience as Careaga's attorney before the 1993 Jury, he argues that the Jury was independent of the governor at the time.[34]

Legislating the Governor's Control of the Impeachment Jury

Law 5102 of 1996 cleared the way for the governor to assume control of the Impeachment Jury. The law purged the Jury, creating nine vacancies. Thus, the governor had the opportunity to replace Jury members such as Pagano and Cacace who had refused to dismiss independent judges whose rulings were sometimes against the administration's interests. The nine new members all had close ties to Rodríguez Saá.[35] In addition, Law 5102 created new reasons to introduce charges against judges, facilitating the dismissal of independent judges. The law stipulates that undermining the judiciary's prestige, or *desprestigio del poder judicial*, is sufficient cause to bring a judge before the Jury. The vagueness of the term *desprestigio* allowed the governor to target judges who challenged his administration. Furthermore, the legislative process behind the passage of Law 5102 was opaque and irregular. The PJ bloc did not provide opposition legislators with a copy of the bill prior to House deliberations, which hindered the opposition's ability to engage in effective debate.[36]

Law 5123 of 1996 gave the governor discretion over who represents lawyers on the Jury. According to the San Luis Constitution, the three attorneys on the Jury are chosen from a list of twenty attorneys compiled each year by the San Luis Colegio Forense. Prior to Law 5123, which abolished the independent San Luis Bar Association, the Colegio Forense was comprised of bar association members. As discussed above, Law 5123 of 1996 abolished the independent bar association and replaced it with Asociaciones de Abogados, which were composed of the governor's allies. After Law 5123, the pro-Rodríguez Saá Asociaciones de Abogados sent representatives to the Colegio Forense. As a result, the governor's allies gained control of the Colegio Forense that selects the lawyers who serve on the Jury.[37]

The Impeachment Jury's 1998 composition demonstrated the governor's use of the legislation to fill the Jury with his allies. All nine members had ties to Rodríguez Saá before joining the Jury. Carlos Sergnese, the governor's close friend and former Minister of Government, presided over the body. Other members included Victor Nicanor Liceda and Julio César Agundez, both of whom had demonstrated their loyalty to the governor during their tenures as State Prosecutor. Liceda had also been the governor's personal attorney. Luis Antonio Amitrano had been Rodríguez Saá's Minister of Industry and a pliant Supreme Court justice. César Carmen Zucco had also served on the docile Court. Atilio Astudillo and Mario Alonso had been members of Rodríguez Saá's cabinet.[38]

The Impeachment Jury and the Removal of Judge Gallo and Judge Careaga

Rodríguez Saá used his control of the Impeachment Jury to remove judges who challenged his interests. The 1998 removals of Gallo and Careaga demonstrated the Jury's willingness to execute the governor's will. The national newspaper *La Nación* reported that the Jury's treatment of Gallo and Careaga was the governor's "political revenge" against independent judges.[39] Argentina's Federation of Bar Associations, the Federación Argentina de Colegios de Abogados (FACA), also denounced the dismissals.[40] According to Zaffaroni, the Jury had no legal basis to remove either judge.[41] Luis Moreno Ocampo, former president of Transparency International Latin America, agreed to represent Gallo before the Jury because he was convinced of her innocence. Christian Courtis of the civil society group Centro de Estudios Legales y Sociales (CELS) represented Careaga for the same reason.[42]

The Rodríguez Saá administration considered Gallo and Careaga to be threats to its interests. The two judges had opposed the 1995 reduction of judges' salaries and signed the San Luis Bar Association denunciation of executive subordination of the courts. Furthermore, Gallo had issued rulings against the governor's economic interests. For instance, she ruled against Edesal, a private electricity company in which the governor owned stock.[43] In July 1998, the Impeachment Jury suspended her for eight years. Careaga faced an even more severe punishment than did Gallo. San Luis Attorney General Domingo Vacca had requested a one-year suspension, but the Jury suspended her for fifteen years. In addition, the Jury passed her case to the San Luis criminal courts where she faced the threat of prosecution. In order to avoid imprisonment, Careaga fled San Luis on the same day that the Jury announced its ruling. According to Careaga, the message to the rest of San Luis judicial community was clear: judges who dare to investigate government officials will suffer grave consequences.[44]

The government's cases against Gallo and Careaga were weak. Attorney General Vacca based his case against Gallo on the retroactive application of a 1996 law. He alleged that in 1994 Gallo had been guilty of undermining the judiciary's prestige, or *desprestigio*, which did not constitute a crime until the 1996 passage of Law 5102. In addition, Vacca revived a charge of bad performance, or *mal desempeño*, of which the 1996 Jury had absolved Gallo. After the governor purged the 1996 Impeachment Jury, Sergnese ordered the new Jury to hide the 1996 absolution of Gallo, which prevented her attorneys from accessing it during the 1998 hearing.[45] The Jury suspended Gallo even though her defense team demonstrated her strong performance in the judiciary. Of all San Luis judges, she issued the most rulings during the 1994–97 period. In addition, she had the second lowest percentage of decisions overruled by an appellate court.[46] In the Careaga case, Vacca based his political militancy charge, *intervención en política*, on her support of the San Luis Bar Association denunciation of the governor's subordination of the courts. The Jury declared her guilty of adhering to an "irrational declaration." Vacca also alleged that Careaga had conducted an unreasonable investigation of a PJ mayor's involvement in an irregular contract that privatized the local parking meter system. Her CELS defense team demonstrated that the investigation was reasonable and did not violate the mayor's rights.[47]

Both Jury processes were replete with irregularities. In Gallo's case, the Impeachment Jury did not provide an explanation for its refusal to admit 70 percent of the defense team's evidence. Moreover, the Jury did not stipulate a clear set of rules at the onset of the hearing. Instead, the Jury added and modified rules on an ad hoc basis throughout the process.[48] During the Careaga hearing, Attorney General Vacca violated the rule that prohibits the prosecution from introducing new charges after the defense has responded to the Attorney General's initial accusation. Vacca added the charge of political militancy after Careaga's defense team responded to the original accusation. In addition, in order to maintain the Jury's pro-Rodríguez Saá composition throughout the hearing, the PJ-controlled Congress extended Jury members' terms by six months, violating the constitutional stipulation that members serve one-year terms. Furthermore, the Jury rejected many CELS witnesses without explanation. For instance, the Jury did not permit FACA president Ángel Fermin Garrote to testify. The CELS team had planned to use Garrote's testimony to demonstrate that like Careaga, FACA had supported the San Luis Bar Association denunciation, suggesting that the statement was reasonable rather than a militant, irrational view.[49]

PJ DOMINANCE AND THE GOVERNOR'S CONTROL OF THE OFFICE OF THE STATE PROSECUTOR

The 1987 San Luis Constitution established the Office of the State Prosecutor, known as the Fiscalía de Estado, which has the formal power to act as an agency of horizontal accountability. The Office has the constitutional authority to declare any law or decree unconstitutional, and the constitution grants the head of the Office, the State Prosecutor, tenure protection.[50] Monolithic party control, however, prevented the Office from exercising its formal power. It acted as Rodríguez Saá's advisory board rather than as a check on the governor's authority.

Unified PJ government coupled with party discipline allowed Rodríguez Saá to subordinate the Office of the State Prosecutor. Due to PJ control of the Senate, the requirement that the Senate approve the governor's nominee failed to reduce executive discretion over who serves as State Prosecutor. Rodríguez Saá appointed only unconditional allies who did not challenge his administration. For instance, Victor Nicanor Liceda was the governor's personal lawyer before becoming State Prosecutor. When Liceda took his oath as State Prosecutor, he delivered a speech praising the governor.[51] The political trajectory of the State Prosecutor in 1999, Eduardo Ángel Estrada, demonstrates the governor's effort to appoint loyal PJ members. Estrada began a long career as a PJ functionary in 1960. The 1976 military coup interrupted his political career, which he resumed in 1986 as Rodríguez Saá's Undersecretary of Government.[52]

Estrada provides a stark contrast with the 1995–99 Mendoza State Prosecutor, Aldo Giordano. The two men had different visions of their roles. In contrast to Giordano, Estrada performed none of the functions of an agent of horizontal accountability. Estrada considered himself to be a government advisor. Unlike Giordano, Estrada believed that the State Prosecutor and the governor should be members of the same party. According to Estrada, in order to perform the State Prosecutor's primary function, defending the governor, the Prosecutor must have close relations with executive officials. Estrada admits that the San Luis Office of the State Prosecutor channeled its work through the executive branch. He acknowledges that although the State Prosecutor has the formal power to declare laws unconstitutional, the San Luis State Prosecutor did not perform this function. According to Estrada, it is the responsibility of the Court rather than the State Prosecutor to challenge the constitutionality of laws and decrees. Unlike Giordano, whose activity as State Prosecutor produced the fall of two cabinet ministers, Estrada never presented a suit against an administration official.[53]

In addition, Rodríguez Saá had the informal power to dismiss the State Prosecutor, as demonstrated by his treatment of Sergio Calderón. Despite his background as a PJ leader, Calderón challenged the governor after assuming the post of State Prosecutor. Thus, the governor requested his resignation. Calderón acquiesced. He knew that if he did not resign, the pliant Impeachment Jury would follow the governor's orders to remove him from office.[54]

The governor used his control of the legislature to consolidate power over the Office of the State Prosecutor. In 1990, the disciplined PJ bloc in Congress approved legislation that permits the governor to replace the State Prosecutor with any lawyer from within the agency whenever the Prosecutor is absent, either temporarily or permanently. In effect, the law created a substitute prosecutor that lacks tenure protection yet has the same responsibilities as the State Prosecutor. Moreover, the governor can appoint the substitute prosecutor without legislative interference. Unlike the State Prosecutor, the substitute does not require Senate approval. Although in theory the substitute prosecutor acts only when the State Prosecutor is absent, the substitute can serve indefinitely. The 1990 law does not require that the governor appoint a State Prosecutor within a specific period of time, a violation of the constitutional stipulation that any position requiring Senate approval be filled within ten days after a vacancy appears.[55]

PJ CONTROL OF THE ACCOUNTING TRIBUNAL

Monolithic PJ control also prevented the Accounting Tribunal from emerging as a competing power center in San Luis. Since the Accounting Tribunal gained constitutional status in 1987, it has had the formal power to review all government expenditures. In theory, the Tribunal is independent of the executive branch. According to the San Luis Constitution, the government cannot reduce Tribunal members' salaries or dismiss members before the end of their two-year terms. Furthermore, the constitution stipulates that the Tribunal manages its own budget and dictates the rules that guide its functioning.[56] Despite constitutional guarantees of autonomy, however, the Tribunal was unable to check the Rodríguez Saá administration's economic activity.

Rodríguez Saá controlled the Tribunal's composition. The 1987 constitution gives the governor the authority to appoint three of the five members with Senate approval. The PJ-controlled Senate never rejected a Rodríguez Saá nominee to the Tribunal. The House selects the other two Tribunal members. The majority party appoints one and the first minority selects the second.[57] During the Rodríguez Saá administration, four of the five Tribunal members were loyal PJ affiliates. According to former PJ Congressman Samper, the Tribunal was a bureaucratic agency that did not fill its constitutional role.[58] In contrast to the Mendoza Accounting Tribunal, which has been dominated by the opposition, the PJ dominated the San Luis Tribunal throughout Rodríguez Saá's governorship. Once again, PJ dominance in Congress was crucial to the governor's ability to subordinate oversight agencies.

EXECUTIVE SUBORDINATION OF THE ATTORNEY GENERAL'S OFFICE

Monolithic PJ control also rendered the San Luis Attorney General's Office unable to act as an agency of horizontal accountability. An effective, autonomous Attorney General's Office was critical in Rodríguez Saá's San Luis due to the high level of government corruption. In theory, public prosecutors initiate proceedings against government functionaries suspected of illegal practices. In San Luis, however, the composition of the Office prevented it from prosecuting administration officials.

The governor appoints the Attorney General with Senate approval. The PJ-controlled Senate never withheld its approval from Rodríguez Saá. Executive discretion over who serves as Attorney General was central to the governor's impunity. The Attorney General can order lower level prosecutors to halt investigations. In addition, the Attorney General acts as the prosecutor against judges who appear before the Impeachment Jury. Thus, the Attorney General was an important player when the governor sought to remove independent judges such as Careaga and Gallo.

Former Attorney General Vacca was representative of the Office's subservience to Rodríguez Saá. The long-time friend of Rodríguez Saá brought Gallo and Careaga before the 1998 Impeachment Jury. At the time, he acknowledged the governor's subordination of his office. When Rosso encountered Vacca at a social event during the Gallo hearing, the Attorney General admitted that he had brought charges against an innocent woman.[59] During a meeting with Moreno Ocampo, Vacca acknowledged that the Office lacked autonomy.[60]

In addition, Rodríguez Saá's control of the Judicial Council gave him discretion over the selection of lower level public prosecutors. The Judicial Council intervenes in the selection of public prosecutors as well as lower court judges. When a vacancy in the Attorney General's Office appears, the Council recommends a *terna* from which the governor selects one public prosecutor with Senate approval.[61] The same laws that weakened the Judicial Council's discretion over the appointment of judges also undermined its discretion over the selection of prosecutors. For instance, the governor can reject all three members of the Council's first *terna*. Rodríguez Saá used his power over the Council to fill the Attorney General's Office with pliant PJ allies. Close ties to Rodríguez Saá prevented public prosecutors from investigating administration officials.[62] Instead, they focused their efforts on investigating the opposition.[63]

The monolithic PJ control that allowed Rodríguez Saá to subordinate all agencies of horizontal accountability gave him absolute power over politics in *Adolfolandia*. In contrast, the province of Mendoza has a robust system of overlapping horizontal accountability agencies, which has been central to the establishment and fortification of the rule of law in the province. Chapter 6 explains the stark contrast between San Luis and Mendoza. It explores how Mendoza's competitive party system has fostered the evolution of effective institutional power centers that reinforce one another and disperse power away from the governor.

CHAPTER 6

Party Competition and the Rule of Law in Mendoza

IN CONTRAST TO the monolithic party control that has favored executive dominance in San Luis, political party competition in Mendoza set the stage for the rule of law. Competitive politics has bolstered the checks and balances that comprise Mendoza's effective system of horizontal accountability. Competition among three strong parties has fostered divided government and the rotation of the party in the governorship. Under divided government, governors have been unable to manipulate the institutional design of the judiciary and other countervailing power centers. The likelihood that the governor's party will lose power in the future has created incentives to strengthen horizontal accountability agencies.

The first section of this chapter traces the evolution of the three-party system that has been fundamental to the dispersal of political power and the establishment of the rule of law in Mendoza. Section II demonstrates that party competition has indeed encouraged divided government and rotation of the party that controls the executive branch. Section III shows that party discipline has been high in Mendoza, but divided government has mitigated the effects of discipline. Section IV demonstrates how three-party balance has limited the executive's partisan powers and compelled governors to respect constitutional limits on their authority. This chapter concludes by documenting how competitive politics has permitted the establishment of durable control organs that constrain Mendoza governors. Along with an autonomous judiciary, the Judicial Council, the Impeachment Jury, the Office of the State Prosecutor, the Accounting Tribunal, and the Attorney General's Office check executive authority in Mendoza. Competition among three parties has encouraged the distribution of power among these agencies of horizontal accountability and away from the executive, thereby promoting the rule of law.

The Three-Party Balance in Mendoza

Mendoza's political system features three political parties that compete aggressively with one another for congressional seats and for control of the governorship: the Partido Justicialista (PJ), the Unión Cívica Radical (UCR), and the Partido Demócrata (PD). No single party has dominated Mendoza politics, and the difference in electoral performance among the parties has been small. As a result of the three-party balance, the parties have had to work together to pass legislation or to block executive initiatives. Legislators from the three parties assert that the party balance has promoted coalitions that check executive power.[1]

The UCR was the first of the three parties to emerge in Mendoza. In contrast to San Luis where the UCR has been weak, the Mendoza UCR has remained a strong political force since the early twentieth century. Historically, the UCR performed better in Mendoza than in other Argentine provinces. Mendoza was the only province where the nation-wide UCR-led Revolution of 1905 triumphed. Moreover, the UCR frequently occupied the Mendoza governorship during the twentieth century. The Lencinista branch of the Mendoza UCR captured the governorship from 1918 until 1930. After twenty-five years of retreat due to internal struggles, the UCR returned to the governorship in 1956. From 1958 until 1961, a UCR faction, the Unión Cívica Radical Intransigente (UCRI), was in power under Ernesto Ueltschi.[2] The UCR captured the governorship again in 1983 under Santiago Felipe Llaver and remained a strong opposition force during the 1987–99 PJ administrations. In 1999, the UCR returned to the governorship under Roberto Iglesias.

The founding of the PD in 1931 and the emergence of the PJ in the 1940s were important steps toward competitive politics and the dispersal of political power in Mendoza. The PD, a descendant of the conservative forces that dominated Mendoza politics until the birth of the UCR, competes only in Mendoza. It has captured much of the middle and upper class vote and has had more affiliates than either the Mendoza PJ or UCR. The PD governed Mendoza from 1931 until 1943. Although the PD experienced a temporary decline when the PJ emerged in the mid-1940s, it had recovered its strength by 1961 when Francisco Gabrielli (PD) assumed the governorship. The PD captured the governorship again from 1970 until 1973. During the 1976–83 military regime, PD leaders collaborated with the regime and occupied key government posts. Following Argentina's 1983 transition to democracy, the PD share of the vote fell because of its association with the military government. In the first election after the transition, the PD received only 13 percent of the vote. Since 1983, however, the PD has steadily regained power. In 1989, the PD joined the Alianza del Centro, a national alliance that included the conservative Unión del Centro Democrático (UCeDé), which received 20 percent of the provincial vote that year. By 1994, the PD had restored its status as a relevant party in Mendoza. In 1994, the PD received 35 percent of the vote, second only to the PJ.[3] In the 1997 legislative elections, the PD outperformed both the PJ and the UCR. In the 1999 gubernatorial election, the PD garnered 33 percent of the vote and came in second to the UCR.

Divided Government and Party Rotation in Mendoza

The three-party balance has encouraged divided government and the rotation of the party in power, which have enhanced the capacity of the Mendoza Congress to check the executive. Divided government has prevented the governor from passing legislation that would dismantle Mendoza's horizontal accountability system.[4] Mendoza has a long history of divided government. For instance, in the 1920s, UCR Governor José Néstor Lencinas was in constant conflict with a conservative legislature that opposed major UCR initiatives. In order to pass legislation, members of Lencinas's UCR had to bargain with the conservative opposition in Congress. During the 1958–61 administration of Ueltschi (UCRI), relations between the executive and the legislative branches became increasingly hostile. After the midterm elections, the number of UCRI seats in both chambers declined. In 1958, Ueltschi's UCRI held 58 percent of seats in the House. The percentage of UCRI House seats fell to 42 percent in 1959 and to 22 percent in 1960. In 1958, the UCRI held 67 percent of Senate seats. The UCRI share fell to 41 percent in 1960.[5]

Divided government has continued in contemporary Mendoza. Unified UCR government characterized the first administration after the 1983 transition, but divided government reemerged in 1987. In contrast to San Luis where Adolfo Rodríguez Saá's PJ controlled both the legislative and executive branches from 1987 through 2003, divided government became the norm in Mendoza after 1987. Although all three governors who served from 1987 through 1999 were PJ members, José Octavio Bordón (1987–91) and Arturo Lafalla (1995–99) faced limits because divided government characterized their terms. The PJ did not dominate the political landscape but rather shared power with the opposition parties in Congress.

The PJ never held a majority in the House during Bordón's term. Even after the 1989 midterm elections when the PJ share of House seats rose from 38 percent to 48 percent, UCR and PD legislators together outnumbered Bordón's PJ by one. Moreover, the PJ did not have a majority in the Senate during Bordón's first two years in office. UCR and PD legislators frequently joined forces to oppose PJ initiatives, which forced Bordón's PJ to bargain

TABLE 6.1

Divided Government in Mendoza, 1983–2003

	Governor	Party of Governor	Percentage of House Seats	Percentage of Senate Seats	Divided Government
1983–85	Llaver	UCR	52.1	50.0	No
1985*–87	Llaver	UCR	56.3	60.5	No
1987–89	Bordón	PJ	37.5	36.8	Yes
1989*–91	Bordón	PJ	47.9	52.6	Yes
1991–93	Gabrielli	PJ	52.1	60.5	No
1993*–95	Gabrielli	PJ	58.3	60.5	No
1995–97	Lafalla	PJ	45.8	44.7	Yes
1997*–99	Lafalla	PJ	43.8	44.7	Yes
1999–2001	Iglesias	UCR (Alianza)	33.3	34.2	Yes
2001*–3	Iglesias	UCR (Alianza)	31.3	26.3	Yes

SOURCE: Data from Centro de Estudios para el Desarrollo Institucional (CEDI) and Omar Pérez Botti.

* Midterm election year.

with the opposition in Congress.[6] Unified government reemerged temporarily under Rodolfo Gabrielli (1991–95) when the PJ regained a majority in both houses. Thus, under Gabrielli, checks on the executive were relatively limited.

Divided government returned under Lafalla in 1995. During his four-year term, Lafalla's PJ never held a majority in the Senate, and after two years in office, his PJ lost its majority in the House. The presence of a strong opposition in Congress encouraged consensus-building among the parties. Cooperation in both chambers permitted the passage of major initiatives, including the privatization of important Mendoza industries.[7] Divided government continued in 1999 when Iglesias (UCR) assumed the governorship. In fact, from 1999 through 2001 both houses were evenly divided among the three parties. Each party had sixteen representatives in the House. In the Senate, both the UCR and the PD had thirteen seats, and the PJ had twelve seats. Table 6.1 traces divided government in post-transition Mendoza.

The three-party balance has also facilitated the rotation of the party in the governorship, which differentiates Mendoza from San Luis where the PJ held the governorship from 1983 through 2003.[8] The rotation among Mendoza's three parties has created incentives to strengthen horizontal accountability agencies in the province. Governors have foreseen the displacement of their parties and therefore have sought the protection of such agencies, including the judiciary. Mendoza Supreme Court justices Jorge Nanclares and Aída Rosa Kemelmajer de Carlucci point to the rotation among parties as a principal factor behind judicial independence.[9] Due to the party rotation and the respect for judges' tenure protection, Mendoza justices serve during the administrations of different parties.

An analysis of electoral results from 1932 through 2003 demonstrates that no single party has dominated politics in Mendoza. Although the PJ held the governorship from 1987 through 1999, the divided government that characterized the Bordón and Lafalla administrations placed limits on PJ power. The return of the UCR to the governorship in 1999 was important for the maintenance of Mendoza's balanced party system and for competitive politics in the province. The following list demonstrates the frequent rotation of the party in the governorship from 1932 through 2003.

1932–43	PD
1943–46	Military
1946–55	PJ
1955–58	Military
1958–61	UCR
1961–66	PD
1966–70	Military
1970–73	PD
1973–76	PJ
1976–83	Military
1983–87	UCR
1987–99	PJ
1999–2003	UCR (Alianza)

Party Discipline in Mendoza

Along with the number of parties, the level of party discipline determines the governor's partisan powers. In Mendoza, however, party competition has offset the effects of party discipline. Although Mendoza governors have wielded significant control over their respective political parties, the governor's party has rarely held a majority in the legislature or maintained control of the executive branch for a prolonged period of time. This divided government and party rotation have attenuated the effects of party discipline. Discipline in Mendoza has not been as detrimental as in San Luis, which was characterized by unified PJ government from 1987 through 2003. In Mendoza, discipline does not guarantee the governor the legislative support necessary to pass laws that would subordinate horizontal accountability agencies.

Mendoza legislators of all parties report a high level of party discipline. Congresswoman Teresa Peltier (PD), Senator Omar Pérez Botti (PJ), and Congressman Sergio Bruni (UCR) explain that party blocs are vertically structured with the party president at the top. The party president determines party stances and can punish legislators who do not vote with their bloc.[10] Jorge Zapata Mercader (PD) and Carlos Balter (PD) report that legislators who disagree with their party's position usually abstain rather than vote against their party.[11]

As in Argentina at the national level and in San Luis, the electoral rules and nomination procedures have created an incentive structure that encourages party discipline. In Mendoza's closed-list system, one important incentive is placement on the party electoral list, which determines legislators' chances of reelection. Legislators who vote against their party risk losing access to electoral lists.[12] Bruni reports that members of a bloc who vote against the official stance on important votes fall on the party list.[13] Senator Alberto Montbrun felt the effect of voting against his party when he cast several votes that were against his UCR bloc during the 1998–99 legislative sessions. These votes led to his isolation from the party and undermined his chances of reelection.[14]

Discipline has been particularly high in the PD. The PD has a stronger party identity than does either the Mendoza PJ or UCR. Adherence to the PD's conservative ideology has contributed to party discipline. In 1993, 30 percent of voters who supported PD candidates based their vote on qualities of the party as compared to 20 percent of UCR voters and 15 percent of PJ voters.[15] In addition, the provincial PD is more tightly organized than are the UCR and PJ with their complex national party organizations. As De Luca, Jones, and Tula argue, internal struggle and disarray are less likely in provincial parties than in national parties. A single individual or group can more easily control a party that operates in a single province.[16]

A high level of discipline characterizes each of Mendoza's three parties, but discipline in the Mendoza PJ does not approach that of the San Luis PJ. The structure of the PJ is much less vertical in Mendoza than in San Luis, where Governor Rodríguez Saá served as PJ president from 1985 through 2003. In Mendoza, PJ governors have respected the party rule that prohibits the governor from serving as party president. Bordón recalls that on the day he assumed the governorship in 1987, he resigned as party president.[17] In addition, the Mendoza PJ became less hierarchical over the three PJ administrations between 1987 and 1999. Discipline was higher during the administrations of Bordón and Gabrielli than it was under Lafalla.[18] This decrease in PJ discipline during the Lafalla administration coincided with the fortification of checks on the governor's power.

Party Balance and Limits on Executive Power

As a result of competitive politics, the executive-legislative balance of power in Mendoza has not favored the governor anywhere near the degree that it has in San Luis. Although the San Luis and Mendoza governors have similar constitutional powers, divided government and party rotation in Mendoza have limited the governor's partisan powers and prevented the governor from seizing informal powers that violate the Mendoza Constitution. Party competition has prevented executive domination of the legislative process. In contrast, as discussed in Chapter 5, monolithic PJ control in San Luis granted Rodríguez Saá tremendous partisan powers and allowed him to overstep constitutional limits and seize informal powers in order to subordinate Congress, the judiciary, and other potential checks on his authority.

In Mendoza, the governor cannot prevent a legislative majority from changing the status quo. The Mendoza governor's rare use of the veto suggests weak reactive powers despite the high override requirement. Due to the three-party balance, opposition parties often have the two-thirds majority in both houses to override vetoes. In addition, party balance has fostered a tradition of consensus-building meetings between opposition legislators and executive officials prior to congressional sessions. The meetings usually result in agreement on the content of bills and render the veto unnecessary.[19]

Mendoza governors have also respected the constitutional restraints on their proactive powers. They cannot enact new legislation without congressional consent. In contrast to Argentina at the national level, the line-item veto does not exist in Mendoza. In addition, the governor can only issue decrees during legislative recess and must submit those decrees to Congress for approval after the legislature reconvenes.[20] Decrees of necessity and urgency (DNUs) are virtually unheard-of in Mendoza. Indeed, none of the first three governors following the 1983 transition issued a DNU. In contrast to Menem who issued 336 of these decrees between July 1989 and August 1994, Lafalla issued only two DNUs during his four-year term, both of which he submitted to Congress for ratification. Moreover, unlike the San Luis governor who has the authority to bypass Congress by classifying bills as urgent, in Mendoza, Congress alone determines what is necessary and urgent.[21]

Divided government in Mendoza has also permitted the legislature to use its constitutional investigative and monitoring powers to check the executive branch. Article 94 of the Mendoza Constitution grants both houses of Congress the authority to demand that cabinet ministers answer congressional queries. Law 1151 gives Congress the power to create investigative commissions.[22] Although both the San Luis and the Mendoza legislatures have the formal authority to form investigative committees, only the Mendoza Congress has exercised this prerogative. In 1998 and 1999, for instance, the Mendoza House of Representatives formed committees that investigated executive officials. Like their counterparts in the House, Senate investigative committees have been effective under divided government. Senate investigations were central to the 1996 prosecution of twenty-six former Bank of Mendoza officials for irregularities during their tenure with the state-owned bank. As discussed in Chapter 4, the 1996 prosecutions were a blow to Lafalla who had been vice-governor at the time of the bank irregularities.[23] Party balance has also permitted the creation of bicameral committees that check the executive. For example, the 1998 Bicameral Committee on Security acted as an effective countervailing power center. When Congress granted Lafalla broad powers to fight rising crime in Mendoza, it created the Bicameral Committee on Security to oversee the government ministry in charge of crime policy, the Ministry of Justice. As a result of its composition, Lafalla's PJ could not control the Bicameral Committee, which blocked several Lafalla administration proposals. PD and UCR legislators demanded that the opposition have a majority on the Committee. Of the ten members (five Senators and five House members), six were opposition members and four were members of Lafalla's PJ.[24]

In addition, Mendoza governors have been unable to eliminate the constitutional clause that prohibits reelection. The governor cannot serve a second consecutive four-year term or become vice-governor immediately following his tenure as governor. As Chapter 4 explains, Bordón's attempt to reform the constitution to permit reelection failed. In addition, after the end of a term, no member of the governor's immediate family and none of the governor's first cousins can be elected to the governorship.[25] These strict restrictions help prevent the concentration of power in the hands of a single actor or family. The restriction on family members sets Mendoza apart from San Luis, La Rioja, Catamarca, and Corrientes, all of which have been dominated by a single family.[26]

Finally, party balance reduced the governor's discretion over judicial appointments even before the Judicial Council gained constitutional status in 1998. Under divided government, Congress has hindered executive attempts to select judges based on partisan preferences rather than professional merit. During the first half of Bordón's administration and throughout the terms of Lafalla and Iglesias, no party had an absolute majority in the Senate. Former UCR Senator León Chade recalls that from 1987 through 1989, UCR and PD senators often joined forces to pressure Bordón to retract his judicial nominees.[27] Under Lafalla, the agreement of two parties often required intense Senate debate. Lafalla could not push through his party's candidate.[28] Furthermore, divided government fostered the creation of an effective Judicial Council that is independent of the executive branch.

Party Competition and Mendoza's Effective Judicial Council

The Mendoza Judicial Council has been part of the development of a transparent and merit-based appointment process that fosters judicial autonomy. For each vacancy in the lower courts, the Council proposes a *terna*, a rank order list of three candidates, from which the governor selects one candidate with Senate approval. With each governor since 1987, the appointment process has become less secretive and politicized. Bordón and Gabrielli issued decrees that called for a Judicial Council, and the Council achieved constitutional status under Lafalla. With each iteration, the Council gained strength. Since it gained constitutional status in 1998, the Council's institutional design has protected its autonomy from encroachments by the governor.

Before the first Judicial Council decree in 1987, unified UCR government permitted Llaver to select judges linked to his party. As discussed in Chapter 4, the UCR majority in the Senate approved Llaver's nominees. All UCR senators voted together without dissent.[29] Senator Montbrun (UCR) recalls, "If you were a judge, you were a friend."[30] According to Judge Alberto Staib, "*amiguismo*," friendship or cronyism, was Llaver's primary consideration when selecting judges.[31] The secrecy of Senate approval sessions enhanced the governor's ability to appoint judges on the basis of partisan loyalty. Llaver's 1987 appointments demonstrate the lack of transparency at the time. In the secret March 1987 session, the UCR-dominated Senate approved twenty-seven lower court nominees without consulting the Constitutional Affairs Committee, which was supposed to interview candidates, review their backgrounds, and then recommend particular candidates to the entire Senate. Opposition members argued that without the Committee's intervention, senators had no knowledge about nominees' career trajectories. The only information available was candidates' identification number, address, and profession.[32]

In response to the 1987 appointments, Mendoza attorneys and judges advocated for more inclusive and public debate. The Mendoza Bar Association argued that the Senate should seek the input of lawyers and judges.[33] The Mendoza Asociación de Magistrados (Association of Judges) also criticized the appointment process. Staib, the Association president in 1987, pushed for the creation of a Judicial Council to enhance objectivity in the designation of judges.[34] Even Chief Justice Elías Baglini declared that a reform of the appointment process was a necessary condition for judicial independence.[35]

THE FIRST ITERATION OF THE JUDICIAL COUNCIL: BORDÓN'S DECREE

Governor Bordón's 1987 decree laid the foundation for today's Judicial Council in Mendoza. The decree called for a five-member Council: an executive official, a Supreme Court justice, an attorney, a lower court judge, and a member of the House of Representatives. By a vote of the absolute majority of all members, the Council recommended a *terna* from which the governor selected one member with Senate approval. This early version with its balanced composition was an important step toward enhancing judicial autonomy. In the words of UCR Congressman Bruni, Bordón's decree placed a "brake" on the governor's appointment power.[36]

The Judicial Council functioned especially well under divided government. Before 1989 when Bordón's PJ gained a majority in the Senate, Bordón chose the first member in the *terna* rather than risk Senate rejection of his nominee. However, the limits on the Mendoza Council's ability to check the governor's appointment power became evident after Bordón's PJ won a majority of Senate seats. After 1989, the PJ-dominated Senate permitted Bordón to choose the last candidate in the *terna*. Unified PJ government also allowed Governor Gabrielli to select the last member of the *terna*. Each Council member had its preferred candidate in the *terna*, and unified PJ government permitted Gabrielli to select the one proposed by the executive representative.[37] By 1993, the Council was close to collapse and was the subject of criticism from attorneys, judges, and members of the opposition.

In late 1993, the Senate approved a PD initiative to modify Senate Rules to require that debate over judicial appointments be public. The 1994 debate over Pedro Funes's promotion from first instance to appellate court judge illustrates the improvement resulting from the 1993 reform of Senate Rules. During Senate deliberations, UCR senators argued that Funes had acted with a notable bias in favor of the executive in his investigations of government officials. Because debate over the appointment was public, citizens had easy access to senators' opinions. The objections of citizens and legislators prevented Funes's promotion to appellate court judge.[38]

THE SECOND ITERATION OF THE JUDICIAL COUNCIL: GABRIELLI'S DECREE

The evolution of the appointment process continued with Gabrielli's 1994 decree that modified the Judicial Council by creating a system of competitive examinations for judicial candidates. The purpose of the decree was to increase objectivity. The decree also created advisory commissions to evaluate the candidates based on their backgrounds and on their theoretical and technical knowledge. The Judicial Council used the evaluations to form the *terna*. The executive did not dominate the seven-member advisory commissions, which were composed of a Supreme Court justice, an executive representative, two law professors, an attorney, a lower court judge, and a public prosecutor. The local newspapers announced upcoming exams. In the first competition, over four hundred attorneys applied for twelve vacancies. Staib, an advisory commission member, reports that the examination system worked well.[39]

The 1994 decree represented another step toward increasing judicial autonomy. Lafalla praised the Gabrielli Judicial Council for its balanced composition. Lafalla emphasized that the executive branch had only one representative on the Council and on the advisory commission.[40] In addition, after the 1994 decree, Gabrielli selected the highest ranking member of the *terna*. Senator Montbrun reports that after the 1994 decree, senators began to vote based on candidates' merits rather than on partisan considerations. Senators no longer voted strictly along party lines. After 1994, in most cases, at least thirty-four of the thirty-eight senators comprised the majority that approved a nominee, whereas in the past, the majority had been comprised of the PJ senators.[41]

1998 GRANT OF CONSTITUTIONAL STATUS TO THE JUDICIAL COUNCIL

The balance among the three parties permitted the 1998 constitutional amendment that institutionalized a Judicial Council with the power to check the executive.[42] At the time, Lafalla's PJ did not hold a majority in either house of Congress. In contrast to the San Luis Judicial Council over which Rodríguez Saá had total control, the balanced composition of the Mendoza Council reduces the chances of politicization. The constitutional amendment called for a seven-member Judicial Council that reflects the equilibrium among Mendoza's three parties. The executive does not dominate the body, which contains a Supreme Court justice, a lower court judge, two lawyers, two House members, and one executive representative. Only three of the seven members are political functionaries. In addition, the two House members must represent different parties. Even if the governor's party holds a majority in Congress, that party is guaranteed only two of the seven seats: the executive representative and one House member.[43]

The binding nature of the *ternas* enhances the Mendoza Judicial Council's autonomy from the executive branch. The constitution stipulates that the Council proposes *ternas vinculantes*, or binding *ternas*, from which the governor must select one of the three members. Furthermore, if the Senate rejects the executive's nominee, the governor must select a different member of the original *terna*; the governor cannot demand that the Council present a new *terna*.[44] The binding nature of the *terna* contrasts with San Luis, where the governor can effectively reject all three members. Although the Mendoza executive can propose any *terna* member regardless of placement in the Council's ranking, party balance in the Senate encourages selection of the highest-ranking member. Otherwise, the Senate can withhold its approval.

The constitutional amendment also retains the competitive examination system, and a provincial law calls for the participation of advisory commissions, which facilitate the appointment of the most qualified candidates.[45] The Judicial Council has the exclusive power to dictate the rules that govern the examinations; the executive has no authority to intervene in the exams. Based on examination results, the advisory commission provides the Judicial Council with the score of each candidate. The commission assigns up to five points for both the oral and the written exam. Thus, when the list reaches the Council, the candidates have already passed through a technical filter. The next phase consists of oral interviews by the Judicial Council. Each of the seven Council members assigns the candidate a score between one and ten. The Council combines the average of the seven scores with the commission's score to produce the final *terna* ranking. Since the first exams in November 1998, the process has been transparent. The Judicial Council publishes the list of candidates and the examination results. Exams are open, and any citizen with an objection can denounce the process. In addition, on the written portion of the exam, a number replaces the candidate's name. Thus, those who grade the exam do not know the identity of the test taker.[46]

The Judicial Council has the exclusive power to set the rules that guide its functioning. The executive cannot enter this terrain.[47] The Mendoza Council's sole discretion in this arena differentiates it from its counterpart in San Luis where the governor has dictated the guidelines that govern the body. Table 6.2 provides a summary comparison of the Mendoza Council with its counterpart in San Luis.

The assessments of Mendoza Council members indicate that it functions as an effective horizontal accountability agency. According to Judicial Council president Pedro Llorente, the Council conducts thorough evaluations of candidates. Both Staib and Oscar Portabella observe that members stress their common interest in selecting the most capable candidates rather than defend narrow personal or partisan interests. Council members use the oral interview to determine candidates' merits rather than their ideological stance. In 1999, Lafalla's representative on the Council, Félix Pesce, reported that the Council had improved the public image of the judiciary. After the Judicial Council gained constitutional status, Mendoza society developed a renewed faith in the appointment process.[48]

TABLE 6.2

The Judicial Council: San Luis versus Mendoza

	San Luis	Mendoza
Balanced composition	No. Dominated by the governor.	Yes. Equilibrium among the three political parties.
Binding *ternas*	No. Law 4872: If the governor does not select a *terna* member within 30 days, the Judicial Council proposes 3 new candidates.	Yes. If the Senate rejects the governor's nominee, the governor must select a different member of the original *terna*.
Exclusive power over internal rules	No. Law 4872 violated the Judicial Council's constitutional power to dictate internal rules.	Yes. Law 6561: The governor cannot intervene in the rules that guide the Judicial Council's functioning.
Competitive exam system	Yes, but violates judges' tenure protection. Aptitude Evaluation Tribunal administers exams to sitting judges rather than to candidates, and the Tribunal dismisses judges who fail exams.	Yes. Transparent exam system enhances objectivity and reduces the governor's discretion over the judicial appointment process.

Competitive Politics and Mendoza's Autonomous Impeachment Jury

Like the appointment process, the mechanism for removing judges has bolstered judicial autonomy in Mendoza. The Impeachment Jury, which has the authority to dismiss lower court judges, has reduced the governor's discretion over the removal of judges. In contrast to provinces where the executive has the power to remove judges, Mendoza judges are unlikely to accept subordinate roles. They do not face the threat of removal from office if they challenge the governor.

The governor's party does not dominate the Impeachment Jury in Mendoza. In contrast to San Luis where monolithic party control permitted Rodríguez Saá to fill the nine-member Jury with loyal PJ members, the composition of the Mendoza Jury reflects the three-party balance. The 21-member Jury is composed of the seven Supreme Court justices, seven senators, and seven House members. The partisan affiliation of the fourteen legislators reflects the balance in Congress. Moreover, as a result of the respect for the life tenure of Supreme Court members, the seven justices are not subordinate to the executive. Mendoza governors have inherited justices from opposition administrations.[49]

The Impeachment Jury's autonomy permits it to fulfill its role as a competing power center. Based on her experience as a Jury member, Kemelmajer concludes that the Jury exercises its constitutional function without executive interference. Justices Kemelmajer, Nanclares, and Carlos Bohm assert that the Jury removes judges who deserve to be removed; partisan considerations are not part of Jury deliberations. The Jury does not dismiss judges when there is insufficient proof.[50] Zapata Mercader, a Jury member during his 1987–91 term as provincial senator, reports that during his tenure, the Jury never received pressure from the governor.[51]

Party Balance and a Strong State Prosecutor

Like the Judicial Council and the Impeachment Jury, the Mendoza Office of the State Prosecutor has the potential to disperse power away from the governor. According to the Mendoza Constitution, the head of the Office, the State Prosecutor, can appear before the provincial judiciary to challenge any law, decree, contract, or resolution on the basis that it is unconstitutional or against Mendoza's economic interests. In addition, the constitution protects the Office's autonomy. The executive appoints the State Prosecutor with Senate approval. Like judges, the State Prosecutor has life tenure during good conduct and is removable only by the Impeachment Jury, an independent body.[52]

The ability of the Office to check executive power depends largely on the appointment and removal process for the State Prosecutor. In contrast to Rodríguez Saá's San Luis, Mendoza governors have respected the tenure protection of the State Prosecutor. In addition, under divided government, the requirement that the Senate approve the governor's nominee has the potential to reduce executive discretion over who serves as State Prosecutor. Indeed, during the Lafalla governorship, a member of the opposition was State Prosecutor, which contributed to the effectiveness of the Office as an agency of horizontal accountability.

From 1983 through 1995, however, most Mendoza governors appointed members of their party who did not challenge executive interests. Prior to the Lafalla administration, the State Prosecutor was little more than an advisor to the governor. As a result, the public viewed the State Prosecutor as a mere extension of the governor. Mendocinos thought of the State Prosecutor as just one more bureaucrat; they rarely knew the name of the person who occupied the post.[53] With the exception of Llaver's appointment of

Rodríguez Lemos, governors did not appoint opposition members to serve as State Prosecutor. Moreover, even Rodríguez Lemos failed to act as a check. He served for less than a year, and he was never an active PJ member. After Rodríguez Lemos resigned in 1987, Bordón replaced him with fellow PJ member Efrain Quevedo Mendoza. According to Aldo Giordano, Quevedo Mendoza was practically Bordón's private secretary; he acted as an advisor to the governor. Bordón acknowledges that he did not have an adversarial relationship with the State Prosecutor.[54] Quevedo Mendoza continued in his post as State Prosecutor during Gabrielli's term. After Lafalla appointed Giordano to the position, however, the State Prosecutor became a household name associated with preventing abuses of power by the executive branch.

Lafalla made a concerted effort to strengthen the Office of the State Prosecutor as a control on the executive. He viewed the State Prosecutor as one of the pillars of transparency that should stand alongside the Supreme Court as a check on the elected branches of government. For Lafalla, the selection of an opposition member to occupy the post of State Prosecutor was of utmost importance. In addition, Lafalla faced a Senate dominated by the opposition, which may have rejected the appointment of a PJ member to the post. After Quevedo Mendoza's 1996 resignation, Lafalla composed a list of ten potential individuals to replace him as State Prosecutor. None of the ten was a member of Lafalla's PJ. Of the ten, Lafalla selected Giordano, who had strong ties to the UCR. Giordano had been an advisor for the Llaver administration and for Mendoza mayor Victor Fayad (UCR). The UCR-PD majority in the Senate approved the appointment of Giordano.[55]

Under Lafalla, the Office of the State Prosecutor emerged as a countervailing power center. Giordano's suits against executive branch functionaries produced the fall of two cabinet ministers, the Minister of Education who resigned in 1997 and the Housing Minister who resigned in 1999. Giordano also initiated proceedings against former PJ Governor Gabrielli regarding the privatization of the Bank of Mendoza. His denunciation of Gabrielli paved the way for Judge Leiva's prosecution and conviction of a group of former Bank of Mendoza officials, which harmed Lafalla's PJ. Giordano also conducted investigations of government housing projects.[56]

Giordano's popularity enhanced his effectiveness as State Prosecutor. During his tenure as State Prosecutor, he was a high-profile figure who sought media attention. A central goal of Giordano was to teach Mendocinos about the constitutional function of the State Prosecutor. As a result of his efforts, Giordano earned a broad base of support in the province. The people of Mendoza elected him "Mendocino of the Year" for two consecutive years.[57] The State Prosecutor entered the public consciousness as a critical check on the governor. This grassroots support has enhanced the

Office of the State Prosecutor's ability to act as a horizontal accountability agency.

Lafalla and Giordano took important steps toward strengthening the Office of the State Prosecutor. Although future governors may not want to appoint an opposition member as State Prosecutor, the public support and expectations generated during Giordano's term will help ensure that the State Prosecutor remains a check on the governor. Mendocinos now demand that governors place the State Prosecutor's Office in the hands of the opposition. Indeed, Lafalla declared that the State Prosecutor's independence would survive beyond his administration. As a result of the transformation of expectations and demands, future governors will have difficulty dismantling the institutional autonomy of the Office of the State Prosecutor.[58] In addition, the opposition witnessed the capacity of the Office to check the governor and therefore is likely to insist that future governors appoint an opposition member as State Prosecutor. Under divided government, the opposition majority in the Senate can withhold its approval if the governor's nominee appears unlikely to challenge the administration.

Three-Party Balance and the Mendoza Accounting Tribunal

The Accounting Tribunal has fulfilled its constitutional role as a control on the Mendoza executive. Party competition has prevented the governor from subordinating the Tribunal by altering its institutional design. The Tribunal is a product of the 1916 Mendoza Constitution, and only the Impeachment Jury, an independent body, has the authority to remove Tribunal members.[59] Article 181 gives the Tribunal the power to oversee government administration of public funds. Article 182 obliges all state agencies, municipalities, and individual functionaries to submit an annual account documenting their spending. The Tribunal uses this account to approve or reject the spending at the end of each year.[60]

Balanced composition has permitted the Tribunal to act as a countervailing power center. Rotation of the party in the governorship and respect for the tenure protection of Tribunal members has contributed to its independence from the executive. During the three PJ administrations from 1987 through 1999, the opposition dominated the Tribunal. Four of the seven Tribunal members had served since the UCR administration of Llaver. In fact, the PJ governors inherited a Tribunal president from Llaver. Like the Chief Justice, the president of the Tribunal was a former provincial UCR senator.[61]

Since the Tribunal began to function by law in 1931, it has acted as a check on the legality of the government's economic activity. Bordón recalls that the UCR-dominated Tribunal was as an effective control on his administration's spending.[62] The strength of the opposition has made it difficult for governors to prevent reforms that bolster the Tribunal's ability to check government spending. At the beginning of 1999, for instance, the Tribunal expanded to incorporate a team of engineers, architects, and specialists in information technology. This team monitors the government's public works contracts. Although the expansion enhanced the capacity of the Tribunal to serve as a watchdog, Lafalla did not resist the reforms.[63]

The Mendoza Office of the Attorney General

In Mendoza, a lack of resources rather than subordination to the governor stands in the way of an effective Attorney General's Office. The Office of the Attorney General is the weakest of Mendoza's agencies of horizontal accountability. A strong Attorney General's Office is an especially critical check where there is a high level of government corruption. Mendoza, however, has a relatively low level of corruption as compared to San Luis or Argentina at the national level.[64]

In addition to insulation from the executive, an effective Attorney General's Office requires adequate resources and a strong infrastructure. In Mendoza, resources do not meet the large number of cases that reach public prosecutors' offices. A shortage of prosecutors contributes to the backlogs. As a result of the personnel shortage, prosecutors cannot conduct efficient investigations. Each prosecutor is understaffed and works with a small team composed of a law clerk and three assistants.[65]

The Mendoza Attorney General is almost unheard-of in the local press and in discussions about the judiciary. The procedural codes that govern the Mendoza Attorney General's Office contribute to its low profile. The Mendoza Attorney General's Office shares some of the procedural weaknesses that undermine its counterpart on the national level. The prosecutor only initiates investigations; the judge actually conducts investigations. Staib explains that conflictive relations with the Mendoza police have contributed to public prosecutors' inactivity. The police do not protect prosecutors who face threats as a result of their investigations. Prosecutors often choose not to initiate investigations rather than risk their personal safety.[66] Nevertheless, the shortcomings of the Attorney's General Office have not eroded the rule of law in Mendoza. In contrast to Rodríguez Saá's San Luis and to Menem's Argentina, Mendoza has other countervailing power centers such as an independent judiciary, a strong State Prosecutor, and an autonomous Accounting Tribunal that compensate for the weak Attorney General's Office.

Mendoza's history since 1983 illustrates how agencies of horizontal accountability are central to the construction and fortification of the rule of law. As a result of the competing institutional power centers, a reform coalition of nonstate actors has not been necessary for the establishment of the rule of law in Mendoza. In contrast to Mendoza with its competitive politics, reform coalitions can be the catalyst for the fragmentation of political power in countries or provinces characterized by monolithic party control and a weak rule of law. The next chapter turns to the role of reform coalitions in Rodríguez Saá's San Luis and in Menem's Argentina.

CHAPTER 7

The Politics of Reform Coalitions

REFORM COALITIONS were central to progress toward the rule of law in Carlos Menem's Argentina and have begun to fracture political power in San Luis.[1] In both cases, a coalition of nonstate actors activated societal power, which helped fragment monopolies in the political realm and disperse resources away from the executive branch. In a country or province where those with a monopoly on power have hardened against the rule of law, dense interaction between civil society and political actors is necessary for change. Ultimately, in order to alter the status quo, the legislature must adopt reform and the executive branch must either approve the reform or be overridden. By providing alternative sources of information and increasing the demand for change, reformist networks have fostered vertical accountability, which is secured through the electoral process. A reform coalition can impose electoral costs on subordination of the courts by mobilizing public opinion against dominant executives and advancing the cause of opposition parties.

The experiences of Argentina at the national level and the province of San Luis demonstrate that the creation of reform networks of nonstate actors is a dynamic process that relies heavily on information politics and leverage politics.[2] Information and leverage have been potent tools for reform coalitions that seek to establish the rule of law. The documentation and dissemination of data about executive subordination of the courts have drawn domestic and international groups into the coalitions. The economic vulnerability of Argentina and San Luis permitted external actors to use material leverage to push the executive to enact reforms.

This chapter demonstrates how nonstate actors in Argentina and San Luis coalesced into well-organized networks of domestic civil society groups, international organizations, and the media. The chapter begins with a discussion of the local civil society groups that served as the foundation for reform coalitions. In both Argentina and San Luis, information has been the principal weapon of civil society to counter the executive's monopoly on political power. The chapter then turns to the incorporation of external actors that wield economic power, providing the coalitions with material leverage, a potent new instrument to help establish the rule of law. Next, the chapter focuses on the role of the media and information politics in the two coalitions. It concludes with a discussion of Mendoza, where competitive politics has rendered a reform coalition unnecessary, yet nonstate actors have at times helped strengthen horizontal accountability agencies, including the courts.

Local Civil Society: The Foundation of Reform Coalitions

In Argentina at the national level and in San Luis, local civil society groups laid the groundwork for reform coalitions. Diverse civil society groups have acted as watchdogs that expose executive subordination of horizontal accountability agencies. As Keck and Sikkink argue, in order to attract members, a coalition must demonstrate that a deliberate wrongdoing has harmed a shared value.[3] Local civil society groups attributed the subordination of the courts to deliberate Menem and Rodríguez Saá policies. By showing how a pliant judiciary undermines shared values such as human rights and economic development, the coalitions recruited a diverse group of local actors with an interest in an independent judicial branch, including human rights groups, lawyers, judges, and business associations. In both Argentina and San Luis, these groups have formed partnerships with one another in the struggle to build the rule of law.

OVERCOMING OBSTACLES TO CIVIL SOCIETY IN ARGENTINA

Argentine civil society groups have grown in strength and number since the country's 1983 transition to democracy. From 1930 through 1983, political instability and repressive military regimes stymied the development of a robust civil society. Nevertheless, in response to the 1976–83 Dirty War, human rights groups with an emphasis on government accountability emerged. After the transition, these groups turned to the courts for recourse. As Argentines witnessed the trials of high-ranking military leaders during the mid-1980s, citizens became optimistic about the ability of the courts to enforce the rule of law by holding powerful state actors accountable for their actions.[4] Journalist Horacio Verbitsky who covered the trials recalls that most Argentines were unaware of the potential role of the judiciary until the military hearings. The trials engendered a consciousness that served as the basis for the demands for judicial independence in the 1990s.[5] The growing knowledge about the importance of the judiciary fueled the reform coalition.

Groups that promote citizen involvement in politics were among the first members of Argentine civil society to emerge. In 1982, a group of Argentine women formed Conciencia (Conscience), a non-partisan organization with the goal of increasing citizen participation in politics: "History shows that in Argentina we are accustomed to the 'don't get involved' attitude, to never-ending complaints without positive actions. However, members of Conciencia believe participation is a right that citizens must exercise if democracy is to mature and endure in a system. 'Become Aware, the Country Needs You' has become our motto."[6] Conciencia founders strove to educate citizens about their rights and duties in a democracy. Since its founding, Conciencia has increased its work on the judiciary and has sponsored conferences across Argentina to educate citizens about the judicial system and its role in a democratic society. In 2001, Conciencia helped publish a comprehensive guidebook about the Argentine judiciary. The guide provides detailed information about the function, structure, personnel, and budget of the federal judiciary as well as of the Judicial Council and the Impeachment Jury.[7]

After its 1989 founding, Poder Ciudadano (Citizen Power) became a leading member of the reform coalition. The Poder Ciudadano program "Citizens for Justice" created an easily accessible database about the judiciary and published *Who's Who in the Judiciary*, which contains detailed information about the professional background and financial assets of federal judges in Argentina. Poder Ciudadano has also conducted research for a *Who's Who* about members of the Judicial Council and the Impeachment Jury.[8] Poder Ciudadano was instrumental in increasing the transparency of the judicial appointment process. The Judicial Council adopted the Poder Ciudadano proposal that appointment hearings be public to ensure citizen participation in the selection of judges. Poder Ciudadano has continued to monitor the Judicial Council and publish reports on its performance.[9]

OVERCOMING OBSTACLES TO CIVIL SOCIETY IN SAN LUIS

Throughout most of Rodríguez Saá's governorship, the concentration of power in the governor extended beyond political institutions to include the private realm in San Luis. Rodríguez Saá took deliberate steps to prevent the growth of independent civil society groups. During his fourth term in office (1995–99), however, provincial civil society emerged to provide the basis for a reform coalition in San Luis. By the late 1990s, the local component of the reform network began to overcome the governor's clientelism, cooptation, and outright repression.

Rodríguez Saá used paternalism and clientelism to immobilize most sectors of San Luis society early during his tenure as governor. Due to their dependence on the provincial government for jobs and housing, citizens were reluctant to challenge or criticize the governor. In contrast to much of northwestern Argentina where clientelism collapsed in the mid 1990s, Rodríguez Saá's San Luis did not experience the shortage of funds that triggers a breakdown of clientelism. Clientelism, the traditional form of control in the Argentine interior, broke down in the provinces of Santiago del Estero, Salta, Jujuy, Corrientes, Chaco, Río Negro, and San Juan during the mid 1990s. As a result of public employee layoffs and the failure to pay salaries, these northwestern provinces experienced growing unrest and violence, and provincial governments faced mounting opposition. For instance, the 1993 riots in Santiago del Estero and the 1999 government standstill in Corrientes were in large part a product of the erosion of clientelistic forms of control. In contrast, federal programs such as Industrial Promotion, which provides tax incentives to companies operating in San Luis, helped keep the San Luis coffers full and permitted the governor to maintain a vast patronage machine. Large-scale public works projects were a major source of employment in San Luis. Between 1983 and 1999, the total kilometers of paved roads in the province skyrocketed from 300 to 2,500 and the total kilometers of aqueducts grew from 30 to 2,100. The public housing program was another element of Rodríguez Saá's political platform, as evident in the PJ campaign slogan, "A home for every family." In 1999, four out of ten families in San Luis lived in government-subsidized houses.[10]

Rodríguez Saá coopted potential members of the reform coalition. Because the San Luis Catholic Church became dependent on government funding, Church leaders answered to the governor. In contrast to the province of Catamarca where an independent Church has challenged the government, the San Luis Church was an unwavering government ally. Between 1993 and 1994, San Luis Bishop Juan Rodolfo Laise's diocese received $600,000 from the Rodríguez Saá administration. Not surprisingly, Laise became one of Rodríguez Saá's most prominent supporters. The bishop defended the governor when his scandalous extra-marital affair became public knowledge in 1993. In addition, the Rodríguez Saá brothers wielded tremendous influence over the athletic clubs that form part of the PJ infrastructure. For instance, Alberto Rodríguez Saá owned the high-profile San Luis basketball club, which recruited and mobilized party members.[11]

When clientelism and cooptation were insufficient to silence challenges from civil society, the governor used repression. In contrast to Argentina at the national level where protests against Menem were frequent, the October 1998 demonstration in San Luis was the first major anti-government protest since Rodríguez Saá assumed power in 1983. Buenos Aires-based journalist Miguel Wiñazki characterizes San Luis as the most repressed province in all of Argentina. While he was conducting research for his 1995 book about the

Rodríguez Saá brothers, many individuals refused to speak on the record for fear of punishment from the governor.[12] The Federation of Argentine Bar Associations denounced the Rodríguez Saá administration's use of death threats to silence opposition members.[13]

Despite multiple challenges, civil society grew in San Luis, and the Rodríguez Saá administration faced an increasing number of protests. Although the public works projects helped keep the populace subdued for over a decade, the government cut spending on key services such as education. Rodríguez Saá's 1998 decision to close several public schools aroused widespread opposition. Citizens began to demand better education, and public employees began to demand higher salaries. The Teachers' Union, the Psychologists' Association, and the San Luis Bar Association became increasingly active.[14] Moreover, civil society in San Luis expanded its focus to include issues involving the rule of law.

THE PIVOTAL ROLE OF LAWYERS AND JUDGES IN THE ARGENTINE COALITION

Lawyers and judges have been on the front line of the national and provincial reform coalitions. They have provided the coalitions with valuable expertise, and their deep commitment to the rule of law has contributed to their effectiveness. Judicial autonomy has been a central concern for these actors who work within the judiciary. For those attorneys and judges who have resisted pressure from the executive, an independent judiciary has been necessary for a successful career. When trying cases, attorneys rely on predictable and unbiased application of laws. Judges who challenge executive interests must not fear retribution. Lawyers and judges have fulfilled multiple roles in the networks. They have acted as watchdogs, built links to other organizations, and provided the reform coalition with leadership.[15]

The most influential of the Argentine lawyers' organizations in the national coalition has been the Federación Argentina de Colegios de Abogados (FACA), the umbrella organization for Argentina's seventy public bar associations. FACA's principal contribution to the reform network has been its effective use of information politics to heighten awareness of the president's interference in the courts. In addition, the provincial bar associations that comprise FACA have acted individually to raise awareness in provinces across Argentina. For instance, the bar associations of Neuquén, Quilmes, Santa Fe, Córdoba, and Buenos Aires engaged in information politics when they documented and denounced Menem's subordination of the federal courts in their respective provincial newspapers.[16]

Throughout Menem's presidency, Buenos Aires was the site of intense activity on the part of lawyers. The public Buenos Aires Bar Association and the two private associations, Asociación de Abogados de Buenos Aires

(AABA) and Colegio de Abogados de la Ciudad de Buenos Aires (CACBA), have been major voices in the reform coalition. The public bar association used its high profile to condemn Menem's Supreme Court expansion, to attack specific Court rulings, and to publicize irregularities in judicial appointments. It continued to denounce Menem appointees on the Court after the end of Menem's second term.[17] The left-leaning AABA, a prestigious association since its establishment in 1934, brought impeachment suits against Menem Supreme Court justices and took part in public demonstrations to demand judicial autonomy.[18] The conservative CACBA has stressed the importance of judicial autonomy since its 1913 founding. Its press releases condemning Menem's treatment of the courts aided the coalition's strategy of information politics. CACBA devoted entire issues of its weekly bulletin, *La Hoja*, to denounce Menem's subordination of the judiciary.[19]

Individual attorneys have worked alongside the bar associations. For instance, in 1977, former CACBA president Horacio Lynch helped found the Foro de Estudios sobre la Administración de Justicia (FORES), a nonprofit group with the goal of improving the administration of justice in Argentina. Lynch served as the link connecting FORES, CACBA, and the Consejo Empresario Argentino (CEA), an association of Argentine business executives, which collaborated to produce reports on the federal and provincial judiciaries.[20] Partners in Argentina's most prominent law firms such as Juan Javier Negri of Negri, Teijeiro & Incera and Jaime Fernández Madero of Bruchou, Fernández Madero, Lombardi & Mitrani denounced Menem's assaults against judicial autonomy.[21] Attorneys have also participated in former Economy Minister Domingo Cavallo's efforts to reform the judiciary. Lawyers dominate the judicial division of Cavallo's Fundación Novum Millennium, which has focused on judicial autonomy.[22]

Argentine judges' associations have also been active in the coalition. The two largest networks of Argentine judges, the Federación Argentina de la Magistratura (FAM) and the Asociación de Magistrados y Funcionarios de la Justicia Nacional, became increasingly vocal during the Menem administration. Since its 1966 founding, FAM, an umbrella organization for judges' associations across the country, has advocated judicial independence and the need to increase society's faith in the courts. The Asociación de Magistrados y Funcionarios shares the goal of judicial autonomy.[23]

In response to Menem's assaults on judicial autonomy, grassroots groups of activist judges joined the coalition. Organizations such as Agrupación para una Justicia Democrática (Justicia Democrática), Encuentro de Jueces, Asociación de Mujeres Jueces de Argentina (AMJA), and Fundación de Estudios para la Justicia (Fundejus) condemned Menem's treatment of the courts. Justicia Democrática and Encuentro de Jueces were major actors in the 1994–97 struggle for legislation creating an effective Judicial Council that would reduce executive discretion over judicial appointments. Encuentro de Jueces formed in 1994 to lobby for the reform of the judicial appointment process. These organizations work together and view themselves as members of a single network. In fact, most AMJA members also belong to Justicia Democrática. AMJA founder Carmen Argibay, for instance, served as vice president of Justicia Democrática and has been a Fundejus member. Fundejus, which focuses its efforts on educating citizens about the judiciary, shares office space with AMJA.[24]

In 1999, lawyers and judges formalized a previously informal network with the goal of promoting judicial reform in Argentina. A diverse group of attorneys and judges from across the political spectrum formed the Foro Social por la Justicia (Social Forum for Justice). During its first meeting, the Forum defined its mission as increasing transparency by gathering and disseminating information about the judiciary. The Forum announced its intent to engage in information politics to advance the cause of judicial autonomy. Participants included former Supreme Court Justice Jorge Bacqué, Roberto de Michele of Poder Ciudadano, FORES founder Horacio Lynch, FORES director Germán Garavano, and Ricardo Gil Lavedra, who would later become President Fernando de la Rúa's Justice Minister.[25]

THE ROLE OF LAWYERS AND JUDGES IN THE SAN LUIS COALITION

As in Argentina at the national level, attorneys and judges have led the struggle for judicial autonomy in San Luis. San Luis Bar Association President Miriam Agundez, Bar Association Secretary Graciela Rosso, and former judges Adriana Gallo and Ana María Careaga are representative of the committed activists who risked punishment by Rodríguez Saá to further the coalition's efforts. The San Luis Bar Association, which was founded in 1944, was among the few civil society groups that challenged Rodríguez Saá throughout his five consecutive terms as governor. After the 1995 reduction of judges' salaries, for instance, the bar association issued a declaration to alert the public about the threat to judicial autonomy. A 1997 bar association condemnation of the Judicial Emergency Law that suspended judgments against the state generated opposition to executive control of the courts.[26] In response to these initiatives, the PJ-controlled Congress abolished the bar association in 1997. Nevertheless, bar association members remained organized and effective. They went underground where they continued to struggle for judicial independence.

Individual San Luis judges worked alongside the bar association members to increase public awareness about Rodríguez Saá's assaults on judicial autonomy. The assertion of independence by select judges has been central to the reform network. Due to their direct experience as victims of subordination of the courts, judges have been important sources of information. Although the majority of San Luis judges opted not to endure the costs of confronting the governor, which included dismissal by the Impeachment Jury and attacks in the government-controlled media, a handful continued to challenge Rodríguez Saá. For instance, five judges known in San Luis as "the samurai" resisted pressure to drop their suits against the unconstitutional reduction of their salaries. Careaga, one of the samurai, declared: "I want to fight despite the high personal cost."[27] Like Careaga and Gallo, Judge Carlos Cacace resisted government pressure for over a decade and publicly denounced executive subordination of the judiciary. Moreover, at times, individual judges have acted together. During Cacace's brief tenure on the San Luis Supreme Court in 1997, the Court issued a resolution condemning the lack of judicial autonomy in the province.[28]

ARGENTINE BUSINESS ORGANIZATIONS

In recognition of the economic costs of executive subordination of the courts, powerful Argentine business organizations joined the national reform coalition and rallied around the call for *seguridad jurídica*, or judicial security. National associations of corporate executives and entrepreneurs lobbied for a predictable judicial environment to encourage investment, protect property rights, and enforce contracts. For example, since its founding in 1963, the Instituto para el Desarrollo de Empresarios en la Argentina (IDEA), a prestigious organization of Argentine business leaders, has focused increasingly on the judiciary. During Menem's decade in the presidency, the director of IDEA's legal division, Juan Ángel Pardo, spoke annually to the IDEA board of directors about how the legal system impacts the economy. He encouraged all IDEA divisions, not just the legal division, to lobby government officials to promote *seguridad jurídica* and judicial autonomy. Pardo also organized biannual meetings between business executives and lawyers to discuss legal issues that affect the business environment. The 1992 annual IDEA colloquium focused on the importance of judicial independence for Argentine business and for the country's economic development.[29]

The Consejo Empresario Argentino (CEA), Fundación de Investigaciones Económicas Latinoamericanas (FIEL), and Asociación Cristiana de Dirigentes de Empresas (ACDE) have also devoted projects to *seguridad jurídica*. For instance, CEA collaborated with FORES and CACBA on a report about the impact of the judiciary on economic development. At a 1996 ACDE conference, members called for a reform of the judicial appointment process and pledged to promote judicial autonomy. The 1997 annual ACDE meeting focused on *seguridad jurídica* and condemned Menem's subordination of the courts.[30]

THE PUBLIC UNIVERSITY IN SAN LUIS

The public university in San Luis, the Universidad Nacional de San Luis, is one of the only institutions in San Luis that had the autonomy necessary to challenge Governor Rodríguez Saá. Because it depends on the federal rather than the provincial government for funds, the university has maintained its independence from the governor and therefore has had the ability to participate in the reform coalition. Like state universities across Argentina, the public university in San Luis defends its status as an autonomous institution. In addition, Rodríguez Saá's PJ has failed to gain a foothold in the university. Instead, the UCR has dominated the university. The Franja Morada, the nation-wide UCR student organization, is strong in all of Argentina's public universities, including the National University of San Luis.

University autonomy and the strong UCR presence enabled university groups to resist pressure from the governor. Government efforts to infiltrate the UCR-dominated associations of students, professors, alumni, and administrators failed. In contrast to Rodríguez Saá's ability to remove judges that he considered to be a threat, he lacked the authority to remove university officials who criticized his policies. Former judge Adriana Gallo and political scientist María Gloria Trocello, an outspoken Rodríguez Saá critic whose publications in national journals have drawn attention to San Luis, retained their teaching posts.[31] In addition, university groups supported the growing number of protests against the governor. Both the Federación Universitaria de San Luis, a student group, and the Asociación Docentes Universitarias, the professors' association, participated in the October 1998 demonstration. The Consejo Superior, the university's highest-ranking administrative organ, supported the San Luis Bar Association's 1997 condemnation of the governor's treatment of the judiciary.[32]

International Organizations and the Boomerang Pattern in Argentina

Domestic members of Argentina's reform network have built relationships with influential international organizations that exerted external pressure on the Menem administration and continue to push for judicial autonomy in the post-Menem era, illustrating what Keck and Sikkink call the "boomerang pattern." Keck and Sikkink argue that "[v]oices that are suppressed in their own societies may find that networks can project and amplify their concerns to an international arena, which in turn can echo back into their own countries. Transnational networks multiply the voices that are heard in international and domestic policies."[33] Indeed, the international component has amplified the call for the rule of law in Argentina. Pressure from outside Argentina's borders countered Menem's initial unresponsiveness to local groups. International organizations aided the reform coalition in two primary ways: they provided material leverage, and they bolstered domestic coalition members by providing training and funding.

Menem's preoccupation with Argentina's image in the international community enhanced the effectiveness of material leverage. Argentina's economic vulnerability permitted external actors to employ aid conditionality and the threat of economic sanctions to push for reform. For instance, financial leverage played a critical role in the 1997 passage of the Judicial Council law. The International Monetary Fund (IMF) demanded that Argentina increase the transparency of the appointment process in exchange for a loan. The IMF loan was conditional on the creation of a Judicial Council. Indeed, ten days after Congress sanctioned the Judicial Council law, the IMF released the money to Argentina.[34]

External participation in the coalition has also taken the form of support for domestic civil society groups that in turn struggle for judicial autonomy from within Argentina. The United States Agency for International Development (USAID) has provided Poder Ciudadano, Conciencia, FORES, and the Centro de Estudios Judiciales de la República Argentina (CEJURA) with funding to support their projects aimed at bolstering the courts. For instance, USAID financed the 1991–95 CEJURA surveys that documented citizens' lack of faith in the judiciary.[35]

External actors have been most successful when they joined forces with local civil society. The support of domestic groups legitimized the international presence. In addition to the USAID-CEJURA project, examples of successful teamwork include the co-sponsored U.S. Embassy-Poder Ciudadano meetings of government officials, judges, and legislators to discuss the Judicial Council law. Poder Ciudadano involvement encouraged opposition members to participate, whereas the U.S. involvement drew members of Menem's PJ to the discussion table.[36]

International actors have continued to take part in the reform coalition in the post-Menem era. The United Nations Development Program (UNDP) has played a key role in supporting the Diálogo Argentino (Argentine Dialogue), which formed in 2002 to address Argentina's deep economic, social, and political crisis. Through the Dialogue, the UN has provided financial and technical aid to supplement domestic efforts. The Dialogue is a broad-based coalition of representatives from the UNDP, the Argentine government, the Argentine Conference of Bishops, and domestic civil society. Within the Dialogue, the group that focuses on judicial reform, the Mesa de Justicia (Judicial Committee), has recognized the need to bolster judicial autonomy. The Judicial Committee is a network of lawyers, civil society actors, and representatives from the federal judiciary, Congress, and the executive branch. Judicial Committee members report that UN support has been critical to the Committee's ability to formulate proposals that would advance judicial independence in Argentina.[37]

The Formation of an Intranational Coalition: The Boomerang Pattern in San Luis

In recognition of the power of pressure from outside of the province, actors in San Luis have drawn national civil society groups into their fight for judicial autonomy, giving rise to an intranational network that spans Argentina. San Luis civil society reacted to the governor's repression by establishing links to national organizations based in Buenos Aires, setting the stage for the boomerang pattern in San Luis. These links show the potential for an intranational advocacy network, which permits application of Keck and Sikkink's framework within the borders of a nation. The case of San Luis demonstrates that national organizations can play the role of external actors in a coalition that pushes for reform at the provincial level. Pressure from powerful groups in Buenos Aires countered the governor's unresponsiveness to local actors in San Luis.

The San Luis Bar Association drew national attention to the situation in San Luis. It first formed a partnership with the Buenos Aires-based FACA, which became an active participant in the San Luis coalition. For example, FACA collaborated with the San Luis Bar Association to issue joint declarations denouncing Rodríguez Saá's subordination of the courts.[38] FACA also worked with the San Luis Bar Association to organize demonstrations in Buenos Aires and in San Luis. For instance, the March 1998 protest, *Día nacional de protesta*, in Buenos Aires drew prominent national figures including former Argentine Supreme Court Justice Jorge Bacqué and national UCR Congresswoman Elisa Carrió.[39] In October 1998, FACA and the Comisión Nacional de Jóvenes Abogados (National Commission of Young Lawyers) staged a protest in San Luis that drew representatives of seventy provincial bar associations from across Argentina.[40]

FACA recruited its member-associations to join the San Luis reform network. Representatives from the Neuquén Bar Association and the General Roca Bar Association attended the 1998 protest in Buenos Aires and criticized Rodríguez Saá's reduction of judges' salaries.[41] The La Plata Bar Association published an announcement in its local press that chronicled Rodríguez Saá's assaults against judicial autonomy.[42] The Buenos Aires Bar Association disseminated information about the situation in San Luis.[43]

National organizations of judges, including FAM, Justicia Democrática, and AMJA, declared their solidarity with the San Luis Bar Association. In 1998, FAM addressed a letter to Rodríguez Saá condemning his treatment of the courts.[44] FAM representatives denounced the Impeachment Jury's removal of independent judges and traveled to San Luis to show their support for Gallo during her hearing before the Jury.[45] In 1998, FAM expelled the San Luis Judges' Association in recognition of San Luis judges' subordination to the governor.[46] Justicia Democrática organized a March 1999 conference to raise consciousness about San Luis, which required the cooperation of a variety of nonstate actors. Gerónimo Sansó, Justicia Democrática president, used his contacts with national and international organizations to fund the conference. The Buenos Aires Bar Association and Spain's Agency for International Cooperation provided funding. Representatives from AMJA, Encuentro de Jueces, Fundejus, and the Spanish organization Judges for Democracy traveled to San Luis to participate in the conference.[47] The conference put San Luis in the national spotlight and heightened awareness about the situation in San Luis.

National civil society groups Poder Ciudadano and Centro de Estudios Legales y Sociales (CELS) also helped expand the San Luis reform coalition. Moreno Ocampo of Poder Ciudadano used his high profile to draw national media attention to San Luis. His role as Gallo's defense attorney before the Impeachment Jury attracted attention to her removal. In addition, Poder Ciudadano held joint press conferences with FACA to condemn Rodríguez Saá's control of the courts.[48] CELS also sought to inform the rest of Argentina about San Luis. A team of CELS lawyers defended Careaga during her 1998 hearing before the Impeachment Jury. Like Poder Ciudadano at Gallo's hearing, CELS presence at Careaga's hearing exposed Rodríguez Saá's attacks against independent judges to national scrutiny.[49]

National civil society groups disseminated information about San Luis beyond Argentina's borders, thereby converting the intranational network into a transnational coalition. Both Poder Ciudadano and CELS denounced Rodríguez Saá's subordination of the courts to powerful international organizations such as Amnesty International. CELS and Poder Ciudadano attorneys appealed the San Luis Impeachment Jury's removals of judges Careaga and Gallo before the Interamerican Commission on Human Rights.[50] The appeals increased international scrutiny. Gallo recognizes the benefits of this attention: "If they [the Rodríguez Saá administration] hope to punish me through the process [the Impeachment Jury hearing], they are mistaken. They have given me the opportunity to expose their abuses outside of the province."[51] An Interamerican Commission ruling against the San Luis Impeachment Jury would damage Rodríguez Saá's image in the eyes of international lenders and investors. Domestic civil society also denounced Rodríguez Saá before the UN Permanent Assembly on Human Rights, which prompted a UN investigation in San Luis.[52]

In addition, powerful foreign companies that provide San Luis with much-needed revenue began to demand a neutral and effective arbiter to enforce contracts and protect property rights, making them a potentially powerful member of the transnational coalition. For instance, in 1995, Procter and Gamble filed a criminal complaint against Rodríguez Saá's personal attorney, Víctor Hissa, upon discovering that he had pocketed the company's tax payments. Hissa's law firm handled the legal side of the federal Industrial Promotion (IP) program in San Luis. The experience of Procter and Gamble damaged Rodríguez Saá's reputation at the national level and within the international business community and drew attention to the governor's corrupt implementation of IP.[53]

The Federal Government in the San Luis Reform Coalition

The federal government has the potential to be a central component of the San Luis reform coalition. Like national civil society groups, the federal government can act as an external actor that pushes for reform at the provincial level. The central government can function as a foreign actor in the boomerang pattern scenario in San Luis. Like international financial institutions, the Argentine government has a potent tool at its disposal: leverage politics. Due to San Luis's economic vulnerability, the federal government can use material leverage to instigate change in the province. The Menem administration did not exercise this power, but the Alianza defeat of the PJ in the 1999 presidential elections provided a new entry point for reform. In contrast to Menem, who supported fellow PJ member Rodríguez Saá, the Alianza administration pressured the governor to strengthen the rule of law in San Luis. Furthermore, after Argentina's 2001 economic meltdown, the federal government faced new limits on its ability to maintain costly subsidies to San Luis.

THE FEDERAL-PROVINCIAL RELATIONSHIP

The federal government's willingness to participate in the San Luis reform coalition depends in part on the relationship between the national and provincial governments. If the same party is at the helm of the national and provincial administrations, the federal government is unlikely to pressure its provincial ally to implement reforms. During Menem's decade in the presidency, PJ control of the national and the San Luis governments prevented the federal government from participating in the reform coalition. The two *caudillos* could not afford to alienate one another. Rodríguez Saá relied on Menem for economic support, and Menem needed the governor's political support. As a result of this codependence, the Menem administration did nothing to remedy the governor's assaults on the rule of law. As provincial challenges to PJ discipline grew during his second term, Menem became increasingly dependent on the support of PJ governors such as Rodríguez Saá. As the opposition gained strength and divisions within the PJ emerged, Menem found himself losing political power. As Levitsky demonstrates, Menem failed to "Menemize" the provinces. Powerful provincial level PJ machines often ignored the president's orders.[54] In his effort to retain the support of the San Luis PJ, Menem wooed Rodríguez Saá by providing him with economic resources.

In contrast to the PJ administration of Menem, the short-lived Alianza government of Fernando de la Rúa (1999–2001) supported reform coalitions in San Luis and other PJ-controlled authoritarian enclaves. In effect, the Alianza victory introduced the federal government as an external actor in the San Luis coalition, providing a new opportunity to fracture Rodríguez Saá's monopoly on power. The same party no longer controlled both the national and the San Luis administrations. Observers of the situation in San Luis agree that the support of the national government is a requisite for reform in San Luis.[55] As one San Luis journalist declared before the 1999 presidential election, "We cannot change things on our own. We need help from the national level. Unless the national order changes, a member of the Rodríguez Saá family will be in power until I die."[56]

MATERIAL LEVERAGE: INDUSTRIAL PROMOTION AND CENTRALIZED TAX AUTHORITY

San Luis's economic dependence on the federal government allows the federal government to exercise leverage politics. The San Luis economy has relied heavily on federal tax revenue and on the IP program that has provided tax exemptions and deferrals to industries that operate in the provinces of San Luis, San Juan, Catamarca, and La Rioja since 1974. During Rodríguez Saá's first term (1983–87), IP drew 773 private enterprises to San Luis.[57] San Luis was not the least developed of the provinces targeted by IP, yet per capita IP spending in San Luis was the second highest in Argentina and five times higher than in the third most favored province.[58] Per capita IP spending in San Luis reached $4,824 annually during Rodríguez Saá's first four years in office.[59] Together, IP and federal tax revenues permitted the governor to maintain the vast public works projects that helped keep the population dependent on the government for jobs and housing and therefore subdued. A withdrawal of federal economic support could lead to a shortage of funds in San Luis and a breakdown of clientelism.

The IP program benefited Rodríguez Saá in numerous ways. Besides permitting him to amass a personal fortune through corrupt implementation of the program, IP was a factor behind his victory in five consecutive elections. The revenues from IP filled the government's coffers, permitting the governor to create jobs and to build houses, roads, and schools. The IP program gave San Luis an advantage over neighboring provinces by providing tax incentives to companies operating in San Luis.[60]

The governor used his discretion over IP to concentrate economic power in his hands. He sold the IP contracts, often to friends and relatives, without conducting the requisite investigation into the companies. Purchasing IP permits from the San Luis government became a method of tax evasion for companies that installed sham factories in San Luis. During his extensive research on IP in San Luis, Wiñazki interviewed only one source who denied that the IP decrees were sold, the governor himself.[61] In 1997, Moreno Ocampo provided the Menem administration with a videotape of Rodríguez Saá functionaries selling IP contracts. Despite the well-known corruption, Menem maintained IP in San Luis.[62]

In addition to IP, the Federal Tax Sharing Law, the Coparticipación Federal de Impuestos, provides the federal government with a potential source of material leverage over the governor of San Luis. Since the 1934 implementation of the Tax Sharing Law, the San Luis economy has depended on the central government for the transfer of tax revenues, exacerbating the province's vulnerability to material leverage. The federal government has collected taxes and then redistributed the revenues to the provinces, centralizing tax authority. Although the tax sharing arrangement has undergone multiple iterations since 1934, presidents have maintained discretion over the distribution of tax revenues, causing a vertical fiscal imbalance.[63] From 1985 through 1995, taxes collected by the federal government financed an average of 80 percent of provincial spending, whereas provincial revenues financed an average of 20 percent. In San Luis, provincial revenues funded only 18 percent of expenditures, as compared to 31 percent in Mendoza.[64] Furthermore, federal transfers to the provinces increased dramatically during the Menem administration. Between 1990 and 1995, they rose from $7.6 billion to $16 billion.[65] Like IP, tax revenues allowed Rodríguez Saá to create jobs and fund public works projects. As Eaton explains, revenue sharing has helped governors expand their patronage machines.[66]

In addition, the Argentine president has discretion over the distribution of non-reimbursable discretionary treasury grants, Aportes del Tesoro Nacional (ATNs), on which provinces have become increasingly dependent. According to a 1988 Tax Sharing Law, the central government retains 42 percent of the tax revenue, 57 percent is earmarked for the provinces, and 1 percent is devoted to unforeseen crises. The Ministry of the Interior distributes this 1 percent in the form of ATNs. In contrast to the 57 percent that is distributed to the provinces according to law, the Ministry of the Interior has discretion over the distribution of the 1 percent designated for provincial crises. Between 1991 and 1995, the share of provincial revenues from ATN grants grew annually by an average of 30 percent and reached 2.3 percent of total provincial revenues in 1995. Although 2.3 percent appears insignificant at first glance, ATN grants became an important source of revenue for San Luis and La Rioja. Although the law stipulates that ATNs go to provinces facing fiscal crisis, in reality, political interests have affected the allocation of these discretionary transfers. During the Menem administration, the president favored San Luis and his home province of La Rioja. In fact, ATNs were the source of 40 percent of the La Rioja government's resources.[67]

In contrast to Menem, the Alianza administration of De la Rúa had no incentive to bolster Rodríguez Saá's position in San Luis through programs such as IP and federal tax sharing. Indeed, during the 1999 presidential campaign, the Alianza pledged to terminate the IP program in San Luis. In 2000, President De la Rúa reduced IP in San Luis. Argentina's economic crisis also led to a reduction in IP benefits and tax revenue earmarked for San Luis.[68]

The Press and Information Politics in Menem's Argentina

During the Menem years, reform coalition members utilized the press to build and sustain support for the rule of law in Argentina. Independent newspapers along with television and radio programs exposed Menem's assaults against judicial autonomy and increased public scrutiny of government. In addition to monitoring the courts, the media publicized the benefits of an independent judiciary. The growing accessibility of information increased the political costs of subordinating the judiciary, and public opinion began to act as a check on the president.

Press coverage of the judiciary increased over the course of Menem's decade in the presidency. Horacio Verbitsky and Adrián Ventura were the first journalists to specialize in coverage of the courts. Verbitsky's articles in *Página 12* and Ventura's pieces in *La Nación* helped create public demand for an independent judiciary. Until 1995, Ventura and Verbitsky were among a handful of journalists who focused on the courts. After 1995, however, the press became a protagonist in the reform coalition. Reporters such as Román Lejtman, Magdalena Ruiz Guiñazú, Nelson Castro, and Eduardo Aliverti joined Ventura and Verbitsky, raising the costs of executive pressure on judges and public prosecutors. According to Aníbal Ibarra, the pressure that he received from Menem during his tenure as public prosecutor in the early 1990s would have received greater press attention later in Menem's term. In the early 1990s, only Verbitsky covered the Ibarra case. In contrast, articles about government pressure on public prosecutor Carlos Stornelli filled the newspapers in 1998, triggering a groundswell of public support for Stornelli. Ultimately, Menem could not stop Stornelli's investigation of the administration's illegal arms sales to Ecuador and Croatia.[69]

Although Menem sometimes used defamation suits and even threats of violence to impede journalists' role as watchdogs, the government faced limits on its ability to act as a censor.[70] The written press and most radio and television stations broadcast freely and are privately owned. Newspapers across Argentina criticized Menem's treatment of the courts. For instance, provincial newspapers in Buenos Aires, Córdoba, Santa Fe, and Misiones published editorials condemning the 1990 expansion of the Supreme Court and the 1993 Olivos Pact that permitted Menem to run for a second consecutive presidential term.[71]

Due to Argentines' faith in the press, the media has been an effective reform coalition member. According to a 1996 survey, the press has the best image of all Argentine institutions including the Catholic Church, Congress, political parties, the judiciary, and labor unions. Sixty-five percent of Argentines have a positive image of the media and only 8 percent have a negative image.[72] In a 1998 survey, 48 percent of respondents reported that the press is the most effective means of combating corruption, more effective than either the judicial process or congressional investigations.[73] Indeed, investigative reporters have proven effective at exposing corruption in the judiciary. For instance, the popular Channel 13 *Telenoche Investiga* used a hidden camera to record judges accepting bribes in exchange for favorable rulings. Independent reporting on government corruption brought about the fall of several Menem functionaries.[74] The press also helped turn public opinion against Menem's bid for reelection in 1999.

In recognition of the importance of the press, Argentine civil society groups have promoted the media's role as watchdog. The 1995 Poder Ciudadano program "Judges and Journalists" brought journalists, judges, and academics together to encourage dialogue among the three sectors.[75] A Social Forum for Justice initiative taught journalists about the fundamentals of the judiciary with the goal of increasing the number of reporters who cover the courts.[76]

The Media and Information Politics in San Luis

National press coverage of San Luis has helped the province's reform coalition expose Rodríguez Saá's subordination of the judiciary. The national media has provided information to the citizens of San Luis as well as to the rest of Argentina. Exposure by the national media has been especially important due to the governor's monopoly on information within San Luis. Rodríguez Saá deliberately undermined press freedom in the province.

In contrast to the information pluralism of Argentina at the national level, Rodríguez Saá's control of the San Luis media aided and abetted his monolithic political power. Before Rodríguez Saá assumed power, San Luis had five local newspapers that represented a variety of political views. After 1983, however, this diversity of viewpoints disappeared. The governor forced three papers into bankruptcy by withholding economic support, and his family purchased the two remaining newspapers: *Diario de la República* and *La Opinión*. In order to compel the owner to sell *Diario de la República* in 1984, Rodríguez Saá refused to place government advertisements and announcements in the paper. When a member of the Rodríguez Saá family purchased *La Opinión* in 1997, the paper eliminated all coverage of opposition views. The 1997 acquisition marked the end of the independence that the paper had enjoyed since 1973.[77]

The administration's policy of rewarding pro-government papers and punishing the independent press made it difficult for the opposition press to survive. Favoritism in government advertising stymied the growth of periodicals with a critical editorial line.[78] San Luis newspapers depended on revenues from advertising by state-owned companies and by the government itself. During the Rodríguez Saá governorship, most public works contracts contained a clause that required companies to advertise in the government-controlled press. For instance, the companies that built the government housing projects had to announce the opening of new projects in the *Diario de la República* and *La Opinión*. This policy provided the Rodríguez Saá family newspapers with a secure source of revenue.[79]

In contrast to the pro-government journalists who reaped rewards such as government-sponsored travel and easy access to executive officials, the government punished the few journalists who criticized administration policies. Punishment took the form of reduced access to government, attacks by the government-controlled press, threats of physical harm, and defamation suits. Rodríguez Saá did not hold open press conferences after a journalist inquired about his alleged tax evasion during a 1992 conference. After 1992, the governor invited only a select group of pro-government reporters, and the state radio station, Radio Nacional, stopped transmitting live press conferences. As a result of his independent stance, journalist Eduardo Olivares lost access to government press conferences, faced attacks in the local newspapers, and received physical threats. The personal attacks in the government-owned newspapers hurt his reputation in the community. When Olivares denounced government officials for involvement in narcotrafficking, the government-controlled press printed unfounded allegations that Olivares was trying to camouflage his own drug use. When Olivares investigated police inaction in a rape case, the papers published stories accusing Olivares of rape. In 1998, Amnesty International condemned government threats against Olivares and his family.[80] Both Miguel Wiñazki and Jaime Emma faced libel suits. In response to a 1990 article that criticized the governor, a San Luis judge ordered the police to arrest Wiñazki, who went into hiding for two days. The arrest order was withdrawn when it was discovered that Rodríguez Saá had paid the judge to authorize the arrest. In 1992, Rodríguez Saá ordered the arrest and imprisonment of Emma after he reported on government corruption. Mario Otero went into temporary hiding as a result of government threats.[81]

Rodríguez Saá's use of the San Luis newspapers to silence independent judges and opposition legislators highlights the importance of the national press's dissemination of balanced and fair reporting. As discussed in Chapter 4, the governor used his control of the *Diario de la República* to secure the resignations of Supreme Court justices in 1996. Rodríguez Saá also used the papers to tarnish the image of judges who opposed the 1995 reduction of their salaries. In addition, opposition Congressmen Juan José Laborda Ibarra and Roberto Pagano were the targets of attacks throughout Rodríguez Saá's governorship. In response to Laborda Ibarra's 1990 allegations of government corruption, the papers published stories that portrayed him as a drug addict. When Laborda Ibarra traveled to the United States in July 1998 with his daughter, the *Diario de la República* reported that he was with his lover. In response to Pagano's victory in a suit against the government, the *Diario de la República* portrayed him as a thief.[82]

The San Luis governor controlled provincial television stations as well as the written press. In the words of Wiñazki, "Rodríguez Saá built an electronic wall around San Luis."[83] The government owned the only news channel that is available to all of San Luis, Channel 13. In addition, the governor's influence encompassed the two privately owned cable news channels, TVC Puntana and Carolina Cable Color (CCC). Victorio Américo Gualtieri, a businessman with strong ties to the San Luis PJ, owned both cable stations. His companies benefited from government construction contracts. As a result of his economic dependence on the governor, Gualtieri did not risk airing programs that challenged government policies. In addition, in order to qualify for government advertising, cable journalists had to follow the government-owned station's editorial line. Both TVC Puntana and CCC were pro-government, and reporters did not address the executive subordination of the judiciary.[84]

Radio is the only sector of the provincial media in which the opposition has had a strong voice. Independent radio stations became important components of the reform coalition by countering the governor's control of information within San Luis. Although most radio shows followed the editorial line of the *Diario de la República*, independent radio stations began to emerge in the early 1990s. Both Otero and Olivares used their programs on the independent station Radio Dimensión to draw attention to the subordination of the courts. In fact, the owner of Radio Dimensión, Enrique Finochietti, instructed his reporters to address the governor's abuse of power. Finochietti is from the province of Córdoba and therefore was independent of the governor. Olivares had another popular program on the independent Radio Máxima, and Otero had a show on the independent Radio Universidad.[85] Because radio was the only part of the San Luis media capable of challenging the governor, the participation of the national media was critical to the strategy of information politics.

In 1997, the national media became an important addition to the San Luis reform coalition. During Rodríguez Saá's first three terms as governor, the national media did not participate in the coalition. The September 1997 dissolution of the San Luis Bar Association was the first of the governor's attacks on the judiciary to receive significant national attention. After 1997, coverage grew. Journalists such as Wiñazki and Lejtman helped expose the situation in San Luis. Wiñazki published two books about Rodríguez Saá's accumulation of power as well as articles in *Clarín* and *Noticias*. Lejtman devoted an issue of the weekly magazine *Tres Puntos* to Rodríguez Saá's violations of the rule of law.[86]

Activists' denunciations of Rodríguez Saá in the national press damaged the governor's reputation. Eugenio Raúl Zaffaroni and Moreno Ocampo, for example, frequently condemned Rodríguez Saá in the media. Zaffaroni arranged a high profile meeting between former Argentine president Raúl Alfonsín and former judge Careaga that received national press attention.[87] Such media attention damaged Rodríguez Saá's image on the national level. National press coverage also exposed the corrupt implementation of IP in San Luis, which increased demand for reform of the program. For instance, the major newspapers covered the 1997 videotape of provincial government officials selling IP contracts.[88]

The national media's extensive coverage of the removal of judges Gallo and Careaga demonstrated its ability to undermine the governor's strategy of misinformation. Press reports about the unjust removals galvanized national public opinion against Rodríguez Saá. In fact, a primary goal of both judges' defense teams was to raise national awareness about the governor's abuse of power. Poder Ciudadano and CELS used their high profiles to draw the national media to the hearings. CELS attorney Alberto Bovino asserts, "We nationalized the case."[89] National reporting favored the two judges over the governor. For instance, *La Nación* reported that Rodríguez Saá used the pliant Impeachment Jury to intimidate other independent judges.[90]

At the time of their trials, Gallo and Careaga appeared on popular television programs filmed in Buenos Aires and broadcast across Argentina as a way to rally public opinion against the governor's subordination of the courts. The two judges shared their personal testimonies on the popular daytime talk show *Almorzando con Mirtha Legrand* that reaches a broad audience.[91] They used national television to inform the Argentine public about their personal experiences, a strategy that enhances the effectiveness of information politics. As Keck and Sikkink note, dramatic personal testimony is a particularly potent tool.[92] The testimony focused attention on individuals rather than on abstract notions about the rule of law.

The Role of Nonstate Actors in Mendoza

As a result of competitive politics in Mendoza, a reform coalition has not been as critical for judicial autonomy as in Rodríguez Saá's San Luis or in Menem's Argentina. Nevertheless, at key moments in Mendoza's history, local civil society and an independent press helped strengthen horizontal accountability agencies, including the courts. However, these elements have not needed to form a sustained coalition with the goal of establishing judicial autonomy. Instead, individual groups have worked on their own as discrete units for limited periods of time.

At different points in Mendoza's history, the assertion of independence from judges helped the province achieve the strong judiciary it has today. The well-organized Mendoza Judges' Association defended the constitutional guarantee of salary protection and advocated for the creation of a Judicial Council in Mendoza. When Governor Llaver attempted to lower salaries in 1984, the president of the Judges' Association, Alberto Staib, mobilized judges in an effective campaign to force the administration to respect salary protection. Ultimately, the Mendoza Supreme Court declared the salary reduction unconstitutional. In addition, the Association's efforts were a factor behind Governor Bordón's 1987 decree that created a Judicial Council. Staib's effective leadership enabled him to convince other judges to join the campaign for a Judicial Council that would reduce the governor's discretion over judicial appointments. As a candidate for governor, Bordón recognized the strength of the Judges' Association. Shortly before the 1987 election, Bordón visited Staib and pledged that if he were to win the election, his first act would be to create a Judicial Council. Staib attributes Bordón's pledge to the judges' victory in the fight with Llaver over their salaries. As a result of that struggle, Mendocinos' opinion of Llaver had fallen. According to Staib, Bordón wanted to avoid such a public conflict with the Judges' Association, which could undermine his popularity. Only three days after assuming the governorship, Bordón sent a copy of the Judicial Council decree to the Association.[93]

Mendoza lawyers have at times struggled for judicial autonomy, but the Mendoza Bar Association no longer emphasizes judicial independence.[94]

During Oscar Portabella's tenure as the bar association president from 1991 until 1996, he never received a complaint regarding executive subordination of the judiciary. Although the provincial bar association continues to function as a watchdog, it focuses on challenges such as backlogs in the courts and inefficiency.[95]

The bar association's lack of attention to judicial independence reflects the situation of broader Mendoza civil society. Judicial autonomy is not a primary concern of provincial civil society groups. Mendoza journalist Andrés Gabrielli explains that these groups focus on more pressing issues such as the rising crime rate.[96] Even civil society groups linked to the judiciary, such as the Association of Public Prosecutors, emphasize efficiency over autonomy.[97]

A small but powerful group of committed activists emerged during Arturo Lafalla's 1995–99 term to fortify the rule of law in Mendoza. Lafalla and Moreno Ocampo were key players in the group. They provided strong leadership as they worked toward their shared goal of increasing transparency in government. Their collaboration produced the Citizen Information Program (CIP), which provides information about government functionaries' income and property. Moreno Ocampo helped create the Inspector General, a control organ unique to Mendoza that monitors and disseminates information about the government. Moreno Ocampo's contributions varied from specific technical proposals to plans for implementation of reform.[98]

In addition, the Mendoza press has played a critical role as a watchdog against government abuses. In contrast to San Luis, Mendoza has a free press. The Mendoza press is independent from the government and does not rely on revenue from government advertising. This autonomy has allowed the press to act as a control on the government. The media has been central to actors who employ the tactic of information politics. For instance, during his tenure as State Prosecutor, Aldo Giordano used the press to build public support for investigations of government officials.[99] According to Mendoza Congressman Sergio Bruni, politicians use the local media to communicate with the electorate. Without such communication, citizens would lack the information necessary to hold legislators accountable.[100] As Lafalla explains, there is a synergy between the government's provision of information and the work of journalists. Mendoza journalists confirm the information provided by government programs such as CIP. If a functionary does not provide accurate information, journalists expose the inaccuracy.[101] In addition, local newspapers conduct investigations and publish editorials that critique the government. The newspaper *Los Andes* has published editorials on violations of human rights in Mendoza's prisons, the government's failure to address increasing crime, and backlogs in the courts.[102]

The cases of San Luis and Argentina at the national level demonstrate how nonstate actors can work alongside the opposition in Congress to fragment political power. In contrast to Rodríguez Saá's San Luis where the nascent reform coalition was the only competing power center, in Mendoza, provincial civil society and the local press are just a small part of a much larger system of overlapping horizontal accountability agencies. As components of a system, they operate alongside and reinforce government organs of control.

Conclusion

Competitive Politics and the Rule of Law in Presidential Systems

THE QUESTION of how nascent democracies construct and fortify the rule of law is fundamentally one of power. The rule of law requires that all state and private actors that wield significant power be subject to legality. By focusing on judicial autonomy, a key component of the rule of law in presidential systems, this book demonstrates that the balanced dispersal of political power among competing actors is a necessary condition for the rule of law. In the ultrapresidential regimes of Latin America where the problem of establishing judicial autonomy is especially acute, party competition can be the catalyst for political fragmentation. In contrast, monolithic party control, defined as a prolonged period of unified government under the control of a highly disciplined party, obstructs the rule of law. But how do political systems generate competitive politics in the first place? The fragmentation of power in two other areas, the economic and the social realms, can lead to the requisite competitive politics. Evidence from the diachronic study of Argentina at the national level and the synchronic comparison of the Argentine provinces of San Luis and Mendoza supports these hypotheses.

This chapter first reviews the main theoretical propositions and empirical findings of the book. The chapter then introduces external case material to contextualize the argument by highlighting the difficulty of establishing and maintaining judicial independence in presidential regimes. It contains a brief discussion of other Argentine provinces, of Chile and the United States at the federal level, and of the state of Louisiana, all of which support the argument that party competition fosters judicial autonomy. Monolithic party control and non-competitive politics, on the other hand, appear to inhibit the judiciary's ability to constrain executive prerogatives. The chapter concludes by exploring the theoretical implications of the findings.

Theoretical Propositions and Empirical Findings

Patterns of power in the political, economic, and social realms explain the different degrees of progress toward the rule of law in Argentina across time, across regime type, and across space. Based on the hypotheses of this study, one would expect to find the rule of law in cases characterized by competitive politics. In particular, a high level of party competition should cultivate judicial autonomy. In contrast, in cases of monolithic party control, one should find an ineffective system of horizontal accountability, which includes courts that are subordinate to the executive branch of government.

Indeed, empirical study of the Argentine experience reveals that party competition set the stage for the establishment of checks and balances at the national and provincial levels. As Chapter 3 demonstrates, party balance early in Argentina's history and from 1983 through 1989 compelled presidents to comply with the formal rules that call for judicial independence. Chapter 6 shows that competition among three strong political parties in Mendoza has fostered divided government and the rotation of the party in power, which, in turn, have promoted respect for the formal rules that protect the autonomy of the courts.

Monolithic party control, on the other hand, impedes the rule of law. In the absence of significant inter-party competition and intra-party dissent, the executive has incentives to concentrate power and has the capacity to do so. By increasing the executive's partisan powers, monolithic control permits the passage of legislation that establishes executive control over horizontal accountability agencies, including the courts. As expected, monolithic party control characterized Argentina under presidents Juan Perón, Arturo Frondizi, and Carlos Menem and San Luis under Governor Adolfo Rodríguez Saá. In addition, the military regimes that governed Argentina had a monopoly on political power that was tantamount to monolithic party control. Chapter 3 argues that unified government and party discipline during the Perón, Frondizi, and Menem administrations and the monolithic control that characterized periods of military rule eroded the system of horizontal accountability at the national level. Chapter 5 reveals how monolithic party control in San Luis enabled that province's governor to dismantle all remnants of the rule of law.

What are the historical roots of the rule of law? Based on the hypothesis that socioeconomic complexity is one path to the requisite competitive politics, one would expect to find the rule of law where economic resources have been distributed among members of a divided elite. As Chapter 4 demonstrates, the histories of San Luis and of Mendoza support this proposition. The dispersal of economic assets among competing actors of comparable strength engendered an independent judiciary in Mendoza. Competing economic groups demanded a neutral body to adjudicate their disputes. In San Luis, the concentration of economic resources has stood in the way of the rule of law. Furthermore, in San Luis, the economic elite has overlapped with the political elite.

What about countries with a high concentration of both economic and political power? Are they trapped without the rule of law? In this case, movement in the direction of judicial autonomy can come from outside of the state apparatus. The mobilization of a reform coalition draws from societal power to disperse resources away from the executive branch. Thus, one would expect to find an active coalition of nonstate actors in cases where both economic and political power are concentrated. Indeed, as Chapter 7 demonstrates, a reform network emerged in Menem's Argentina and in Rodríguez Saá's San Luis to fracture the executive's monopoly on political power. Such a coalition has not been vital in Mendoza, where a competitive party system has promoted an effective system of checks and balances that supports the rule of law.

A Return to the Comparative Perspective

This section explains how the theoretical framework might be applied to additional cases. It serves as an invitation to others to move beyond the Argentine case. The plausibility probes of Argentina at the provincial level, of Chile and the United States at the national level, and of the state of Louisiana have been formulated to encourage application in different contexts.[1]

PARTY COMPETITION AND JUDICIAL INDEPENDENCE IN THE ARGENTINE PROVINCES

Preliminary research on Argentine provinces other than San Luis and Mendoza supports the argument that party competition is a key explanatory variable behind variations in judicial autonomy.[2] Monolithic party control has characterized the Argentine provinces with the lowest level of judicial autonomy: Catamarca, Corrientes, and La Rioja. Like San Luis, all three became provincial oligarchies dominated by a single family after the 1983 democratic transition: the Saadi family in Catamarca, the Romero Feris family in Corrientes, and the Menem family in La Rioja. The province of Córdoba also demonstrates that monolithic party control leads to executive subordination of the courts. Córdoba has an economy and a democratic political culture that are similar to those of Mendoza, yet Córdoba has had a much lower level of judicial independence. Unified UCR government coupled with party discipline undermined the rule of law in

Córdoba despite the province's socioeconomic complexity and vibrant civil society. Sixteen years of monolithic UCR control led to a decline in judicial autonomy evidenced by the violations of judges' salary protection during the 1990–95 period.[3]

Competitive politics, on the other hand, is the trademark of provinces with independent judicial branches. Party competition has helped provinces overcome the concentration of economic resources and build the rule of law. The socioeconomic history of the province of La Pampa resembles that of San Luis more than that of Mendoza, yet the La Pampa judiciary enjoys a high degree of independence from the executive. La Pampa is representative of Argentina's fertile *pampa húmeda* that has a long history of large-scale landholdings and wealth concentration, yet the La Pampa judiciary is renowned for its autonomy and for its transparent and merit-based appointment process. A competitive party system appears to have facilitated this judicial independence in La Pampa.[4]

PARTY COMPETITION AND THE RULE OF LAW IN CHILE

The historical experience of Chile also suggests that competitive politics promotes judicial autonomy.[5] Chile and Argentina share the Spanish colonial legacy and civil law tradition, and they both recently experienced transitions from harsh military rule. Nevertheless, Chile has had more success than Argentina in establishing a strong rule of law that includes a judiciary that is independent of the executive branch.[6] Party competition has been an operative variable behind Chile's relative success. Valenzuela describes the pre-Pinochet courts as "largely insulated from political control and partisan battles" and argues that they "exercised important governmental functions drawing on formal authority and institutional clout."[7] In the wake of the 1973 coup, however, General Augusto Pinochet's monopoly on political power permitted him to subordinate the courts, demonstrating once again that the construction of the rule of law is not a linear process.

A long history of competition among highly institutionalized political parties set the stage for the rule of law in Chile.[8] No single party has dominated the Chilean political landscape and party discipline has been lower than in neighboring Argentina. Unlike most of Latin America, monolithic party control did not characterize the Chilean political landscape for most of the country's history. Competitive politics provided the judiciary with insularity from the political branches.

Party balance and electoral rules in pre-Pinochet Chile encouraged the frequent rotation of the party in power and divided government, which permitted the legislature to check the president and prevented executive manipulation of the courts. As in the Argentine province of Mendoza, competition among at least three relevant parties has prevented the executive's party from holding a majority in Congress for a sustained period of time. For most of the twentieth century, five relevant parties competed for seats in Congress. As a result, coalition government was common.[9]

The pre-Pinochet electoral rules contributed to divided government. Along with multipartism, Chile's modified d'Hondt system of proportional representation made it difficult for a single party to hold over one-third of the seats in the House or the Senate. Nonsimultaneous legislative and executive elections and the partial reelection of the Senate also fostered divided government. Indeed, as a result of the competitive party system and electoral rules, divided government was the norm, forcing presidents to bargain with the opposition in Congress. In fact, from 1932 through 1973, no single party captured the executive and both houses of the legislative branch at the same time. Divided government was the norm.[10] Moreover, the Chilean electoral system discouraged party discipline. Unlike Argentina, Chile has used open-list ballots. In addition, adequate independent sources of campaign finance have undermined threats of punishment from party leaders.[11]

The 1973 coup brought an abrupt end to competitive politics, but the balanced dispersal of political power and party competition appear to have reemerged in post-authoritarian Chile. Despite the military regime's electoral engineering, which was meant to reduce multipartism and over-represent the right, Chile's political parties survived with their distinct identities and platforms intact. The two main electoral forces, the Concertación por la Democracia on the left and the Renovación Nacional-Unión Demócrata Independiente alliance on the right, are loose coalitions rather than unified parties. For instance, four distinct parties comprise the Concertación. Even under unified Concertación government, the undisciplined nature of the coalition would likely preclude monolithic party control.[12]

COMPETITIVE POLITICS AND JUDICIAL AUTONOMY IN THE UNITED STATES

Political observers often point to the United States as the only presidential regime that has never suffered a breakdown. Like Argentina and Chile, however, the experience of the U.S. shows that when the executive branch and Congress have been united unambiguously under a single party for a sustained period of time, the Supreme Court has reflected the executive's partisan preferences. In contrast, judicial autonomy has characterized eras of divided government. Prior to World War II, with the exception of the 1874–96 period, one party tended to dominate the political landscape. As a result of similar congressional and presidential preferences, judicial autonomy was lower during this period than in the post–World War II era. The increase in party competition and divided government since 1946 has bolstered the separation of powers.[13]

Between 1860 and 1932, the Republican Party dominated national politics. Government was unified under the Republicans for over half of the 36 congressional periods. In contrast, government was unified under the Democrats for only four of the 36 periods. During this 72-year period, the Supreme Court generally issued decisions in line with Republican policy preferences.[14]

The 1932 elections marked a transformation in the U.S. political landscape as the Democratic Party gained a strong foothold in government for the first time since 1860. During Franklin Roosevelt's first term from 1932 to 1936, the Supreme Court was able to maintain its independence and opposed the redefinition of the federal government's role in the economy. Until the landslide election of 1936, it was unclear that 1932 marked the end of Republican hegemony. Thus, the Court was able to retain its Republican, laissez-faire stance for four years. During Roosevelt's first term, the New Deal program suffered a series of defeats in the Supreme Court. For example, the Court ruled against the Railroad Retirement Act of 1934, the National Industrial Recovery Act of 1933, the Agricultural Adjustment Act of 1933, and the Bituminous Coal Conservation Act of 1935.[15]

After only four years, however, the recalcitrant Court buckled in the face of a government unified under the Democrats. The Democrats gained representation in Congress in the 1934 mid-term elections. After the Democrats won a two-thirds majority in both the House and the Senate along with almost three-quarters of the state legislatures in 1936, Supreme Court Justice Owen Roberts changed his position and began to support the New Deal. In 1936, the federal government was clearly unified under the Democratic Party, thus ending the conflict between Roosevelt and the Court. It had become clear that the 1932 elections did not mark a temporary electoral shift but rather the beginning of an era of Democratic hegemony that lasted until 1946. In 1946, divided government became the norm and the Supreme Court once again began to assert its autonomy.[16]

HUEY LONG AND MONOLITHIC PARTY CONTROL: THE RODRÍGUEZ SAÁ OF LOUISIANA

Like the provincial-level analysis of Argentina, state-level analysis of the United States has the potential to reveal patterns of power that undermine judicial independence. The U.S. standard is often stated in theoretical terms without delving into the very mixed record of individual states. It is here that the selection and analysis of Louisiana is relevant. The inability of the judiciary to check the executive in Governor Huey Long's Louisiana illustrates the dynamics of non-competitive politics at the subnational level in the United States. Like San Luis in Argentina, Jim Crow Louisiana was an authoritarian enclave embedded in a democratic national system. The courts were notorious for their subordination to the Democrat-controlled state legislative and executive branches. As in contemporary San Luis, where the PJ has dominated provincial politics since 1983, the Democratic Party dominated the South until the 1960s. Between 1932 and 1958, Democrats won 80 percent of the vote in gubernatorial and state legislative elections across the South. It was not until the Democrats lost their monopoly on power that the construction of the rule of law began in states like Louisiana. The Democrats' share of the vote fell to 63 percent in 1966, to 55 percent in 1972, and to 44 percent in 1996.[17] As the Republican Party gained a foothold in the South, the courts began to challenge the executive.

As in San Luis, prolonged unified government under a highly disciplined party undermined the rule of law in Huey Long's Louisiana. Louisiana's one-party system encouraged the development of highly personalized, authoritarian political leadership under Governor Long.[18] Long's accumulation of power was not unlike the concentration of power in Latin American presidents. Schlesinger likens Long to Perón.[19] Key's description of Long could be used to describe Perón or Rodríguez Saá: "He dominated the legislature. He ripped out of office mayors, parish officials, and judges who raised a voice against him. Weapons of economic coercion were employed to repress opposition. . . . Huey, at the height of his power, brooked no opposition and those who could not be converted were ruthlessly suppressed."[20]

Like Perón and Rodríguez Saá, Long relied on a powerful patronage machine to garner support. His large-scale public works programs included building roads, bridges, schools, and hospitals. When Long assumed power in 1928, Louisiana had 476 kilometers of concrete road and 56 kilometers of asphalt roads. By 1935, Louisiana had 3,936 kilometers of concrete roads and 2,105 kilometers of asphalt roads. Under Rodríguez Saá, the total miles of paved roads in San Luis grew from 300 to 2,500 kilometers. In addition, like Rodríguez Saá, Long used his control over the local economy to create vested interests that would support him. Long used his control of petroleum and gambling concessions; Rodríguez Saá used his discretion over the tax incentives from the Industrial Promotion program.[21]

Long subordinated both the legislature and the judiciary. Over two-thirds of the Louisiana state congress was pro-Long. Long's partisan powers permitted him to dominate the legislative process. At one point, he pushed 44 bills through the legislature in just 22 minutes. During seven special sessions between August 1934 and September 1935, the legislature passed 463 bills.[22] Long took deliberate steps to subordinate the state Supreme Court and ensure the appointment of pliant judges. Long controlled a four-member majority in the seven-member Louisiana Supreme Court throughout his governorship. In order to maintain a majority on the Court, Long intervened in the 1934 Supreme Court elections and even violated state law.[23]

In addition, like Rodríguez Saá, Long recognized the importance of the press. Early in his term, Long faced criticism from newspapers across the state. In order to undermine these independent voices, Long founded *The Louisiana Progress* in 1930. Much like Rodríguez Saá's use of the *Diario de la República*, Long used the paper to attack his critics. For instance, he waged personal attacks against the editors of independent newspapers and against his political rivals. Moreover, he used his control of the state legislature to pass legislation that created a tax on advertising to drive the opposition press out of business. In recognition that the pliant state courts would uphold the law, the independent newspapers appealed to the federal judiciary. Unlike the state courts that had refused to challenge the Long law, the federal courts declared the tax unconstitutional.[24] As in the case of San Luis where the Argentine federal government is now poised to impose reform, the U.S. federal government was critical to the establishment of the rule of law in Louisiana.

Conclusion

The diachronic study of Argentina at the national level and the synchronic comparison of San Luis and Mendoza illustrate that the same formal system of checks and balances may have different consequences—depending on the dispersal of power and competitive politics. In particular, effective party competition promotes the rule of law in presidential regimes. A major theoretical implication of this finding is that the rule of law is endogenous to other variables. Although usually treated as independent, the rule of law is not independent of other aspects of the political system, such as legislative and electoral institutions.

A second important lesson of this study is that divided government can foster the rule of law in presidential systems. Authors who focus on electoral and legislative politics stress the negative effects of multipartism and divided government in presidential systems—consequences such as stalemate and inflexibility. By expanding analysis from the executive and legislative branches to include the judiciary, however, one sees that divided government can strengthen democracy by promoting judicial independence.[25]

Another lesson is that comparativists would benefit from more subnational analysis, which is a powerful tool for political scientists who study Latin America as well as other regions, including the United States. The tendency in comparative politics has been to focus on institutional factors and their consequences at the national level. However, as the case studies of San Luis, Mendoza, and Louisiana demonstrate, institutional features—including judicial autonomy and party competition—can vary significantly at the local level. For example, each of Argentina's twenty-four provinces reflects a different degree of judicial autonomy, and the number of relevant political parties varies across the country. These subnational units helped identify conditions that foster the rule of law in nascent democracies. By supplementing the study of national politics with a systematic look at the subnational level, comparativists will find rich new laboratories for theory building.

APPENDIX

A Spatial Model of Supreme Court Independence

WHEN WILL JUDGES act independently of elected officials? When do judges have incentives to cave rather than issue rulings that challenge the government? This appendix introduces a spatial model to graphically illustrate the logic behind the argument that when the executive and legislative branches are united against the courts, the judiciary has few resources with which to defend an independent course and therefore typically caves. In contrast, when significant disagreements arise among elected officials, such as occur under divided government, judges have the ability to challenge the state and to sustain an independent course.[1]

A spatial model of Supreme Court independence sheds light on why particular presidents are able to subordinate the judiciary. The model indicates that in presidential systems, unified party control of the executive and legislative branches hinders judicial independence. When the president's party controls a disciplined majority in Congress, the executive and legislative branches together can overrule court decisions or punish judges. Divided government, on the other hand, facilitates judicial autonomy. It permits the legislature to check the president and vice versa, creating a climate in which an independent judiciary can emerge.

Spatial models similar to those that help explain U.S. judicial doctrine and statutory interpretation are useful in explaining the presence or absence of Supreme Court independence.[2] This appendix employs a spatial model that assumes a one-dimensional policy space and identifies the ideal point of the President as P, of Congress as C, and of the Supreme Court as SC.[3] The model assumes that the President, Congress, and the Supreme Court all have coherent and consistent policy preferences. Movement from left to right along the axis represents a shift in preferences, for instance, from state intervention in the economy to more laissez faire economic policies. When the

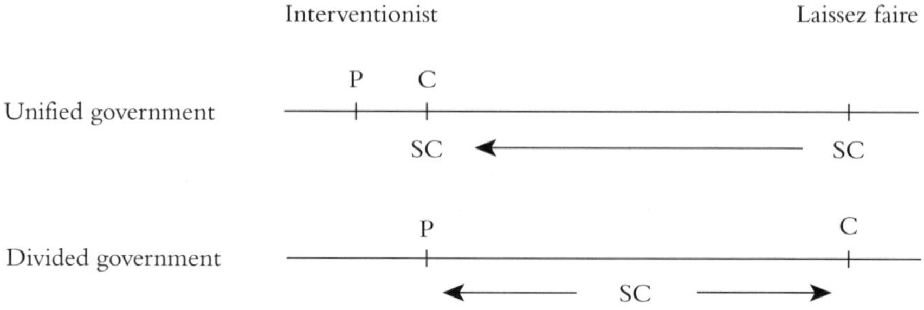

FIGURE A.1 Spatial models of unified and divided government.
Ideal points:

P President
C Congress
SC Supreme Court

preferences of the President and Congress are close together for a sustained period of time, as they tend to be under unified government, the Court is likely to cave.

On the other hand, if the gap between the President's preferences and Congress's preferences is large, the Court can more easily challenge government policies. The interval between P and C during divided government gives the Court the freedom to issue rulings that challenge the other branches. In this scenario, the Court can issue a ruling anywhere within the space between P and C.

In ruling on government initiatives of questionable constitutionality, judges make a strategic choice: either cave under government pressure or assert autonomy by challenging the policy. The judge's choice is contingent upon how the other two branches would respond to a challenge. If a judge foresees that the government will "overrule" rather than accept a decision, the judge is likely to cave. For the purposes of this model, the term "overrule" encompasses a variety of possible actions, such as packing the Court with new members, forcing members to resign, withholding funds from the judiciary, or simply ignoring judicial rulings. On the other hand, judges who foresee that the government will accept their rulings are more likely to issue adversarial decisions.

The following game illustrates the strategic dilemma facing the Court. In T1, the government has enacted a policy of dubious constitutionality. The Court has two options: to challenge or to cave. When making a choice, the Court considers what is likely to happen after its decision. In T2, the Presi-

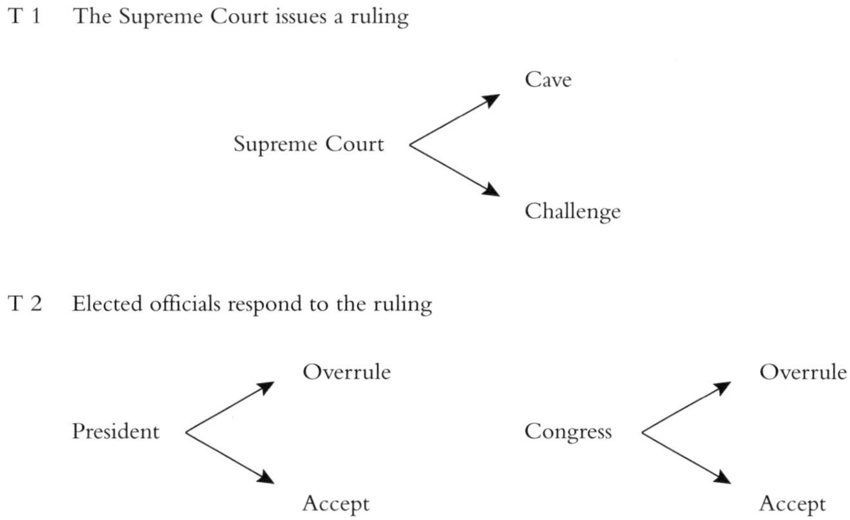

FIGURE A.2 The sequential game

dent and Congress are the players. To overrule the Court, both the President and Congress must agree. If the Court foresees that both the president and Congress will overrule its decision, the Court is likely to cave. This outcome is more likely under unified government because unified government permits members of the same party to coordinate their actions against the Court.[4] In contrast, divided government allows the opposition party to prevent the typical strategies for overruling the Court. An opposition Senate, for example, can block presidential plans to expand the Court or to impeach judges for political reasons. If the Court predicts that the President will overrule but that Congress will accept the decision or vice versa, it can challenge the government. Acting on its own, neither the President nor Congress has the power to overrule a decision.

This spatial model indicates that to bolster judicial autonomy, reformers must address the problematic nature of prolonged periods of unified government, especially when there is a high level of party discipline, the second element of monolithic party control. It also suggests the potential value of integrating the field of comparative politics with tools from positive political theory.

Notes

Introduction

1. Larry Diamond, "Democracy in Latin America: Degrees, Illusions, and Directions for Consolidation," in *Beyond Sovereignty: Collectively Defending Democracy in the Americas*, ed. Tom Farer (Baltimore: Johns Hopkins University Press, 1996), 52–104; Guillermo O'Donnell, "Delegative Democracy," *Journal of Democracy* 5 (January 1994): 55–69; Fareed Zakaria, "The Rise of Illiberal Democracy," *Foreign Affairs* 6 (November-December 1997): 22–43.

2. The "third wave" refers to the most recent trend toward democracy that began with the 1974 overthrow of the Salazar-Caetano dictatorship in Portugal. Since then, the wave has spread from Southern Europe to Latin America, Asia, Eastern Europe, the former Soviet Union, and parts of Africa. See Samuel Huntington, *The Third Wave: Democratization in the Late Twentieth Century* (Norman: University of Oklahoma Press, 1991).

3. For a discussion of the sequence in Germany, see Juan Linz, "Democracy Today: An Agenda for Students of Democracy," *Scandinavian Political Studies* 20 (1997): 118–20.

4. Huntington, *Third Wave*, 6. Przeworski also employs the minimalist definition of democracy. See Adam Przeworski et al., "What Makes Democracies Endure?" *Journal of Democracy* 7 (January 1996): 39. The decision whether to treat democracy as a continuous or a dichotomous variable depends upon the goals of the study. See David Collier and Steven Levitsky, "Democracy with Adjectives: Conceptual Innovation in Comparative Research," *World Politics* 49 (April 1997): 430–51.

5. Robert A. Dahl, *Polyarchy: Participation and Opposition* (New Haven: Yale University Press, 1971). Dahl's nonelectoral components of "polyarchy" or democracy include alternative sources of information and freedom of organization.

6. Terry Lynn Karl, "Imposing Consent? Electoralism versus Democratization in El Salvador," in *Elections and Democratization in Latin America, 1980–1985*, ed. Paul W. Drake and Eduardo Silva (San Diego: Center for Iberian and Latin American Studies and Center for U.S.-Mexican Studies, University of California at San Diego, 1986), 34.

7. Linz, "Democracy Today," 118. See Karl, "Dilemmas of Democratization in Latin America," *Comparative Politics* 23 (October 1990): 2.

8. Juan Linz and Alfred Stepan, "Toward Consolidated Democracies," *Journal of Democracy* 7 (April 1996): 16. Their third component of democratic consolidation is behavioral, meaning that there are no relevant anti-system actors.

9. Indeed, public opinion polls reveal that citizen faith in democracy has declined over the past decade in Latin America. The 2000 Latinobarómetro survey revealed that citizen trust in democratic institutions has declined as government corruption has risen. Only 34 percent of the public trusts the courts. In addition, only 37 percent of respondents reported that they are satisfied with the way that democracy works. See Marta Lagos, "How People View Democracy: Between Stability and Crisis in Latin America," *Journal of Democracy* 12 (January 2001): 137–45.

10. Diamond, *Developing Democracy: Toward Consolidation* (Baltimore: Johns Hopkins University Press, 1999), 12.

11. Charles de Montesquieu, *The Spirit of the Laws*, Book 11, chapt. 6, ed. Anne M. Cohler, Basia Carolyn Miller, and Harold Samuel Stone (Cambridge: Cambridge University Press, 1989), 157.

12. James Madison, "Federalist No. 47," in *The Federalist: A Commentary on the Constitution of the United States*, from the original text of Alexander Hamilton, John Jay, and James Madison, Modern Library Edition (New York: Random House, 1937), 313.

13. Harry Eckstein, "Case Study and Theory in Political Science," in *Handbook of Political Science*, ed. Fred Greenstein and Nelson Polsby (Reading, Mass.: Addison-Wesley, 1975), 7: 105–6.

14. Gary King, Robert O. Keohane, and Sidney Verba, *Designing Social Inquiry* (Princeton: Princeton University Press, 1994), 24–46.

15. John Stuart Mill, "Two Methods of Comparison," in *Comparative Perspectives: Theories and Methods*, ed. Amitai Etzioni and Frederic L. Dubow (Boston: Little, Brown, 1970), 206–12; Adam Przeworski and Henry Teune, *The Logic of Comparative Social Inquiry* (New York: Wiley Interscience, 1970), 33.

16. Arend Lijphart, "Comparative Politics and the Comparative Method," *American Political Science Review* 65 (September 1971): 686–88. Lijphart advocates focusing on comparable cases to overcome the "many variables, small-n problem." See Neil J. Smelser, "The Methodology of Comparative Analysis of Economic Activity," in *Essays in Sociological Interpretation*, ed. Smelser (Englewood Cliffs, N.J.: Prentice Hall, 1968), 62–75.

17. King, Keohane, and Verba, *Social Inquiry*, 46.

18. Bruce Bueno de Mesquita, Stephen Krasner, and Robert Jervis, "Symposium: Methodological Foundations of the Study of International Conflict," *International Studies Quarterly* 29 (June 1985): 128.

19. Process tracing helps determine causality and illuminates detail about how a theory works. See Stephen Van Evera, *Guide to Methods for Students of Political Science* (Ithaca: Cornell University Press, 1997), 64–67.

20. Michael Mann, *The Sources of Social Power: A Historical Comparison* (Cambridge: Cambridge University Press, 1986), 174.

21. See Theda Skocpol and Margaret Somers, "The Uses of Comparative History in Macrosocial Inquiry," *Comparative Studies in Society and History* 22 (April 1980): 178.

22. Lijphart, "The Comparable-Cases Strategy in Comparative Research," *Comparative Political Studies* 8 (July 1975): 168.

Chapter 1

1. John Henry Merryman, *The Civil Law Tradition: An Introduction to the Legal Systems of Western Europe and Latin America*, 2d ed. (Stanford: Stanford University Press, 1985), 140–41.

2. For instance, Linz and Stepan write, "It [the rule of law] is the important continuous and routine way in which the elected government and the state administration are subjected to a network of laws, courts, semiautonomous review and control agencies, and civil society norms." Juan Linz and Alfred Stepan, "Toward Consolidated Democracies," *Journal of Democracy* 7 (April 1996): 18–19.

3. Harold J. Berman, *Law and Revolution: The Formation of the Western Legal Tradition* (Cambridge: Harvard University Press, 1983), 292. Note that laws are not necessarily good. Much of the rule of law literature is based on the problematic assumption that law is fair and respects human rights. The rules themselves may be unjust, undemocratic, or even unconstitutional. For instance, Jim Crow laws mandated racial segregation in the U.S. South from Reconstruction through the 1950s. Laws that forbid citizens from criticizing or showing contempt for a public official (*desacato*) have been commonplace in Latin America.

4. The writings of the sixteenth century French thinker Jean Bodin illustrate this problem. Bodin's "sovereign" is a ruler who requires absolute power to maintain order. According to Bodin's theory of sovereignty, power is indivisible. Bodin rejects the separation of powers and calls for an elimination of enforceable restraints on the king. Without any form of lawful resistance to the all-powerful, unified sovereign, Bodin's sovereign is accountable to no one. See Bodin, *On Sovereignty: Four Chapters from the Six Books of the Commonwealth*, trans. and ed. Julian Franklin (Cambridge: Cambridge University Press, 1992).

5. Guillermo O'Donnell, "Delegative Democracy," *Journal of Democracy* 5 (January 1994): 61–62.

6. Owen Fiss, "The Right Degree of Independence," in *Transition to Democracy in Latin America: The Role of the Judiciary*, ed. Irwin P. Stotzky (Boulder: Westview, 1993), 56.

7. Barry Weingast, "The Political Foundations of Democracy and the Rule of Law," *American Political Science Review* 91 (June 1997): 249–51.

8. Oliver E. Williamson, *The Economic Institutions of Capitalism: Firms, Markets, Relational Contracting* (New York: Free Press, 1985), 48–49.

9. See Douglass North and Barry Weingast, "Constitutions and Commitment: The Evolution of Institutions Governing Public Choice in Seventeenth-Century England," *Journal of Economic History* 49 (December 1989): 803–32.

10. Hilton Root, "Tying the King's Hands: Credible Commitments and Royal Fiscal Policy during the Old Regime," *Rationality and Society* 1 (October 1989): 240–58.

11. For instance, as Boris Yeltsin accumulated power during his tenure as presi-

dent, he dismantled the system of checks and balances. He had the authority to dissolve the Duma, and he filled the courts with his loyal supporters.

12. Ameen Jan, "Pakistan on a Precipice," *Asian Survey* 34 (September-October 1999): 699–719. Until the 1999 coup, the executive branch represented the major hazard to the rule of law. Both Benazir Bhutto and Nawaz Sharif subordinated the courts.

13. The argument put forth in this book treats history and culture as endogenous. Although the colonial legacy provides a strong starting point in explaining the development of Latin America's institutional framework, the colonial heritage must be supplemented with an examination of more recent history. Latin American nations followed different developmental paths after independence and vary in their level of judicial autonomy, suggesting the need to look beyond the colonial legacy and to consider other explanatory variables.

14. See David Abernethy, *Dynamics of Global Dominance: European Overseas Empires: 1415–1980* (New Haven: Yale University Press, 2000).

15. C. H. Haring, *The Spanish Empire in America* (New York: Harcourt, Brace & World, 1947), 94–109, 138–46; Luz Estella Nagle, "Evolution of the Colombian Judiciary and the Constitutional Court," *Indiana International and Comparative Law Review* 6 (1995): 63–65.

16. Brian Loveman, *The Constitution of Tyranny: Regimes of Exception in Spanish America* (Pittsburgh: University of Pittsburgh Press, 1993), 34–35; Daniel Poneman, *Argentina: Democracy on Trial* (New York: Paragon House, 1987), 135.

17. For instance, in the Spanish tradition, Argentina's "Father of the Constitution," Juan Baustista Alberdi, advocated concentrating power in the president. See Alberdi, *Bases y puntos de partido para la organización política de la República Argentina*, 2d ed. (Buenos Aires: Cultura Argentina, 1915), 166. The Latin American framers based their conception of the executive on the 1812 Cádiz Constitution's constitutional monarch who was considered to be "sacred and inviolable, the king is not responsible [liable for actions]." See Loveman, *Constitution*, 41–42, 55. This executive supremacy also reflects the influence of *caudillismo* in Latin America. The *caudillo*, a strong, personalistic leader who often rules above the law, was the predecessor of the Latin American president.

18. See William C. Banks and Alejandro D. Carrió, "Presidential Systems in Stress: Emergency Powers in Argentina and the United States," *Michigan Journal of International Law* 15 (fall 1993): 7–9.

19. Argentina's 1815 Provisional Statute and 1819 Constitution granted the executive broad powers and contained provisions for "regimes of exception," in which the president could suspend civil liberties. Loveman, *Constitution*, 266–75.

20. McCloskey argues that the common law perception of judges contributed to the strength of the U.S. Supreme Court. See Robert G. McCloskey, *The American Supreme Court* (Chicago: University of Chicago Press, 1960), 12–13.

21. Arthur Taylor Von Mehren, *The Civil Law System: Cases and Materials for the Comparative Study of Law* (Englewood Cliffs, N.J.: Prentice-Hall, 1957), 840; Carlos Fayt, *La supremacía constitucional y la independencia de los jueces* (Buenos Aires: Depalma, 1994), 61–62; Merryman, *Civil Law*, 38.

22. Merryman, *Civil Law*, 2.

23. Alexander T. Edelmann, *Latin American Government and Politics: The Dynamics of a Revolutionary Society* (Homewood, Ill.: Dorsey Press, 1969), 466.

24. See Appendix, "A Spatial Model of Supreme Court Independence," for a graphic representation of the argument put forth in this section. The spatial model illustrates the logic behind the argument that divided government facilitates judicial autonomy.

25. Matthew Soberg Shugart, "The Electoral Cycle and Institutional Sources of Divided Presidential Government," *American Political Science Review* 89 (June 1995): 327–43.

26. Adam Przeworski, *Democracy and the Market* (Cambridge: Cambridge University Press, 1991).

27. The number of relevant parties in Congress and the level of party discipline determine the executive's "partisan powers." See Scott Mainwaring and Matthew Soberg Shugart, "Introduction," in *Presidentialism and Democracy in Latin America*, ed. Mainwaring and Shugart (Cambridge: Cambridge University Press, 1997), 4–10.

28. Argentina, Peru, El Salvador, Panama, Costa Rica, Colombia, Paraguay, and Ecuador recently amended their constitutions to create a Judicial Council. Chile, Guatemala, Honduras, and Nicaragua are considering the creation of such an organ. See Eugenio Raúl Zaffaroni, *Estructuras judiciales* (Buenos Aires: Ediar Sociedad Anónima Editora, 1994), 147–65.

29. Glendon Schubert, *Judicial Policy Making* (Glenview, Ill.: Scott, Foresman and Co., 1974), 14–25.

30. Richard D. Schwartz and James C. Miller, "Legal Evolution and Societal Complexity," *American Journal of Sociology* 70 (September 1964): 165. See also Theodore L. Becker, *Comparative Judicial Politics: The Political Functionings of Courts* (Chicago: Rand McNally, 1970), 99–105.

31. Alexis de Tocqueville, *Democracy in America*, Everyman's Library Edition (New York: Alfred A. Knopf, 1994), 1: 4–5.

32. Tocqueville, *Democracy*, 1: 3–4.

33. Karl, "Economic Inequality and Democratic Instability," *Journal of Democracy* 11 (January 2000): 151.

34. Tocqueville, *Democracy*, 1: 48.

35. John A. Booth, "Costa Rica: The Roots of Democratic Stability," in *Democracy in Developing Countries*, vol. 4, *Latin America*, ed. Diamond, Linz, and Lipset (Boulder: Lynne Rienner, 1989), 387–89.

36. Tocqueville, *Democracy*, 1: 29.

37. Margaret E. Keck and Kathryn Sikkink, *Activists beyond Borders: Advocacy Networks in International Politics* (Ithaca: Cornell University Press, 1998), 26–29, 206–8. A reform coalition that instigates change in the judicial arena has elements of Keck and Sikkink's "transnational advocacy network" and of Haas's "epistemic community." All three are composed of transnational nonstate actors that influence policy. Epistemic communities and reform coalitions use similar tactics: the community or coalition identifies the problem, creates channels of access to key players, provides information, and pushes for change. See Peter M. Haas, "Banning Chlorofluorocar-

bons: Epistemic Community Efforts to Protect Stratospheric Ozone," *International Organization* 46 (winter 1992): 187–224.

38. See Jennifer A. Widner, *Building the Rule of Law: Francis Nyalali and the Road to Judicial Independence in Africa* (New York: W.W. Norton & Co., 2001). Widner shows how individual judges who provided strong leadership have helped build the rule of law in Africa.

39. Diamond, "Rethinking Civil Society: Toward Democratic Consolidation," *Journal of Democracy* 5 (July 1994): 5.

40. Reed Brody, "International Aspects of Current Efforts at Judicial Reform: Undermining Justice in Haiti," in *The (Un)Rule of Law and the Underprivileged in Latin America*, ed. Juan E. Méndez, Guillermo O'Donnell, and Paulo Sérgio Pinheiro (Notre Dame: University of Notre Dame Press, 1999), 234–36; Harry Blair and Gary Hansen, *Weighing in on the Scales of Justice: Strategic Approaches for Donor-Supported Rule of Law Programs*, USAID Program and Operations Assessment Report No. 7 (February 1994), 1–15; Linn A. Hammergren, *Politics of Justice and Justice Reform in Latin America: The Peruvian Case in Comparative Perspective* (Boulder: Westview, 1998), 215–19. Brody attributes the failure of United States Agency for International Development (USAID) projects in Haiti in part to the lack of local actor input. Blair and Hansen use USAID case studies to show that the participation of domestic actors is critical to the success of international rule of law projects. Hammergren illustrates how the decision to sideline local actors hindered judicial reform in El Salvador. See also Thomas Carothers, "The Rule of Law Revival," *Foreign Affairs* 77 (March-April 1998): 103–6.

41. Keck and Sikkink, *Activists*, 12–13.

42. Keck and Sikkink, *Activists*, 16–29.

43. See Julio Faundez, "Legal Technical Assistance," in *Good Government and Law: Legal and Institutional Reform in Developing Countries*, ed. Faundez (New York: St. Martin's Press, 1997), 1–24; Christopher Sabatini, "Whom Do International Donors Support in the Name of Civil Society?" (paper presented at the annual Latin American Studies Association meeting, Miami, Fla., March 2000). Sabatini reports that in 1999, USAID and the National Endowment for Democracy provided Latin American civil society groups with $22.4 million in support.

44. Keck and Sikkink, *Activists*, 26–29. See Carothers, *In the Name of Democracy: United States Policy Toward Latin America in the Reagan Years* (Berkeley: University of California Press, 1991).

45. Tocqueville, *Democracy*, 2: 111–14.

46. Robert Putnam, *Making Democracy Work: Civic Traditions in Modern Italy* (Princeton: Princeton University Press, 1993), 92–93.

47. See Horacio Verbitsky, *Un mundo sin periodistas* (Buenos Aires: Planeta, 1997), 13–16. In his discussion of the media's role in exposing government abuses, O'Donnell refers to the media as a "surrogate court." See O'Donnell, "Horizontal Accountability in New Democracies," in *The Self-Restraining State: Power and Accountability in New Democracies*, ed. Andreas Schedler, Larry Diamond, and Marc F. Plattner (Boulder: Lynne Rienner, 1999), 30.

48. The emphasis on the role of informal judicial institutions in shaping incentives and behavior in Latin America was introduced in Rebecca Bill Chavez [Re-

becca Ann Bill], "Countervailing Power Centers and Judicial Autonomy in San Luis and Mendoza" (paper presented at the annual Latin American Studies Association meeting, Miami, Fla., March 2000). See also Chavez, "The Construction of the Rule of Law in Nascent Democracies: Judicial Autonomy in Latin America" (Ph.D. diss., Stanford University, 2001).

49. Alexander J. Groth, *Comparative Politics: A Distributive Approach* (New York: Macmillan, 1971), 221.

50. James Madison, "Federalist No. 48," in *The Federalist: A Commentary on the Constitution of the United States*, from the original text of Alexander Hamilton, John Jay, and James Madison, Modern Library Edition (New York: Random House, 1937), 321.

51. Becker, for instance, suggests looking at statute books and aggregating guarantees of judicial independence to determine the level of autonomy. See Becker, *Judicial Politics*, 148.

52. See John W. Meyer and Brian Rowan, "Institutionalized Organizations: Formal Structure in Myth and Ceremony," in *The New Institutionalism in Organizational Analysis*, ed. Paul J. DiMaggio and Walter W. Powell (Chicago: University of Chicago Press, 1991), 41–62; Nils Brunsson, *The Organization of Hypocrisy: Talk, Decisions, and Actions in Organizations*, trans. Nancy Adler (New York: Wiley, 1989).

53. Herman Schwartz, "Eastern Europe's Constitutional Courts," *Journal of Democracy* 9 (October 1998): 113.

54. In fact, 87 percent of U.S. Supreme Court nominees have been members of the president's political party. Sixty percent of appointees in the U.S. have known the president who nominated them. See Jeffrey A. Segal and Harold J. Spaeth, *The Supreme Court and the Attitudinal Model* (Cambridge: Cambridge University Press, 1993), 127–30.

55. The career of Nixon Supreme Court appointee Harry A. Blackmun illustrates the importance of life tenure. During his twenty-four years on the Court, Blackmun, a Republican before his appointment, changed his stance on major issues, including the death penalty. By the time of his retirement, Blackmun was one of the most liberal justices on the Court. Three years after he assumed his seat, he signed the *Roe v. Wade* opinion. In addition, he supported affirmative action in his partial dissent to the 1978 *California v. Bakke* decision and gay rights in the 1986 *Bowers v. Hardwick* decision.

56. Hamilton, "Federalist No. 78," 503.

57. Robert E. Biles, "The Position of the Judiciary in the Political Systems of Argentina and Mexico," *Lawyer of the Americas* 8 (1976): 294.

58. Hamilton, "Federalist No. 79," 512. Even Brutus recognizes the importance of salary protection in certain contexts: "While the judges held their places at the will and pleasure of the king, on whom they depended not only for their offices, but also for their salaries, they were subject to every undue influence. If the crown wished to carry a favorite point, to accomplish which the aid of the courts of law was necessary, the pleasure of the king would be signified to the judges. And it required the spirit of a martyr to determine contrary to the king's will." Quoted in Bernard Bailyn, *The Debate on the Constitution* (New York: Library of America, 1993), 373–74.

59. In the case of Argentina at the federal level, most presidents have respected judges' salary protection. Thus, Chapter 2, which traces the level of judicial auton-

omy in Argentina from 1862 through 1999, uses the de facto doctrine rather than respect for salary protection as an indicator of executive subordination of the courts. The de facto doctrine refers to courts' acceptance of laws passed by military regimes that came to power by force rather than by election.

60. The standard procedure among political scientists and lawyers for measuring judicial independence is to focus on court rulings in which the government is a party. For instance, in her important study of the relationship between the president and the Supreme Court, Helmke bases her conclusions about the degree of judicial autonomy on a large-*n* statistical study of rulings in which the government is a party. She uses the percent of rulings against the government to determine whether the Argentine judiciary has been independent. The percentage of rulings against the government is not, however, an accurate proxy for judicial autonomy. For instance, most statistical studies of rulings do not take into account that courts often refuse to hear cases in which the government has an interest. A high percentage of rulings against the executive may obscure the fact that courts rule only on issues of little political significance to the government. Moreover, the difficulties in assessing a ruling's importance to the government lead to problems in weighting cases. Although a good start, a large-*n* study is not enough on its own. Such a study would be useful in conjunction with a consideration of the other four indicators put forth in this book. See Gretchen Helmke, "The Logic of Strategic Defection: Court-Executive Relations in Argentina Under Dictatorship and Democracy," *American Political Science Review* 96 (June 2002): 291–303. For another excellent quantitative analysis of Supreme Court independence in Argentina, see Matías Iaryczower, Pablo T. Spiller, and Mariano Tommasi, "Judicial Independence in Unstable Environments, Argentina 1935–98," *American Journal of Political Science* 46 (October 2002): 699–719.

61. Becker, *Judicial Politics*, 214. See M. J. C. Vile, *Constitutionalism and the Separation of Powers* (Oxford: Oxford University Press, 1967), 158.

62. U.S. history illustrates that judicial autonomy requires neutrality not just from the president but detachment from partisan politics. As Supreme Court rulings during Franklin Roosevelt's first term illustrate, a Court can be relentlessly hostile to the president because it favors an opposing ideological view. Because this has not been the major problem in the ultrapresidential systems of Latin America, this book uses rulings against the executive branch as an indicator.

63. Jerome Alan Cohen, "The Chinese Communist Party and 'Judicial Independence,' 1949–59," *Harvard Law Review* 82 (March 1969): 972. Although often considered ideal, the U.S. judiciary has at times demonstrated subservience to the other branches of government.

Chapter 2

1. It is important to keep in mind that judicial autonomy is a continuous rather than a dichotomous variable. The judiciary did not shift from total autonomy to total subordination in 1946. Instead, the decline in independence began in 1930 when the Court embraced the de facto doctrine and began to show some restraint in exercising judicial review. As this chapter illustrates, however, practices such as purging

and packing the Supreme Court did not emerge until 1946. Because the decline began with the first military coup in 1930, some scholars treat the 1862–1930 period rather than the 1862–1946 period as an era of high judicial autonomy. See Jonathan Miller, "Judicial Review and Constitutional Stability: A Sociology of the U.S. Model and its Collapse in Argentina," *Hastings International and Comparative Law Review* 21 (fall 1998): 79–80; Mariano Grondona, *La realidad: El despertar del sueño argentino* (Buenos Aires: Planeta, 2001), 160–62. Note also that until 1912, Argentina was what Dahl calls a "competitive oligarchy." Gibson refers to pre-1912 Argentina as an "oligarchic regime." The 1912 Sáenz Peña law granted universal male suffrage, and women gained the right to vote in 1947. In addition, electoral fraud was commonplace during this early era of Argentine history. See Edward Gibson, *Class and Conservative Parties: Argentina in Comparative Perspective* (Baltimore: Johns Hopkins University Press, 1996); Robert A. Dahl, *Polyarchy: Participation and Opposition* (New Haven: Yale University Press, 1971), 133–34.

2. Santos Primo Amadeo, *Argentine Constitutional Law: The Judicial Function in the Maintenance of the Federal System and the Preservation of Individual Rights* (New York: Columbia University Press, 1943), 55. In 1944, Argentine legal scholar Luis Méndez Calzada echoed Amadeo's assessment when he described the judiciary as Argentina's strongest institution and as a source of pride for the Argentine people. See Méndez Calzada, *La función judicial en las primeras épocas de la independencia: Estudio sobre la formación evolutiva del poder judicial argentino* (Buenos Aires: Editorial Losada, 1994), 9.

3. Raúl Alfonsín, "'Never Again' in Argentina," *Journal of Democracy* 4 (January 1993): 15.

4. Because most Argentine presidents have respected judges' salary protection, this chapter uses the de facto doctrine rather than respect for salary protection as the fifth indicator of executive subordination of the courts.

5. Amadeo, *Constitutional Law*, 6, 12–23. General Juan Manuel de Rosas, who ruled Argentina from 1829 until 1852, temporarily abolished the formal institutions providing for judicial independence.

6. The only period during which the 1853 constitution did not guide Argentina was under Perón's short-lived 1949 constitution that was repealed in 1956. The 1949 constitution bolstered Perón's dominance by permitting his indefinite reelection and expanding his emergency powers. The 1853 constitution has been amended five times: 1860, 1866, 1898, 1957, and 1994.

7. Amadeo, *Constitutional Law*, 33. See Segundo V. Linares Quintana, *El espíritu de la constitución* (Buenos Aires: Ad Hoc, 1993), 47–52.

8. *Constitución de la República Argentina* (1853), art. 96.

9. See Chapter 3 for a discussion of the 1994 reform, including an analysis of the Judicial Council and the Impeachment Jury.

10. N. Guillermo Molinelli, M. Valeria Palanza, and Gisela Sin, *Congreso, presidencia y justicia en Argentina: Materiales para su estudio* (Buenos Aires: Temas Grupo Editorial, 1999), 686. This percentage is even higher than in the United States where 63 percent of Supreme Court nominees have had previous experience as jurists. See Jeffrey A. Segal and Harold J. Spaeth, *The Supreme Court and the Attitudinal Model* (Cambridge: Cambridge University Press, 1993), 128.

11. Roberto Repetto, "Corte Suprema," *Nación* (Buenos Aires), 28 September 1989. See Clodomiro Zavalía, *Historia de la Corte Suprema de Justicia de la República Argentina en relación con su modelo americano* (Buenos Aires: Talleres Casa Jacobo Peuser, 1920), 61. All translations in this book are mine.

12. Zavalía, *Historia de la Corte Suprema*, 57–74; Miller, "Courts and the Creation of a 'Spirit of Moderation': Judicial Protection of Revolutionaries in Argentina, 1863–1929," *Hastings International and Comparative Law Review* 20 (fall 1997): 242–44; Silvestre Aquino, "1863: Corte Suprema," *El Liberal* (Santiago del Estero), 15 January 1992.

13. Félix Luna, Argentine historian, interview by author, Buenos Aires, 3 November 1998; Alejandro Carrió, *La Corte Suprema y su independencia* (Buenos Aires: Abeledo-Perrot, 1996), 50–52. Luna illustrates the loyalty of Perón's appointees with an anecdote: When the federal government intervened in the province of Córdoba, Perón designated a Supreme Court justice, Felipe Pérez, to restructure the provincial judiciary. Pérez compelled the new Córdoba justices to declare their allegiance to Perón.

14. Molinelli, Palanza, and Sin, *Congreso, presidencia y justicia*, 686. See Carrió, *Corte*, 79; Adolfo R. Gabrielli, *La Corte Suprema de Justicia y la opinión pública: 1976–1983* (Buenos Aires: Abeledo-Perrot, 1986), 19–21.

15. D'Alessio, former Supreme Court clerk (1980–82), interview by author, Buenos Aires, 23 November 1998; Gelli, interview by author, Buenos Aires, 2 December 1998; Durrieu, interview by author, Buenos Aires, 15 October 1998; Gabrielli, interview by author, Buenos Aires, 1 December 1998.

16. As Chapter 1 argues, scholars who base their conclusions about the level of judicial independence solely on the percentage of rulings against the government overlook other important indicators, such as respect for judges' tenure protection.

17. Arslanian, interview by author, Buenos Aires, 7 December 1998. Arslanian reports that he never felt pressure from the government during his 1983–88 tenure as an appellate court judge.

18. Gil Lavedra, interview by author, Buenos Aires, 14 March 2003.

19. When D'Alessio asked Alfonsín about the mistaken assumption, Alfonsín responded, "I don't know why, but I was convinced you were a Peronist." D'Alessio, interview; Ibarra, interview by author, Buenos Aires, 9 December 1998.

20. Supreme Court Justice, interview by author, Buenos Aires. When the name of an interviewee is not provided, it is because he or she wished to be identified only by profession. Occasionally, the date of the interview is also omitted in order to further protect the anonymity of the interviewee.

21. "La justicia en la Argentina," *Ámbito Financiero* (Buenos Aires), 11 September 1989.

22. "Se van tres ministros," *Ámbito Financiero*, 1 August 1989.

23. "Se completó la Corte," *Nuevo Sur* (Buenos Aires), 21 April 1990; "Renunció Bacqué," *Cronista* (Buenos Aires), 18 April 1990; "Jura hoy Moliné O'Connor," *Cronista*, 6 August 1990. In contrast to Moliné O'Connor, Oyhanarte had an extensive publication record and a long judicial career. In fact, he had served as a Supreme Court justice during the 1958–62 administration of Arturo Frondizi.

24. Horacio Verbitsky, *Hacer la Corte: La construcción de un poder absoluto sin justicia ni control* (Buenos Aires: Planeta, 1993), 52; "Acuerdo para los nuevos integrantes," *Clarín* (Buenos Aires), 20 April 1990; "Senado: radicales ausentes," *Nación*, 20 April 1990.

25. Barra, interview by author, Buenos Aires, 13 November 1998. Barra acknowledges that Bauzá and Corach were his *padrinos*, his godfathers or patrons.

26. Raúl Baglini et al., *Juicio a la Corte* (Buenos Aires: Mecanografix, 1993), 101; Marcela Goldin, "Una Corte descartable," *Noticias*, 10 October 1993, 78.

27. Verbitsky, *Hacer la Corte*, 56.

28. Baglini, *Juicio*, 101–02.

29. Baglini, *Juicio*, 81; Verbitsky, *Hacer la Corte*, 53–56.

30. Cavagna Martínez, interview by author, Buenos Aires, 27 November 1998. Cavagna Martínez speaks with pride of his father's post as Perón's Foreign Minister before the 1955 coup and points to photographs of Perón displayed prominently in his office.

31. "Buen amigo de Eduardo Menem," *Nación*, 22 December 1993; Eduardo Bocco, "Resignado a que lo llamen menemista," *La Voz del Interior* (Córdoba), 17 November 1996; Enrique Llamas de Madariaga, "Quién es quién," *Ámbito Financiero*, 11 April 1990. Like Cavagna Martínez, however, Levene was a prestigious legal scholar.

32. Corporate attorney, interview by author, Buenos Aires, 1998; "Apoyo de la iglesia," *Página 12* (Buenos Aires), 24 April 1993; Andrea Rodríguez, "El turno de Boggiano," *Página 12*, 24 April 1993. Boggiano had been a law professor since 1971. In 1981, he became an Appellate Court judge.

33. "Después del terremoto," *Río Negro* (General Roca), 18 December 1993; Dolores Olveira, "La renovación de la Corte," *Cronista*, 20 December 1993; Adrián Ventura, "Continúa en crisis," *Nación*, 22 February 1994.

34. "Vázquez admitió que fue nombrado en la Corte por ser amigo de Menem," *Prensa* (Buenos Aires), 29 November 1995; Alberto Amato, "Un operativo que aún no se aclara," *Clarín*, 30 November 1995.

35. "Senado prepara calvarios," *Ámbito Financiero*, 29 November 1995; "Vázquez a la Corte," *Río Negro*, 8 December 1995.

36. "Vázquez admitió," *Prensa*, 29 November 1995; "Vázquez," *Diario Popular* (Buenos Aires), 16 December 1995. Vázquez's poor performance in law school also suggests that the criterion for his appointment was friendship rather than merit. He graduated from law school with an average score of five out of a possible ten. See "Vázquez ya es tema," *Prensa*, 6 December 1995; Jorge Rodríguez Duval, "Vázquez dijo que le costó sangre ser abogado," *Nación*, 7 December 1995.

37. "Un juez de la Corte," *Página 12*, 2 July 1996.

38. Lucas Guagnini, Santiago O'Donnell, and Ernesto Semán, "El Estado contra Vázquez," *Tres Puntos*, 25 September 1997, 10. Vázquez acknowledged his bias on the Argentine television program *Hora Clave*.

39. Jorge Maiorano, National Ombudsman, interview by author, Buenos Aires, 25 November 1998.

40. Bindo Caviglione Fraga, Federal Judge, interview by author, Buenos Aires, 22

October 1998; Andrea Campbell, "Scandals Hit Argentine Judiciary," *Financial Times*, 13 May 1998.

41. "No hay seguridad," *Crónica*, 24 February 1993; Baglini, *Juicio*, 9–12; Melchor Rene Cruchaga, UCR Congressman, interview by author, Buenos Aires, 7 December 1998.

42. "Frepaso presses for S. Court's impeachment," *Buenos Aires Herald*, 6 June 1998. Bossert, Belluscio, Petracchi, and Fayt were not considered part of the automatic majority.

43. Calculated from data in Molinelli, Palanza, and Sin, *Congreso, presidencia y justicia*, 678–81, 690.

44. Rosendo Fraga, *Los 90: La ilusión perdida* (Buenos Aires: El Ateneo, 2001), 179–83.

45. Calculated from data in Molinelli, Palanza, and Sin, *Congreso, presidencia y justicia*, 690.

46. Hugo Gambini, *Historia del Peronismo: El poder total, 1943–1951* (Buenos Aires: Planeta, 1999), 92–98; Luna, *La Argentina era una fiesta, 1946–49*, vol. 1 of *Perón y su tiempo* (Buenos Aires: Editorial Sudamericana, 1984), 58–62.

47. Eugenio Raúl Zaffaroni, *Estructuras judiciales* (Buenos Aires: Ediar Sociedad Anónima Editora, 1994), 64–65, 267; "Corte en tiempo de los militares," *Prensa*, 24 March 1996.

48. Robert E. Biles, "The Position of the Judiciary in the Political Systems of Argentina and Mexico," *Lawyer of the Americas* 8 (1976): 291, 314.

49. Biles, "Position," 290–91; Gabriel Negretto and Mark Ungar, "Independencia del poder judicial y estado de derecho en América Latina: Los casos de Argentina y Venezuela," *Política y Gobierno* 4 (1997): 99–100; Carrió, *Corte*, 43; Nélida Rebollo, "Suprema Corte," *Diario de Cuyo*, 10 October 1993.

50. Cited in Celia Szusterman, *Frondizi and the Politics of Developmentalism in Argentina, 1955–62* (London: Macmillan, 1993), 143–44.

51. Rosenn, "Judicial Review in Latin America," *Ohio State Law Journal*, 35 (1974): 810; Zaffaroni, *Estructuras*, 264–67.

52. Alejandro M. Garro, "The Role of the Argentine Judiciary in Controlling Governmental Action under a State of Siege," *Human Rights Law Journal* 4 (1983): 315; Verbitsky, *Hacer la Corte*, 18–19; Bindo Caviglione Fraga, interview by author, Buenos Aires, 22 October 1998. Judge Caviglione Fraga recalls his fear of removal by the junta.

53. Christopher Larkins, "Judicial Independence and Democratization: A Theoretical and Conceptual Analysis," *American Journal of Comparative Law* 44 (fall 1996): 621–24. In 1983, the Argentine civil society group FORES led a campaign calling on Alfonsín to remove judges through constitutional channels. FORES, *Por el poder judicial: La estabilidad de los jueces como principio esencial* (Buenos Aires: FORES, 1983). Alfonsín's defenders stress that the military regime did not use the judiciary in accordance with constitutional norms. Fiss asserts that life tenure should be "regime-relative," meaning that after democratic transitions, civilian administrations should dismiss judges inherited from military regimes. See Owen Fiss, "The Right Degree of Independence," in *Transition to Democracy in Latin America: The Role of the Judiciary*, ed. Irwin P. Stotzky (Boulder: Westview, 1993), 63–64.

54. Fayt, interview by author, Buenos Aires, 29 October 1998; Héctor Simeoni, "Rompecabezas judicial," *Somos* (Buenos Aires), 16 August 1989. In response to the ambassadorship offer, Fayt gave Menem's messenger a copy of his book, *Teoría de política*, and pointed the chapter entitled "Ethics and Politics," declaring he would not consider the unethical offer.

55. "Barra acató la orden," *Crónica*, 2 December 1993; Ventura, "Jurarán Bossert y López," *Nación*, 29 March 1994; "'Jubilarán' a miembros de la Corte," *Crónica*, 23 November 1993.

56. Barra, interview; Cavagna Martínez, interview.

57. Nancy Pazos, "Levene aún no se quiere ir," *Clarín*, 27 February 1994; Vicente Muleiro, "La resistencia de Levene no afecta al pacto," *Clarín*, 2 March 1994; "Levene sin salida por el juicio," *Ámbito Financiero*, 19 March 1994. Interior Minister Bauzá ordered the head of the House Impeachment.Committee, Alberto Balestrini (PJ), to dismiss all charges against Levene. Balestrini resisted the order, but the PJ majority in the Committee ultimately absolved all Menem appointees. "La Corte ya tiene tres nuevos miembros," *Prensa*, 11 December 1993; Orlando Baratta, "Absolvieron a la Corte," *Ámbito Financiero*, 21 June 1995.

58. Szusterman, *Frondizi*, 143–44.

59. Barry Weingast, "The Political Foundations of Democracy and the Rule of Law," *American Political Science Review* 91 (June 1997): 254. Court-packing is a viable policy in cases of "asymmetric equilibrium," meaning that citizens have not resolved the coordination dilemma or established a social consensus regarding limits on the state.

60. See José A. Coronel, "El poder legislativo y la Corte," *Nueva Provincia*, 2 October 1989.

61. Verbitsky, *Hacer la Corte*, 35; "Compás de espera hasta diciembre," *Somos*, 4 October 1989.

62. "El texto completo de la acordada," *Nación*, 23 September 1989; "Reiteró la Corte su oposición," *Clarín*, 8 February 1990; Román Lejtman, "Los informes de la Corte," *Página 12*, 9 February 1990.

63. Supreme Court justice, interview by author, Buenos Aires.

64. Daniel Lupa, "Corte Suprema," *Prensa*, 27 September 1989; "Oposición a la reforma," *Nación*, 9 February 1990; Ernesto Tenembaum, "Para Durañona y Vedia el siete es buen número," *Página 12*, 2 February 1990.

65. "Argentina: Controversy Surrounding the Judiciary." *International Commission of Jurists Review* 45 (1990): 5. See Baglini, *Juicio*, 53–56; Verbitsky, "Argentina Retreats from Democracy," *New York Times*, 3 October 1992; Verbitsky, *Hacer la Corte*, 47–51.

66. This occurred in Buenos Aires. First instance courts in Argentina are the equivalent of district courts in the United States.

67. Federal prosecutor, interview by author, Buenos Aires. See Gustavo Beliz, "Corrupción: ¿El fin de la política?" in *No robarás: ¿Es posible ganarle a la corrupción?* ed. Beliz (Buenos Aires: Editorial de Belgrano, 1997), 144–46.

68. Arslanian, interview.

69. Amadeo, *Constitutional Law*, 73–74; Miller, "Courts," 238–42. See Humberto Quiroga Lavié, *Constitución de la nación argentina comentada*, 3d ed. (Buenos Aires: Zavalía, 2000), 698.

70. *Constitución de la República Argentina* (1853), art. 31; *Constitución de la República Argentina* (1994), art. 31.

71. *Constitución de la República Argentina* (1853), art. 100; *Constitución de la República Argentina* (1994), art. 116.

72. See Fayt, *La supremacía constitucional y la independencia de los jueces* (Buenos Aires: Depalma, 1994), 26–27.

73. Phanor J. Eder, "Judicial Review in Latin America," *Ohio State Law Journal* 21 (1960): 576; Rosenn, "Judicial Review," 787–88.

74. Fayt, *Supremacía*, 125–28, 162; Biles, "Position," 308; Eder, "Judicial Review," 576.

75. In *Ríos*, the Court ruled that the president cannot exercise or delegate judicial powers. The president had granted judicial authority to a military official, allowing the official to rule on a murder committed on board a ship. Carrió, *Corte*, 33–34; Eder, "Judicial Review," 576; Fayt, *Supremacía*, 29; Carlos S. Nino, "On the Exercise of Judicial Review in Argentina," in *Transition to Democracy in Latin America: The Role of the Judiciary*, ed. Irwin P. Stotzky (Boulder: Westview, 1993), 316–17.

76. Cited in Nino, "Judicial Review," 316–17. See Carrió, *Corte*, 36; Fayt, *Supremacía*, 29–30.

77. Fayt, *Supremacía*, 69. Eduardo Sojo, a newspaper editor, had appealed directly to the Supreme Court after Congress had ordered his imprisonment for publishing a drawing considered offensive to the legislature. Sojo bypassed the lower courts and went directly to the Supreme Court with his habeas corpus plea. According to the constitution, the Court has original jurisdiction only in cases concerning ambassadors, foreign diplomats, or an Argentine province. In order to bypass first instance and appellate courts, Sojo claimed that an 1863 law extended the Court's original jurisdiction. The Court ruled that the constitution prevails when in conflict with a law.

78. Miller, "Courts," 259–62. Miller makes the important point that the Court did not review electoral results or take other steps to reduce the electoral fraud that characterized this early period of Argentina's history.

79. For an analysis of Supreme Court protection of the press, see Miller, "Judicial Review," 113–30.

80. Carrió, *Corte*, 47–50; Kenneth L. Karst and Keith S. Rosenn, *Law and Development in Latin America: A Case Book* (Berkeley: University of California Press, 1975), 196–98.

81. Carrió, *Corte*, 51–53.

82. Cited in Margaret Popkin, "Efforts to Enhance Judicial Independence in Latin America," in U.S. Agency for International Development, *Guidance for Promoting Judicial Independence and Impartiality*, rev. ed., Technical Publication Series, January 2002, 101.

83. Marguerite Feitlowitz, *A Lexicon of Terror: Argentina and the Legacies of Terror* (Oxford: Oxford University Press, 1998), 257, note 1.

84. Zaffaroni, *Estructuras*, 268; Zaffaroni, interview by author, Buenos Aires, 1 July 1999. Zaffaroni explains that by killing lawyers who introduced habeas corpus cases, the government reduced the number of lawyers who would present such cases. Between March 1976 and January 1978, junta security forces murdered 23 lawyers, detained 109 lawyers, and "disappeared" 41 lawyers. See Garro, "Argentine Judiciary,"

316. For more on the Timerman case, see Carrió, *Corte*, 105–8; Gabrielli, *Corte*, 101–26.

85. Former president Jimmy Carter and the Vatican were among the high profile international actors that advocated for Timerman's release.

86. See Mariano Grondona, "Peligro en la Corte Suprema," *Nación*, 27 August 1989.

87. Nino, *Fundamentos de derecho constitucional* (Buenos Aires: Astrea, 1992), 668–73; Carlos Manuel Garrido, "Informe sobre Argentina," in *Situación y políticas judiciales en América Latina*, ed. Jorge Correa Sutil (Santiago: Escuela de Derecho, Universidad Diego Portalis, 1993), 67–68; Stotzky and Nino, "The Difficulties of the Transition Process," in *Transition to Democracy in Latin America*, 12; Enrique Zuleta Puceiro, "Justicia y política," *El Economista* (Buenos Aires), 6 October 1989.

88. Bacqué, interview by author, Buenos Aires, 13 October 1998; Belluscio, interview by author, Buenos Aires, 13 March 2003; Petracchi, interview by author, Buenos Aires, 13 March 2003. According to Bacqué, "No official ever asked me for anything—not Alfonsín, not the Justice Minister, not a special messenger."

89. Supreme Court Justice, interview by author, Buenos Aires.

90. Bacqué, interview.

91. Carrió, *Corte*, 160–68; Baglini, *Juicio*, 147–49. In his dissenting opinion, Petracchi wrote, "The members of this Court did not take our oaths to facilitate or obstruct government proposals; we took our oaths for the sole purpose of deciding whether those proposals are constitutional." Cited in Baglini, *Juicio*, 18.

92. Fernando J. Cafferata, *Nuevas instituciones en la constitución nacional* (Córdoba, Argentina: Marcos Lerner Editora Córdoba, 1996), 125–32; Carrió, *Corte*, 174–77; Alberto B. Bianchi, "La Corte Suprema ha establecido su tesis oficial sobre la emergencia económica," *La Ley* 41 (1991): 141–91. The Plan Bonex decree was part of Menem's economic plan to address hyperinflation. Before 1990, economic emergency had served as a justification for congressional laws rather than presidential decrees. In recognition that *Peralta* involved an executive decree, the Court asserted need to interpret the doctrine of separation of powers in a "flexible" way, thereby degrading the important principle. See Chapter 3 for an in-depth discussion of decrees of necessity and urgency.

93. "Crítica a la aplicación del recurso," *Nación*, 19 September 1990; Armando Vidal, *El Congreso en la trampa: Entretelones y escándalos de la vida parlamentaria* (Buenos Aires: Planeta, 1995), 73–75; Bianchi, "¿Ha llegado la Corte Suprema al final de su lucha por una jurisdicción discrecional?" *El Derecho* 172 (1997): 935–37; "Vía libre al 'per saltum,'" *Somos*, 12 September 1990; Fabián Doman, "Per saltum," *Ámbito Financiero*, 9 August 1990. For Fayt's dissenting opinion, see Fayt, *Supremacía*, 104–15.

94. Colegio de Abogados de General Roca, "El fin no justifica los medios," *Río Negro*, 6 October 1993; "Dos miembros del alto tribunal," *Crónica*, 10 October 1993. The lawyer sought payment for his work for a bank that was in liquidation, Banco Patagónico. He turned to the bank in charge of the liquidation, Argentina's Central Bank, because Banco Patagónico could not pay his fees. The Menem administration argued that the June 8 ruling would have caused enormous financial damage to the Central Bank because it would have provoked similar cases. Economy Minister

Domingo Cavallo admitted that he had warned Boggiano that the original ruling would have hurt the Argentine economy. Hearings on the lost ruling revealed that Boggiano's assistant had removed the ruling from the records. See Verbitsky, "La suprema justificación," *Página 12*, 1 October 1993; Sergio Crivelli, "¿Otro parodia?" *Prensa*, 8 March 1994; "Acusan a secretario de Boggiano," *Crónica*, 25 November 1993; Ventura, "Investigan en la Corte," *Nación*, 20 September 1993; Alberto Amato, "Tensión en la Corte," *Clarín*, 11 November 1993; "Auditores avalan que faltó una sentencia," *Crónica*, 10 November 1993; "Abren periodo de pruebas," *Diario Popular*, 14 October 1993; Diego Llumá, "No aparece una salida para la crisis," *La Capital* (Rosario), 25 October 1993.

95. Baglini, *Juicio*, 151–55; Carrió, *Corte*, 186–98; Verbitsky, *Hacer la Corte*, 211–18; "Corte Suprema a la cuestión 'Corrientes,'" *El Litoral* (Corrientes), 14 January 1992. The Buenos Aires Bar Association argued that the unconstitutional intervention in Corrientes was a clear example of executive subordination of the Court. "Corrientes: Dudas del Colegio de Abogados," *Nación*, 23 September 1992.

96. "Severa crítica," *Prensa*, 13 January 1992; Ricardo V. Canaletti, "La balanza de la justicia," *Clarín*, 12 January 1992; Verbitsky, *Hacer la Corte*, 191–97. Note that this chapter addresses only a few of the high profile cases that suggest executive subordination of the judiciary. Other such decisions include *Unión Ferroviaria* (Court intervened in the elections of a private entity to ensure that a Menemist remained union president); *Radio Nacional* (Court overturned a lower court decision that had ordered a public radio station to reinstate a program, which had been cancelled because it criticized Menem policies); and *Soengas* (Court sided with the Menem administration by ruling that economic emergency was sufficient justification for the government to restrict workers' rights). See Julio C. Fernández, "Los abogados laboralista piden juicio político," *El Informador Público*, 25 September 1992 and Baglini, *Juicio*, 156–62.

97. Linares Quintana, "Comparison of the Constitutional Basis of the United States and the Argentine Political Systems," *University of Pennsylvania Law Review* 97 (April 1949): 658; Banks and Carrió, "Presidential Systems," 27. For the text of the ruling, see Fayt, *Nuevas fronteras del derecho constitucional: La dimensión político-institucional de la Corte Suprema de la Nación* (Buenos Aires: La Ley, 1995), 111–12.

98. Carrió, *Corte*, 46; Fayt, *Nuevas fronteras*, 113; Linares Quintana, "Comparison," 658.

99. Cited in Nino, "Judicial Review," 318; Fayt, *Nuevas fronteras*, 115.

100. Karst and Rosenn, *Law and Development*, 196

101. Garro, "Argentine Judiciary," 314, note 6.

102. Nino, "Judicial Review," 319; Stotzky and Nino, "Difficulties," 13; Baglini, *Juicio*, 126–28.

103. Baglini, *Juicio*, 126–28; Nino, "Judicial Review," 319.

104. Department of State, *Country Reports on Human Rights Practices for 1995*, report submitted to the Committee on International Relations, U.S. House of Representatives and the Committee on Foreign Relations, U.S. Senate, April 1996, 316. See James H. Andrews, "Lawyers and Judges Worldwide Risk Their Lives for Human Rights," *Christian Science Monitor*, 2 May 1994; "The Meaning of Menemism," *Economist*, 26 November 1994; Freedom House, *Freedom in the World 1994–1995* (New York: Freedom House, 1995), 107.

105. World Economic Forum and Center for International Development at Harvard University, *Global Competitiveness Report 2000* (Oxford: Oxford University Press, 2000), 248.

106. Lynch, interview by author, Buenos Aires, 5 October 1998; Mustapic, interview; Smulovitz, interview by author, Buenos Aires, 20 October 1998; Gelli, interview. FORES formed in 1977 with the goal of improving the administration of justice in Argentina.

107. "Cavallo," *Ámbito Financiero*, 31 October 1996; "Cavallo desató un terremoto," *La Capital* (Mar del Plata), 16 October 1996; "El contragolpe de Cavallo," *El Día* (La Plata), 16 October 1996.

108. Carrió, interview by author, Buenos Aires, 26 November 1998; Vanossi, interview by author, Buenos Aires, 4 November 1998; Cruchaga, interview.

109. "Casi 6 de cada 10 personas desconfían," *La Maga* (Buenos Aires), 16 September 1992.

110. Centro de Estudios Judiciales de la República Argentina (CEJURA), *Estudio de opinión acerca de la administración de justicia*, Study conducted by Instituto Gallup Argentina (Buenos Aires: La Ley, 1994), 17.

111. Elena Highton with Elias Jassan, "Judicial Reform in Argentina," in *Judicial Reform in Latin America and the Caribbean*, ed. Malcolm Rowat, Waleed H. Malik, and Maria Dakolias (Washington, D.C.: World Bank, 1995), 176.

112. CEUNM, "Imagen específica del poder judicial," *La imagen de la justicia en la Argentina*, June 1996.

113. Grondona, "Cómo pasar del descreimiento," *Nación*, 20 October 1996.

114. Andrea Rodríguez, "Hacete amigo," *Página 12*, 13 December 1992. In the survey, 66 percent of attorneys admitted to having witnessed or participated in a corrupt act such as paying a judge for a favorable ruling.

115. Federal prosecutor, interview by author, Buenos Aires; Federal judge, interview by author, Buenos Aires; Supreme Court justices, interviews by author, Buenos Aires. Bossert attributed his 2002 resignation from the Supreme Court to "*hartazgo espiritual*," or spiritual exhaustion, stemming from the subordination of the judiciary that he witnessed during his tenure on the Court. Bossert, resignation letter to Eduardo A. Duhalde, President of Argentina, 21 October 2002.

Chapter 3

1. Collier and Collier define "critical juncture" as a "period of significant change, which typically occurs in distinct ways in different countries and which is hypothesized to produce different legacies." Ruth Berins Collier and David Collier, *Shaping the Political Arena: Critical Junctures, the Labor Movement, and Regime Dynamics in Latin America* (Princeton: Princeton University Press, 1991), 29.

2. Karen L. Remmer, *Party Competition in Argentina and Chile: Political Recruitment and Public Policy, 1890–1930* (Lincoln: University of Nebraska Press, 1984), 24–33; Jeane Kirkpatrick, *Leader and Vanguard in Mass Society: A Study of Peronist Argentina* (Cambridge: MIT Press, 1971), 21–24.

3. Remmer, *Party Competition*, 27–31; Susan Calvert and Peter Calvert, *Argentina: Political Culture and Instability* (Pittsburgh: University of Pittsburgh Press, 1989), 90–

91; Guillermo Molinelli, *Presidentes y congresos en Argentina: Mitos y realidades* (Buenos Aires: Grupo Editor Latinoamericano, 1991), 104; Paula Alonso, *Between Revolution and the Ballot Box: The Origins of the Argentine Radical Party* (Cambridge: Cambridge University Press, 2000), 163.

4. Alonso, *Revolution*, 162–67.

5. James R. Scobie, *Argentina: A City and a Nation*, 2d ed. (Oxford: Oxford University Press, 1971), 205.

6. Cited in Alonso, *Revolution*, 164.

7. Molinelli, "Sobre 'gobierno unificado / dividido' en América Latina," unpublished manuscript, 4 April 1998, 23.

8. Mark Falcoff and Ronald H. Dolkart, "Political Developments," in *Prologue to Perón: Argentina in Depression and War, 1930–1943*, ed. Falcoff and Dolkart (Berkeley: University of California Press, 1975), 32–36.

9. Chapter 2 demonstrates that the decline in judicial independence began in the wake of the 1930 coup. As the theory of competitive politics predicts, the decline began during a period of monolithic control.

10. Félix Luna, *La Argentina era una fiesta, 1946–49*, vol. 1 of *Perón y su tiempo* (Buenos Aires: Editorial Sudamericana, 1984), 58–62; Robert J. Alexander, *Juan Domingo Perón: A History* (Boulder: Westview, 1979), 48–61; Robert E. Scott, "Legislatures and Legislation," in *Government and Politics in Latin America*, ed. Harold Eugene Davis (New York: Ronald Press, 1958), 321.

11. Cited in Robert D. Crassweller, *Perón and the Enigmas of Argentina* (New York: W.W. Norton & Co., 1987), 189.

12. Hugo Gambini, *Historia del Peronismo: El poder total, 1943–1951* (Buenos Aires: Planeta, 1999), 81–88; Alexander, *Perón*, 48–50, 57–61; Crassweller, *Perón*, 186–97. In his study of roll-call votes, Smith demonstrates that the connection between partisan affiliation and legislative voting grew more pronounced over the course of Perón's first term. Peter H. Smith, *Argentina and the Failure of Democracy: Conflict among Political Elites, 1904–1955* (Madison: University of Wisconsin Press, 1974), 60–87.

13. Peter G. Snow, *Political Forces in Argentina*, rev. ed. (New York: Praeger, 1979), 46–47; Daniel Rodríguez Lamas, *La presidencia de Frondizi* (Buenos Aires: Centro Editor de América Latina, 1984), 72–73; Celia Szusterman, *Frondizi and the Politics of Developmentalism in Argentina, 1955–62* (London: Macmillan, 1993), 131–43. The 1960 bill allowed private companies to invest in Argentina's natural resources.

14. Luigi Manzetti, *Institutions, Parties, and Coalitions in Argentine Politics* (Pittsburgh: University of Pittsburgh Press, 1993), 43, 93–94. In the 1950s, the UCR split into two parties: the UCRI and the Unión Cívica Radical del Pueblo (UCRP).

15. Guillermo Molinelli, interview by author, Buenos Aires, 28 September 1998. In 1984, the Senate rejected an unprecedented sixteen nominees for appellate court judges.

16. Verbitsky, interview by author, Buenos Aires, 3 December 1998; Elisa Carrió, UCR Congresswoman, interview by author, Buenos Aires, 26 November 1998.

17. Joaquín Morales Solá, *Asalto a la ilusión* (Buenos Aires: Planeta, 1990), 82–85.

18. Delia Ferreira Rubio and Matteo Goretti, "Cuando el presidente gobierna solo: Menem y los decretos de necesidad y urgencia hasta la reforma constitucional," *Desarrollo Económico* 36 (April–June 1996): 444–45; Ana María Mustapic, "Oficialis-

tas y diputados: Las relaciones ejecutivo-legislativo en la Argentina" (paper presented at the conference on Legislaturas en América Latina: Perspectivas Comparadas, Mexico City, February 1998), 2.

19. Steven Levitsky, "An Organized Disorganization: Informal Structures and the Persistence of Mass Organization in Argentine Peronism" (paper presented at the annual Latin American Studies Association meeting, Miami, Fla., March 2000), 3–4, 12–20.

20. Morales Solá, *Asalto*, 92–93; Miguel De Luca, Mark P. Jones, and María Inés Tula, "Argentine Political Parties and Their Candidate Nomination Procedures: 1983–89," (paper presented at the annual Latin American Studies Association meeting, Miami, Fla., March 2000), 7–11. De Luca, Jones, and Tula characterize Menem as a strong party leader in the style of Perón. See James W. McGuire, *Peronism Without Perón: Unions, Parties, and Democracy in Argentina* (Stanford: Stanford University Press, 1997).

21. Jones, "Explaining the High Level of Party Discipline in the Argentine Congress," in *Legislative Politics in Latin America*, ed. Scott Morgenstern and Benito Nacif (Cambridge: Cambridge University Press, 2002), 151–58; Jones, "Evaluating Argentina's Presidential Democracy: 1983–95," in *Presidentialism and Democracy in Latin America*, ed. Scott Mainwaring and Matthew Soberg Shugart (Cambridge: Cambridge University Press, 1997), 279. See Ana M. Mustapic y Matteo Goretti, "Gobierno y oposición en el Congreso: La práctica de la cohabitación durante la presidencia de Alfonsín (1983–89)," *Desarrollo Económico* 32 (July-September 1992): 251–69.

22. Carrió, interview; Vanossi, interview by author, Buenos Aires, 4 November 1998.

23. Levitsky, "Organized Disorganization," 3–4, 12–20.

24. Mustapic, "Oficialistas y diputados," 12.

25. Aguirre Lanari, interview by author, Buenos Aires, 23 October 1998.

26. Supreme Court Justice, interview by author, Buenos Aires; Mariano Obarrio, "Punto final de Menem a la reelección," *Nación*, 1 April 1999; "Frepaso presses for S. Court's impeachment," *Buenos Aires Herald*, 6 June 1998; Clifford Krauss, "Argentine Chief Drops Bid for Third Term," *New York Times*, 22 July 1998.

27. Jorge Urien Berri, "Armas: Maniobra para apartar al juez Urso," *Nación*, 10 November 1998.

28. Jones, "Evaluating Argentina's Presidential Democracy," 271–75.

29. Edgardo Catterberg, *Argentina Confronts Politics: Political Culture and Public Opinion in the Argentine Transition to Democracy* (Boulder: Lynne Rienner, 1991), 50–55; Jones, "Evaluating Argentina's Presidential Democracy," 264; Jones, "Explaining Party Discipline," 150.

30. Gerardo Adrogué, "El nuevo sistema partidario argentino," in *La nueva matriz política argentina*, ed. Carlos H. Acuña (Buenos Aires: Nueva Visión, 1995), 34.

31. See Adrogué, "Sistema partidario," 37, 51–52; Jones, "Evaluating Argentina's Presidential Democracy," 267–69.

32. See De Luca, Jones, and Tula, "Argentine Political Parties," 12–13.

33. David Mayhew, *Congress: The Electoral Connection* (New Haven: Yale University Press, 1974); Bruce Cain, John Ferejohn, and Morris Fiorina, *The Personal Vote: Con-*

stituency Service and Electoral Independence (Cambridge: Harvard University Press, 1987).

34. Lee C. Fennell, "Congress in the Argentine Political System: An Appraisal," in *Latin American Legislatures: Their Role and Influence*, ed. Weston H. Agor (New York: Praeger, 1971), 164–66. For more on closed-list versus open-list systems, see Barry Ames, "Electoral Strategy under Open-List Proportional Representation," *American Journal of Political Science* 30 (May 1995), 406–33; John M. Carey and Matthew Soberg Shugart, "Incentives to Cultivate a Personal Vote: A Rank Ordering of Electoral Systems," *Electoral Studies* 14 (December 1995): 417–40.

35. Austin F. Macdonald, *Government of the Argentine Republic* (New York: Thomas Y. Cromwell, 1942), 205.

36. Jones, "Explaining Party Discipline," 167–77; Jones, "Evaluating Argentina's Presidential Democracy," 262, 283. Jones provides an excellent discussion of the sources of party discipline in Argentina.

37. Jones, "Explaining Party Discipline," 179–83; Mustapic, "Oficialistas y diputados," 8.

38. Jones, "Explaining Party Discipline," 179–83; Fennell, "Congress," 154–57; National Democratic Institute for International Affairs, "Committees in Legislatures: A Division of Labor," Legislative Research Series, Paper no. 2 (Washington, D.C.: National Democratic Institute for International Affairs, 1996), 16–19.

39. Jones, "Explaining Party Discipline," 177–78, 183–84; Peter Ranis, "Profile Variables among Argentine Legislators," in *Latin American Legislatures*, 203.

40. Mustapic, interview by author, Buenos Aires, 27 November 1998.

41. Levitsky, "Organized Disorganization," 11.

42. Mainwaring and Shugart, "Introduction," in *Presidentialism and Democracy*, 4–5.

43. The line-item veto supplemented presidents' strong constitutional veto power, a reactive power. Article 72 of the 1853 constitution and Article 83 of the 1994 constitution stipulate that a two-thirds majority in each house is required to overturn a presidential veto. Under unified government, reaching the high override requirement has been virtually impossible.

44. Molinelli, "El veto parcial: ¿Qué hacer?" *Sentencia* (December 1992): 54–55; Molinelli, "Las relaciones presidente-congreso en Argentina '83-'95," *PostData* 2 (November 1996): 68–70.

45. Molinelli, "Veto parcial," 54–56; Molinelli, "Relaciones," 68–71; Gregorio Badeni, *Reforma constitucional e instituciones políticas* (Buenos Aires: Ad Hoc, 1994), 402–03; Mustapic, "Tribulaciones del Congreso en la nueva democracia argentina: El veto presidencial bajo Alfonsín y Menem," *Agora* 3 (winter 1995): 65–66; María Angélica Gelli, "Veto y promulgación parcial en la reforma constitucional de 1994," in *Estudios sobre la reforma constitucional de 1994*, ed. Germán Bidart Campos and H. R. Sandler (Buenos Aires: Ediciones Depalma, 1995), 185. In *Colella*, the Court declared a line-item veto unconstitutional because President Illia had promulgated only four of 63 articles in a labor contract law. The Court ruled that Illia had undermined the unity of the bill, suggesting that the line-item veto would be valid if this were not the case. In contrast to Argentina, U.S. presidents did not acquire line-item veto authority until the 1996 Line-item Veto Act, which the Supreme Court declared unconstitutional in 1998.

46. Mustapic and Natalia Ferretti, "El veto presidencial bajo Alfonsín and Menem (1983–95)" (paper presented at the annual Latin American Studies Association meeting, Washington, D.C., September 1995), 2; Jones, "Evaluating Argentina's Presidential Democracy," 289.

47. *Constitución de la República Argentina* (1994), art. 82.

48. *Constitución de la República Argentina* (1994), art. 80.

49. *Constitución de la República Argentina* (1994), art. 99.

50. Mainwaring and Shugart, "Introduction," 46–47.

51. Jones, "Evaluating Argentina's Presidential Democracy," 288. Jones points to Menem's 1993 threat to implement a pension reform law by decree if the House did not approve his bill.

52. Ferreira Rubio and Goretti, "Cuando el presidente," 443–56; Molinelli, "Relaciones," 75–77.

53. Ferreira Rubio and Goretti, "Cuando el presidente," 455–66; Molinelli, "Relaciones," 77.

54. Vanossi, "Reglamentación legal de los decretos de necesidad y urgencia," Proyecto de Ley, *Tramite Parlamentario*, no. 32, 12 June 1992, 1843–44. Vanossi proposed that the executive be required to submit DNUs to Congress for approval and to call an extraordinary session during congressional recess. Congress would have ten days to rule on the decree's validity, and congressional inaction would be tantamount to rejection of the DNU.

55. Carrió, interview.

56. *Constitución de la República Argentina* (1994), art. 99.

57. See Mark Ungar, *Elusive Reform: Democracy and the Rule of Law in Latin America* (Boulder: Lynne Rienner, 2002), 169–86.

58. See Adrián Ventura, *Consejo de la Magistratura y Jurado de Enjuiciamiento en el derecho comparado y nacional* (Buenos Aires: Ediciones Depalma, 1998), 205–8.

59. Granillo Ocampo, interview by author, Buenos Aires, 18 November 1998; Cruchaga, "Los riesgos en el proyecto del gobierno," *Agrupación para una Justicia Democrática* 3 (1996): 15–17; Vanossi, "La Constitución evanescente," *La Ley* 58 (2 December 1994): 2. See Eugenio Raúl Zaffaroni, *Estructuras judiciales* (Buenos Aires: Ediar Sociedad Anónima Editora, 1994), 75–77.

60. Critics argue that the high number of politicians (nine of twenty members) violates equilibrium among sectors. Mariano Cavagna Martínez and Rafael Bielsa advocated increasing the number of lawyers and judges, pointing to Spain where twelve of the twenty Judicial Council members are judges. Cavagna Martínez, former Supreme Court justice, interview by author, Buenos Aires, 27 November 1998; Rafael Bielsa and Luis Francisco Lozano, "Apostillas relativas a las Leyes 24.937 y 24.939," *La Ley* 62 (12 November 1998): 2.

61. Carrió, interview; Nilda Garré, Frepaso Congresswoman, interview by author, Buenos Aires, 12 March 2003; "Acuerdo para el Consejo," *Cronista*, 11 October 1996. Congresswomen Carrió and Garré were among the primary authors of the Judicial Council law. Both argue that the 1997 law was a significant improvement over the initial Senate bill.

62. Argentine Law 24,937, Title I, chapt. IV, art. 13. See Carlos Manuel Garrido,

"Informe sobre Argentina," in *Situación y políticas judiciales en América Latina*, ed. Jorge Correa Sutil (Santiago: Universidad Diego Portalis, 1993), 56–57.

63. Bindo Caviglione Fraga, Judicial Council member, interview by author, Buenos Aires, 22 October 1998; Humberto Quiroga Lavié, Judicial Council member, interview by author Buenos Aires, 10 March 2003; Adrián Ventura, journalist, interview by author, Buenos Aires, 12 March 2003, Ricardo Gil Lavedra, Justice Minister (1999–2000), interview by author, Buenos Aires, 14 March 2003. Caviglione Fraga reports that "a positive atmosphere" has characterized Council meetings. Quiroga Lavié explains that the distinct sectors that comprise the Council act as "reciprocal controls that check one another."

64. Orlando Baratta, "Absolvieron a la Corte," *Ámbito Financiero*, 21 June 1995; "Oyarbide," *Clarín*, 8 October 1998.

65. Atilio Bieta, "Otro retraso por la elección de jueces," *Clarín*, 16 November 1996; Andrea Rodríguez, "Yo los pongo, yo los saco," *Página 12*, 30 October 1996; Ventura, "Impulso oficialista," *Nación*, 29 October 1996.

66. Argentine Law 24,937, title II, chapt. 1, arts. 22–26; Caviglione Fraga, interview. Caviglione Fraga declared, "Before, removal was pure politics." Although they commend the depoliticization of the removal process, Garré, Gil Lavedra, Quiroga Lavié, and Ventura report that the Impeachment Jury has been inefficient and slow. Garré, interview; Gil Lavedra, interview; Quiroga Lavié, interview; Ventura, interview.

67. Irwin Stotzky and Carlos Nino, "The Difficulties of the Transition Process," in *Transition to Democracy in Latin America: The Role of the Judiciary*, ed. Stotzky (Boulder: Westview, 1993), 8.

68. Alejandro Carrió, *La Corte Suprema y su independencia* (Buenos Aires: Abeledo-Perrot, 1996), 163; Claudio Andrada, "Procurador se busca," *Clarín*, 24 August 1989.

69. See Alejandro M. Garro, "Staffing the Judiciary and Prosecutorial Offices in Argentina: Trials and Tribulations in Search of Merit, Integrity, and Accountability" (paper presented at the annual Latin American Studies Association meeting, Miami, Fla., March 2000), 5–6.

70. D'Alessio, interview by author, Buenos Aires, 23 November 1998.

71. D'Alessio, interview; "D'Alessio denunció presiones," *Cronista*, 17 October 1996; Carrió, *Corte*, 168.

72. D'Alessio, interview.

73. "La Corte se opone a su ampliación," *Nación*, 22 September 1989; "Roger volcó en libro sus defensas penales," *Voz del Interior*, 10 December 1999; "Un perdido del procurador," *Página 12*, 7 March 1992; Verbitsky, "Los amigos del jefe," *Página 12*, 27 October 1996; Jorge Urien Berri and Alejandra Florit, "La procuración, centro de críticas," *Nación*, 15 October 1996; Verbitsky, "Un Ángel para los funcionarios," *Página 12*, 27 October 1996.

74. Quantín, interview by author, Buenos Aires, 2 July 1999.

75. Ibarra, interview by author, Buenos Aires, 9 December 1998.

76. Federal prosecutors, interviews by author, Buenos Aires, 1998 and 1999.

77. Alejandro Diglio, "Fiscales rigurosamente descuidados," *Nación*, 27 October

1996; "Corach y Jassan manejan a los jueces," *La Arena* (La Pampa), 16 October 1996.

78. "No investigarán al fiscal Stornelli," *Nación*, 5 November 1998; "Un verdadero tiro por la culata," *Clarín*, 5 November 1998; Diego Schurman, "Menem quiere la cabeza de Stornelli," *Página 12*, 4 November 1998; "La Alianza propondrá una oxigenación del poder judicial," *Nación*, 28 October 1997.

79. *Constitución de la República Argentina* (1994), art. 114. Due to widespread concern about the weakness of the Attorney General's Office, representatives at the 1994 Constitutional Convention introduced over thirty proposals to strengthen the Office. Cavagna Martínez, *Labor constituyente: Trabajos desarrollados en la convención nacional constituyente* (Buenos Aires: La Ley, 1995), 39–44.

80. "Nuevo régimen," *Nación*, 3 November 1996; Carlos Pagni, "Fiscales perderían su estabilidad," *Ámbito Financiero*, 1 November 1996; "La cámara alta aprobó la ley," *Nación*, 8 November 1996; "Todo tiene su precio," *Página 12*, 8 November 1996; "Agüero Iturbe en la cuerda floja," *Clarín*, 8 November 1996.

81. Before the Attoney General's Office Law, there was a general consensus that the Attorney General's Office was part of the executive branch. See Garro, "Staffing," 6–8.

82. Ley del Ministerio Público, Ley 24,946, arts. 5–6; José Barbaccia, federal prosecutor, interview by author, Buenos Aires, 29 June 1999; León Carlos Arslanian, former Justice Minister, interview by author, Buenos Aires, 7 December 1998.

83. Decreto 1757, 9 February 1956, art. 248.

84. Raúl Baglini et al., *Juicio a la Corte* (Buenos Aires: Mecanografix, 1993), 146–47; Verbitsky, *Hacer la Corte: La construcción de un poder absoluto sin justicia ni control* (Buenos Aires: Planeta, 1993), 90–98.

85. Verbitsky, *Hacer la Corte*, 92–97; Alfonsín, *La reforma constitucional de 1994* (Buenos Aires: Tiempo de Ideas, 1994), 26. Although the contract with the company Herrera Hermanos specified payment upon receipt, the administration paid for the uniforms before receiving them. In addition, due to Menem's personal links to Herrera Hermanos, he did not fulfill the requirement of public competition for government contracts. In fact, Herrera Hermanos charged more for school jackets than did competitors.

86. Baglini, *Juicio*, 146–47; Verbitsky, *Hacer la Corte*, 90–98.

87. "La Fiscalía," *Nación*, 29 October 2000.

88. Verbitsky, *Hacer la Corte*, 99–106; Carrió, *Corte*, 160–62; "La Fiscalía," *Nación*, 29 October 2000.

89. Verbitsky, *Hacer la Corte*, 99–106; Carrió, *Corte*, 160–62.

90. "Justicia: Un reclamo de muchos años," *Revista La Nación* (21 September 1997): 42–43; Verbitsky, *Hacer la Corte*, 99–106; Carrió, *Corte*, 160–62.

91. Ley del Ministerio Público, Ley 24,946.

Chapter 4

1. Monolithic party control in San Luis continued beyond 2003 when Adolfo's brother, Alberto Rodríguez Saá, assumed the governorship.

2. The current Mendoza Constitution has been in effect since 1916 except for the 1949–56 period. For a discussion of the short-lived 1949 constitution, see Claudia Lacoste, "El proceso de reforma constitucional de Mendoza (1943–56)," in *La legislatura y las ciencias sociales* (Mendoza: Cámara de Senadores, 1995), 127–47.

3. Elvecia Gatica, Supreme Court justice, interview by author, San Luis, 9 October 1998; Beatriz Tardieu de Quiroga, Appellate Court judge, interview by author, San Luis, 9 October 1998; María Bona, First Instance judge, interview by author, San Luis, 9 October 1998.

4. This chapter and the subsequent two chapters build and expand upon Rebecca Bill Chavez, "The Construction of the Rule of Law in Argentina: A Tale of Two Provinces," *Comparative Politics* 35 (July 2003): 417–37.

5. See John A. Booth, "Costa Rica: The Roots of Democratic Stability," in *Democracy in Developing Countries: Latin America*, ed. Larry Diamond, Juan Linz, and Seymour Martin Lipset (Boulder, Lynne Rienner, 1989), 387–89.

6. La Rosa, interview by author, Mendoza, 6 May 1999. See William Fleming, "The Cultural Determinants of Entrepreneurship and Economic Development: A Case Study of Mendoza Province, Argentina, 1861–1914," *Journal of Economic History* 39 (March 1979): 216–18; Larry Sawers, *The Other Argentina: The Interior and National Development* (Boulder: Westview, 1996), 82–83; David J. Keeling, *Contemporary Argentina: A Geographical Perspective* (Boulder: Westview, 1997), 255–57.

7. Sixty-five percent of vineyards in Mendoza are less than five hectares in size. Keeling, *Contemporary Argentina*, 255.

8. Fleming, "Determinants," 216–22; Sawers, *Argentina*, 82–86. Among the major families were the Villanueva, Ceretti, Civit, Serú, Bombal, and Giol families.

9. Lehman Brothers, *Offering Circular, Province of Mendoza*, 2 August 1996, 41–42. The largest economic sectors in Mendoza are manufacturing, which includes a diverse array of products such as wine, food, oil, chemicals, machinery, paper, medical tools, and textiles; commerce, which includes the restaurant, hotel, and tourism industries; community, social, and personal services; financial services; mining; agriculture and livestock, which includes vegetable and fruit production; transportation and communication; construction; and electricity, gas, and water. Note that Mendoza remains Argentina's main producer of wine. Wine production constitutes 50 percent of the total foods and beverages manufactured in Mendoza.

10. Natalio Botana, Argentine historian, interview by author, Buenos Aires, 25 November 1998. Botana uses the term "provincial oligarchy" for provinces controlled by a single family.

11. Néstor Pedro Menéndez, "La vera historia de los Rodríguez Páez o Rodríguez-Rodríguez y Páez-Montero, alias Rodríguez Saá," Appendix 1 in *San Luis: La cárcel de los Rodríguez Saá*, by Jaime Emma (Buenos Aires: Ediciones de la Urraca, 1992), 114–15. Ironically, the brothers' family name was Mendoza.

12. See Chapter 7 for a detailed discussion of the Rodríguez Saá family's control of the provincial press.

13. Rodríguez Saá's salary alone does not account for the growth in his wealth. In 1983, he owned one small house. By 1987, he had acquired two mansions in San Luis worth over $2.5 million and property in Buenos Aires. In addition, Rodríguez Saá controlled the two San Luis law firms that handled the legal side of IP. His close

friends ran both firms. Fabián Álvarez, "Un feudo bajo sospecho," *Los Andes*, 25 September 1997. For more on IP, see Chapter 7.

14. Sawers, *Argentina*, 233. See Miguel Wiñazki, *El último feudo: San Luis y el caudillismo de los Rodríguez Saá* (Buenos Aires: Planeta, 1995), 90–95.

15. Emma, *San Luis*, 208–9; Wiñazki, *El último feudo*, 54, 108; José Samper, *San Luis: La (in)dependencia de los poderes* (San Luis: Alta Editorial, 1993), 36–37.

16. Colegio de Abogados y Procuradores de Villa Mercedes, "Comunicado," 23 February 1998.

17. Chade, interview by author, Mendoza, 7 May 1999. After Gustavo Bossert resigned from the federal Supreme Court in 2002, leaders of the Buenos Aires Bar Association proposed Kemelmajer as a possible replacement. Hugo Germano, Buenos Aires Bar Association President, interview by author, Buenos Aires, 11 March 2003.

18. Pablo Lacoste, "Ueltschi, gobernador (1958–61)," in *San Rafael: Historia y perspectivas*, ed. Lacoste (Mendoza: Universidad de Congreso, Universidad Nacional de Cuyo, *Uno*, 1996), 69; Pablo Lacoste, "El gobierno de Llaver se pone en marcha (1983–84)," chapter in *Santiago Felipe Llaver, gobernador de Mendoza, 1983–1987* (forthcoming); Nanclares, interview by author, Mendoza, 4 May 1999.

19. Lafalla, interview by author, Mendoza, 7 May 1999.

20. Both constitutions provide for tenure protection. *Constitución de la Provincia de San Luis*, art. 201; *Constitución de la Provincia de Mendoza*, art. 151.

21. See "Los judiciales se preparan," *Diario de la República*, 22 November 1996; Daniel Casas, "Amo y señor de San Luis," *Tres Puntos*, 16 September 1998, 46.

22. *Constitución de la Provincia de San Luis*, art. 191; Ley Orgánica de Tribunales no. 4929, art. 40, 2 December 1991.

23. Cacace, interview by author, San Luis, 9 October 1998; Suriani, interview by author, San Luis, 9 October 1998. See Superior Tribunal de Justicia, Resolución, 5 February 1997.

24. Samper, *San Luis*, 46–50; Colegio de Abogados y Procuradores de Villa Mercedes, "Comunicado;" Horacio Verbitsky, "El último emperador," *Página 12*, 8 March 1998.

25. Superior Tribunal de Justicia, Acuerdo no. 25, San Luis, 9 February 1998.

26. Adriana Carranza de Carrió, former *secretario*, San Luis, 11 October 1998; Estela Aragón Zwiener, former *secretario*, San Luis, 8 October 1998; Santiago O'Donnell, "San Luis," *Nación*, 2 November 1998; Colegio de Abogados de San Luis, "Situación institucional en San Luis," 1998, 7–8; Justicia Democrática, "Conclusiones del Seminario sobre la independencia de los poderes judiciales provinciales" (paper presented at the conference Seminario sobre la independencia de los poderes judiciales provinciales, San Luis, Argentina, March 1999), 2.

27. Pablo Lacoste, "Llaver," 13–14; Chade, interview. See Chapter 2 for an assessment of Alfonsín's dismissal of a Court inherited from a military regime.

28. Because he respected the life tenure of judges, Lafalla was only able to designate one Supreme Court justice. When a vacancy appeared in 1997, Lafalla complied with a transparent, merit-based appointment process. The new justice, Carlos Bohm, had ties to the governor, but the opposition-controlled Senate made sure that the appointment was based on professional qualifications. In fact, due to Bohm's profes-

sional background and experience, 80 percent of the Senate voted in favor of his appointment. Bohm came from a long judicial career and was a prominent appellate court judge at the time of his 1997 appointment. Both Lafalla and Bohm acknowledge their friendship, which Bohm asserts is irrelevant to his performance on the Court. He renounced his PJ affiliation when he became a public prosecutor fourteen years before assuming his seat on the Supreme Court. Lafalla, interview; Bohm, interview by author, Mendoza, 4 May 1999.

29. Kemelmajer, interview by author, Mendoza, 4 May 1999, Nanclares, interview; Llorente, interview by author, Mendoza, 4 May 1999. Nanclares and Chief Justice Llorente concur with Kemelmajer.

30. *Constitución de la Provincia de San Luis*, art. 192; *Constitución de la Provincia de Mendoza*, art. 151.

31. Judge Alberto Staib, interview by author, Mendoza, 11 May 1999; "La situación existente con el poder judicial," *Los Andes*, 2 May 1985.

32. Colegio de Abogados de San Luis, "Situación institucional," 2; Justicia Democrática, "Conclusiones," 5; Colegio de Abogados y Procuradores de Villa Mercedes, "Comunicado."

33. *Constitución de la Provincia de San Luis*, art. 191.

34. *Constitución de la Provincia de Mendoza*, art. 143.

35. Emma, *San Luis*, 208–9; Wiñazki, *El último feudo*, 108; Samper, *San Luis*, 34–35.

36. Ley Orgánica de Tribunales no. 4929, art. 40, 2 December 1991; Ley Orgánica de la Administración de Justicia de San Luis no. 5158, art. 38, 15 December 1998.

37. Bordón, interview by author, Buenos Aires, 12 March 2003.

38. Nanclares, interview.

39. Gallo, interview by author, Mendoza, 11 October 1998; Relly, interview by author, San Luis, 21 May 1999; Relly, letter addressed to the president of the Impeachment Jury, San Luis, April 1999. In her letter of resignation, Relly wrote, "I have no guarantee of facing an impartial Impeachment Jury, and I will not submit myself to be judged by a Jury that was composed unconstitutionally." See Chapter 5 for details on the 1998 removal of Careaga and Gallo.

40. "San Luis, sin justicia," *Nación*, 19 July 1997; Colegio de Abogados y Procuradores de Villa Mercedes, "Comunicado."

41. Sup. Corte Just. Mendoza, Merga, Fernando y otra c/ Municip. de Las Heras, 15 February 1994, *Jurisprudencia Argentina*, 1994-II, 486–509; Sup. Corte Just. Mendoza, Campoy, Gustavo A. c/ Mendoza, 17 October 1994, *Jurisprudencia Argentina*, 1995-I, 384–91.

42. Emma, *San Luis*, 209.

43. See Chapter 5 for an in-depth discussion of the reelection clause in the San Luis Constitution.

44. *Constitución de la Provincia de Mendoza*, art. 221.

45. The Court did not intervene in previous plebiscites on constitutional reform. For instance, after the 1947 referendum that set the stage for the 1949 constitution, reform went forward although only 34 percent of eligible voters participated in the referendum. See Claudia Lacoste, "Proceso," 138–40; "Se pidió a la Corte de Mendoza la nulidad," *Prensa*, 30 March 1989.

46. Bordón recalls, "I didn't agree with the Mendoza Court, but it has the last word." Bordón, interview.

47. Samper, *San Luis*, 38.

48. Casas, "Amo," 48. Rodríguez Saá intervened in the case to avoid the scrutiny of the national press. The governor wanted to prevent the *catamarquización* of the case, a reference to the province of Catamarca where the judiciary's treatment of a young woman's murder led to national protests and ultimately to the governor's downfall.

49. Zaffaroni, interview by author, Buenos Aires, 1 July 1999.

50. Leiva, interview by author, Mendoza, 10 May 1999; "Mendoza," *Clarín*, 5 December 1996; "PJ quiere a Leiva fuera de la causa," *Ámbito Financiero*, 28 November 1996; "Niegan la excarcelación," *Clarín*, 28 November 1996.

51. Sistema Público de Evaluación de la Calidad (SIPEC), "Grado de acuerdo con la detención de ex-directivos del Banco," December 1996, 76; SIPEC, "¿Qué representa la acción iniciada por Leiva?" December 1996, 82.

52. "Preparan denuncia contra el juez federal," *Los Andes*, 17 May 1998; "Procesan a dirigentes del PJ," *Nación*, 27 September 1996; "Procesamiento," *El Cronista*, 26 September 1996.

53. CEA and FORES, *Proyecto justicia y desarrollo económico: Anexo I, La justicia de las provincias argentinas* (Buenos Aires, 1998), 5–6, 31–32.

54. Mario Otero, "La autoría de las sentencias," *El Decamerón*, 4 November 1998, 14.

55. Carmen Argibay, AMJA founder, interview by author, Buenos Aires, 24 June 1999; Gerónimo Sansó, Justicia Democrática president, interview by author, Buenos Aires, 18 June 1999; Justicia Democrática, "Conclusiones."

56. FACA, Resolución, San Rafael, Mendoza, 4 April 1997; Ángel Fermin Garrote (FACA president), letter to presidents of provincial bar associations, 26 February 1998.

57. Declaration signed by FACA, Colegio de Abogados de Corrientes, Colegio de Abogados de Córdoba, Colegio de Abogados de Mendoza, Colegio Forense de San Luis, 6 March 1998.

58. Staib, interview.

59. Graciela Rosso, interview by author, San Luis, 8 October 1998.

60. Courtis, interview by author, Buenos Aires, 28 June 1999.

61. Abregú, interview by author, Buenos Aires, 15 June 1999.

62. Juan Pablo Mortarotti, attorney at Pérez Alati, Grondona, Benites, Arntsen & Martínez de Hoz, interview by author, Mendoza, 4 May 1999.

63. Mortarotti, interview. Other major firms, including Marval, O'Farrell & Mairal, conducted a decision-making process similar to that of Pérez Alati.

64. Former San Luis Supreme Court Justice, interview by author, San Luis, 1999.

65. Cacace, interview; San Luis judges and bar association members, interviews by author, San Luis, 1999.

66. Ceballos, 1999 Alianza candidate for governor, interview by author, San Luis, 19 May 1999; Samper, interview by author, San Luis, 21 May 1999.

67. Olivares, interview by author, San Luis, 26 May 1999; Otero, interview by au-

thor, San Luis, 24 May 1999; Wiñazki, interview by author, Buenos Aires, 22 June 1999.

68. University administrator, interview by author, San Luis, 1999.

69. Leiva, interview.

70. Llorente, interview; Kemelmajer, interview. Kemelmajer reports that the government never tried to influence her rulings.

71. Portabella, interview by author, Mendoza, 10 May 1999; Pérez Hualde, interview, Mendoza, 7 May 1999.

72. Balter, interview by author, Buenos Aires, 27 April 1999; Mosso de Mortarotti, interview by author, Buenos Aires, 29 June 1999.

73. La Rosa, interview; Gabrielli, interview by author, Mendoza, 5 May 1999.

Chapter 5

1. Following President Fernando de la Rúa's resignation in December 2001, Rodríguez Saá stepped down as governor and began a one-week stint as Argentina's interim president. Rodríguez Saá's resignation from the governorship did not, however, mark the end of his control of provincial politics. With the help of his brother Alberto, Rodríguez Saá continued to dominate the political landscape of San Luis despite his replacement by María Alicia Lemme. Lemme, a long-time Rodríguez Saá ally, had been vice-governor since 1999. In the 1990s, she had been a PJ mayor and a provincial congresswoman representing the Partido Unión y Libertad (PUL), a party allied with the PJ and founded by Rodríguez Saá's brother. After returning to San Luis after only one week as president, Rodríguez Saá resumed his post as provincial PJ president. The Rodríguez Saá brothers continued to dominate provincial politics during Adolfo's unsuccessful bid at Argentina's presidency in 2003. In 2003, Alberto Rodríguez Saá assumed the governorship.

2. Jean Bodin, *On Sovereignty: Four Chapters from the Six Books of the Commonwealth*, trans. and ed. Julian H. Franklin (Cambridge: Cambridge University Press, 1992).

3. Miguel Wiñazki, *El último feudo: San Luis y el caudillismo de los Rodríguez Saá* (Planeta: Buenos Aires, 1995), 113. The governor's sister-in-law made the statement.

4. José Samper, *San Luis: La (in)dependencia de los poderes* (San Luis: Alta Editorial, 1993), 58–62; Eugenio Raúl Zaffaroni, interview by author, Buenos Aires, 1 July 1999. When conservative parties were a relevant force in Congress, the judiciary enjoyed greater independence than it did under Rodríguez Saá. Based on his 1969–73 experience as a San Luis Appellate Court judge and as the San Luis Attorney General from 1973 through 1975, Zaffaroni asserts that until 1976, San Luis was closer to Mendoza on the judicial autonomy continuum.

5. The historical weakness of the UCR in San Luis is evident in its poor electoral performance throughout the twentieth century. In 1973, for instance, the UCR came in a distant third, receiving only 10 percent of the vote as compared to the PJ's 41 percent and conservative parties' 27 percent. Samper, *San Luis*, 58–60. See Pablo Lacoste, *La Unión Cívica Radical en Mendoza y en la Argentina, 1890–1946* (Mendoza: Ediciones Culturales de Mendoza, 1995).

6. Néstor Pedro Menéndez, "La vera historia de los Rodríguez Páez o Rodríguez-Rodríguez y Páez-Montero, alias Rodríguez Saá," Appendix 1 in *San Luis: La cárcel de los Rodríguez Saá*, by Jaime Emma (Buenos Aires: Ediciones de la Urraca, 1992), 125.

7. Samper, *San Luis*, 60–61; Samper, interview by author, San Luis, 21 May 1999.

8. Pagano, former UCR congressman, interview by author, San Luis, 19 May 1999; Rosso, interview by author, San Luis, 20 May 1999; Fernando Rodríguez, "Crisis judicial en la provincia," *Nación*, 24 November 1998.

9. Samper, interview; Pagano, interview.

10. According to Article 118 of the San Luis Constitution, a majority of legislators must support the initiative to begin a congressional investigation. After the PJ gained a majority in 1987, the number of opposition members was insufficient to initiate investigations of PJ functionaries, contributing to the impunity of government officials. For instance, the PJ rejected Congressman Juan José Laborda Ibarra's proposal to investigate allegations that Rodríguez Saá had used provincial funds to finance his 1999 presidential campaign. Pagano, interview; Laborda Ibarra, San Luis congressman (Frepaso), interview by author, San Luis, 18 May 1999.

11. Samper, interview; Eduardo Ángel Estrada, president of the Constitutional Convention (PJ), interview by author, San Luis, 26 May 1999. Both Samper and Estrada support proposals that would increase minority representation in the Senate and that would limit the governor's reelection to two consecutive terms. Such reforms would be a step toward overcoming monolithic party control and extreme executive dominance in San Luis.

12. Emma, *San Luis*, 208; Samper, *San Luis*, 32–33.

13. The constitutional reform in Santa Cruz permitted Néstor Kirchner to hold the governorship from 1991 until he became Argentina's president in 2003. He was first elected in 1991, and then reelected in 1995 and 1999. Like Rodríguez Saá, Kirchner packed the provincial Supreme Court with loyalists. Not surprisingly, the pro-Kirchner Supreme Court did nothing to prevent the 1998 reform that permitted the governor's indefinite reelection. The reigning model in Argentina permits reelection but only for a second consecutive term. Fifteen provinces permit two consecutive terms: Buenos Aires (art. 123), Chaco (art. 133), Chubut (art. 149), Ciudad de Buenos Aires (art. 98), Córdoba (art. 136), Formosa (art. 129), Jujuy (art. 127), La Pampa (art. 74), Misiones (art. 110), Neuquén (art. 114), Río Negro (art. 175), Salta (art. 140), San Juan (art. 175), Santiago del Estero (art. 139), and Tierra del Fuego (art. 126). Five provinces prohibit reelection: Corrientes (art. 102), Entre Ríos (art. 120), Mendoza (art. 115), Santa Fe (art. 64), and Tucumán (art. 76).

14. See Chapter 6 on Mendoza's no-reelection clause.

15. Natalio Botana, interview by author, Buenos Aires, 25 November 1998; Botana, *El orden conservador: La política argentina entre 1880 y 1916* (Buenos Aires: Editorial Sudamericana, 1977).

16. Román Lejtman, "Tradición, familia, propiedades," *Tres Puntos*, 6 September 1998, 45; Laborda Ibarra, Comunicado de prensa, "Adolfo senador nacional . . . Un 'enroque' por nepotismo y impunidad," 15 September 1998; Menéndez, "Historia," 114–15.

17. Menéndez, "Historia," 123–25; Samper, *San Luis*, 46–53; Miriam Agundez, interview by author, San Luis, 24 May 1999; Mario Otero, journalist, interview by author, San Luis, 24 May 1999. Agundez served as a cabinet minister from the opposition Orange List from 1983 until 1985. She resigned in response to Rodríguez Saá's declaration that he planned to govern for another forty years. Otero recounts a similar story. When Otero's friend told the governor that his young son hoped to be the next governor, Rodríguez Saá responded, "Yes, the boy will be the right age in forty years when I step down."

18. Samper, interview.

19. Carlos Cacace, interview by author, San Luis, 9 October 1998.

20. Laborda Ibarra, interview; Samper, interview; Samper, *San Luis*, 29–30.

21. Mainwaring and Shugart focus on two types of executive authority: constitutional (formal) and partisan. Like Menem, Rodríguez Saá exercised a third type: informal power. See Scott Mainwaring and Matthew Soberg Shugart, eds., *Presidentialism and Democracy in Latin America* (Cambridge: Cambridge University Press, 1997), 4–5.

22. Pagano, interview; Laborda Ibarra, interview.

23. Régimen Disciplinario del Cuerpo, chapt. XIX, art. 139.

24. *Constitución de la República Argentina*, art. 60; *Constitución de la Provincia de San Luis*, art. 128.

25. Samper, interview; Laborda Ibarra, interview.

26. *Constitución de la Provincia de San Luis*, art. 196.

27. *Constitución de la Provincia de San Luis*, art. 196.

28. Colegio de Abogados de San Luis, "Situación institucional en la provincia de San Luis," 1998, 2; Justicia Democrática, "Conclusiones del Seminario sobre la independencia de los poderes judiciales provinciales," San Luis, March 1999, 2.

29. Agundez, Judicial Council member (1991–93), interview.

30. *Constitución de la Provincia de San Luis*, arts. 199–200; Colegio de Abogados de San Luis, "Situación institucional," 3–4.

31. *Constitución de la Provincia de San Luis*, art. 197–98.

32. Fifty-seven of the sixty attorneys that comprised two Associaciones de Abogados had close ties to the governor. Pagano, interview; Colegio de Abogados y Procuradores de la Ciudad de San Luis, "Declaración a la opinión pública," 19 November 1997.

33. *Constitución de la Provincia de San Luis*, art. 224.

34. Pagano, interview; Zaffaroni, interview; Pagano, "Jurado de Enjuiciamiento de la Provincia de San Luis, su brutal conquista, propuesta para su liberación" (paper presented at Seminario sobre la independencia de los poderes judiciales provinciales, San Luis, March 1999).

35. Colegio de Abogados y Procuradores de Villa Mercedes, "Comunicado," 23 February 1998; Cacace, interview.

36. Pagano, interview; Rosso, interview.

37. "Acusan a Rodríguez Saá de manejar el poder judicial," *Voz del Interior*, 11 March 1998; Casas, "Amo y señor de San Luis," *Tres Puntos* 2 (16 September 1998), 49; Pagano, interview.

38. Casas, "Amo y señor," 48; Santiago O'Donnell, "Final anunciado para un fallo

discutible," *Nación*, 7 November 1998; Colegio de Abogados y Procuradores de San Luis y Villa Mercedes y Colegio Forense de la Provincia de San Luis, "Declaración a la opinión pública," 26 February 1998.

39. Claudia San Martín, "Destruyeron a la jueza enfrentada con Rodríguez Saá," *Nación*, 18 December 1998. The national newspapers *Nación*, *Clarín*, and *Página 12* condemned the San Luis Impeachment Jury. For examples of national press coverage, see Laura Zommer, "Para la ex jueza Gallo, 'hay un San Luis sin ley,'" *Nación*, 10 November 1998, on the Gallo hearing. See Martín Granovsky, "Su señoría," *Página 12*, 2 September 1998, on Careaga's hearing.

40. "Adhesiones y críticas en el ámbito judicial," *Nación*, 19 December 1998.

41. Zaffaroni, interview. Zaffaroni defended Careaga before the 1993 Impeachment Jury that absolved her.

42. Moreno Ocampo, interview by author, Buenos Aires, 4 November 1998; Courtis, interview by author, Buenos Aires, 28 June 1999; Guillermo Jorge, member of Adriana Gallo's defense team, interview by author, Buenos Aires, 4 November 1998.

43. Adriana Gallo, declaration before the Impeachment Jury, San Luis, 2 November 1998.

44. Fernando Rodríguez, "Careaga está dispuesta a dar batalla," *Nación*, 19 December 1998.

45. Domingo Vacca, statement before the Impeachment Jury, San Luis, 2 November 1998; Otero, "La vara distinta," *El Decamerón*, 15 November 1998, 11; Gallo, interview by author, San Luis, 11 October 1998; Pagano, interview. Pagano was a member of the 1996 Impeachment Jury that absolved Gallo.

46. Moreno Ocampo, statement before the Impeachment Jury, San Luis, 2 November 1998.

47. Courtis, interview; Otero, "El juicio que viene," *El Decamerón*, 15 November 1998, 17.

48. Rosso, interview; Moreno Ocampo, interview.

49. Courtis, interview; Alberto Bovino, CELS defense team member, interview by author, Buenos Aires, 23 June 1999. Bovino reports that he never felt such *impotencia*, or powerlessness, as he did before the San Luis Impeachment Jury.

50. *Constitución de la Provincia de San Luis*, arts. 236–37. According to Article 236, only the Impeachment Jury has the power to remove the head prosecutor before the end of his or her four-year term.

51. Laborda Ibarra, interview.

52. Estrada, interview.

53. Estrada, interview; Giordano, interview by author, Mendoza, 3 May 1999. See chapter 6 for a detailed discussion of the Mendoza State Prosecutor.

54. Samper, *San Luis*, 29.

55. Samper, *San Luis*, 42–43, 69; *Constitución de la Provincia de San Luis*, art. 168.

56. *Constitución de la Provincia de San Luis*, arts. 238–46.

57. *Constitución de la Provincia de San Luis*, art. 242.

58. Samper, *San Luis*, 43–44. Samper calls the Tribunal a *burocracia decorativa*, a mere decorative bureaucracy.

59. Rosso, interview.

60. Moreno Ocampo, interview.

61. *Constitución de la Provincia de San Luis*, art. 196.

62. For instance, public prosecutor Sandra Pipoillen formerly served as an attorney for PUL. Prosecutor Sonya Fernandez found her first job after law school in the office of the Rodríguez Saá brothers. Eduardo Olivares, journalist, interview by author, San Luis, 26 May 1999; Pagano, interview.

63. Prosecutor José Liseda, for example, worked with the government-controlled press. When Rodríguez Saá used the media to publish false allegations about an opposition member, Liseda brought formal charges against that member based on the press report. Fabián Álvarez, "Un feudo bajo sospecho," *Los Andes*, 25 September 1997; Pagano, interview.

Chapter 6

1. Omar Pérez Botti, PJ Senator, interview by author, Mendoza, 4 May 1999; Sergio Bruni, UCR Congressman, interview by author, Mendoza, 6 May 1999; Teresa Peltier, PD Congresswoman, interview by author, Mendoza, 5 May 1999.

2. Pablo Lacoste, *La Unión Cívica Radical en Mendoza y en la Argentina, 1890–1946* (Mendoza: Ediciones Culturales de Mendoza, 1995), 17; Pablo Lacoste, "Ueltschi, gobernador (1958–61)," in *San Rafael: Historia y perspectivas*, ed. Lacoste (Mendoza: Universidad de Congreso, Universidad Nacional de Cuyo, *Uno*, 1996), 68–71.

3. Lacoste, *Los "gansos" de Mendoza: Aporte para el estudio de los partidos provincianos y del modelo conservador, 1880–1943* (Buenos Aires: Centro Editor de América Latina, 1991), 7–8; Gerardo Adrogué, "El nuevo sistema partidario argentino," in *La nueva matriz política argentina*, ed. Carlos H. Acuña (Buenos Aires: Nueva Visión, 1995), 35–36, 43.

4. Mendoza legislators from the three parties agree that their power relative to the executive branch has been greatest under divided government. Carlos Balter, PD Congressman (1987–91), interview by author, Buenos Aires, 27 April 1999; León Victor Chade, UCR Senator (1987–91), interview by author, Mendoza, 7 May 1999; Jorge Zapata Mercader, PD Senator (1987–91), interview by author, Buenos Aires, 27 April 1999; Peltier, interview.

5. Lacoste, "El gobierno de Llaver se pone en marcha, 1983–84," in *Santiago Felipe Llaver, gobernador de Mendoza, 1983–1987* (forthcoming), 2; Lacoste, "Ueltschi," 68–71.

6. Chade, interview; Bordón, interview by author, Buenos Aires, 12 March 2003.

7. Lehman Brothers, *Offering Circular, Province of Mendoza*, 2 August 1996, 40; Ana María Mosso de Mortarotti, Mendoza Minister of Economy (1995–97), interview by author, Buenos Aires, 29 June 1999.

8. When Alberto Rodríguez Saá (PJ) assumed office in 2003, it marked the sixth four-year term that the PJ has held the governorship in San Luis.

9. Nanclares, interview by author, Mendoza, 4 May 1999; Kemelmajer, interview by author, Mendoza, 4 May 1999. See Chapter 4 for an in-depth discussion of judicial autonomy in Mendoza.

10. Laura Inzirillo, advisor to the Mendoza PJ bloc, interview by author, Mendoza, 4 May 1999; Pérez Botti, interview; Bruni, interview; Peltier, interview. Inzi-

rillo reports that the PJ bloc gathers before each legislative session to determine how to vote.

11. Zapata Mercader, interview; Balter, PD bloc president in the national House, interview.

12. See Barry Ames, "Electoral Strategy under Open-List Proportional Representation," *American Journal of Political Science* 30 (May 1995), 406–33; John M. Carey and Matthew Soberg Shugart, "Incentives to Cultivate a Personal Vote: A Rank Ordering of Electoral Systems," *Electoral Studies* 14 (December 1995): 417–40.

13. Bruni, interview; Pérez Botti, interview. The PJ rewarded Pérez Botti for voting with the party during his 1995–99 term in the Mendoza Senate. In 1999, he was the first candidate on the PJ list for the Mendoza House of Representatives.

14. Montbrun, UCR senator (1991–99), interview by author, Mendoza, 6 May 1999.

15. Adrogué, "Sistema partidario," 43, 67.

16. Miguel De Luca, Mark P. Jones, and María Inés Tula, "Argentine Political Parties and Their Candidate Nomination Procedures: 1983–89" (paper presented at the annual Latin American Studies meeting, Miami, Fla., March 2000), 15.

17. Bordón, interview. Sociologist Carlos La Rosa concurs that discipline in the Mendoza PJ is lower than in the San Luis PJ. La Rosa, interview by author, Mendoza, 6 May 1999.

18. Mosso de Mortarotti, interview.

19. Chade, interview.

20. *Constitución de la Provincia de Mendoza*, arts. 129–30.

21. Bordón, interview; Susana Becerra, Sistema Público de Evaluación de la Calidad (SIPEC), interview by author, Mendoza, 10 May 1999; María Cristina Poj, SIPEC, interview by author, Mendoza, 10 May 1999. See Chapter 5 for a discussion of the clause in the San Luis Constitution that permits the governor to bypass Congress by classifying bills as "urgent" or "very urgent."

22. *Reglamento, Cámara de Diputados, Provincia de Mendoza, 1998*, chapt. 17, arts. 193–97; *Reglamento de la Honorable Cámara de Senadores, Provincia de Mendoza*, chapt. 19, arts. 212–17, June 1995; *Constitución de la Provincia de Mendoza*, art. 94. Both the House and Senate Rules refer to Article 94 of the Mendoza Constitution.

23. Leiva, interview by author, Mendoza, 10 May 1999.

24. Bruni, head of Bicameral Committee on Security, interview; Peltier, Bicameral Committee on Security member, interview; Luis Alejandro Cazaban, Justice Minister (1998–99), interview by author, Mendoza, 3 May 1999. In 1999, the Lafalla administration created the Inspección General de Seguridad (Inspector General of Security) to monitor the police. The opposition dominated the bicameral committee that oversaw the Inspector General. Two of the three members were from the opposition.

25. *Constitución de la Provincia de Mendoza*, art. 115.

26. The provincial politics of La Rioja, Catamarca, and Corrientes are controlled by the Menem family, the Saadi family, and the Romero Feris family respectively.

27. Chade, interview. Opposition senators warned Bordón that they would withhold approval if he did not retract his nominee.

28. Pérez Botti points to the May 4, 1999, Senate session when the PD and UCR

joined forces to reject the governor's candidate. Pérez Botti arrived late for our interview that day because of the extended Senate session and intense debate over Lafalla's nominee. Pérez Botti, interview.

29. Chade, Llaver's Minister of Government, interview; Lafalla, interview by author, Mendoza, 7 May 1999.

30. Montbrun, interview.

31. Staib, interview by author, Mendoza, 11 May 1999.

32. "Designación de magistrados," *Hoy*, 28 March 1987; "Aprobaron nominaciones para cargos judiciales," *Los Andes*, 20 November 1987.

33. "Los abogados opinan sobre designación," *Los Andes*, 17 October 1987; "Citan al Senado a sesión secreta," *Los Andes*, 24 October 1987.

34. "Debe hacer una carrera judicial," *Los Andes*, 24 October 1987.

35. "Baglini rechazó elección popular de magistrados," *Los Andes*, 3 February 1987.

36. Bruni, interview.

37. Montbrun, interview; Staib, interview.

38. "Serán públicos los debates para designación de jueces," *Los Andes*, 31 December 1993; José Luis Toso, "Sin secretos y con bastante oposición," *Los Andes*, 13 June 1994; Balter, interview.

39. Staib, interview. See "Jueces por concurso," *Los Andes*, 21 November 1994; "El PE no tiene cálculos políticos con las designaciones," *Los Andes*, 11 June 1994; Flavio Arjona, Sergio Olivieri, and Fernanda MacIntosh, "Mendoza: La administración de justicia," *Novedades Económicas*, June 1996, 38–39; "Concurso para la selección," *Los Andes*, 14 July 1994; "Concursos para jueces," *Los Andes*, 1 July 1994.

40. Lafalla, Address before first meeting of Mendoza's legislature, 1997 (photocopy).

41. Montbrun, interview. Montbrun was a member of the Senate at the time of Gabrielli's decree.

42. Before the Judicial Council gained constitutional status, governors could eliminate it by decree.

43. *Constitución de la Provincia de Mendoza*, art. 150. In addition, the attorneys on the Council must practice in different districts, which gives the Council geographic balance.

44. *Constitución de la Provincia de Mendoza*, art. 150.

45. Law 6561, art. 4, inc. 3.

46. Bruni, Judicial Council member, interview; Claudia Pagliarulo, "Comienzan los exámenes para cargos judiciales," *Uno*, 13 September 1998.

47. Alejandro Pérez Hualde, "El Consejo de la Magistratura en la Constitución de Mendoza," unpublished manuscript, 25 May 1998 (photocopy), 12–13; *Constitución de la Provincia de Mendoza*, art. 144.

48. Llorente, interview; Staib, interview; Portabella, representative of the attorneys on the Judicial Council, interview by author, Mendoza, 10 May 1999; Pesce, interview by author, Mendoza, 4 May 1999; "Ya arrancó Consejo de la Magistratura," *Ámbito Financiero*, 23 February 1999.

49. *Constitución de la Provincia de Mendoza*, art. 164.

50. Bohm, interview by author, Mendoza, 4 May 1999; Nanclares, interview; Llorente, interview; Kemelmajer, interview.

51. Zapata Mercader, interview.

52. *Constitución de la Provincia de Mendoza*, arts. 177, 180.

53. Andrés Gabrielli, journalist, interview by author, Mendoza, 5 May 1999; Alejandro Pérez Hualde, attorney, interview by author, Mendoza, 7 May 1999; Cazaban, interview.

54. Giordano, Mendoza State Prosecutor, interview by author, Mendoza, 6 May 1999; Bordón, interview. Until the Lafalla administration, Mendocinos did not recognize the State Prosecutor's potential role as a control organ. Thus, the opposition majority in the Senate did not block Bordón's appointment of Quevedo Mendoza.

55. Lafalla, interview; Giordano, interview. See Andrés Gabrielli, "Arturo y la gata Flora," *Uno*, 28 July 1998.

56. Giordano, interview; Andrés Gabrielli, interview, Julio Gómez, former Mendoza Undersecretary of Justice, Mendoza, 5 May 1999. As discussed in Chapter 4, a majority of the former bank officials had been part of the PJ administrations of Bordón and Gabrielli. The prosecutions damaged the image of the Mendoza PJ.

57. Gabrielli, interview.

58. Giordano, interview; Lafalla, interview. Giordano reports that during his first months in office, his investigations of Governor Gabrielli aroused opposition from PJ officials. As the citizens of Mendoza learned the benefits of an independent State Prosecutor, however, the criticism decreased. After Giordano had gained the support of civil society, politicians were less likely to accept the costs of attacking him. Citizens now defend their State Prosecutor.

59. *Constitución de la Provincia de Mendoza*, art. 185.

60. *Constitución de la Provincia de Mendoza*, arts. 182–83.

61. Lafalla, interview; Cazaban, interview.

62. Bordón, interview.

63. Gómez, legal advisor to the Accounting Tribunal, interview.

64. Mendocinos report a lower level of government corruption in their province than on the national level. In a 1996 survey, 71 percent of Mendocinos reported a high level of corruption in the national government, whereas 40 percent reported a high level in the provincial government. SIPEC, "Percepción de niveles de corrupción en distintos ámbitos," September 1996, 56.

65. Leiva, interview; Alejandra Obregón, Mendoza public prosecutor, interview by author, 10 May 1999; Portabella, interview; Staib, interview.

66. Staib, interview.

Chapter 7

1. The 2003 transfer of power from Adolfo Rodríguez Saá to his brother Alberto did not diminish the need for a reform coalition in San Luis. Little changed other than the name of the brother who holds the governorship. Monolithic PJ control and executive dominance continued to characterize San Luis politics, and Alberto, who was Adolfo's advisor and closest political ally, is likely to govern in the same style as his brother.

2. Margaret E. Keck and Kathryn Sikkink, *Activists beyond Borders: Advocacy Net-*

works in International Politics (Ithaca: Cornell University Press, 1998), 16–25. Keck and Sikkink develop a typology of coalition strategies: information politics, leverage politics, accountability politics, and symbolic politics.

3. Keck and Sikkink, *Activists*, 26–29, 206–8.

4. Catalina Smulovitz, "Constitución y poder judicial en la nueva democracia argentina: La experiencia de las instituciones," in *La nueva matriz política argentina*, ed. Carlos H. Acuña (Buenos Aires: Nueva Visión, 1995), 72.

5. Verbitsky, interview by author, Buenos Aires, 3 December 1998.

6. María Rosa S. de Martini, "Civil Participation in the Argentine Democratic Process," in *The Democratic Revolution: Struggles for Freedom and Pluralism in the Developing World*, ed. Larry Diamond (New York: Freedom House, 1992), 47–48.

7. *Mapa del estado argentino 2000: Poder judicial nacional* (Buenos Aires: United Nations Development Program, 2001); Silvia Rueda de Uranga, Director of Conciencia, interview by author, Buenos Aires, 10 March 2003.

8. Poder Ciudadano, *Quién es quién en la justicia* (Buenos Aires: Fundación Poder Ciudadano, 1997); Marta Oyhanarte, *Cómo ejercer su Poder Ciudadano: Autoayuda democrática* (Buenos Aires: Tesis-Grupo Editorial Norma, 1992).

9. María Julia Pérez Tort, "The Citizens for Justice Program," in *Civil Society Initiatives for Transparency in the Justice Sector*, ed. Due Process of Law Foundation (Washington, D.C.: Due Process of Law Foundation, 2003), 74–76.

10. José Samper, PJ Congressman, interview by author, San Luis, 21 May 1999. However, by the 2001 culmination of Argentina's economic crisis, clientelism in San Luis had begun to falter.

11. Miguel Wiñazki, journalist, interview by author, Buenos Aires, 22 June 1999; Wiñazki, *El último feudo: San Luis y el caudillismo de los Rodríguez Saá* (Buenos Aires: Planeta, 1995), 71–84, 162–65.

12. Wiñazki, interview; Wiñazki, *El último feudo*, 184–85. For the same reason, many of the people that I interviewed for this book spoke off the record or requested that I substitute their professions for their names.

13. Ángel Fermín Garrote (FACA president) and Pedro Valle (FACA secretary), letter to bar associations throughout Argentina, 26 February 1998.

14. Germán Eduardo Arias, Dean of Social Sciences at Universidad Nacional de San Luis, interview by author, San Luis, 24 May 1999.

15. For an excellent discussion of the role of judges, see Jennifer A. Widner, *Building the Rule of Law: Francis Nyalali and the Road to Judicial Independence in Africa* (New York: W.W. Norton & Co., 2001). Using the experience of Africa, Widner shows how individual judges moved the cause of judicial autonomy forward.

16. Colegio de Abogados de Buenos Aires, "Restaurar la confianza perdida," *Nación*, 13 October 1993; Colegio de Abogados de Neuquén, *Río Negro*, 17 October 1993; "Se pronunció el Colegio," *El Litoral* (Santa Fe), 18 October 1993; "Denuncian crisis en la Corte," *El Sol* (Quilmes), 13 October 1993; "Córdoba," *Cronista Comercial*, 28 October 1993. For examples of FACA's role, see FACA, "Resolución," 4 April 1997; "Corte Suprema, acusada por los abogados," *Nación*, 28 October 1993.

17. Hugo Germano, Buenos Aires Bar Association president, interview by author, Buenos Aires, 11 March 2003. See "Declaración del Colegio," *Nación*, 27 September

1989; "Abogados: Opinión contraria al aumento," *La Prensa*, 10 February 1990; Ángel Anaya, "La punta de una crisis," *Nación*, 28 September 1989; "Crítica a la aplicación del recurso," *Nación*, 19 September 1990; "Seguridad jurídica," *Uno* (Mendoza), 9 December 1995.

18. "Abogados enjuician a la Corte," *Crónica*, 21 December 1993; "Frepaso no logró ayer rodear los tribunales," *Ámbito Financiero*, 10 October 1996.

19. Ignacio Alperín Bruvera, CACBA director, interview by author, Buenos Aires, 2 October 1998; Horacio Lynch, former CACBA president, interview by author, Buenos Aires, 23 September 1998. See *La Hoja*, 31 December 1997; 23 April 1998; 28 September 1998.

20. CEA, CACBA, and FORES, *Justicia y desarrollo económico,* Buenos Aires, September 1997; CEA and FORES, *Proyecto justicia y desarrollo económico: Anexo I, La justicia de las provincias argentinas,* Buenos Aires, 1998; Horacio Lynch and Silvana M. Stanga, *Reformas en la Corte Suprema* (Buenos Aires: FORES, 1987).

21. Miguel Ángel Rouco, "Piden arbitraje internacional por inseguridad jurídica," *Clarín*, 21 October 1996; Negri, interview by author, Buenos Aires, 21 October 1998.

22. Adolfo Casabal, Novum Millennium member, interview by author, Buenos Aires, 4 December 1998. See Teodoro Kreckler and Franco Caviglia, eds., *Justicia para todos: Políticas de consenso para la recuperación de la justicia argentina* (Buenos Aires: Fundación Novum Millennium, 1999).

23. Bindo Caviglione Fraga, former Asociación de Magistrados y Funcionarios de la Justicia Nacional president, interview by author, 22 October 1998; "Que el ciudadano confíe," *Semanario Jurídico* (Córdoba), September 1998. For more on Argentine judges' associations, see Carlos Manuel Garrido, "Informe sobre Argentina," in *Situación y políticas judiciales en América Latina*, ed. Jorge Correa Sutil (Santiago: Escuela de Derecho Universidad Diego Portalis, 1993), 63.

24. Argibay, interview by author, Buenos Aires, 24 June 1999; Gerónimo Sansó, Justicia Democrática president, interview by author, Buenos Aires, 18 June 1999; "No puedo mostrar con orgullo mi condición de juez," *Revista La Nación*, (21 September 1997), 48.

25. Social Forum for Justice, First Organizational Meeting, University of Buenos Aires Law School, 30 June 1999. De la Rúa selected Gil Lavedra to be Justice Minister in November 1999.

26. Daniel Casas, "Amo y señor de San Luis," *Tres Puntos*, 16 September 1998, 46; Martín Granovsky, "Su señoría," *Página 12*, 2 September 1998. See Chapter 4 for details on the Judicial Emergency Law, which declared the judiciary in a state of emergency for a one-year period that the Supreme Court extended for another 180 working days. During this period, the San Luis courts abstained from ruling on suits against the state and on suits that challenged the constitutionality of laws and decrees.

27. Fernando Rodríguez, "Careaga está dispuesta," *Nación*, 19 December 1998; Santiago O'Donnell, "San Luis: El caso que revela la crisis judicial," *Nación*, 2 November 1998. Five of the ninety-four judges and judicial functionaries that initially sued the government continued to litigate despite the government-controlled newspapers' effort to discredit them. The *Diario de la República* portrayed the five judges

as obstacles to the delivery of justice. See "Firmarán un acuerdo para terminar con los juicios," *Diario de la República*, 10 October 1998.

28. Superior Tribunal de Justicia, "Resolución," 5 February 1997; Cacace, interview by author, San Luis, 9 October 1998. In response to the resolution, Rodríguez Sáa purged the 1997 Court.

29. Pardo, interview by author, Buenos Aires, 10 December 1998; Verbitsky, *Hacer la Corte*, 16.

30. Fernando Flores, "Preocupación por la crisis," *Cronista*, 15 October 1996; Flores, "Inseguridad jurídica," *Cronista*, 9 December 1996; "Amenazadores modificaciones," *Cronista*, 9 December 1996. See CEA, CACBA, and FORES, *Justicia y desarrollo económico* (Buenos Aires: FORES, 1997).

31. See Trocello, "El discurso del régimen patrimonialista puntano," *Escenarios Alternativos* (autumn 1998): 63–74.

32. Arias, interview.

33. Keck and Sikkink, *Activists*, x.

34. Elisa Carrió, UCR Congresswoman, interview by author, 26 November 1998; Jorge Sosa and Martín Dinatale, "Menem busca mejorar la imagen de la justicia," *Cronista*, 25 October 1996.

35. Jorge Schvarstein, former CEJURA president, interview by author, Buenos Aires, 12 June 1998; USAID Office of Democracy and Governance, "Achievements in Building and Maintaining the Rule of Law," Occasional Papers Series, November 2002, 33–36.

36. Fernando González, "Justicia, bajo la lupa de EE.UU.," *Clarín*, 1 November 1996.

37. The Committee's proposals include monitoring and disseminating information about the Judicial Council and the Impeachment Jury, working with domestic civil society groups to increase the transparency of judicial appointments, and defending the tenure protection of judges. Ricardo Gil Lavedra, former Justice Minister, interview by author, Buenos Aires, 14 March 2003; Nilda Garré, Frepaso Congresswoman, interview by author, Buenos Aires, 12 March 2003; Enrique Petracchi, Supreme Court Justice, interview by author, Buenos Aires, 13 March 2003; Rueda de Uranga, interview; Germano, interview. Gil Lavedra, Garré, Petracchi, Rueda de Uranga, and Germano are members of the Judicial Committee within the Dialogue.

38. Miriam Agundez, San Luis Bar Association president, interview by author, San Luis, 24 May 1999; Ángel Fermín Garrote, FACA president, interview by author, Buenos Aires, 7 July 1999; "Denuncian persecución," *Ámbito Financiero*, 10 March 1998; Junta de Gobierno de FACA, "Resolución," 3 April 1998; "Acusan a Rodríguez Saá de manejar el poder judicial," *La Voz del Interior*, 11 March 1998.

39. "Denuncian maniobras en la Justicia de San Luis," *La Prensa*, 20 March 1998; "San Luis: 'Se está velando a la justicia,'" *Ámbito Financiero*, 25 March 1998; Comité Ejecutivo de la Provincia Distrito de San Luis, UCR, Resolución no. 04/98, 17 March 1998.

40. "Protesta de los abogados por la falta de justicia," *La Prensa*, 11 October 1998; "Más rachazos de abogados," *Los Andes*, 25 September 1997.

41. Ángel Fermín Garrote (FACA President) and Pedro Valle (FACA Secretary),

letter to bar associations throughout Argentina, 26 February 1998; Colegio de Abogados de General Roca, letter to San Luis Bar Association, 2 March 1998; Colegio de Abogados y Procuradores de Neuquén, "Por una justicia independiente en San Luis," 18 March 1998.

42. "San Luis sin justicia," *Hoy* (La Plata), 19 March 1998.

43. Diego May Zubiria (Buenos Aires Bar Association Secretary), letter to Miriam Agundez, 12 March 1998.

44. Carlos Alberto Huespe (FAM president) and Jorge Eduardo Vivas (FAM secretary), letter to Adolfo Rodriquez Saá, February 1998.

45. O'Donnell, "San Luis," *Nación*, 2 November 1998.

46. "Una mordaza para jueces independientes," *Nación*, 24 November 1998.

47. Sansó, interview; Argibay, interview; Justicia Democrática, "Conclusiones del Seminario sobre la independencia de los poderes judiciales provinciales" (paper presented at the conference Seminario sobre la independencia de los poderes judiciales provinciales, San Luis, Argentina, March 1999). Argibay explains that AMJA, an association of Argentine women judges, took part in the 1999 conference to support judges Careaga, Gallo, and Relly.

48. Poder Ciudadano-FACA press conference, "San Luis sin justicia," Buenos Aires, 25 September 1998.

49. Christian Courtis, CELS attorney, interview by author, Buenos Aires, 28 June 1999; Martín Abregú, CELS director, interview by author, Buenos Aires, 15 June 1999. The 1999 CELS report on human rights in Argentina included a chapter about violations in San Luis.

50. Abregú, interview.

51. Laura Zommer, "Para la ex jueza Gallo, 'hay un San Luis sin ley,'" *Nación*, 10 November 1998.

52. "Denuncian al gobierno de San Luis," *Noticias de Radio* (San Luis), año 11, no. 290, 10 April 1998.

53. Wiñazki, *El Adolfo: Crónicas del fascismo mágico en la Argentina* (Buenos Aires: Planeta, 2002), 24–26; Olga Wornat, "El Adolfo de San Luis," *Poder*, 27 November 2002; Verbitsky, "El último emperador," *Página 12*, 8 March 1998.

54. Steven Levitsky, "An Organized Disorganization: Informal Structures and the Persistence of Mass Organization in Argentine Peronism" (paper presented at the annual Latin American Studies Association meeting, Miami, Fla., March 2000), 3–4, 12–20.

55. Zaffaroni, interview by author, Buenos Aires, 1 July 1999; Walter Ceballos, San Luis Congressman (UCR), interview by author, San Luis, 19 May 1999; Juan José Laborda Ibarra, San Luis Congressman (Frepaso), interview by author, 18 May 1999; Eduardo Olivares, journalist, interview by author, San Luis, 26 May 1999.

56. Mario Otero, interview by author, San Luis, 24 May 1999.

57. Rubén Lijteroff, Virgilio Cortinez, and Julio Raba, "Urban Development and Air Quality in San Luis City, Argentina," *Environmental Monitoring and Assessment* 17 (1999): 170. See Fundación Capital, *Ranking Productivo Provincial*, Buenos Aires, March 1998, 17–18. Fundación Capital highlights the incentives to invest in provinces with IP.

58. Larry Sawers and Raquel Massacane, "Structural Reform and Industrial Promotion in Argentina," *Journal of Latin American Studies* 33 (2001): 108. Sawers and Massacane provide a history of IP in Argentina.

59. Sawers, *The Other Argentina: The Interior and National Development* (Boulder: Westview, 1996), 237–38. For a discussion of the shortcomings of IP, see Sawers, *Argentina*, 231–39.

60. Wiñazki, *El último feudo*, 92–99; "Repercusiones de una interna agitada," *Cronista*, 12 March 1999; "Mendoza: Legisladores amenazan con no votar el presupuesto," *Ámbito Financiero*, 21 September 1999; Ceballos, interview; Wiñazki, interview.

61. Wiñazki, *El último feudo*, 90; Wiñazki, interview. In 1998, the level of tax evasion in San Luis was second only to that of Menem's home province of La Rioja. "Evasión por $827 millones," *Clarín*, 12 March 1999.

62. Moreno Ocampo, interview by author, Buenos Aires, 19 April 1999. As Sawers and Massacane point out, however, Menem began to reform IP and reduced the number of new IP programs. Sawers and Massacane, "Structural Reform," 123–29.

63. See Kent Eaton, "Decentralisation, Democratisation, and Liberalisation: The History of Revenue Sharing in Argentina, 1934–99," *Journal of Latin American Studies* 33 (2001): 1–28. See also Sawers, *Argentina*, 218–26.

64. Sebastián Saiegh and Mariano Tommasi, "Argentina's Federal Fiscal Institutions: A Case Study in the Transaction-Cost Theory of Politics" (paper presented at conference on Modernization and Institutional Development in Argentina, UNDP, Buenos Aires, May 1998); Mark P. Jones, Pablo Sanguinetti, and Mariano Tommasi, "Politics, Institutions, and Public-Sector Spending in the Argentine Provinces," in *Fiscal Institutions and Fiscal Performance*, ed. James M. Poterba and Jurgen von Hagen (Chicago: University of Chicago Press, 1999), 136–37; Sawers, *Argentina*, 218. Menem's home province of La Rioja was even more dependent on federal transfers. Only 7 percent of La Rioja's expenditure came from provincial revenues.

65. Edward L. Gibson and Ernesto Calvo, "Federalism and Low-Maintenance Constituencies: Territorial Dimensions of Economic Reform in Argentina," *Studies in Comparative International Development* 35 (fall 2000): 42–43; Sawers, *Argentina*, 224–26. Sawers reports that in 1991 San Luis received $793 per capita from the federal government in revenue sharing, as compared to the national average of $284 per capita.

66. Eaton, "Decentralisation," 7. Discretionary transfers from the federal government to the provinces almost doubled between 1990 and 1995. See Gibson and Calvo, "Federalism," 42–43.

67. Moritz Kraemer, "Intergovernmental Transfers and Political Representation: Empirical Evidence from Argentina, Brazil and Mexico," Inter-American Development Bank, Office of the Chief Economist, Working Paper 345, January 1997, 12–22.

68. "Primer enfrentamiento de Alianza," *Ámbito Financiero*, 9 November 1999; "De la Rúa suspendió la promoción," *Ámbito Financiero*, 11 January 2000, "Malestar en provincias," *Ámbito Financiero*, 12 January 2000.

69. Ibarra, interview by author, Buenos Aires, 9 December 1998; Ventura, interview by author, Buenos Aires, 2 December 1998; Verbitsky, interview; "No investi-

garán al fiscal Stornelli," *Nación*, 5 November 1998; "Un verdadero tiro por la culata," *Clarín*, 5 November 1998; Diego Schurman, "Menem quiere la cabeza de Stornelli," *Página 12*, 4 November 1998. See Chapter 3 on the Ibarra and Stornelli incidents.

70. The Menem administration is widely suspected to have been involved in the 1997 murder of José Luis Cabezas, a photographer for the magazine *Noticias*.

71. "More isn't always better," *Buenos Aires Herald*, 7 April 1990; "Corte como prenda negociable," *El Litoral* (Santa Fe), 5 December 1993; "Cuánto vale una Corte," *Río Negro*, 16 October 1993; "El manoseo de la Corte," *El Popular* (Olavarria), 23 November 1993; "La Corte en entredicho," *Voz del Interior*, 1 December 1995; "Corte Suprema en entredicho," *El Territorio* (Posadas), 9 December 1995; "La designación del nuevo ministro," *La Capital* (Rosario), 5 December 1995.

72. Centro de Estudios Unión Para la Nueva Mayoria (CEUNM), Cuaderno No. 189, *La imagen de la justicia en la Argentina*, June 1996.

73. CEUNM, "La opinión pública cree más en las denuncias de los medios que en la justicia para combatir la corrupción," March 1998.

74. Laura G. Koch, "Old Democratic Pitfalls Dog the New Argentina," *Wall Street Journal*, 27 March 1992. Lawyers also utilize the media to aid the reform coalition. When Menem used a presidential plane to transport a cake from Buenos Aires to La Rioja in 1997, a Radio Plata reporter broadcast attorney Ricardo Monner Sans's assessment that the incident represented a misuse of public funds. The reporter called on listeners to present a suit against the government. Despite three days of pouring rain, approximately four hundred people signed the suit. Monner Sans, interview by author, Buenos Aires, 2 July 1999.

75. Poder Ciudadano, *Jueces y periodistas: Cómo se informa y cómo se juzga* (Buenos Aires: Fundación Poder Ciudadano, 1996).

76. Daniel Sabsay, Social Forum for Justice member, interview by author, 5 July 1999; Social Forum for Justice meeting, 30 June 1999.

77. Mario Otero, interview by author, San Luis, 24 May 1999.

78. Independent papers such as Otero's *El Decamerón* look more like pamphlets than newspapers. Nevertheless, they have helped the reform coalition disseminate information. *El Decamerón* contains extensive coverage of the judiciary and devoted entire issues to the removal of Gallo and Careaga. See "El más político de los juicios," *El Decamerón*, 2 November 1998; "La destitución de la jueza," *El Decamerón*, 15 November 1998; "Careaga: Dificil de acusar y dificil de defender," *El Decamerón*, 16 December 1998.

79. Otero, interview; Laborda Ibarra, interview.

80. Amnesty International, "Argentina: 'Occupational Hazards'? Attacks, Threats and Harassment against Journalists," May 1998, AI Index: AMR13/05/98; Olivares, interview.

81. Jaime Emma, *San Luis: La cárcel de los Rodríguez Saá* (Buenos Aires: Ediciones de la Urraca, 1992); Otero, interview; Wiñazki, interview.

82. Verbitsky, "El último emperador," *Página 12*, 8 March 1998; Graciela Rosso, interview with author, San Luis, 8 October 1998; Laborda Ibarra, interview; Pagano, interview by author, San Luis, 19 May 1999.

83. Wiñazki, interview.

84. Wiñazki, *El Adolfo*, 80–81; Yamila Fernández, TVC Puntana reporter, interview by author, San Luis, 19 May 1999; Otero, interview.

85. Olivares, interview; Otero, interview.

86. Lejtman, "Tradición, familia, propiedades," *Tres Puntos*, 16 September 1998; Wiñazki, *El último feudo* and *El Adolfo*.

87. Zaffaroni, interview.

88. Moreno Ocampo, interview.

89. Bovino, interview by author, Buenos Aires, 23 June 1999; Moreno Ocampo, interview.

90. "Echan a la jueza," *Nación*, 7 November 1998; O'Donnell, "San Luis," *Nación*, 2 November 1998; Claudia San Martín, "Destruyeron a la jueza," *Nación*, 18 December 1998; Martín Granovsky, "Su señoría," *Página 12*, 2 September 1998.

91. Almorzando con Mirtha Legrand, "Cinco mujeres que luchan por la justicia," 9 October 1998.

92. Keck and Sikkink, *Activists*, 16–25, 88–89.

93. Alberto Staib, interview by author, Mendoza, 11 May 1999; Aída Rosa Kemelmajer de Carlucci, Mendoza Supreme Court Justice, interview by author, Mendoza, 4 May 1999; "Se refirió también a la situación existente con el poder judicial," *Los Andes*, 2 May 1985. See Chapter 6 on the evolution of the Judicial Council in Mendoza.

94. Early in Mendoza's history, lawyers' associations struggled actively for judicial independence. For instance, after the 1928 federal intervention in Mendoza, a lawyers' association condemned the federal government's manipulation of the provincial judiciary. Pablo Lacoste, *La Unión Cívica Radical en Mendoza y en la Argentina 1890–1946* (Mendoza: Ediciones Culturales de Mendoza, 1995), 90–91. The Mendoza Bar Association denounced the May 1949 reform of the provincial constitution, arguing that it violated the separation of powers. Claudia Lacoste, "El proceso de reforma constitucional de Mendoza (1943–56)," in *La legislatura y las ciencias sociales* (Mendoza: Cámara de Senadores, 1995), 143–44.

95. Portabella, interview by author, Mendoza, 10 May 1999; Alejandro Pérez Hualde, interview by author, Mendoza, 7 May 1999. For instance, the Mendoza Bar Association works with other provincial groups to organize courses aimed at improving the performance of those who work in Mendoza's judiciary. See "Sobre 'responsibilidad profesional' darán curso," *Los Andes*, 14 September 1985; "Actualización en materia procesal," *Los Andes*, 22 May 1995.

96. Gabrielli, interview by author, Mendoza, 5 May 1999.

97. See "Encuentro de procuradores y fiscales," *Los Andes*, 11 May 1994.

98. Moreno Ocampo, interview; Luis Alejandro Cazaban, interview, Mendoza, 3 May 1999. The Lafalla administration, Transparency International, and Poder Ciudadano collaborated on the Isla de la Integridad (Island of Integrity) to make Mendoza a model of government transparency for other provinces. See "Mendoza, 'isla de la integridad,'" *Uno*, 29 July 1996.

99. Andrés Gabrielli, interview by author, Mendoza, 5 May 1999; Carlos la Rosa,

interview by author, Mendoza, 6 May 1999. See Chapter 6 for a detailed discussion of the Mendoza State Prosecutor (Fiscal de Estado).

100. Sergio Bruni, San Luis Congressman (UCR), interview by author, 6 May 1999; La Rosa, interview. La Rosa's survey on Mendocinos' opinion regarding various institutions revealed that they rely heavily on the press. They ranked the church as the most reliable institution followed by the press.

101. Lafalla, interview by author, Mendoza, 7 May 1999.

102. For instance, "Necesidad de construir una nueva penitenciaría," *Los Andes*, 9 August 1994, addressed inhumane prison conditions. "Un sentimiento de inseguridad jurídica," *Los Andes*, 2 September 1991, addressed the problems that confront the federal judiciary. "Necesidad de asegurar la administración de la justicia," *Los Andes*, 29 March 1987, stressed the backlog in Mendoza's courts. "La justicia y los tribunales del sur," *El Atuel* (San Rafael), 3 August 1988, focused on the shortage of funds available to courts.

Conclusion

1. The case of Mexico also suggests that the theoretical framework advanced in this book can travel beyond Argentina. Non-competitive politics inhibited the judiciary's ability to constrain the president in Mexico under the Partido Revolucionario Institucional (PRI), which dominated Mexico from 1929 until 2000.

2. See Rebecca Bill Chavez, "The Construction of the Rule of Law in Argentina: A Tale of Two Provinces," *Comparative Politics* 35 (July 2003): 417–37.

3. Colegio de Abogados de la Ciudad de Buenos Aires (CACBA) and Foro de Estudios para la Justicia (FORES), *La justicia de las provincias argentinas* (Buenos Aires: FORES, 1998). Eduardo Angeloz (UCR) served three consecutive terms as governor beginning in 1983.

4. CACBA and FORES, *Justicia*; Leonardo Jorge Schvarstein, former director of Centro de Estudios Judiciales de la República Argentina (CEJURA), interview by author, Buenos Aires, 12 June 1998.

5. For a more detailed discussion of the relationship between competitive politics and the rule of law in Chile, see Chavez, "The Construction of the Rule of Law in Nascent Democracies: Judicial Autonomy in Latin America" (Ph.D. diss., Stanford University, 2001).

6. In Chile, the Supreme Court intervenes in both the appointment and removal of lower court judges. Thus, in contrast to Argentina, the threat to judicial autonomy comes from within the judiciary itself rather than from the executive. Although the Chilean judiciary is independent of the political branches, what Carlos Peña González calls "external independence," the judiciary lacks "internal independence," meaning that lower courts are not autonomous of higher courts. Carlos Peña González, Dean of Universidad Diego Portalis Law School, interview by author, Santiago, 14 May 1999. On the appointment and removal process in Chile, see Jorge Correa Sutil, "The Judiciary and the Political System in Chile: The Dilemmas of Judicial Independence during the Transition to Democracy," in *Transition to Democracy*

in Latin America: The Role of the Judiciary, ed. Irwin P. Stotzky (Boulder: Westview, 1993), 96–101; Peña González, "Informe sobre Chile," in *Situación y políticas judiciales en América Latina*, ed. Correa Sutil (Santiago: Escuela de Derecho Universidad Diego Portalis, 1993), 328–30.

7. Arturo Valenzuela, *The Breakdown of Democratic Regimes: Chile* (Baltimore: Johns Hopkins University Press, 1978), 14.

8. See Scott Mainwaring and Timothy R. Scully, "Introduction," in *Building Democratic Institutions: Party Systems in Latin America*, ed. Mainwaring and Scully (Stanford: Stanford University Press, 1995), 6–17.

9. For an analysis of the Chilean party system, see Scully, *Rethinking the Center: Cleavages, Critical Junctures, and Party Evolution in Chile* (Stanford: Stanford University Press, 1992).

10. Weston H. Agor, *The Chilean Senate: Internal Distribution of Influence*, Latin American Monographs Series, no. 23, Institute of Latin American Studies (Austin: University of Texas Press, 1971), 22, 77–78; Valenzuela and Alexander Wilde, "Presidential Politics and the Decline of the Chilean Congress," in *Legislatures and Development: Dynamics of Change in New and Old States*, ed. Joel Smith and Lloyd D. Musolf (Durham: Duke University Press, 1979), 197–99; Valenzuela, *Breakdown*, 37, 70–72.

11. See Ronald H. McDonald and J. Mark Ruhl, *Party Politics and Elections in Latin America* (Boulder: Westview, 1989), 193; Alfredo Rehren, Chilean political scientist, interview by author, Santiago, 12 May 1999.

12. Peter M. Siavelis, *The President and Congress in Post-Authoritarian Chile: Institutional Constraints to Democratic Consolidation* (University Park: Pennsylvania State University Press, 2000), 122–35. See Patricio Navia and José Miguel Sandoval, "Binomial Electoral Law and Multi-Party System: The Chilean Contradiction" (paper presented at the annual Latin American Studies Association meeting, Chicago, Ill., September 1998).

13. Following the defeat of the Federalist Party in the 1800 elections, the Democratic party established itself as the dominant governmental party until 1856, controlling one or both branches during much of the period. For an in-depth analysis of the evolution of judicial autonomy over the course of U.S. history, see Chavez, John A. Ferejohn, and Barry R. Weingast, "A Theory of the Politically Independent Judiciary" (paper presented at the annual American Political Science Association meeting, Philadelphia, Pa., August 2003). The paper applies the theory of competitive politics to four eras of U.S. history: the period from the 1800 election until the Civil War; the period from the Civil War to the New Deal; the period from the New Deal to 1980; and the period since 1980.

14. Mathew McCubbins, Roger Noll, and Barry Weingast, "Politics and the Courts: A Positive Theory of Judicial Doctrine and the Rule of Law," *Southern California Law Review* 68 (September 1995), 1669.

15. McCubbins, Noll, and Weingast, "Politics and the Courts," 1668–69; William Cohen and Jonathan D. Varat, *Constitutional Law: Cases and Materials*, 9th ed. (Westbury, N.Y.: Foundation Press, 1993), 204.

16. Cohen and Varat, *Constitutional Law*, 205.

17. Alexander Lamis, "The Two-Party South: From the 1960s to the 1990s," in

Southern Politics in the 1990s, ed. Lamis (Baton Rouge: Louisiana State University Press, 1999), 1–9.

18. Key argues that the one-party system in the U.S. South fostered "lone-wolf operators" and "spectacular demagogues." V. O. Key Jr., *Southern Politics: In State and Nation* (New York: Alfred A. Knopf, 1950), 16.

19. Arthur M. Schlesinger Jr., *The Age of Upheaval* (New York: Houghton Mifflin, 1960), 68.

20. Key, *Southern Politics*, 156.

21. T. Harry Williams, "The Gentleman from Louisiana: Demagogue or Democrat," in *Huey P. Long: Southern Demagogue or American Democrat*, ed. Henry C. Dethloff (Boston: D.C. Heath & Co., 1967), 70; Key, *Southern Politics*, 162–63.

22. Williams, "Gentleman," 72; Williams, "Huey Long and the Politics of Realism," in *Essays on Recent Southern Politics*, ed. Harold M. Hollingsworth (Austin: University of Texas Press, 1970), 98–99.

23. Williams, *Huey Long* (New York: Alfred A. Knopf, 1969), 733–36. See William Ivy Hair, *The Kingfish and His Realm: The Life and Times of Huey P. Long* (Baton Rouge: Louisiana State University Press, 1991), 179–80, 248–50.

24. Richard C. Cortner, *The Kingfish and the Constitution: Huey Long, the First Amendment, and the Emergence of Modern Press Freedom in America* (Westport, Conn.: Greenwood Press, 1996), 35–40; Williams, *Huey Long*, 454–60; Key, *Southern Politics*, 162–63.

25. See Juan Linz, "The Perils of Presidentialism," *Journal of Democracy* 1 (1990), 51–69; Scott Mainwaring, "Presidentialism, Multipartism, and Democracy: The Difficult Combination," *Comparative Political Studies* 26 (1993), 198–228; Linz and Valenzuela, eds., *The Failure of Presidential Democracy*, vols. 1–2 (Baltimore: Johns Hopkins University Press, 1994).

Appendix

1. For an application of the spatial model to the evolution of judicial autonomy over time in the U.S. and in Argentina, see Rebecca Bill Chavez, John A. Ferejohn, and Barry R. Weingast, "A Theory of the Politically Independent Judiciary" (paper presented at the annual American Political Science Association meeting, Philadelphia, Pa., August 2003).

2. See Mathew McCubbins, Roger Noll, and Barry Weingast, "Politics and the Courts: A Positive Theory of Judicial Doctrine and the Rule of Law," *Southern California Law Review* 68 (September 1995): 1631–65; Ferejohn and Weingast, "A Positive Theory of Statutory Interpretation," *International Review of Law and Economics* 12 (1992): 263–79; Ferejohn and Weingast, "Limitation of Statutes: Strategic Statutory Interpretation," *Georgetown Law Journal* 80 (February 1992): 565–82. Major works on positive political theory and the judiciary include Pablo T. Spiller and Rafael Gely, "Congressional Control or Judicial Independence: The Determinants of U.S. Supreme Court Labor Decisions, 1949–88," *Rand Journal of Economics* 23 (1992): 463–92; William N. Eskridge, Jr., and John Ferejohn, "Making the Deal Stick: Enforcing the Original Constitutional Structure of Lawmaking in the Modern Regulatory State," *Journal of Law, Economics and Organization* 8 (March 1992): 165–89; Gely and

Spiller, "A Rational Choice Theory of Supreme Court Statutory Decisions with Applications to the *State Farm* and *Grove City* Cases," *Journal of Law, Economics and Organization* 6 (1990): 263–300; Brian A. Marks, "A Model of Judicial Influence on Congressional Policymaking: *Grove City College v. Bell*" (Ph.D. diss., Washington University, 1989).

3. C represents the position of the median member of Congress. It combines the House and the Senate and therefore does not reflect bicameralism.

4. Note that coordination is most likely when there is a high degree of party discipline, the second element of monolithic party control. As Chapter 1 argues, without discipline, copartisanship does not guarantee legislative acquiescence to the president's will. Legislators and presidents who are members of the same party may have competing ambitions. By compelling members of Congress to respond to the executive, strict discipline can eliminate competing executive-legislative preferences.

Selected Bibliography

Books, Journal Articles, and Conference Papers

Abernethy, David. *Dynamics of Global Dominance: European Overseas Empires, 1415–1980.* New Haven: Yale University Press, 2000.

Adrogué, Gerardo. "El nuevo sistema partidario argentino." In *La nueva matriz política argentina,* edited by Carlos H. Acuña, 27–70. Buenos Aires: Nueva Visión, 1995.

Agor, Weston H. *The Chilean Senate: Internal Distribution of Influence.* Latin American Monograph Series, no. 23. Institute of Latin American Studies, University of Texas at Austin. Austin: University of Texas Press, 1971.

Alberdi, Juan Bautista. *Bases y puntos de partido para la organización política de la República Argentina.* 2a reedición. Buenos Aires: La Cultura Argentina, 1915.

Alexander, Robert J. *Juan Domingo Perón: A History.* Boulder: Westview, 1979.

Alfonsín, Raúl. "The Function of Judicial Power During the Transition." In *Transition to Democracy in Latin America: The Role of the Judiciary,* edited by Irwin P. Stotzky, 41–52. Boulder: Westview, 1993.

———. *La reforma constitucional de 1994.* Buenos Aires: Tiempo de Ideas, 1994.

———. "'Never Again' in Argentina." *Journal of Democracy* 4 (January 1993): 15–19.

Alonso, Paula. *Between Revolution and the Ballot Box: The Origins of the Argentine Radical Party.* Cambridge: Cambridge University Press, 2000.

Amadeo, Santos Primo. *Argentine Constitutional Law: The Judicial Function in the Maintenance of the Federal System and the Preservation of Individual Rights.* New York: Columbia University Press, 1943.

Ames, Barry. "Electoral Strategy under Open-List Proportional Representation." *American Journal of Political Science* 30 (May 1995): 406–33.

"Argentina: Controversy Surrounding the Judiciary." *International Commission of Jurists Review* 45 (1990): 1–6.

Arjona, Flavio, Sergio Olivieri, and Fernanda MacIntosh. "Mendoza: La administración de justicia." *Novedades Económicas* (June 1996): 33–42.

Badeni, Gregorio. *Reforma constitucional e instituciones políticas.* Buenos Aires: Ad Hoc, 1994.

Baglini, Raúl, et al. *Juicio a la Corte.* Buenos Aires: Mecanografix, 1993.

Bailyn, Bernard. *The Debate on the Constitution.* New York: Library of America, 1993.

Baldez, Lisa, and John M. Carey. "Presidential Agenda Control and Spending Policy: Lessons From General Pinochet's Constitution." *American Journal of Political Science* 43 (January 1999): 29–55.

Banks, William C., and Alejandro D. Carrió. "Presidential Systems in Stress: Emergency Powers in Argentina and the United States." *Michigan Journal of International Law* 15 (fall 1993): 1–76.

Becker, Thomas L. *Comparative Judicial Politics: The Political Functionings of Courts.* Chicago: Rand McNally, 1970.

Beliz, Gustavo. *No robarás: ¿Es posible ganarle a la corrupción?* Buenos Aires: Editorial de Belgrano, 1997.

Berman, Harold J. *Law and Revolution: The Formation of the Western Legal Tradition.* Cambridge: Harvard University Press, 1983.

Bianchi, Alberto B. "¿Ha llegado la Corte Suprema al final de su lucha por una jurisdicción discrecional?" *El Derecho* 172 (1997): 923–41.

———. "La Corte Suprema ha establecido su tesis oficial sobre la emergencia económica." *La Ley (Jurisprudencia)* 41 (1991): 141–91.

Bielsa, Rafael, and Luis Francisco Lozano. "Apostillas relativas a las Leyes 24.937 y 24.939." *La Ley* 62 (12 November 1998): 1–3.

Biles, Robert E. "The Position of the Judiciary in the Political Systems of Argentina and Mexico." *Lawyer of the Americas* 8 (1976): 287–318.

Blair, Harry, and Gary Hansen. *Weighing in on the Scales of Justice: Strategic Approaches for Donor-Supported Rule of Law Programs.* USAID Program and Operations Assessment Report, no. 7. February 1994.

Bodin, Jean. *On Sovereignty: Four Chapters from the Six Books of the Commonwealth.* Translated and edited by Julian H. Franklin. Cambridge: Cambridge University Press, 1992.

Booth, John A. "Costa Rica: The Roots of Democratic Stability." In *Democracy in Developing Countries.* Vol. 4, *Latin America*, edited by Larry Diamond, Juan Linz, and Seymour Martin Lipset, 387–422. Boulder: Lynne Rienner, 1989.

Botana, Natalio. *El orden conservador: La política argentina entre 1880 y 1916.* Buenos Aires: Editorial Sudamericana, 1977.

Brody, Reed. "International Aspects of Current Efforts at Judicial Reform: Undermining Justice in Haiti." In *The (Un)Rule of Law and the Underprivileged in Latin America*, edited by Juan E. Méndez, Guillermo O'Donnell, and Paulo Sérgio Pinheiro, 227–42. Notre Dame: University of Notre Dame Press, 1999.

Brunsson, Nils. *The Organization of Hypocrisy: Talk, Decisions, and Actions in Organizations.* Translated by Nancy Adler. New York: Wiley, 1989.

Bueno de Mesquita, Bruce, Stephen Krasner, and Robert Jervis. "Symposium: Methodological Foundations of the Study of International Conflict." *International Studies Quarterly* 29 (June 1985): 119–54.

Buscaglia, Edgardo Jr., Maria Dakolias, and William Ratliff. *Judicial Reform in Latin America: A Framework for National Development.* Essays in Public Policy. Hoover Institution on War, Revolution and Peace, Stanford University, 1995.

Cafferata, Fernando J. *Nuevas Instituciones en la Constitución Nacional.* Córdoba, Argentina: Marcos Lerner Editora Córdoba, 1996.

Cain, Bruce, John Ferejohn, and Morris Fiorina. *The Personal Vote: Constituency Service and Electoral Independence*. Cambridge: Harvard University Press, 1987.

Calvert, Susan, and Peter Calvert. *Argentina: Political Culture and Instability*. Pittsburgh: University of Pittsburgh Press, 1989.

Carey, John M., and Matthew Soberg Shugart. "Incentives to Cultivate a Personal Vote: A Rank Ordering of Electoral Systems." *Electoral Studies* 14 (December 1995): 417–40.

Carothers, Thomas H. *In the Name of Democracy: U.S. Policy Toward Latin America in the Reagan Years*. Berkeley: University of California Press, 1991.

———. "The Rule of Law Revival." *Foreign Affairs* 77 (March-April 1998):95–106.

Carrió, Alejandro. *La Corte Suprema y su independencia*. Buenos Aires: Abeledo-Perrot, 1996.

Casas, Daniel. "Amo y señor de San Luis," *Tres Puntos* 2 (16 September 1998): 46–50.

Catterberg, Edgardo. *Argentina Confronts Politics: Political Culture and Public Opinion in the Argentine Transition to Democracy*. Boulder: Lynne Rienner, 1991.

Cavagna Martínez, Mariano Augusto. *Labor constituyente: Trabajos desarrollados en la convención nacional constituyente*. Buenos Aires: La Ley, 1995.

Cavagna Martínez, M. A., R. A. Bielsa, and E. R. Graña. *El poder judicial de la nación: Una propuesta de reconversión*. Buenos Aires: La Ley, 1994.

Cea Engaña, José Luis. "El Consejo de la Magistratura en el derecho constitucional comparado." In *Proposiciones para la reforma judicial*, edited by Eugenio Valenzuela S., 331–64. Santiago: Centro de Estudio Públicos, 1991.

Centro de Estudios Judiciales de la República Argentina (CEJURA). *El poder judicial en las constituciones provinciales de la Argentina*. Buenos Aires: La Ley, 1994.

———. *Estudio de opinión acerca de la administración de justicia*. Study conducted by Instituto Gallup Argentina. Buenos Aires: La Ley, 1994.

Chavez, Rebecca Bill. "The Construction of the Rule of Law in Argentina: A Tale of Two Provinces." *Comparative Politics* 35 (July 2003): 417–37.

———. "The Construction of the Rule of Law in Nascent Democracies: Judicial Autonomy in Latin America." Ph.D. dissertation, Stanford University, 2001.

Chavez, Rebecca Bill [Rebecca Ann Bill]. "Countervailing Power Centers and Judicial Autonomy in San Luis and Mendoza." Paper presented at the annual Latin American Studies Association meeting, Miami, Fla., March 2000.

Chavez, Rebecca Bill, John A. Ferejohn, and Barry R. Weingast. "A Theory of the Politically Independent Judiciary." Paper presented at the annual American Political Science Association meeting, Philadelphia, Pa., August 2003.

Ciancaglini, Sergio, and Gabriela Cerruti. *El octavo círculo*. Buenos Aires: Planeta, 1991.

Close, David, ed. *Legislatures and the New Democracies in Latin America*. Boulder: Lynne Rienner, 1995.

Cohen, Jerome Alan. "The Chinese Communist Party and 'Judicial Independence,' 1949–59." *Harvard Law Review* 82 (March 1969): 967–1006.

Cohen, William, and Jonathan D. Varat. *Constitutional Law: Cases and Materials*. 9th ed. Westbury, N.Y.: Foundation Press, 1993.

Colegio de Abogados de la Ciudad de Buenos Aires (CACBA), and Foro de Estudios para la Justicia (FORES). *La justicia de las provincias argentinas*. Buenos Aires: FORES, 1998.

Collier, David, and Steven Levitsky. "Democracy with Adjectives: Conceptual Innovation in Comparative Research." *World Politics* 49 (April 1997): 430–51.

Collier, Ruth Berins, and David Collier. *Shaping the Political Arena: Critical Junctures, the Labor Movement, and Regime Dynamics in Latin America*. Princeton: Princeton University Press, 1991.

Consejo Empresario Argentina (CEA), and Foro de Estudios para la Justicia (FORES). *Proyecto justicia y desarrollo económico: Anexo I, La justicia de las provincias argentinas*. Buenos Aires: FORES, 1998.

Consejo Empresario Argentina (CEA), Colegio de Abogados de la Ciudad de Buenos Aires (CACBA), and FORES. *Justicia y desarrollo económico*. Buenos Aires: FORES, 1997.

Correa Sutil, Jorge. "The Judiciary and the Political System in Chile: The Dilemmas of Judicial Independence during the Transition to Democracy." In *Transition to Democracy in Latin America: The Role of the Judiciary*, edited by Irwin P. Stotzky, 89–106. Boulder: Westview, 1993.

Cortner, Richard C. *The Kingfish and the Constitution: Huey Long, the First Amendment, and the Emergence of Modern Press Freedom in America*. Westport, Conn.: Greenwood Press, 1996.

Crassweller, Robert D. *Perón and the Enigmas of Argentina*. New York: W.W. Norton & Co., 1987.

Cruchaga, Melchor. "Los riesgos en el proyecto del gobierno." *Agrupación para una Justicia Democrática* 3 (1996): 15–17.

Dahl, Robert A. *Polyarchy: Participation and Opposition*. New Haven: Yale University Press, 1971.

D'Alessio, Andrés José. "The Function of the Prosecution in the Transition to Democracy in Latin America." In *Transition to Democracy in Latin America: The Role of the Judiciary*, edited by Irwin P. Stotzky, 187–201. Boulder: Westview, 1993.

De Luca, Miguel, Mark P. Jones, and María Inés Tula. "Argentine Political Parties and Their Candidate Nomination Procedures: 1983–89." Paper presented at the annual Latin American Studies Association meeting, Miami, Fla., March 2000.

De Martini, María Rosa S. "Civil Participation in the Argentine Democratic Process." In *The Democratic Revolution: Struggles for Freedom and Pluralism in the Developing World*, edited by Larry Diamond, 29–48. New York: Freedom House, 1992.

Diamond, Larry. "Democracy in Latin America: Degrees, Illusions, and Directions for Consolidation." In *Beyond Sovereignty: Collectively Defending Democracy in the Americas*, edited by Tom Farer, 52–104. Baltimore: Johns Hopkins University Press, 1996.

———. *Developing Democracy: Toward Consolidation*. Baltimore: Johns Hopkins University Press, 1999.

———. "Promoting Democracy in the 1990s: Actors and Instruments, Issues and Imperatives." A Report to the Carnegie Commission on Preventing Deadly Conflict, Carnegie Corporation of New York. New York: Carnegie Corporation, 1995.

———. "Rethinking Civil Society: Toward Democratic Consolidation." *Journal of Democracy* 5 (July 1994): 4–17.

Diamond, Larry, Juan J. Linz, and Seymour Martin Lipset, eds. *Politics in Developing Countries: Comparing Experiences with Democracy*. 2d ed. Boulder: Lynne Rienner, 1995.

Domingo, Pilar. "Judicial Independence and Judicial Reform in Latin America." In *The Self-Restraining State: Power and Accountability in New Democracies*, edited by Andreas Schedler, Larry Diamond, and Marc F. Plattner, 151–75. Boulder: Lynne Rienner, 1999.

Eaton, Kent. "Decentralisation, Democratisation, and Liberalisation: The History of Revenue Sharing in Argentina, 1934–99." *Journal of Latin American Studies* 33 (2001): 1–28.

Eckstein, Harry. "Case Study and Theory in Political Science." In vol. 7 of *Handbook of Political Science: Strategies of Inquiry*, edited by Fred Greenstein and Nelson Polsby, 79–137. Reading, Mass.: Addison-Wesley, 1975.

Edelmann, Alexander T. *Latin American Government and Politics: The Dynamics of a Revolutionary Society*. Homewood, Ill.: Dorsey Press, 1969.

Eder, Phanor J. "Judicial Review in Latin America." *Ohio State Law Journal* 21 (1960): 570–615.

Ehrenberg, John. *Civil Society: The Critical History of an Idea*. New York: New York University Press, 1999.

Emma, Jaime. *San Luis: La cárcel de los Rodríguez Saá*. Buenos Aires: Ediciones de la Urraca, 1992.

Eskridge, William N. Jr., and John Ferejohn. "Making the Deal Stick: Enforcing the Original Constitutional Structure of Lawmaking in the Modern Regulatory State." *Journal of Law, Economics and Organization* 8 (March 1992): 165–89.

Falcoff, Mark, and Ronald H. Dolkart. "Political Developments." In *Prologue to Perón: Argentina in Depression and War, 1930–1943*, edited by Mark Falcoff and Ronald H. Dolkart, 31–56. Berkeley: University of California Press, 1975.

Faundez, Julio, ed. *Good Government and Law: Legal and Institutional Reform in Developing Countries*. New York: St. Martin's Press, 1997.

Fayt, Carlos. *La supremacía constitucional y la independencia de los jueces*. Buenos Aires: Depalma, 1994.

———. *Nuevas fronteras del derecho constitucional: La dimensión político-institucional de la Corte Suprema de la Nación*. Buenos Aires: La Ley, 1995.

Feitlowitz, Marguerite. *A Lexicon of Terror: Argentina and the Legacies of Terror*. Oxford: Oxford University Press, 1998.

Fennell, Lee C. "Congress in the Argentine Political System: An Appraisal." In *Latin American Legislatures: Their Role and Influence*, edited by Weston H. Agor, 139–72. New York: Praeger, 1971.

Ferejohn, John, and Barry Weingast. "A Positive Theory of Statutory Interpretation." *International Review of Law and Economics* 12 (1992): 263–79.

———. "Limitation of Statutes: Strategic Statutory Interpretation." *Georgetown Law Journal* 80 (February 1992): 565–82.

Ferreira Rubio, Delia, and Matteo Goretti. "Cuando el presidente gobierna solo:

Menem y los decretos de necesidad y urgencia hasta la reforma constitucional, julio 1989-agosto 1994." *Desarrollo Económico* 36 (April-June 1996): 443–74.

Ferreira Rubio, Delia, and Matteo Goretti. "¿La reforma constitucional argentina: Un presidente menos poderoso?" *Contribuciones* 1 (1995): 60–89.

Fiss, Owen. "The Right Degree of Independence." In *Transition to Democracy in Latin America: The Role of the Judiciary*, edited by Irwin P. Stotzky, 55–72. Boulder: Westview, 1993.

Fitzgibbon, Russell H., ed. *The Constitutions of the Americas*. Chicago: University of Chicago Press, 1948.

Fleming, William. "The Cultural Determinants of Entrepreneurship and Economic Development: A Case Study of Mendoza Province, Argentina, 1861–1914." *Journal of Economic History* 39 (March 1979): 211–24.

Foro de Estudios para la Justicia (FORES). *Por el poder judicial: La estabilidad de los jueces como principio esencial*. FORES: Buenos Aires, 1983.

Fraga, Rosendo. *Los 90: La ilusión perdida*. Buenos Aires: El Ateneo, 2001.

Freedom House. *Freedom in the World 1994–1995*. New York: Freedom House, 1995.

Friedman, Barry. "'Things Forgotten' in the Debate Over Judicial Independence." *Georgia State University Law Review* 14 (July 1998): 737–66.

Fundación Capital. *Ranking productivo provincial*. Buenos Aires: Fundación Capital, March 1998.

Gabrielli, Adolfo R. *La Corte Suprema de Justicia y la opinión pública: 1976–1983*. Buenos Aires: Abeledo-Perrot, 1986.

Gambini, Hugo. *Historia del Peronismo: El poder total, 1943–1951*. Buenos Aires: Planeta, 1999.

García Lema, Alberto. "El Consejo de la Magistratura." In *El Consejo de la Magistratura*. Colección Temas Jurídicas. Buenos Aires: Fundación Omega Seguros, 1993.

———. "El Consejo de la Magistratura y el Jurado de Enjuiciamiento de jueces en la teoría de la división de poderes." *La Ley* 59 (26 April 1995): 1–5.

———. *La reforma por dentro: La difícil construcción del consenso constitucional*. Buenos Aires: Planeta, 1993.

Gargarella, Roberto. "Después del diluvio: El perfeccionismo conservador en la nueva jurisprudencia de la Corte Suprema, 1990–97." *Desarrollo Económico* 38 (April-June 1998): 439–56.

Garrido, Carlos Manuel. "Informe sobre Argentina." In *Situación y políticas judiciales en América Latina*, edited by Jorge Correa Sutil, 31–120. Santiago: Escuela de Derecho Universidad Diego Portalis, 1993.

Garro, Alejandro M. "The Role of the Argentine Judiciary in Controlling Governmental Action Under a State of Siege." *Human Rights Law Journal* 4 (1983): 311–37.

———. "Staffing the Judiciary and Prosecutorial Offices in Argentina: Trials and Tribulations in Search of Merit, Integrity, and Accountability." Paper presented at the annual Latin American Studies Association meeting, Miami, Fla., March 2000.

Gelli, María Angélica. "Veto y promulgación parcial en la reforma constitucional de

1994." In *Estudios sobre la reforma constitucional de 1994*, edited by Germán Bidart Campos and H. R. Sandler, 181–90. Buenos Aires: Ediciones Depalma, 1995.

Gely, Rafael, and Pablo T. Spiller. "A Rational Choice Theory of Supreme Court Statutory Decisions with Applications to the *State Farm* and *Grove City* Cases." *Journal of Law, Economics and Organization* 6 (1990): 263–300.

Gibson, Edward. *Class and Conservative Parties: Argentina in Comparative Perspective*. Baltimore: Johns Hopkins University Press, 1996.

Gibson, Edward L., and Ernesto Calvo. "Federalism and Low-Maintenance Constituencies." *Studies in Comparative International Development* 35 (fall 2000): 32–55.

Grondona, Mariano. *La realidad: El despertar del sueño argentino*. Buenos Aires: Planeta, 2001.

Groth, Alexander J. *Comparative Politics: A Distributive Approach*. New York: Macmillan, 1971.

Guagnini, Lucas, Santiago O'Donnell, and Ernesto Semán. "El estado contra Vázquez." *Tres Puntos* 1 (25 September 1997): 10–11.

Haas, Peter M. "Banning Chlorofluorocarbons: Epistemic Community Efforts to Protect Stratospheric Ozone." *International Organization* 46 (winter 1992): 187–224.

Hair, William Ivy. *The Kingfish and His Realm: The Life and Times of Huey P. Long*. Baton Rouge: Louisiana State University Press, 1991.

Hammergren, Linn A. *Politics of Justice and Justice Reform in Latin America: The Peruvian Case in Comparative Perspective*. Boulder: Westview, 1998.

Haring, C. H. *The Spanish Empire in America*. New York: Harcourt, Brace & World, 1947.

Helmke, Gretchen. "The Logic of Strategic Defection: Court-Executive Relations in Argentina Under Dictatorship and Democracy." *American Political Science Review* 96 (June 2002): 291–303.

Highton, Elena, and Elias Jassan. "Judicial Reform in Argentina." In *Judicial Reform in Latin America and the Caribbean*, edited by Malcolm Rowat, Waleed H. Malik, and Maria Dakolias. World Bank Technical Paper Series, no. 280. Washington, D.C.: World Bank, 1995.

Huntington, Samuel. *The Third Wave: Democratization in the Late Twentieth Century*. Norman: University of Oklahoma Press, 1991.

Iaryczower, Matías, Pablo T. Spiller, and Mariano Tommasi. "Judicial Independence in Unstable Environments, Argentina, 1935–98." *American Journal of Political Science* 46 (October 2002): 699–719.

Inglehart, Ronald, and Marita Carballo. "Does Latin America Exist? (And is there a Confucian Culture?) A Global Analysis of Cross-Cultural Differences." *Political Science and Politics* 30 (March 1997): 34–46.

Jan, Ameen. "Pakistan on a Precipice." *Asian Survey* 34 (September-October 1999): 699–719.

Jones, Mark P. "Evaluating Argentina's Presidential Democracy: 1983–95." In *Presidentialism and Democracy in Latin America*, edited by Scott Mainwaring and Matthew Soberg Shugart, 259–99. Cambridge: Cambridge University Press, 1997.

———. "Explaining the High Level of Party Discipline in the Argentine Congress." In *Legislative Politics in Latin America*, edited by Scott Morgenstern and Benito Nacif, 147–84. Cambridge: Cambridge University Press, 2002.

Jones, Mark P., Pablo Sanguinetti, and Mariano Tommasi. "Politics, Institutions, and Public-Sector Spending in the Argentine Provinces." In *Fiscal Institutions and Fiscal Performance*, edited by James M. Poterba and Jurgen von Hagen, 135–50. Chicago: University of Chicago Press, 1999.

Justicia Democrática. "Conclusiones del Seminario sobre la independencia de los poderes judiciales provinciales." Paper presented at the conference Seminario sobre la independencia de los poderes judiciales provinciales, San Luis, Argentina, March 1999.

Karl, Terry Lynn. "Dilemmas of Democratization in Latin America." *Comparative Politics* 23 (October 1990): 1–21.

———. "Economic Inequality and Democratic Instability." *Journal of Democracy* 11 (January 2000): 149–56.

———. "Imposing Consent? Electoralism versus Democratization in El Salvador." In *Elections and Democratization in Latin America, 1980–1985*, edited by Paul W. Drake and Eduardo Silva. San Diego: Center for Iberian and Latin American Studies and Center for U.S.-Mexican Studies, University of California at San Diego, 1986.

Karst, Kenneth L. "The Study of Latin American Law and Legal Institutions." In *Social Science Research on Latin America*, edited by Charles Wagley, 290–333. New York: Columbia University Press, 1964.

Karst, Kenneth L., and Keith S. Rosenn. *Law and Development in Latin America: A Case Book*. Berkeley: University of California Press, 1975.

Keck, Margaret E., and Kathryn Sikkink. *Activists beyond Borders: Advocacy Networks in International Politics*. Ithaca: Cornell University Press, 1998.

Keeling, David J. *Contemporary Argentina: A Geographical Perspective*. Boulder: Westview, 1997.

Key, V. O. Jr. *Southern Politics: In State and Nation*. New York: Alfred A. Knopf, 1950.

King, Gary, Robert O. Keohane, and Sidney Verba. *Designing Social Inquiry*. Princeton: Princeton University Press, 1994.

King, Preston. *The Ideology of Order: A Comparative Analysis of Jean Bodin and Thomas Hobbes*. London: Frank Cass, 1999.

Kirkpatrick, Jeane. *Leader and Vanguard in Mass Society: A Study of Peronist Argentina*. Cambridge: MIT Press, 1971.

Kraemer, Moritz. "Intergovernmental Transfers and Political Representation: Empirical Evidence from Argentina, Brazil and Mexico." Inter-American Development Bank, Office of the Chief Economist, Working Paper no. 345, January 1997.

Kreckler, Teodoro, and Franco Caviglia, eds. *Justicia para todos: Políticas de consenso para la recuperación de la justicia argentina*. Buenos Aires: Fundación Novum Millennium, 1999.

Lacoste, Claudia. "El proceso de reforma constitucional de Mendoza (1943–56) a través de la prensa y los debates constituyentes." In *La legislatura y las ciencias sociales*, 127–47. Mendoza: Cámara de Senadores, 1995.

Lacoste, Pablo. *El socialismo en Mendoza y en la Argentina.* Vol. 1. Buenos Aires: Centro Editor de América Latina, 1993.

———. *La generación del '80 en Mendoza, 1880–1905.* Mendoza: Editorial de la Universidad Nacional de Cuyo, 1995.

———. *La Unión Cívica Radical en Mendoza y en la Argentina, 1890–1946.* Mendoza: Ediciones Culturales de Mendoza, 1995.

———. *Los "gansos" de Mendoza: Aporte para el estudio de los partidos provincianos y del modelo conservador, 1880–1943.* Buenos Aires: Centro Editor de América Latina, 1991.

———. *Santiago Felipe Llaver, gobernador de Mendoza, 1983–1987.* Forthcoming.

———. "Ueltschi, gobernador (1958–61)." In *San Rafael: Historia y perspectivas,* 60–81. Edited by Pablo Lacoste. Serie Territorios de la Provincia de Mendoza, no. 10. Mendoza: Universidad de Congreso, Facultad de Ciencias Políticas Universidad Nacional de Cuyo, *Uno,* 1996.

Lagos, Marta. "How People View Democracy: Between Stability and Crisis in Latin America." *Journal of Democracy* 12 (January 2001): 137–45.

Lamis, Alexander, ed. *Southern Politics in the 1990s.* Baton Rouge: Louisiana State University Press, 1999.

Larkins, Christopher. "Judicial Independence and Democratization: A Theoretical and Conceptual Analysis." *American Journal of Comparative Law* 44 (fall 1996): 605–26.

Lehman Brothers. *Offering Circular, Province of Mendoza.* 2 August 1996.

Levitsky, Steven. "An Organized Disorganization: Informal Structures and the Persistence of Mass Organization in Argentine Peronism." Paper presented at the annual Latin American Studies Association meeting, Miami, Fla., March 2000.

Levy, Daniel C., and Kathleen Bruhn. "Mexico: Sustained Civilian Rule Without Democracy." In *Politics in Developing Countries: Comparing Experiences with Democracy.* 2d ed., edited by Larry Diamond, Juan J. Linz, and Seymour Martin Lipset, 171–218. Boulder: Lynne Rienner, 1995.

Lijphart, Arend. "The Comparable-Cases Strategy in Comparative Research." *Comparative Political Studies* 8 (July 1975): 158–77.

———. "Comparative Politics and the Comparative Method." *American Political Science Review* 65 (September 1971): 682–93.

———. *Electoral Systems and Party Systems: A Study of Twenty-Seven Democracies, 1945–1990.* Oxford: Oxford University Press, 1994.

Lijteroff, Rubén, Virgilio Cortinez, and Julio Raba. "Urban Development and Air Quality in San Luis City, Argentina," *Environmental Monitoring and Assessment* 17 (1999): 169–82.

Linares Quintana, Segundo V. "Comparison of the Constitutional Basis of the United States and the Argentine Political Systems." *University of Pennsylvania Law Review* 97 (April 1949): 641–64.

———. *El espíritu de la constitución.* Buenos Aires: Ad Hoc, 1993.

Linz, Juan J. "Democracy Today: An Agenda for Students of Democracy." *Scandinavian Political Studies* 20 (1997): 115–34.

———. "The Perils of Presidentialism." *Journal of Democracy* 1 (1990): 51–69.

Linz, Juan J., and Alfred Stepan. "Toward Consolidated Democracies." *Journal of Democracy* 7 (April 1996): 14–33.

Linz, Juan J., and Arturo Valenzuela, eds. *The Failure of Presidential Democracy*. 2 vols. Baltimore: Johns Hopkins University Press, 1994.

Loveman, Brian. *The Constitution of Tyranny: Regimes of Exception in Spanish America*. Pittsburgh: University of Pittsburgh Press, 1993.

Luna, Félix. *La Argentina era una fiesta, 1946–49*. Vol. 1 of *Perón y su tiempo*. Buenos Aires: Editorial Sudamericana, 1984.

Lynch, Horacio M., and Enrique V. Del Carril. *La Justicia: Un plan integral de reformas al sistema judicial argentina*. Buenos Aires: Fundación Banco de Boston, 1993.

Lynch, Horacio M., and Silvana M. Stanga. *Reformas en la Corte Suprema*. Buenos Aires: FORES, April 1987.

Macdonald, Austin F. *Government of the Argentine Republic*. New York: Thomas Y. Cromwell, 1942.

Madison, James, Alexander Hamilton, and John Jay. *The Federalist: A Commentary on the Constitution of the United States*. Modern Library Edition. New York: Random House, 1937.

Mainwaring, Scott. "Presidentialism, Multipartism, and Democracy: The Difficult Combination." *Comparative Political Studies* 26 (1993): 198–228.

Mainwaring, Scott, and Timothy R. Scully, eds. *Building Democratic Institutions: Party Systems in Latin America*. Stanford: Stanford University Press, 1995.

Mainwaring, Scott, and Matthew Soberg Shugart, eds. *Presidentialism and Democracy in Latin America*. Cambridge: Cambridge University Press, 1997.

Mann, Michael. *The Sources of Social Power: A Historical Comparison*. Cambridge: Cambridge University Press, 1986.

Manzetti, Luigi. *Institutions, Parties, and Coalitions in Argentine Politics*. Pittsburgh: University of Pittsburgh Press, 1993.

Mapa del estado argentino 2000: Poder judicial nacional. Buenos Aires: United Nations Development Program, 2001.

Marquardt, Ronald G. "Judicial Politics in the South: Robed Elites and Recruitment." In *Contemporary Southern Politics*, edited by James F. Lea, 242–62. Baton Rouge: Louisiana State University Press, 1988.

Mayhew, David. *Congress: The Electoral Connection*. New Haven: Yale University Press, 1974.

McCloskey, Robert G. *The American Supreme Court*. Chicago: University of Chicago Press, 1960.

McCubbins, Mathew, Roger Noll, and Barry Weingast. "Politics and the Courts: A Positive Theory of Judicial Doctrine and the Rule of Law." *Southern California Law Review* 68 (September 1995): 1631–89.

McDonald, Ronald H., and J. Mark Ruhl. *Party Politics and Elections in Latin America*. Boulder: Westview, 1989.

McGuire, James W. *Peronism Without Perón: Unions, Parties, and Democracy in Argentina*. Stanford: Stanford University Press, 1997.

Mecham, J. Lloyd. "Latin American Constitutions: Nominal and Real." *Journal of Politics* 21 (1959): 258–75.

Méndez Calzada, Luis. *La función judicial en las primeras épocas de la independencia: Estudio sobre la formación evolutiva del poder judicial argentino*. Buenos Aires: Editorial Losada, 1994.

Menéndez, Néstor Pedro. "La vera historia de los Rodríguez Páez o Rodríguez-Rodríguez y Páez-Montero, alias Rodríguez Saá." Appendix to *San Luis: La cárcel de los Rodríguez Saá*, by Jaime Emma. Buenos Aires: Ediciones de la Urraca, 1992.

Merryman, John Henry. *The Civil Law Tradition: An Introduction to the Legal Systems of Western Europe and Latin America*. 2d ed. Stanford: Stanford University Press, 1985.

Meyer, John W., and Brian Rowan. "Institutionalized Organizations: Formal Structure in Myth and Ceremony." In *The New Institutionalism in Organizational Analysis*, edited by Paul J. DiMaggio and Walter W. Powell, 41–62. Chicago: University of Chicago Press, 1991.

Mill, John Stuart. "Two Methods of Comparison." In *Comparative Perspectives: Theories and Methods*, edited by Amitai Etzioni and Frederic L. Dubow, 205–12. Boston: Little, Brown, 1970. Originally published in John Stuart Mill, *A System of Logic* (New York: Harper and Row, 1888).

Miller, Jonathan M. "Courts and the Creation of a 'Spirit of Moderation': Judicial Protection of Revolutionaries in Argentina, 1863–1929." *Hastings International and Comparative Law Review* 20 (fall 1997): 231–329.

———. "Judicial Review and Constitutional Stability: A Sociology of the U.S. Model and its Collapse in Argentina." *Hastings International and Comparative Law Review* 21 (fall 1998): 77–176.

Molinelli, N. Guillermo. "El veto parcial: ¿Qué hacer?" *Sentencia* (December 1992): 54–57.

———. "Las relaciones presidente-congreso en Argentina '83-'95." *PostData* 2 (November 1996): 59–90.

———. *Presidentes y congresos en Argentina: Mitos y realidades*. Buenos Aires: Grupo Editor Latinoamericano, 1991.

———. "Sobre 'gobierno unificado / dividido' en América Latina." 4 April 1998. Photocopy.

Molinelli, N. Guillermo, M. Valeria Palanza, and Gisela Sin. *Congreso, presidencia y justicia en Argentina: Materiales para su estudio*. Buenos Aires: Temas Grupo Editorial, 1999.

Montesquieu, Charles. *The Spirit of the Laws*. Edited by Anne M. Cohler, Basia Carolyn Miller, and Harold Samuel Stone. Cambridge: Cambridge University Press, 1989.

Morales Solá, Joaquín. *Asalto a la ilusión*. Buenos Aires: Planeta, 1990.

Morgenstern, Scott, and Benito Nacif, eds. *Legislative Politics in Latin America*. Cambridge: Cambridge University Press, 2002.

Mustapic, Ana María. "Oficialistas y diputados: Las relaciones ejecutivo-legislativo en la Argentina." Paper presented at the conference on Legislaturas en América Latina: Perspectivas Comparadas, Mexico City, February 1998.

———. "Tribulaciones del Congreso en la nueva democracia argentina: El veto presidencial bajo Alfonsín y Menem." *Agora* (winter 1995): 61–74.

Mustapic, Ana María, and Natalia Ferretti. "El veto presidencial bajo Alfonsín and Menem (1983–95)." Paper presented at the annual Latin American Studies Association meeting, Washington, D.C., September 1995.

Mustapic, Ana María, and Matteo Goretti. "Gobierno y oposición en el Congreso: La práctica de la cohabitación durante la presidencia de Alfonsín, 1983–89." *Desarrollo Económico* 32 (July-September 1992): 251–69.

Nagle, Luz Estella. "Evolution of the Colombian Judiciary and the Constitutional Court." *Indiana International and Comparative Law Review* 6 (1995): 59–90.

National Democratic Institute for International Affairs. "Committees in Legislatures: A Division of Labor." Legislative Research Series, no. 2. Washington, D.C.: National Democratic Institute for International Affairs, 1996.

Navia, Patricio, and José Miguel Sandoval. "Binomial Electoral Law and Multi-Party System: The Chilean Contradiction." Paper prepared for the annual Latin American Studies Association meeting, Chicago, Ill., September 1998.

Negretto, Gabriel L. "Constitution-Making and Institutional Design: The Reform of Presidentialism in the Argentine Constitution of 1994." Paper prepared for the annual Latin American Studies Association meeting, Chicago, Ill., September 1998.

Negretto, Gabriel, and Mark Ungar. "Independencia del poder judicial y estado de derecho en América Latina: Los casos de Argentina y Venezuela." *Política y Gobierno* 4 (1997): 81–114.

Nino, Carlos S. *Fundamentos de derecho constitucional.* Buenos Aires: Astrea, 1992.

———. "Hyperpresidentialism and Constitutional Reform in Argentina." In *Institutional Design in New Democracies: Eastern Europe and Latin America*, edited by Arend Lijphart and Carlos H. Waisman, 161–74. Boulder: Westview, 1996.

———. "On the Exercise of Judicial Review in Argentina." In *Transition to Democracy in Latin America: The Role of the Judicary*, edited by Irwin P. Stotzky, 309–35. Boulder: Westview, 1993.

———. *Un país al margen de la ley: Estudio de la anomia como componente del subdesarrollo argentino.* Buenos Aires: Emecé Editores, 1992.

North, Douglass, and Barry Weingast. "Constitutions and Commitment: The Evolution of Institutions Governing Public Choice in Seventeenth-Century England." *Journal of Economic History* 49 (December 1989): 803–32.

O'Donnell, Guillermo. "Delegative Democracy." *Journal of Democracy* 5 (January 1994): 55–69.

———. "Horizontal Accountability in New Democracies." In *The Self-Restraining State: Power and Accountability in New Democracies*, edited by Andreas Schedler, Larry Diamond, and Marc F. Plattner, 29–51. Boulder: Lynne Rienner, 1999.

Oyhanarte, Julio. "Historia del poder judicial." *Todo es Historia* (May 1972): 88–121.

Oyhanarte, Marta. *Cómo ejercer su Poder Ciudadano: Autoayuda democrática.* Buenos Aires: Tesis-Grupo Editorial Norma, 1992.

Packenham, Robert A. "Legislatures in Political Development." In *Legislatures in Developmental Perspective*, edited by Allan Kornberg and Lloyd D. Musolf, 81–96. Durham: Duke University Press, 1970.

Pagano, Roberto. "Jurado de Enjuiciamiento de la Provincia de San Luis, su brutal conquista, propuesta para su liberación." Paper presented at the conference Seminario sobre la independencia de los poderes judiciales provinciales, San Luis, Argentina, March 1999.

Peña González, Carlos. "Informe sobre Chile." In *Situación y políticas judiciales en América Latina*, edited by Jorge Correa Sutil, 285–381. Santiago: Escuela de Derecho Universidad Diego Portalis, 1993.

Pérez Tort, María Julia. "The Citizens for Justice Program." In *Civil Society Initiatives for Transparency in the Justice Sector*, edited by Due Process of Law Foundation, 73–78. Washington, D.C.: Due Process of Law Foundation, 2003.

Persson, Torsten, Gerard Roland, and Guido Tabellini. "Separation of Powers and Political Accountability." *Quarterly Journal of Economics* 112 (1997): 1163–1202.

Piedrabuena Richards, Guillermo. *La reforma constitucional*. Santiago: Ediciones Encina, 1970.

Poder Ciudadano. *Jueces y periodistas: Cómo se informa y cómo se juzga*. Buenos Aires: Fundación Poder Ciudadano, 1996.

———. *Quién es quién en la justicia*. Buenos Aires: Fundación Poder Ciudadano, 1997.

Poneman, Daniel. *Argentina: Democracy on Trial*. New York: Paragon House, 1987.

Popkin, Margaret. "Efforts to Enhance Judicial Independence in Latin America." In *Guidance for Promoting Judicial Independence and Impartiality*. Rev. ed. U.S. Agency for International Development, Technical Publication Series, January 2002.

Przeworski, Adam. *Democracy and the Market*. Cambridge: Cambridge University Press, 1991.

Przeworski, Adam, and Henry Teune. *The Logic of Comparative Social Inquiry*. New York: Wiley Interscience, 1970.

Przeworski, Adam, et al. "What Makes Democracies Endure?" *Journal of Democracy* 7 (January 1996): 39–55.

Puryear, Jeffrey M. *Thinking Politics: Intellectuals and Democracy in Chile, 1973–1988*. Baltimore: Johns Hopkins University Press, 1994.

Putnam, Robert. *Making Democracy Work: Civic Traditions in Modern Italy*. Princeton: Princeton University Press, 1993.

"¿Qué es CEJURA?" *CEJURA*. Boletín no. 1 (February 1995): 7–10.

Quiroga Lavié, Humberto. *Constitución de la nación argentina comentada*. 3d ed. Buenos Aires: Zavalía, 2000.

Ranis, Peter. "Profile Variables Among Argentine Legislators." In *Latin American Legislatures: Their Role and Influence*, edited by Weston H. Agor, 173–258. New York: Praeger, 1971.

Remmer, Karen L. *Party Competition in Argentina and Chile: Political Recruitment and Public Policy, 1890–1930*. Lincoln: University of Nebraska Press, 1984.

Rock, David. *Argentina 1516–1987: From Spanish Colonization to Alfonsín*. Berkeley: University of California Press, 1987.

Rodríguez Lamas, Daniel. *La presidencia de Frondizi*. Buenos Aires: Centro Editor de América Latina, 1984.

Root, Hilton. "Tying the King's Hands: Credible Commitments and Royal Fiscal Policy During the Old Regime." *Rationality and Society* 1 (October 1989): 240–58.

Rosenn, Keith S. "Judicial Review in Latin America." *Ohio State Law Journal*, 35 (1974): 785–819.

Rustow, Dankwart. "Transitions to Democracy: Toward a Dynamic Model." *Comparative Politics* 2 (April 1970): 337–63.

Sabatini, Christopher. "Whom Do International Donors Support in the Name of Civil Society?" Paper presented at the annual Latin American Studies Association meeting, Miami, Fla., March 2000.

Saiegh, Sebastián, and Mariano Tommasi. "Argentina's Federal Fiscal Institutions: A Case Study in the Transaction-Cost Theory of Politics." Paper presented at the Conference on Modernization and Institutional Development in Argentina, Programa de las Naciones Unidas para el Desarrollo (PNUD), Buenos Aires, May 1998.

Samper, José. *San Luis: La (in)dependencia de los poderes*. San Luis: Alta Editorial, 1993.

Sansó, Gerónimo. "Comentario crítico sobre el proyecto de ley del Consejo." *Agrupación para una Justicia Democrática Revista* 3 (1996): 19–20.

Sawers, Larry. *The Other Argentina: The Interior and National Development*. Boulder: Westview, 1996.

Sawers, Larry, and Raquel Massacane. "Structural Reform and Industrial Promotion in Argentina." *Journal of Latin American Studies* 33 (2001): 101–32.

Schedler, Andreas, Larry Diamond, and Marc F. Plattner, eds. *The Self-Restraining State: Power and Accountability in New Democracies*. Boulder: Lynne Rienner, 1999.

Schlesinger, Arthur M. Jr. *The Age of Upheaval*. New York: Houghton Mifflin, 1960.

Schmitter, Philippe. "Comments on O'Donnell." In *The Self-Restraining State: Power and Accountability in New Democracies*, edited by Andreas Schedler, Larry Diamond, and Marc F. Plattner, 59–62. Boulder: Lynne Rienner, 1999.

Schubert, Glendon. *Judicial Policy Making*. Glenview, Ill.: Scott, Foresman & Co., 1974.

Schwartz, Herman. "Eastern Europe's Constitutional Courts." *Journal of Democracy* 9 (October 1988): 100–114.

———. *Packing the Courts: The Conservative Campaign to Rewrite the Constitution*. New York: Charles Scribner's Sons, 1988.

Schwartz, Richard D., and James C. Miller. "Legal Evolution and Societal Complexity." *American Journal of Sociology* 70 (September 1964): 159–69.

Scobie, James R. *Argentina: A City and a Nation*. 2d ed. Oxford: Oxford University Press, 1971.

Scott, Robert E. "Legislatures and Legislation." In *Government and Politics in Latin America*, edited by Harold Eugene Davis. New York: Ronald Press, 1958.

Scully, Timothy. *Rethinking the Center: Cleavages, Critical Junctures, and Party Evolution in Chile*. Stanford: Stanford University Press, 1992.

Segal, Jeffrey A., and Harold J. Spaeth. *The Supreme Court and the Attitudinal Model*. Cambridge: Cambridge University Press, 1993.

"Sesiones plenarias." *Obra de la convención nacional constituyente de 1994*. Vol. 5. Centro de Estudios Constitucionales y Políticos. Ministerio de Justicia de la Nación (Argentina).

Shugart, Matthew Soberg. "The Electoral Cycle and Institutional Sources of Divided Presidential Government." *American Political Science Review* 89 (June 1995): 327–43.

Shugart, Matthew S., and John M. Carey. *Presidents and Assemblies: Constitutional Design and Electoral Dynamics*. Cambridge: Cambridge University Press, 1992.

Shumway, Nicolas. *The Invention of Argentina*. Berkeley: University of California Press, 1991.

Siavelis, Peter M. *The President and Congress in Post-Authoritarian Chile: Institutional Constraints to Democratic Consolidation*. University Park: Pennsylvania State University Press, 2000.

Skocpol, Theda, and Margaret Somers. "The Uses of Comparative History in Macrosocial Inquiry." *Comparative Studies in Society and History* 22 (April 1980): 174–97.

Smelser, Neil J. "The Methodology of Comparative Analysis of Economic Activity." In *Essays in Sociological Interpretation*, edited by Neil J. Smelser, 62–75. Englewood Cliffs, N.J.: Prentice Hall, 1968.

Smith, Peter H. *Argentina and the Failure of Democracy: Conflict among Political Elites, 1904–1955*. Madison: University of Wisconsin Press, 1974.

Smulovitz, Catalina. "Constitución y poder judicial en la nueva democracia argentina: La experiencia de las instituciones." In *La nueva matriz política argentina*, edited by Carlos H. Acuña, 71–114. Buenos Aires: Nueva Visión, 1995.

Snow, Peter G. *Political Forces in Argentina*. Rev. ed. New York: Praeger, 1979.

Snow, Peter G., and Luigi Manzetti. *Political Forces in Argentina*. 3rd ed. Westport, Conn.: Praeger, 1993.

Spiller, Pablo T., and Rafael Gely. "Congressional Control or Judicial Independence: The Determinants of U.S. Supreme Court Labor Decisions, 1949–88." *Rand Journal of Economics* 23 (1992): 463–92.

Stepan, Alfred, and Cindy Skach. "Constitutional Frameworks and Democratic Consolidation: Parliamentarism and Presidentialism." *World Politics* 46 (October 1993): 1–22.

Stotzky, Irwin P., ed. *Transition to Democracy in Latin America: The Role of the Judiciary*. Boulder: Westview, 1993.

Stotzky, Irwin P., and Carlos S. Nino. "The Difficulties of the Transition Process." In *Transition to Democracy in Latin America: The Role of the Judiciary*, edited by Irwin P. Stotzky, 3–20. Boulder: Westview, 1993.

Szusterman, Celia. *Frondizi and the Politics of Developmentalism in Argentina, 1955–62*. London: Macmillan, 1993.

Tocqueville, Alexis de. *Democracy in America*. Everyman's Library Edition. New York: Alfred A. Knopf, 1994.

Trocello, María Gloria. "El discurso del régimen patrimonialista puntano." *Escenarios Alternativos* 3 (autumn 1998): 63–74.

Ungar, Mark. *Elusive Reform: Democracy and the Rule of Law in Latin America*. Boulder: Lynne Rienner, 2002.

Urbanski, Edmund Stefan. *Angloamérica e Hispanoamérica: Análisis de dos civilizaciones*. Madrid: Ediciones Studium, 1965.

Valenzuela, Arturo. *The Breakdown of Democratic Regimes: Chile*. Baltimore: Johns Hopkins University Press, 1978.

Valenzuela, Arturo, and Alexander Wilde. "Presidential Politics and the Decline of the Chilean Congress." In *Legislatures and Development: Dynamics of Change in New and Old States*, edited by Joel Smith and Lloyd D. Musolf, 189–215. Durham: Duke University Press, 1979.

Van Evera, Stephen. *Guide to Methods for Students of Political Science*. Ithaca: Cornell University Press, 1997.

Vanossi, Jorge. "El asiento de la decisión política en el régimen de la democracia constitucional." *Pensamiento Constitucional* 4 (1997): 55–77.

———. "El porvenir de la reforma constitucional." *Revista del Colegio de Abogados de la Ciudad de Buenos Aires* 58 (July 1998): 9–22.

———. "La constitución evanescente." *La Ley* 58 (2 December 1994): 1–3.

———. "Reglamentación legal de los decretos de necesidad y urgencia." Proyecto de Ley. *Tramite Parlamentario*, no. 32, 12 June 1992.

Ventura, Adrián. *Consejo de la Magistratura y Jurado de Enjuiciamiento en el derecho comparado y nacional*. Buenos Aires: Ediciones Depalma, 1998.

Vera Villalobos, Enrique. *El poder de nuestro voto: Todo lo que hay que saber sobre la reforma que exige el régimen electoral argentino*. Buenos Aires: Planeta, 1994.

Verbitsky, Horacio. *Hacer la Corte: La construcción de un poder absoluto sin justicia ni control*. Buenos Aires: Planeta, 1993.

———. *Un mundo sin periodistas*. Buenos Aires: Planeta, 1997.

———. *Robo para la corona: Los frutos prohibidos del árbol de corrupción*. Buenos Aires: Planeta, 1991.

Vidal, Armando. *El Congreso en la trampa: Entretelones y escándalos de la vida parlamentaria*. Buenos Aires: Planeta, 1995.

Vile, M. J. C. *Constitutionalism and the Separation of Powers*. Oxford: Oxford University Press, 1967.

Von Mehren, Arthur Taylor. *The Civil Law System: Cases and Materials for the Comparative Study of Law*. Englewood Cliffs, N.J.: Prentice Hall, 1957.

Weingast, Barry. "The Political Foundations of Democracy and the Rule of Law." *American Political Science Review* 91 (June 1997): 245–63.

Widner, Jennifer A. *Building the Rule of Law: Francis Nyalali and the Road to Judicial Independence in Africa*. New York: W.W. Norton & Co., 2001.

Williams, T. Harry. "The Gentleman from Louisiana: Demagogue or Democrat." In *Huey P. Long: Southern Demagogue or American Democrat*, edited by Henry C. Dethloff, 63–75. Boston: D.C. Heath & Co., 1967.

———. *Huey Long*. New York: Alfred A. Knopf, 1969.

———. "Huey Long and the Politics of Realism." In *Essays on Recent Southern Politics*, edited by Harold M. Hollingsworth, 95–115. Austin: University of Texas Press, 1970.

Williamson, Oliver E. *The Economic Institutions of Capitalism: Firms, Markets, Relational Contracting*. New York: Free Press, 1985.

Wiñazki, Miguel. *El Adolfo: Crónicas del fascismo mágico en la Argentina*. Buenos Aires: Planeta, 2002.

———. *El último feudo: San Luis y el caudillismo de los Rodríguez Saá.* Buenos Aires: Planeta, 1995.

World Economic Forum, and Center for International Development at Harvard University. *Global Competitiveness Report 2000.* Oxford: Oxford University Press, 2000.

Wynia, Gary W. "Argentina's New Democracy: Presidential Power and Legislative Limits." In *Legislatures and the New Democracies in Latin America*, edited by David Close, 71–87. Boulder: Lynne Rienner, 1995.

Zaffaroni, Eugenio Raúl. *Estructuras judiciales.* Buenos Aires: Ediar Sociedad Anónima Editora, 1994.

Zakaria, Fareed. "The Rise of Illiberal Democracy." *Foreign Affairs* 6 (November-December 1997): 22–43.

Zavalía, Clodomiro. *Historia de la Corte Suprema de Justicia de la República Argentina en relación con su modelo americano.* Buenos Aires: Talleres Casa Jacobo Peuser, 1920.

Government Documents

Cámara de Diputados, Provincia de Mendoza. *Reglamento, Cámara de Diputados.* 1998.

Constitución de la República Argentina, 1853.

Constitución de la República Argentina, 1994.

Constitución de la Provincia de San Luis, 1987.

Constitución de la Provincia de Mendoza, 1916.

Honorable Cámara de Senadores, Provincia de Mendoza. *Reglamento Interno de la Honorable Cámara de Senadores.* June 1995.

Ley Orgánica de la Administración de Justicia de la Provincia de San Luis. Ley no. 5158. 15 December 1998.

Ley Orgánica del Ministerio Público. Ley no. 24,946. 23 March 1998.

Ley Orgánica de Tribunales de San Luis. Ley no. 4929. 2 December 1991.

Superior Tribunal de Justicia de San Luis. Acuerdo no. 25. 9 February 1998.

Superior Tribunal de Justicia de San Luis. Informe Ley no. 5113. 15 April 1998.

Superior Tribunal de Justicia de San Luis. Resolución. 5 February 1997.

U.S. Agency for International Development, Office of Democracy and Governance. "Achievements in Building and Maintaining the Rule of Law." Occasional Papers Series, November 2002.

U.S. Department of State. *Country Reports on Human Rights Practices for 1995.* Report Submitted to the Committee on International Relations, U.S. House of Representatives and the Committee on Foreign Relations, U.S. Senate in accordance with Sections 116(d) and 502B(b) of the Foreign Assistance Act of 1996, as amended. April 1996. 104th Cong., 2d Sess.

———. *1999 Country Reports on Human Rights Practices.* Released by the Bureau of Democracy, Human Rights, and Labor, 25 February 2000.

Periodicals Cited

ABC Político. Buenos Aires, Argentina.

Ámbito Financiero. Buenos Aires, Argentina.

Buenos Aires Herald. Buenos Aires, Argentina.
Christian Science Monitor.
Clarín. Buenos Aires, Argentina.
Crónica. Buenos Aires, Argentina.
Diario de Cuyo. San Juan, Argentina.
Diario Popular. Buenos Aires, Argentina.
Economist.
El Atuel. Mendoza, Argentina.
El Cronista Comercial. Buenos Aires, Argentina.
El Decamerón. San Luis, Argentina.
El Día. La Plata, Argentina.
El Diario de la República. San Luis, Argentina.
El Economista. Buenos Aires, Argentina.
El Informador Público. Buenos Aires, Argentina.
El Liberal. Santiago del Estero, Argentina.
El Litoral. Corrientes, Argentina.
El Litoral. Santa Fe, Argentina.
El Popular. Olavarria, Argentina.
El Sol. Quilmes, Argentina.
El Territorio. Posadas, Argentina.
El Tribuno. Salta, Argentina.
Extra. Buenos Aires, Argentina.
Financial Times.
Hoy. La Plata, Argentina.
La Arena. La Pampa, Argentina.
La Capital. Rosario, Argentina.
La Hoja. Buenos Aires, Argentina.
La Maga. Buenos Aires, Argentina.
La Nación. Buenos Aires, Argentina.
La Nueva Provincia. Bahía Blanca, Argentina.
La Opinión. San Luis, Argentina.
La Prensa. Buenos Aires, Argentina.
La Voz del Interior. Córdoba, Argentina.
Los Andes. Mendoza, Argentina.
New York Times.
Noticias. Buenos Aires, Argentina.
Noticias de Radio. San Luis, Argentina.
Nuevo Sur. Buenos Aires, Argentina.
Página 12. Buenos Aires, Argentina.
Río Negro. General Roca, Argentina.
Semanario Jurídico. Córdoba, Argentina.
Somos. Buenos Aires, Argentina.
Tres Puntos. Buenos Aires, Argentina.
Uno. Mendoza, Argentina.
Wall Street Journal.

Washington Post.
XXI. Buenos Aires, Argentina.

Unpublished Material

Bossert, Gustavo. Resignation letter to Eduardo A. Duhalde, President of Argentina. 21 October 2002. Photocopy.

Centro de Estudios Unión Para la Nueva Mayoría (CEUNM). *Crisis de credibilidad del poder judicial.* Studies from Cuaderno No. 69, December 1993. Photocopy.

———. *La imagen de la justicia argentina.* Studies from Cuaderno No. 88, June 1994. Photocopy.

———. *La imagen de la justicia en la Argentina.* Studies from Cuaderno No. 189, June 1996. Photocopy.

Colegio de Abogados de General Roca. Letter to San Luis Bar Association. 2 March 1998. Photocopy.

Colegio de Abogados de San Luis. "Situación institucional en la provincia de San Luis." 1998. Photocopy.

Colegio de Abogados y Procuradores de la Ciudad de San Luis, Directorio. "Declaración a la opinión pública." 19 November 1997.

Colegio de Abogados y Procuradores de San Luis y Villa Mercedes y Colegio Forense de la Provincia de San Luis. "Declaración a la opinión pública." 26 February 1998.

Colegio de Abogados y Procuradores de Villa Mercedes. "Comunicado." 23 February 1998.

Federación Argentina de Colegios de Abogados (FACA). "Resolución." San Rafael, Mendoza, 4 April 1997.

Garrote, Ángel Fermín (FACA President), and Pedro Valle (FACA Secretary). Letter to bar associations throughout Argentina. 26 February 1998. Photocopy.

Huespe, Carlos Alberto (FAM president), and Jorge Eduardo Vivas (FAM secretary). Letter to Adolfo Rodriquez Saá. February 1998. Photocopy.

Laborda Ibarra, Juan José. "Adolfo Senador Nacional . . . Un 'enroque' por nepotismo y impunidad." Comunicado de prensa. 15 September 1998.

Pérez Hualde, Alejandro. "El Consejo de la Magistratura en la Constitución de Mendoza." 25 May 1998. Photocopy.

Zubiria Diego May (Buenos Aires Bar Association Secretary). Letter to Miriam Agundez. 12 March 1998. Photocopy.

Personal Interviews

The following list of interviews represents a fraction of the total number of interviews that were conducted by the author between 1998 and 2003. It does not include the names of those who spoke off the record.

Abregú, Martín. Executive director of Centro de Estudios Legales y Sociales (CELS). Buenos Aires. 15 June 1999.

Aguirre Lanari, Juan. Argentine Senator. Buenos Aires. 23 October 1998.

Agundez, Miriam. President of the San Luis Bar Association. San Luis. 24 May 1999.

Ahumada, Roberto. Coordinator of Judicial Affairs, Argentine Ministry of the Interior. Buenos Aires. 14 June 1999 and 15 June 1999.

Alperín Bruvera, Ignacio. Executive Director of Colegio de Abogados de la Ciudad de Buenos Aires. Buenos Aires. 2 October 1998.

Aragón Zwiener, Estela. Former San Luis *secretario*. San Luis. 8 October 1998.

Argibay, Carmen. President of Asociación de Mujeres Jueces de la Argentina (AMJA). Buenos Aires. 24 June 1999.

Arias, Germán Eduardo. Dean of Social Sciences at the National University of San Luis. San Luis. 24 May 1999.

Arslanian, León Carlos. Former Argentine Justice Minister. Buenos Aires. 7 December 1998.

Bacqué, Jorge. Former Argentine Supreme Court Justice. Buenos Aires. 13 October 1998.

Badeni, Gregorio. Constitutional Law Professor at University of Buenos Aires. Buenos Aires. 13 October 1998.

Balter, Carlos M. Argentine Congressman. Buenos Aires. 27 April 1999.

Barbaccia, José C. Federal Prosecutor. Buenos Aires. 29 June 1999.

Barra, Rodolfo Carlos. Former Argentine Supreme Court Justice. Buenos Aires. 13 November 1998.

Becerra, Susana. Sistema Público de Evaluación de la Calidad (SIPEC). Mendoza. 10 May 1999.

Beliz, Gustavo. Former Argentine Minister of Interior. Buenos Aires. 15 October 1998.

Belluscio, Augusto. Argentine Supreme Court Justice. Buenos Aires. 13 March 2003.

Bincaz, Germán. Federal Prosecutor. Buenos Aires. 1 December 1998.

Bohm, Carlos. Mendoza Supreme Court Justice. Mendoza. 4 May 1999.

Bohmer, Martín. Law Professor at the Universidad de Palermo. Buenos Aires. 5 October 1998.

Bona, María Eugenia. San Luis Judge. San Luis. 9 October 1998.

Bordón, José Octavio. Former Mendoza Governor. Buenos Aires. 12 March 2003.

Bossert, Gustavo. Former Argentine Supreme Court Justice. Buenos Aires. 13 March 2003.

Botana, Natalio. History Professor at the Universidad Di Tella. Buenos Aires. 25 November 1998.

Bovino, Alberto. CELS. Buenos Aires. 23 June 1999.

Bruni, Sergio. Mendoza Congressman, member of Mendoza Judicial Council. Mendoza. 6 May 1999.

Bustos Herrera, Gabriel. Director of the *Revista de la Bolsa de Comercio de Mendoza*. Mendoza. 11 May 1999.

Cacace, Carlos Jorge. San Luis Appellate Court Judge. San Luis. 9 October 1998.

Cafferata, Fernando J. Foro de Estudios sobre la Administración de Justicia (FORES). Buenos Aires. 11 June 1998.

Careaga, Ana María. Former San Luis Judge. San Luis. 10 October 1998.

Carranza de Carrió Adriana. Former San Luis *secretario*. San Luis. 11 October 1998.

Carrió, Elisa. Argentine Congresswoman. Buenos Aires. 26 November 1998.

Casabal, Adolfo. Fundación Novum Millennium. Buenos Aires. 4 December 1998.

Castro, Patricia Estela. Argentine Supreme Court *secretario*. Buenos Aires. 26 October 1998.

Cavagna Martínez, Mariano Augusto. Former Argentine Supreme Court Justice. Buenos Aires. 27 November 1998.

Cavallo, Gabriel R. Argentine Federal Judge. Buenos Aires. 3 December 1998.

Cazaban, Luis Alejandro. Mendoza Justice Minister. Mendoza. 3 May 1999.

Ceballos, Walter. San Luis Congressman. San Luis. 19 May 1999.

Chade, León Victor. Former Mendoza Minister of Government. Mendoza. 7 May 1999.

Coria, Martín. Assistant to Mendoza Governor Arturo Lafalla. Mendoza. 7 May 1999.

Correa Sutil, Jorge. Law Professor at Universidad Diego Portalis. Santiago. 13 May 1999.

Courtis, Christian. CELS. Buenos Aires. 28 June 1999.

Cruchaga, Melchor Rene. Argentine Congressman. Buenos Aires. 7 December 1998.

D'Alessio, Andrés J. Former Argentine Attorney General. Buenos Aires. 23 November 1998.

De Michele, Roberto. Poder Ciudadano. Buenos Aires. 23 September 1998.

Di Tella, Torcuato. Sociology Professor at Universidad Di Tella. Buenos Aires. 14 November 1998.

Duce, Mauricio. Law Professor at Universidad Diego Portalis. Stanford, Calif. 3 March 1999.

Durrieu, Roberto. Former Argentine Undersecretary of Justice. Buenos Aires. 15 October 1998.

Estrada, Eduardo Ángel. San Luis State Prosecutor. San Luis. 26 May 1999.
Fayt, Carlos. Argentine Supreme Court Justice. Buenos Aires. 29 October 1998.
Fernández, Yamila. San Luis journalist. San Luis. 19 May 1999.
Ferreira Rubio, Delia. Director of Centro de Estudios para Políticas Públicas Aplicadas. Buenos Aires. 16 June 1998.
Fraga, Bindo Caviglione. Argentine Federal Judge, Judicial Council member. Buenos Aires. 22 October 1998.
Fraga, Rosendo. Director of Centro de Estudios Unión Para la Nueva Mayoría. Buenos Aires. 16 November 1998.
Gabrielli, Aldolfo. Former Argentine Supreme Court Justice. Buenos Aires. 1 December 1998.
Gabrielli, Andrés. Mendoza journalist. Mendoza. 5 May 1999.
Gallo, Adriana. Former San Luis Judge. San Luis. 11 October 1998.
Garavano, Germán C. Director of FORES. Buenos Aires. 26 October 1998, 5 November 1998, and 30 November 1998.
García Lema, Alberto. Former Legal Advisor to President Carlos Menem, former Procurador del Tesoro. Buenos Aires. 20 October 1998.
Garré, Nilda. Frepaso Congresswoman. Buenos Aires. 12 March 2003.
Garrote, Ángel Fermín. President of Federación Argentina de Colegios de Abogados (FACA). Buenos Aires. 7 July 1999.
Gatica, Elvecia. San Luis Supreme Court Justice. San Luis. 9 October 1998.
Gelli, María Angélica. Constitutional Law Professor at University of Buenos Aires. Buenos Aires. 2 December 1998.
Germano, Hugo. President of Buenos Aires Bar Association. Buenos Aires. 11 March 2003.
Gil Lavedra, Ricardo. Former Federal Judge, former Justice Minister. Buenos Aires. 10 December 1998 and 14 March 2003.
Giordano, Aldo. Mendoza State Prosecutor. Mendoza. 3 and 6 May 1999.
Gómez, Julio. Former Mendoza Undersecretary of Justice. Mendoza. 5 May 1999.
Granillo Ocampo, Raúl. Argentine Justice Minister. Buenos Aires. 18 November 1998.
Guarna, Eduardo. Fiscales sin Fronteras. Buenos Aires. 30 June 1999.
Guevara, Alfredo. Attorney. Mendoza. 10 May 1999.
Ibarbia, José María. Former Argentine Congressman. Buenos Aires. 17 June 1998.
Ibarra, Aníbal. Former Federal Prosecutor. Buenos Aires. 9 December 1998.
Inzirillo, Laura. Advisor to the PJ bloc in the Mendoza Congress. Mendoza. 4 May 1999.
Jorge, Guillermo. Member of Adriana Gallo's defense team. Buenos Aires. 4 November 1998.
Kemelmajer de Carlucci, Aída Rosa. Mendoza Supreme Court Justice. Mendoza. 4 May 1999.
Laborda Ibarra, Juan José. San Luis Congressman. San Luis. 18 May 1999.
Lafalla, Arturo. Governor of Mendoza. Mendoza. 7 May 1999.
La Rosa, Carlos. Mendoza sociologist and journalist. Mendoza. 6 May 1999.
Leiva, Luis. Federal Judge in Mendoza. Mendoza. 10 May 1999.
Li Rosi, Ricardo. Argentine Judge. Buenos Aires. 21 October 1998.

Llorente, Pedro. Mendoza Supreme Court Justice. Mendoza. 4 May 1999.
Longhi, María. Former Public Prosecutor. Buenos Aires. 21 October 1998.
Luna, Félix. Argentine historian. Buenos Aires. 3 November 1998.
Lynch, Horacio. Founder of FORES. Buenos Aires. 23 September 1998 and 5 October 1998.
Maiorano, Jorge Luis. National Ombudsman, former Argentine Justice Minister. Buenos Aires. 25 November 1998.
Molinelli, Guillermo. Law Professor at University of Buenos Aires. Buenos Aires. 28 September 1998, 29 October 1998, and 18 November 1998.
Monner Sans, Ricardo. Attorney. Buenos Aires. 2 July 1999.
Montbrun, Alberto. Mendoza Senator. Mendoza. 6 May 1999.
Mooney, Lelia. Conciencia. Buenos Aires. 19 June 1998.
Moreno Ocampo, Luis. Poder Ciudadano founder, former president of Transparency International Latin America. Buenos Aires. 29 September 1998, 4 November 1998, 19 April 1999, and 23 June 1999.
Mortarotti, Juan Pablo. Attorney. Mendoza. 4 May 1999.
Mosso de Mortarotti, Ana María. Argentine Congresswoman, former Mendoza Economy Minister. Buenos Aires. 29 June 1999.
Mustapic, Ana María. Professor of Political Science at Universidad Torcuato di Tella. 27 November 1998.
Nanclares, Jorge. Mendoza Supreme Court Justice. Mendoza. 4 May 1999.
Negri, Juan Javier. Attorney. Buenos Aires. 21 October 1998.
Obregón, Alejandra. Mendoza Public Prosecutor. Mendoza. 10 May 1999.
Olivares, Eduardo. San Luis journalist. San Luis. 26 May 1999.
Oro, Carlos. Director of information technology for Mendoza government. Mendoza. 7 May 1999.
Otero, Mario. San Luis journalist. San Luis. 24 May 1999.
Pagano, Roberto Eduardo. Former San Luis Congressman. San Luis. 19 May 1999.
Pardo, Juan Ángel. Director of the legal division of Instituto para el Desarrollo de Empresarios en la Argentina (IDEA). Buenos Aires. 10 December 1998
Peltier, Teresa. Mendoza Congresswoman. Mendoza. 5 May 1999.
Peña González, Carlos. Dean of the Universidad Diego Portalis Law School. Santiago. 14 May 1999.
Pérez Botti, Omar. Mendoza Senator. Mendoza. 4 May 1999.
Pérez Hualde, Alejandro. Attorney. Mendoza. 7 May 1999.
Pesce, Félix. Mendoza Minister of Government, member of the Mendoza Judicial Council. Mendoza. 4 May 1999.
Petracchi, Enrique. Argentine Supreme Court Justice. Buenos Aires. 13 March 2003.
Poj, María Cristina. SIPEC. Mendoza. 10 May 1999.
Portabella, Oscar N. Attorney, member of the Mendoza Judicial Council. Mendoza. 10 May 1999.
Quantín, Norberto. Public Prosecutor. Buenos Aires. 2 July 1999.
Quiroga Lavié, Humberto. Member of Argentine Judicial Council. Buenos Aires. 10 March 2003.
Ramón Fernández, Ventura. San Luis *secretario*. San Luis. 9 October 1998.

Rehren, Alfredo. Professor of Political Science at Universidad Católica. Santiago. 12 May 1999.
Relly de Closa, Ruth. Former San Luis Judge. San Luis. 21 May 1999.
Rodríguez Estévez, Juan María. FORES. Buenos Aires. 18 June 1998.
Roja de Scacciaté, Dora Larese. Conciencia. Buenos Aires. 19 June 1998.
Rojas, Ricardo Manuel. Argentine Judge. Buenos Aires. 17 June 1998.
Rosso, Graciela. Secretary of the San Luis Bar Association. San Luis. 8 October 1998 and 20 May 1999.
Rueda de Uranga, Silvia. Director of Conciencia. Buenos Aires. 10 March 2003.
Saba, Roberto. Law Professor at Universidad de Palermo. Buenos Aires. 9 December 1998.
Sabsay, Daniel A. Social Forum for Justice. Buenos Aires. 5 July 1999.
Samper, José. San Luis Congressman. San Luis. 21 May 1999.
Sansó, Gerónimo. President of Justicia Democrática. Buenos Aires. 18 June 1999.
Schvarstein, Leonardo Jorge. Former president of Centro de Estudios Judiciales de la República Argentina (CEJURA). Buenos Aires. 12 June 1998.
Smulovitz, Catalina. Professor of Political Science at Universidad Di Tella. Buenos Aires. 20 October 1998.
Staib, Alberto. Mendoza Judge, former president of Mendoza Asociación de Magistrados. Mendoza. 11 May 1999.
Suriani, Osvaldo. San Luis Judge. San Luis. 9 October 1998.
Tardieu de Quiroga, Beatriz. San Luis Judge. San Luis. 9 October 1998.
Vanossi, Jorge Reinaldo. Former Argentine Congressman. Buenos Aires. 23 October 1998 and 4 November 1998.
Vargas, Juan Enrique. Director of Centro de Investigación at Universidad Diego Portalis Law School. Santiago. 13 May 1999.
Ventura, Adrián. Journalist. Buenos Aires. 2 December 1998 and 12 March 2003.
Verbitsky, Horacio. Journalist. Buenos Aires. 3 December 1998.
Wiñazki, Miguel. Journalist. Buenos Aires. 22 June 1999.
Zaffaroni, Eugenio Raúl. Law Professor at University of Buenos Aires, former San Luis Attorney General. Buenos Aires. 1 July 1999.
Zapata Mercader, Jorge. Former Mendoza Senator. Mendoza. 27 April 1999.

Index

AABA. *See* Asociación de Abogados de Buenos Aires
Abregú, Martín, 96
Accounting Tribunal (Argentina), 17, 54, 71, 77–78; tenure protection for, 77
Accounting Tribunal (Mendoza), 113–14, 116, 131–32; tenure protection for, 131
Accounting Tribunal (San Luis), 100, 107, 113–14; vs. Mendoza, 113–14, 132; salaries of, 113; tenure protection for, 113
ACDE. *See* Asociación Cristiana de Dirigentes de Empresas
Acordada 44, 42
Agrupación para una Justicia Democrática, 96, 139–40, 144, 145
Agüero Iturbe, Ángel, 75, 77
Aguirre Lanari, Juan, 64
Agundez, Miriam, 108, 140, 200n17
Alberdi, Juan Bautista, 174n17
Alfonsín, Raúl, 153; and Accounting Tribunal, 77; decrees issued by, 70; and de facto doctrine, 49; divided government under, 32, 41, 54, 59, 61, 78; and Federal Prosecutor of Administrative Investigations (FNIA), 78; line-item vetoes by, 69; vs. Menem, 6, 28, 29, 33, 37, 38, 39–40, 41, 45–46, 49, 50, 53, 54, 59, 69, 70, 77; and Olivos Pact, 30, 107; relations with judiciary, 6, 28–29, 32–33, 36, 37, 39–40, 41, 45–46, 49, 50, 53, 54, 59, 70, 89, 180n19, 182n53
Alianza del Centro, 117–18
Alianza para el Trabajo, la Justicia y la Educación (Alianza), 66, 119, 120; 1997 election victory of, 71, 72, 73–74, 77, 79; 1999 election victory of, 146, 147, 149
Alsina, Valentín, 31
Alsogaray, María Julia, 78
Amadeo, Santos Primo, 179n2; on Supreme Court of Argentina, 28, 42
American Bar Association, 41
AMJA. *See* Asociación de Mujeres Jueces de Argentina
Amnesty International, 145, 151
Los Andes, 155
Anzorreguy, Hugo, 33–34
Anzorreguy, Jorge, 34
Aportes del Tesoro Nacional (ATNs), 148–49
appointment process for judges: under Alfonsín, 32–33, 50, 59, 61; under Menem, 33–36, 50, 74–75; under military government of 1976–83, 31–32, 50; under Perón, 31, 50; relationship to judicial autonomy, 24, 27, 31–36, 37, 50; in San Luis vs. Mendoza, 81, 82, 85–87, 95
Aramburu, Pedro Eugenio, 38, 39, 60
Argentina: vs. Chile, 23, 160–61, 175n28, 213n6; civil law tradition in, 5, 7, 160; vs. Costa Rica, 23, 175n28; executive-judicial relations 1862–1946, 6, 28, 29–30, 31, 41, 50; executive-judicial relations 1946–83, 6, 7, 28, 31–32, 38–39, 41, 44, 45, 48–49, 50, 53–54, 58–59, 178n1; executive-judicial relations 1983–89, 6, 28, 41, 45–46, 50, 59; executive-judicial relations 1989–99, 6, 7, 28, 30, 41–42, 46–49, 50, 61–64; legacy of Spanish colonialism in, 5, 7, 160; vs. Mexico, 39; military governments in, 28, 30, 31–32, 39, 41, 44, 48–49, 55–56, 58–59, 60, 117, 120, 158, 178n1, 184n84, 188n9; 1930 coup, 28, 30–31, 39, 44, 48, 55–56, 178n1, 188n9; reelection of gover-

nors in, 199n13; vs. Russia, 5; suffrage in, 179n1; tradition of ultrapresidentialism in, 5, 28, 61–62; vs. United States, 39, 41, 66, 161; vs. Uruguay, 23. *See also* Argentina and Mendoza, comparisons between; Argentina and San Luis, comparisons between; Constitution of Argentina; Supreme Court of Argentina
Argentina and Mendoza, comparisons between, 4–5, 26, 132, 157, 164; regarding economic resources, 83; regarding electoral rules, 121; regarding executive dominance, 6; regarding line-item veto, 122; regarding reform coalitions, 154
Argentina and San Luis, comparisons between, 4–5, 26, 90, 157, 164; regarding Congress, 106, 107; regarding elites, 83–84; regarding executive dominance, 6, 100, 104; regarding Menem and Rodríguez Saá, 100, 104, 106, 107, 200n21; regarding party discipline, 121; regarding per saltum, 92; regarding reform coalitions, 8, 137, 154, 156; regarding Supreme Courts, 87, 88
Argentine Bar Associations, 38, 47, 96, 108, 109–10, 138–40, 144. *See also* Buenos Aires Bar Association; Mendoza Bar Association; San Luis Bar Association
Argentine Conference of Bishops, 143
Argentine Truth Commission, 45
Argibay, Carmen, 140, 209n47
Arias, César, 73
Arslanian, León Carlos, 32–33, 42, 180n17
Asia, fragmentation of economic power, 19, 20
Asociación Cristiana de Dirigentes de Empresas (ACDE), 141
Asociación de Abogados de Buenos Aires (AABA), 138–39
Asociación de Magistrados y Funcionarios de la Justicia National, 139
Asociación de Mujeres Jueces de Argentina (AMJA), 96, 139, 140, 144, 145, 209n47
Attorney General's Office (Argentina), 17, 39, 54, 71, 74–77, 79, 132, 193nn79,81; appointment process for, 74–75; tenure protection for, 74–75
Attorney General's Office (Mendoza), 116, 132
Attorney General's Office (San Luis), 100, 107, 114–15, 132
Autonomist Party, 54, 55
Avellaneda, Nicolás, 55

Bacqué, Jorge, 33, 37, 42, 45–46, 140, 144
Baglini, Elías, 86, 125
Balbín, Ricardo, 45
Balter, Carlos, 98, 121, 202n4
Bank of Mendoza, 94, 123, 130
Barra, Rodolfo, 34, 35, 37, 40, 42, 47
Barros Pazos, José, 31, 38
Bauzá, Eduardo, 34, 42, 183n57
Bazán, Abel, 38
Becerra, Nicolás, 76
Belluscio, Augusto, 32, 37, 40, 42, 45–46, 47
Bermejo, Antonio, 38
Biles, Robert E., 39
Blackmun, Harry A., 177n55
Blackstone, Sir William, 2
Bodin, Jean, 99, 173n4
Boggiano, Antonio, 35, 37, 40, 47, 186n94
Bohm, Carlos, 129, 195n28
Bolivia, 1
Bordón, José Octavio, 118, 119, 120, 122, 123–24, 130, 131–32, 203n27, 205nn54,56; and Bank of Mendoza, 94; relations with judiciary, 89, 90–91, 93, 125, 154, 197n46
Bossert, Gustavo, 35, 37, 187n115, 195n17
Bovino, Alberto, 153, 201n49
Brazil, 2
Bruni, Sergio, 121, 125, 155
Bueno de Mesquita, Bruce, 5
Buenos Aires Bar Association, 47, 138–39, 144, 145, 186n95, 195n17

Caballero, José Severo, 32, 37, 40
Cacace, Carlos, 87, 97, 102, 109, 141
CACBA. *See* Colegio de Abogados de la Ciudad de Buenos Aires
Cafiero, Antonio, 62
Cámpora, Héctor, 38–39, 40, 60
Careaga, Ana María, 140, 141; impeachment of, 91–92, 109, 110–12, 114, 145, 153–54, 201n41, 209n47
Carolina Cable Color (CCC), 152
Carreras, Francisco de las, 31, 38
Carríl, Salvador María del, 31, 38
Carrío, Elisa, 51, 63, 70, 144, 191n61
Casares, Tomás, 38
Catamarca, province of, 104, 123, 137, 147, 159, 197n48, 203n26

Cavagna Martínez, Mariano Augusto, 34, 35, 37, 40, 42, 181n30, 191n60
Cavallo, Domingo, 51, 76, 139, 186n94
Caviglione Fraga, Bindo, 182n52, 192n63
CEA. *See* Consejo Empresario Argentino
Ceballos, Walter, 97
CEJURA. *See* Centro de Estudios Judiciales de la República Argentina
CELS. *See* Centro de Estudios Legales y Sociales
Central America, 23
Central Bank of Argentina, 47
Centro de Estudios Judiciales de la República Argentina (CEJURA), 143
Centro de Estudios Legales y Sociales (CELS), 96, 110, 111, 145, 153, 209n49
Chaco, province of, 137, 199n13
Chade, León Victor, 86, 124, 202n4
Chile: vs. Argentina, 23, 160–61, 175n28, 213n6; Concertación por la Democracia, 161; coup of 1973, 160, 161; distribution of economic resources in, 19; divided government in, 161; informal practices vs. formal rules in, 23; vs. Mendoza, 160–61; party competition in, 157, 159, 160–61; party discipline in, 160, 161; Renovación Nacional-Unión Demócrata Independiente, 161; rule of law in, 160–61; Supreme Court in, 213n6; third parties in, 160–61; vs. United States, 161
civil law, 5, 7, 9, 13–14, 80, 160
civil society groups: business associations, 141; judges in, 139–40, 141, 144–45; lawyers in, 138–39, 140, 144, 212n94; relations between local and national organizations, 144–45; relations with international organizations, 142–44, 176n40,43; students in, 142
Clarín, 153
clientelism, 20, 96, 136–37, 147–48, 163
Colegio de Abogados de la Ciudad de Buenos Aires (CACBA), 139, 141
Colombia, 1, 12, 175n28
Comisión Nacional de Jóvenes Abogados, 144
common law, 13, 14
competitive politics. *See* party competition
Conciencia (Conscience), 136, 143
Concordancia, 56
Congress. *See* House of Representatives (Argentina); House of Representatives (Mendoza); House of Representatives (San Luis); legislative branch; Senate (Argentina); Senate (Mendoza); Senate (San Luis)
Consejo Empresario Argentino (CEA), 94, 96, 139, 141
Constitution of Argentina, 28–30; Article 17, 46; Article 32, 44; Article 72, 190n43; Article 80, 69; Article 82, 69; Article 83, 190n43; Article 86, 48; Article 99, 70; Article 101, 47; Article 105, 47–48; Article 114, 71–72; Article 115, 73; Article 120, 76–77; vs. Constitution of the United States, 30, 42; and decrees of necessity and urgency (DNUs), 70–71; 1811 Organic Regulations, 29–30; 1815 Provisional Statute, 174n19; 1819 Constitution, 30, 174n19; 1826 Constitution, 30; 1853 Constitution, 29, 30, 68, 179n6, 190n43; judicial autonomy in, 29–30; and judicial review, 42–43; and line-item vetoes, 68–69, 70; 1949 Constitution, 68, 179n6; 1994 Constitution, 29, 30, 35–36, 69, 70, 71–72, 73, 76–77, 190n43, 193n79; Supreme Court provisions in, 30, 41
Constitution of Mendoza, 126–27, 129, 154, 197n46; Article 94, 123; Article 181, 131; Article 182, 131; Article 221, 93; vs. Constitution of San Luis, 80–81, 90, 93, 98, 107, 122, 195n20; 1916 Constitution, 131, 194n2; 1949 Constitution, 196n45, 212n94
Constitution of San Luis, 106; Article 118, 199; Article 138, 103; Article 196, 107; Article 236, 201n50; Constitution of 1905, 104; Constitution of 1987, 102–4, 108, 113; vs. Constitution of Mendoza, 80–81, 90, 93, 98, 107, 122, 195n20; urgent bills in, 103–4, 122, 203n21
Constitution of the United States, 13, 30, 42
contract enforcement, 17, 43, 81–82, 85, 141, 146
Controladuría y Auditoría de la Nación (National Comptroller and Auditor), 78
Corach, Carlos, 34, 51
Córdoba, province of, 97, 153, 159–60, 180n13, 199n13
Corrientes, province of, 47–48, 100, 123, 137, 159, 186n95, 199n13, 203n26
corruption in government, 3, 17, 26,, 42; in

Mendoza, 132, 205n64; under Menem, 42, 51, 73, 74, 76, 77; under Rodríguez Saá, 91, 93, 95, 106, 114, 146, 147–49, 151, 152, 199n10
Costa Rica: vs. Argentina, 23, 175n28; distribution of economic resources in, 18, 19, 83; informal practices vs. formal rules in, 23; vs. Mendoza, 83
Council of Indies, 13
Courtis, Christian, 96, 110
court-packing, 168, 179n1, 183n59; by Menem, 33, 34, 40, 41–42, 50, 59, 62, 90, 139, 150; by Rodríguez Saá, 81, 82, 90, 95, 199n13
Croatia, 64, 76, 149
Cruchaga, Melchor, 51

Dahl, Robert A., 171n5, 179n1
D'Alessio, Andrés, 32, 33, 74–75, 180n19
El Decamerón, 211n78
decrees of necessity and urgency (DNUs), 46, 69–71, 122, 191nn51,54; and Joint Standing Committee, 69, 70
de facto doctrine, 32, 48–49, 50, 178nn1,59, 179n4
Delgado, Francisco, 31
democracy: constitutional component of democratic consolidation, 2–3; definitions of, 2, 171n4,5; faith in, 2–3, 172n9; as illiberal/delegative, 1; in Latin America, 1; liberal vs. electoral, 2–3; relationship to elections, 1, 2; relationship to freedom of expression, 2; relationship to judicial autonomy, 2, 3, 23; relationship to rule of law, 1–4
Diálogo Argentino (Argentine Dialogue), 143–44, 208n37
Diamond, Larry, on rule of law, 3
Diario de la República, 85, 87, 92, 151, 152, 164, 208n27
Dirty War of 1976–83, 45, 135
divided government: under Alfonsín, 32, 41, 54, 59, 61, 78; in Chile, 161; in Mendoza, 100, 116, 118–21, 122–24, 125, 129–32, 158, 160–61; under Menem, 54, 71, 72, 73–74, 76, 77, 79; relationship to party competition, 15–16, 53, 54–55, 59, 61, 64, 79, 116; relationship to rule of law/judicial autonomy, 32, 41, 53–55, 58, 59, 72–74, 76, 77, 79, 116, 118–21, 122–24, 125, 158, 164, 167–69, 175n24; vs. unified government, 41, 53–54, 55, 56, 57, 58, 64, 70–71, 72, 73–74, 76, 77, 78, 79, 158, 159–60, 161, 167–69; in United States, 161, 162
DNUs *See* decrees of necessity and urgency
Dromi, Roberto, 47, 78
Durrieu, Roberto, 32

Eaton, Kent, 148
Eckstein, Harry, 4
economic patterns of power: relationship to party competition, 14–15, 17–20, 81; relationship to rule of law, 3–4, 7, 9, 14–15, 17–20, 81–85; in San Luis vs. Mendoza, 81–85
Ecuador, 64, 76, 149, 175n28
Edelmann, Alexander T., 14
elections: electoral rules, 15–16, 65, 66–67, 105–6, 121, 160, 161; relationship to democracy, 1, 2; in San Luis, 100–102, 105–6, 121; and Supreme Court, 47–48; as vertical accountability, 134
El Salvador, 175n28, 176n40
Emma, Jaime, 151–52
Encuentro de Jueces, 139–40, 145
England: Revolution Settlement in, 11–12; rule of law in, 2, 11–12
Estrada, Eduardo Ángel, 112, 199n11
Europe, Western, rule of law in, 2
executive branch: emergency powers of, 46, 69–71, 103–4, 122, 191nn51,54, 203n21; executives as party leader, 16, 63–64, 105–6, 121; party rotation in, 15–16, 116, 119–20, 121, 122, 131, 158, 160–61; relationship to legislative branch, 12, 13, 15, 16–17, 53–54, 58, 61–64, 67–73, 79, 100–104, 106–15, 122–24, 167–69; relations with judicial branch, 2, 3, 4, 5–6, 7, 8, 13–14, 24–27, 28–52, 31–36, 37, 38–49, 50, 51–52, 53–54, 56, 58–59, 61–64, 67, 70, 71–77, 78, 79, 81, 82, 88, 89, 90–94, 95, 104, 128–29, 132, 138–40, 141, 149, 167–69, 178nn1,60,62, 180nn13,16,19, 182n53, 183n57, 185nn86,94,95,96, 198n4. *See also* Alfonsín, Raúl; Menem, Carlos; Perón, Juan Domingo; Rodríguez Saá, Adolfo

FACA. *See* Federación Argentina de Colegios de Abogados

FAM. *See* Federación Argentina de la Magistratura
Fayad, Victor, 130
Fayt, Carlos, 32, 37, 40, 42, 47, 183n54
Federación Argentina de Colegios de Abogados (FACA; Federation of Argentine Bar Associations), 96, 110, 111–12, 138, 144, 145
Federación Argentina de la Magistratura (FAM), 96, 139, 144–45
Federación Universitaria de San Luis, 142
Federal Prosecutor of Administrative Investigations (Fiscalía Nacional de Investigaciones Administrativas) (FNIA), 46, 54, 71; tenure protection for, 78–79
Federal Tax Sharing Law (Coparticipación Federal de Impuestos), 148
FIEL. *See* Fundación de Investigaciones Económicas Latinoamericanas
field reseach, 6–7
Figueroa Alcorta, José, 55
Figueroa Alcorta, Roberto, 38
Fiscalía de Estado. *See* State Prosecutor
FNIA. *See* Federal Prosecutor of Administrative Investigations
Fontela, Moisés, 47
Foro de Estudios para la Justicia (FORES), 51, 96, 139, 140, 141, 143, 182n53
France: civil law in, 13–14; concentration of assets in, 18; French Revolution, 13–14; Old Regime in, 11, 12
Franja Morada, 142
freedom of expression, 2, 45; freedom of the press, 44, 149–52, 154, 155
Frente por un País Solidario (Frepaso), 65–66
Frondizi, Arturo: line-item vetoes by, 68; monolithic party control under, 58, 60, 158; vs. Perón, 58, 60, 61, 68; relations with judiciary, 39, 40, 58, 60
Fundación de Estudios para la Justicia (Fundejus), 139, 140, 145
Fundación de Investigaciones Económicas Latinoamericanas (FIEL), 141
Fundación Novum Millenium, 139
Funes, Pedro, 125

Gabrielli, Adolfo, 32, 94
Gabrielli, Andrés, 98, 155
Gabrielli, Francisco, 117
Gabrielli, Rodolfo, 89, 119, 122, 124, 125–26, 130, 205nn56,58
Gallo, Adriana, 140, 141, 142; impeachment of, 91–92, 109, 110–12, 114, 145, 153–54, 209n47
Garavano, Germán, 140
Garré, Nilda, 191n61, 192n66
Garrote, Ángel Fermín, 111–12
Gatica, Eduardo, 87
Gelli, María Angélica, 32, 51
Germany, 2
Gil Lavedra, Ricardo, 33, 140, 192n66
Giordano, Aldo, 112, 130–31, 205n58
Gorostiaga, José Benjamín, 31, 38
Granillo Ocampo, Raúl, 33, 72, 78
Guardapolvos case, 77–78
Guatemala, 175n28
Guido, José María, 60

habeas corpus, 45, 184n84
Haiti, 176n40
Hamilton, Alexander, 30, 177n58; on judges' salary protection, 25; on judges' tenure protection, 24–25; on judicial autonomy, 3, 24–25
Hissa, Victor, 146
Honduras, 175n28
House of Representatives (Argentina), 42, 68; distribution of seats in, 61, 63, 65; House Impeachment Committee, 36
House of Representatives (Mendoza), 118–19, 123
House of Representatives (San Luis), 103, 106, 123
human rights, 3, 10, 20, 32, 135
Huntington, Samuel, 2

Ibarra, Aníbal, 33, 75–76, 149
Iglesias, Roberto, 89, 117, 119, 123
Illia, Arturo, 58, 60, 190n45
impeachment (Argentina), 36, 38, 39, 40–41, 44, 47, 139
Impeachment Jury (Argentina), 17, 30, 54, 71, 73–74, 76, 136, 192n66, 208n37
Impeachment Jury (Mendoza), 116, 128–29, 131
Impeachment Jury (San Luis), 91, 92, 100, 107, 108–12, 113, 114, 141, 145, 153, 196n39, 201nn41,49,50
induction and deduction, 4–5

Industrial Promotion program (IP), 84, 137, 146, 147–48, 149, 153, 163, 195n13, 210n62
informal powers and practices, 176n48; vs. formal powers, 7, 9, 23–24, 28, 30–31, 54, 67–68, 80–81, 85, 87, 94, 95, 106–15, 122; line-item veto, 68–69, 70–71, 122, 190nn43,45
information politics, 134, 135, 140, 145, 149–54, 155
Instituto para el Desarrollo de Empresarios en la Argentina (IDEA), 141
Interamerican Commission on Human Rights, 145
International Monetary Fund (IMF), 143
Iran, 12
Irigoyen, Bernardo de, 55
Isla de la Integridad (Mendoza), 212n98

Japan, 20
Jones, Mark P., 63, 66–67, 70, 121
judicial autonomy: in Argentina's provinces, 6, 159–60, 164–65; as continuous variable, 178n1; indicators of, 7, 24–27, 81, 95; informal practices vs. formal rules regarding, 7, 9, 23–24, 28, 30–31, 54, 67–68, 80–81; in Mendoza, 4–5, 6–8, 26, 79, 81–82, 83, 85, 86–87, 90, 94–98, 115, 116, 126–28, 132, 135, 165; relationship to appointment process, 24, 27, 31–36, 37, 50; relationship to democracy, 2, 3, 23; relationship to divided government, 32, 41, 53–55, 58, 59, 72–74, 76, 77, 79, 116, 118–21, 122–24, 125, 158, 164, 167–69, 175n24; relationship to judicial review, 25–26, 36, 42–49, 50; relationship to party competition, 3–4, 7–8, 9, 14, 15–17, 53, 54, 79, 81, 98, 115, 116, 124–31, 157, 158, 159–62, 164, 188n9; relationship to rule of law, 9–12, 157; relationship to rulings against executive branch, 25–26,36, 42–49, 50, 64, 81, 82, 90–94, 95, 128, 178nn60,62, 180n16, 185n95; relationship to salary protection, 25, 80; relationship to Supreme Court size, 25, 27, 33, 34, 40, 41–42, 50, 58, 59, 62, 82, 139; relationship to tenure protection, 24–25, 27, 36, 38–41, 50, 80; spatial model of, 167–69
Judicial Council (Argentina), 17, 30, 54, 71–73, 76, 136, 139–40, 143, 191nn60,61, 208n37
Judicial Council (Mendoza), 85, 107, 116, 123, 124–28, 154
Judicial Council (San Luis), 85, 107–8, 114, 126, 127, 128
judicial review: under Alfonsín, 45–46, 49, 50; under Menem, 46–49, 50; under military governments, 44, 45, 48–49, 50; under Perón, 44–45, 48–49, 50, 51; relationship to judicial autonomy, 25–26, 27, 36, 42–49, 50; in San Luis vs. Mendoza, 81, 82, 90–94, 95, 128–29, 198n4; spatial model of, 167–69
Jujuy, province of, 137, 199n13
Justicia Democrática, 96, 139–40, 144, 145
Justo, Agustín, 56, 57

Karl, Terry Lynn, 2
Keck, Margaret E., 20, 21, 22, 135, 142, 144, 154, 175n37, 206n2
Kemelmajer de Carlucci, Aída, 86, 89, 98, 120, 129, 195n17
Keohane, Robert O., 5
Key, V. O., Jr., 163, 215n18
King, Gary, 5
Kirchner, Néstor, 199n13
Korea, 20

Laborda Ibarra, Juan José, 106, 152, 199n10
Lafalla, Arturo, 118, 119, 120, 122, 123–24, 127, 129, 130–31, 132, 155, 204n28, 205n54, 212n98; and Bank of Mendoza, 94, 123; relations with judiciary, 86–87, 89, 98, 126, 195n28
Laise, Juan Rodolfo (bishop of San Luis), 137
Lanusse, Pablo, 76
La Pampa, province of, 160, 199n13
La Rioja, province of, 34–35, 75, 78, 104, 123, 147, 149, 159, 203n26, 210nn61,64
La Rosa, Carlos, 83, 98, 203n17, 213n100
Latin America: civil law tradition in, 5, 7, 9, 13–14; distribution of economic resources in, 18–19, 20; Spanish colonialism in, 5, 7, 9, 12–13, 14, 18–19, 174n13; ultrapresidentialism in, 2, 3, 5, 9, 11, 12–13, 14, 20, 157, 174n17, 178n62; vs. United States, 1–2; vs. Western Europe, 1–2
legislative branch: relationship to rule of law, 3, 54, 67; relations with executive branch, 12, 13, 15, 16–17, 53–54, 58, 61–64, 67–

73, 79, 100–104, 106–15, 122–24, 167–69. *See also* House of Representatives (Argentina); House of Representatives (Mendoza); House of Representatives (San Luis); legislative branch; Senate (Argentina); Senate (Mendoza); Senate (San Luis)
Leiva, Luis, 94, 98, 130
Lejtman, Román, 149, 153
Lemme, María Alicia, 198n1
Lencinas, José Néstor, 118
Levene, Ricardo Eugenio Gabriel, 34–35, 37, 40–41, 42, 47, 183n57
leverage politics, 134, 135, 143, 146, 147–49
Levitsky, Steven, 67, 147
line-item veto, 68–69, 70–71, 122, 190nn43,45
Linz, Juan J.: on rule of law, 2–3, 172n8, 173n2
Llaver, Santiago Felipe, 86, 117, 119, 124, 130, 131; relations with judiciary, 89, 154
Llorente, Pedro, 86, 89, 98, 127
Long, Huey, 162–64, 165
López, Guillermo, 35, 37
Louisiana, state of, 8, 157, 159; *The Louisiana Progress*, 164; vs. San Luis, 162–64, 165
lower courts, 52, 180n17, 188n15; in Mendoza, 85, 87, 89, 98; and per saltum, 47, 64, 92; in San Luis, 85, 87, 88, 93–94; vs. Supreme Court, 39, 42, 43, 46, 47, 64. *See also* Impeachment Jury (Argentina); Impeachment Jury (Mendoza); Impeachment Jury (San Luis); Judicial Council (Argentina); Judicial Council (Mendoza); Judicial Council (San Luis)
Luder, Italo, 32
Lynch, Horacio, 51, 139, 140

Macdonald, Austin F., 66
Madison, James, 23
Mainwaring, Scott: on executive authority, 67, 175n27, 200n21; on executive decrees, 69–70
Mann, Michael, 5
Masnatta, Héctor, 35
McCubbins, Mathew, 162
media, 176n47; newspapers, 22–23, 85, 87, 92, 149–53, 211n78, 213n100; radio, 151, 152–53; and reform coalitions, 22–23, 134, 135, 149–54; in San Luis, 85, 87, 92, 150–54, 164, 202n63, 208n27; television, 150, 152, 153–54
Mendoza, province of: appointment process for judges, 81, 85–87, 95; vs. Argentina, 4–5, 6, 8, 26, 83, 121, 122, 132, 154, 157, 164; Citizen Information Program (CIP) in, 155; civil law tradition in, 5, 80; civil society groups in, 154–56; vs. Córdoba, 159–60; corporate firms in, 96–97; vs. Costa Rica, 83; divided government in, 100, 116, 118–21, 122–24, 125, 129–32, 158, 160–61; economic resources in, 7, 81–83, 158–59, 194n9; electoral rules in, 121; government corruption in, 132, 205n64; informal practices vs. formal rules in, 80–81, 85, 87, 94, 95; judicial autonomy in, 4–5, 6–8, 26, 79, 81–82, 83, 85, 86–87, 90, 94–98, 115, 116, 126–28, 132, 135, 165; judicial review in, 81, 82, 90–94, 95, 128–29; lower courts in, 85, 87, 89, 98; Office of the State Prosecutor in, 112; Partido Demócrata (PD) in, 117–33, 204n28; Partido Justicialista (PJ) in, 117–33, 203n13, 205n56; party competition in, 8, 79, 80, 85, 98, 100, 107, 115, 116–33, 159, 160–61, 165, 203nn13,17; party discipline in, 120–22; party rotation in governorship, 116, 119–20, 121, 122, 131, 158, 160–61; the press in, 154, 155, 156; salary protection for judges in, 81, 89–90, 95, 154; Spanish colonial legacy in, 5, 80; tenure of judges in, 81, 87–89, 95; third parties in, 100, 116, 117–33, 160–61; unified government in, 86, 124; Unión Cívica Radical Intransigente (UCRI) in, 117, 118; Unión Cívica Radical (UCR) in, 86, 89, 117–33, 124, 204n28; Unión del Centro Democrático (UCeDé) in, 118. *See also* San Luis and Mendoza, comparisons between; Senate (Mendoza); Supreme Court of Mendoza
Mendoza Bar Association, 96, 124–25, 154–55, 212nn94,95
Mendoza brothers, 84, 104
Mendoza Judges' Association (Mendoza Asociación de Magistrados), 124–25, 154
Menem, Carlos: and Accounting Tribunal, 77–78; vs. Alfonsín, 6, 28, 29, 33, 37, 38, 39–40, 41, 45–46, 49, 50, 53, 54, 59, 69, 70, 77; corruption in government of, 42, 51, 73, 74, 76, 77; court-packing by, 33, 34,

40, 41–42, 50, 59, 62, 90, 139, 150; decrees issued by, 70, 122, 191n51; and de facto doctrine, 49; divided government under, 54, 71, 72, 73–74, 76, 77, 79; and Federal Prosecutor of Administrative Investigations (FNIA), 71, 78–79; and *guardapolvos* case, 77–78; line-item vetoes by, 68–69; monolithic party control under, 53, 54, 59, 61–64, 65, 67, 71–79, 133, 146–47, 158; and Olivos Pact, 30, 35, 40, 71, 107, 150; as party leader, 63–64; vs. Perón, 7, 29, 30, 33, 51, 53, 61, 64, 67, 68, 74; Plan Bonex decree, 46; public opinion polls regarding, 51–52; reelection of, 30, 64, 71, 104, 150; reform coalition in opposition to, 8, 134–36, 137, 138–40, 141–44, 149–50, 159; relationship with Rodríguez Saá, 146, 148, 149; relations with judiciary, 6, 7, 8, 28, 29, 30, 33–36, 37, 39–42, 49, 50, 51–52, 53, 54, 59, 61–62, 64, 67, 71–77, 78, 79, 88, 90, 93–94, 104, 132, 138–40, 141, 149, 183n57, 185n94, 186n96; relations with Partido Justicialista (PJ), 40–42, 54, 59, 61–64, 70, 146–47; relations with press, 149–50, 211n74; vs. Rodríquez Saá, 100, 104, 106, 107, 137, 146–47, 200n21; sales of arms to Croatia and Ecuador, 64, 76, 149

Menem, Eduardo, 40

Merryman, John Henry, 10

methodology and case selection, 4–7

Mexico, 18, 39, 213n1

Michele, Roberto de, 140

military government of 1976–83, 31–32, 39, 45, 49, 62, 117, 120, 135, 184n84

Mill, John Stuart: Method of Difference, 4–5

Miller, Jonathan M., 42, 44, 184n78

Mitre, Bartolomé, 31, 54

Molinas, Ricardo, 46, 78–79

Molinelli, N. Guillermo, 68

Moliné O'Connor, Eduardo, 33, 37, 47, 180n23

Monner Sans, Ricardo, 211n74

monolithic party control, 65–79; and Accounting Tribunal (Argentina), 77–78; in Córdoba, 159–60; definition of, 16, 53, 157; under Frondizi, 58, 60, 158; impact on judicial autonomy, 7–8, 41, 53, 56, 58, 59, 61–62, 67, 71–79, 80, 85–86, 87, 89–91, 98, 99–100, 107–12, 116, 128, 133, 158, 159–60, 188n9; and Impeachment Jury (Argentina), 73–74; under Long, 162–64, 165; under Menem, 53, 54, 59, 61–64, 65, 67, 71–79, 133, 146–47, 158; under military governments, 55–56, 58–59, 60, 158, 188n9; under Perón, 41, 53, 56, 58, 60, 67, 79, 158, 163, 188n12; under Rodríguez Saá, 80, 85–86, 87, 89–90, 91, 98, 99–115, 116, 128, 133, 146–47, 158, 159, 163, 193n1, 199n11, 200n17, 202n8. *See also* party discipline; unified government

Montbrun, Alberto, 121, 124, 126

Montesquieu, Charles de, 30; on judicial autonomy, 3; *The Spirit of the Laws*, 3

Moreno Ocampo, Luis, 110, 114, 145, 148, 153, 155

Mosso de Mortarotti, Ana María, 98

Movimiento de Integración y Desarrollo (MID), 88

Moyano, Carlos Eduardo, 86, 89

Mustapic, Ana María, 51, 67

La Nación, 149, 153

Nanclares, Jorge, 86, 89, 91, 120, 129

National Endowment for Democracy, 176n43

Nationalist Party, 54, 55

National Party, 54

Nazareno, Julio Salvador, 34, 37, 42, 47

Negri, Arturo, 101

Negri, Juan Javier, 139

Neuquén Bar Association, 138, 144

newspapers, 22–23, 85, 87, 92, 149–53, 211n78, 213n100

Nicaragua, 175n28

Noll, Roger, 162

North, Douglass, 11–12

Noticias, 153

Nuestro Compromiso, 100, 106

Ochoa, Néstor, 93

O'Donnell, Guillermo, 10, 176n47

Olivares, Eduardo, 97, 151, 152–53

Olivos Pact, 30, 35, 40, 71, 107, 150

Onganía, Juan Carlos, 38, 49; relations with judiciary, 39, 41, 60

Orgaz, Alfredo, 41

Otero, Mario, 97, 152–53, 211n78

Oyhanarte, Julio, 33, 35, 37, 180n23

Pacto Autonomista Liberal (PAL), 47–48
Pagano, Roberto, 102, 106, 109, 152
Página 12, 149
Pakistan, 12, 174n12
Panama, 175n28
Paraguay, 175n28
Pardo, Juan Ángel, 141
Partido Autonomista Nacional (PAN), 55, 56
Partido Demócrata (PD), 117–33, 204n28
Partido Intransigente (PI), 65
Partido Justicialista (PJ): in Corrientes, 47–48; defeat in 1997 federal elections, 54, 71, 72, 73–74, 76, 77, 79; and Impeachment Jury, 73–74, 75; in Mendoza, 117–33, 203n13, 205n56; and Olivos Pact of 1993, 30, 35; origin of, 58, 65; party discipline in, 53, 56, 58, 61–64, 65–68, 79, 99, 100, 104, 105–6, 146–47, 158, 163, 188n12, 203nn13,17; relations with Menem, 40–42, 54, 59, 61–64, 70, 146–47; relations with Perón, 56, 58; relations with Rodríguez Saá, 99–100, 105–6, 107, 108–15, 122; relations with UCR, 30, 59, 61, 65, 100–102, 106; in San Luis, 80, 85–86, 87, 89–90, 91, 98, 99–115, 118, 121, 122, 128, 140, 142, 146–47, 158, 163, 199n10, 202n8; and Supreme Court nominees, 33, 34–35, 36, 37, 41–42, 59; unified government under, 53, 61–64, 67–68, 99–104. *See also* Menem, Carlos; Perón, Juan Domingo
Partido Laborista, 58
Partido Revolucionario Institucional (PRI), 213n1
Partido Unión y Libertad (PUL), 88, 198n1, 202n62
party competition: under Alfonsín, 41, 54, 59, 61; and Attorney General's Office (Argentina), 74–77; and Federal Prosecutor in Charge of Administrative Investigations, 78–79; and Judicial Council (Argentina), 71–73; in Mendoza, 8, 79, 80, 85, 98, 100, 107, 115, 116–33, 159, 160–61, 165, 203nn13,17; after 1997 federal elections, 54, 71, 72, 73–74, 76, 77, 79; relationship to divided government, 15–16, 53, 54–55, 59, 61, 64, 79, 116; relationship to fragmentation of economic power, 14–15, 17–20, 81; relationship to party rotation in governorship, 116; relationship to rule of law/judicial autonomy, 3–4, 7–8, 9, 14, 15–17, 53, 54, 79, 81, 98, 115, 116, 124–31, 157, 158, 159–62, 164, 188n9, 198n4; in San Luis, 7–8, 100–102, 104, 105–6, 107; third parties, 100, 116, 117–33, 160–61
party discipline, 7–8, 15, 16, 52, 54, 157, 169, 216n4; in Chile, 160; in Córdoba, 159–60; in Mendoza, 120–22; in Partido Justicialista (PJ), 53, 56, 58, 61–64, 65–68, 79, 99, 100, 104, 105–6, 146–47, 158, 163, 188n12, 203nn13,17; relationship to electoral rules, 66–67; in Unión Cívica Radical Intransigente (UCRI), 58; in Unión Cívica Radical (UCR), 55, 65–67, 159–60. *See also* monolithic party control
party leaders, 16, 63–64, 65, 67, 105–6, 121, 161
party rotation in executive branch, 121, 122, 131, 158, 160–61; in Mendoza, 116, 119–20
Paz, Benjamín, 38
Peltier, Teresa, 121
Pérez Botti, Omar, 121, 203n13, 204n28
Pérez Hualde, Alejandro, 98
Perón, Juan Domingo, 181n30; and Constitution of 1949, 179; vs. Frondizi, 58, 60, 61, 68; indefinite reelection of, 179n6; line-item vetoes by, 68; vs. Long, 163; vs. Menem, 7, 29, 30, 33, 51, 53, 61, 64, 67, 68, 74; monolithic party control under, 41, 53, 56, 58, 60, 67, 79, 158, 163, 188n12; relations with judiciary, 6, 7, 28, 30, 31, 33, 38, 39, 40, 41, 44–45, 48–49, 50, 51, 53, 54, 56, 67, 180n13; relations with Partido Justicialista (PJ), 56, 58
Peronist Party. *See* Partido Justicialista
per saltum, 47, 64, 92
Peru, 64, 175n28
Pesce, Félix, 127
Petracchi, Enrique, 32, 37, 40, 42, 45, 47, 185n91
Pinochet, Augusto, 160
Pinzón, Jorge Néstor, 79
Poder Ciudadano (Citizen Power), 136, 140, 143, 145, 150, 153, 212n98
Portabella, Oscar, 98, 127, 155
Portugal, 171n2
positive political theory, 169
primogeniture, 18–19
Procedural Code of Argentina: Article 196 of, 75

property rights, 10, 17, 18, 20, 43, 81, 141, 146, 181–82
proportional representation (PR), 66–67, 121, 161
Przeworski, Adam, 16, 171n4
public prosecutors. *See* Attorney General's Office
Putnam, Robert, 22

Quantín, Norberto, 75
Quevedo Mendoza, Efrain, 130, 205n54
Quiroga Lavié, Humberto, 192nn63,66

radio: Radio Dimensión, 152–53; Radio Máxima, 153; Radio Nacional, 151
Rechtsstaat, 2
reform coalitions, 134–65; and civil society groups, 21, 134, 135–42, 144–46; and federal government, 146–49, 164; and information politics, 134, 135, 140, 145, 149–54; and international organizations, 134, 142–46; Keck and Sikkink on, 20, 21, 22, 135, 142, 144, 154, 175n37, 206n2; lawyers and judges in, 138–41, 144–45; and material leverage, 134, 135, 143, 146, 147–49; and the media, 22–23, 134, 135, 149–54; relationship to rule of law, 4, 8, 9, 15, 20–23, 133, 138, 159
Relly de Closa, Ruth, 91–92, 196n39, 209n47
Repetto, Roberto, 38
Reyes, Cipriano, 58
Río Negro, province of, 137, 199n13
Roberts, Owen, 162
Roca, Julio, 55
Rodríguez Saá, Adolfo: corruption in government of, 91, 93, 95, 106, 114, 146, 147–49, 151, 152, 199n10; court-packing by, 81, 82, 90, 95, 199n13; decrees used by, 108, 122; and *Diario de la República*, 85, 87, 92, 151, 152, 164, 208n27; and federal tax revenues, 148, 210n65; indefinite reelection of, 102, 103, 104, 107; and Industrial Promotion (IP) program, 84, 137, 146, 147–48, 149, 153, 163, 195n13; informal powers of, 106–15, 122, 200n21; vs. Long, 162–64; vs. Menem, 100, 104, 106, 107, 137, 146–47, 200n21; monolithic party control under, 80, 85–86, 87, 89–90, 91, 98, 99–115, 116, 128, 133, 146–47, 158, 159, 163, 193n1, 199n11, 200n17, 202n8; and *La Opinión*, 151; as party leader, 121; personal wealth of, 194n13; policies toward civil society groups, 136–38; policies toward the press, 150–52, 164, 202n63, 208n27; as president of Argentina, 198n1; reform coalition in opposition to, 8, 134–35, 136–38, 140–41, 142, 144–49, 150–54, 156, 159, 205n1; relations with Congress, 100–104, 106–15, 118, 122; relations with judiciary, 81, 85–86, 87–88, 91–92, 93–94, 96, 97, 98, 102, 104, 107, 110–12, 122, 126–27, 128, 132, 140–41, 142, 144–45, 153–54, 197n48, 198n4, 199n13; relations with Partido Justicialista (PJ), 99–100, 105–6, 107, 108–15, 122; relations with Unión Cívica Radical (UCR), 101–2
Rodríguez Saá, Alberto, 84, 104, 105, 137, 193n1, 198n1, 202n8, 205n1
Roger, Oscar Eduardo, 75
Roosevelt, Franklin, 41, 162, 178n62
Root, Hilton, 12
Rosas, Juan Manuel de, 179n5
Rosso, Graciela, 102, 114, 140
Rúa, Fernando de la, 140, 147, 149, 198n1
rule of law: construction of, 1, 3–5, 6, 7, 11, 14–23, 26, 28; definition of, 9, 10; Linz on, 2–3, 172n8, 173n2; relationship to balanced dispersal of power, 9, 14–20; relationship to civil society, 21; relationship to contract enforcement, 17, 43, 81–82, 85, 141, 146; relationship to democracy, 1–4; relationship to distribution of economic resources, 3–4, 7, 9, 14–15, 17–20, 81–85; relationship to divided government, 32, 41, 53–55, 58, 59, 72–74, 76, 77, 79, 116, 118–21, 122–24, 125, 158, 164, 167–69, 175n24; relationship to horizontal accountability, 10–11, 15–17; relationship to judicial autonomy, 9–12, 157; relationship to legislative branch, 3, 54, 67; relationship to party competition, 3–4, 7, 8, 9, 14, 15–17, 53, 54, 79, 81, 98, 115, 116, 124–31, 157, 158, 159–62, 164, 188n9; relationship to property rights, 10, 17, 18, 20, 43, 81, 141, 146, 181–82; relationship to reform coalitions, 4, 8, 9, 15, 20–23, 133, 138, 159; Stepan on, 2–3, 172n8, 173n2; in United States vs. Latin America, 1–2

Russia: vs. Argentina, 5; elections in, 2; ultra-presidentialism in, 5, 12; Yeltsin in, 173n11

Saadi, Vicente, 59
Sáenz Peña law of 1912, 179n1
salary protection, judges': in Constitution of Argentina, 30, 44; in Constitution of Mendoza, 80, 154; in Constitution of San Luis, 80; relationship to judicial autonomy, 25, 80; respect for, 44, 177n59, 179n4; in San Luis vs. Mendoza, 80, 81, 82, 89–90, 95
Salta, province of, 137, 199n13
Salvini, Hernán Amilton, 89
Samper, José, 97, 102, 105, 113, 199n11
San Juan, province of, 137, 147, 199n13
San Luis, province of: appointment process for judges in, 81, 82, 85–87, 95; Aptitude Evaluation Tribunal, 88; vs. Argentina, 4–5, 6, 8, 26, 83–84, 87, 90, 92, 100, 104, 106, 107, 134–35, 137, 157, 164; Asociaciones de Abogados, 110; Catholic Church in, 137; CELS report on, 209n49; civil law tradition in, 5, 80; concentration of economic power in, 7, 81, 83–85, 158–59, 160; Congress of, 100–104, 106, 107–15, 123; Constitutional Convention of 1987, 102–4; Economic Emergency Law, 90, 92, 95; elections in, 100–102, 105–6, 121; government corruption in, 91, 93, 95, 106, 114, 132, 146, 147–49, 152, 153, 199n10; informal practices vs. formal rules in, 80–81, 85, 87, 94, 95; Judicial Emergency Law of 1998, 88, 92, 95, 140, 207n26; judicial review in, 81, 82, 90–94, 95, 128–29, 198n4, 207n26; vs. Louisiana, state of, 162–64, 165; lower courts in, 85, 87, 88, 93–94; the media in, 85, 87, 92, 150–54, 164, 202n63, 208n27; monolithic party control in, 80, 85–86, 87, 89–90, 91, 98, 99–115, 116, 128, 133, 146–47, 158, 159, 163, 193n1, 199n11, 202n8; Nuestro Compromiso in, 100, 106; Partido Justicialista (PJ) in, 80, 85–86, 87, 89–90, 91, 98, 99–115, 118, 121, 122, 128, 140, 142, 146–47, 158, 163, 199n10, 202n8; party competition in, 7–8, 100–102, 104, 105–6, 107, 198n4; reform coalition in, 8, 134–35, 136–38, 140–41, 142, 144–49, 150–54, 156, 159, 205n1; relations with federal government, 146–49, 164; salary protection for judges in, 81, 89–90, 95, 140, 141, 144, 152; Spanish colonial legacy in, 5, 80; tenure of judges in, 81, 82, 87–89, 95, 128; Unión Cívica Radical (UCR) in, 100–104, 106, 142, 198n5. *See also* House of Representatives (San Luis); Rodríguez Saá, Adolfo; San Luis and Mendoza, comparisons between; Senate (San Luis); Supreme Court of San Luis
San Luis and Mendoza, comparisons between, 120, 154, 156, 157, 164; regarding Accounting Tribunals, 113–14, 132; regarding appointment process for judges, 81, 82, 85–87, 95; regarding constitutions, 80–81, 90, 93, 98, 107, 122, 195n20; regarding divided/unified government, 100, 116, 118, 122; regarding economic resources, 81–85; regarding executive branch, 122; regarding judicial autonomy, 4–5, 6–8, 26, 79, 81–82, 83, 85, 86–87, 90, 94–98, 115, 126–28, 132, 165; regarding judicial review, 81, 82, 90–94, 95, 128–29, 198n4; regarding Partido Justicialista (PJ), 105, 121–22; regarding salary protection for judges, 80, 81, 82, 89–90, 95; regarding Senates, 123; regarding State Prosecutors, 112, 129, 132; regarding Supreme Courts, 81, 89, 92–93, 95; regarding tenure of judges, 81, 82, 87–89, 95, 128, 195n20
San Luis Bar Association, 86, 108, 109–10, 111–12, 138, 140–41, 142, 144, 153
San Luis Colegio Forense, 109–10
San Luis Judges' Association, 145
San Luis Psychologists' Association, 138
San Luis Teachers' Union, 138
Sansó, Gerónimo, 145
Santa Cruz, province of, 104, 199n13
Santiago del Estero, province of, 137, 199n13
Sarmiento, Domingo, 54
Sawers, Larry, 84, 210n58,59,62,65
Schlesinger, Arthur M., Jr., 163
Schumpeter, Joseph, 2
Schwartz, Herman, 24
Secretaría de Inteligencia del Estado (SIDE), 33–34
Senate (Argentina): approval of FNIA head by, 78; approval of lower court nominees by, 188n15; approval of Supreme Court nominees by, 30, 34, 35–36, 62, 71; distri-

bution of seats in, 61, 62; and Judicial Council, 72
Senate (Mendoza), 118–19, 123–24, 125, 126–27, 129, 131, 205n54
Senate (San Luis), 103, 112, 113, 114, 123
Sergnese, Carlos, 88, 110, 111
Shugart, Matthew Soberg: on executive authority, 67, 175n27, 200n21; on executive decrees, 69–70
Sikkink, Kathryn, 20, 21, 22, 135, 142, 144, 154, 175n37, 206n2
Smulovitz, Catalina, 51
Social Forum for Justice (Foro Social por la Justicia), 140, 150
spatial model of Supreme Court independence, 167–69
Staib, Alberto, 124–25, 126, 127, 132, 154
State Prosecutor, 17; in Mendoza, 112, 116, 129–31, 205nn54,58; in San Luis, 100, 107, 132; tenure protection for, 112–13, 129
Stepan, Alfred: on rule of law, 2–3, 172n8, 173n2
Stornelli, Carlos, 64, 76, 149
Supreme Court of Argentina, 7, 28–52, 184nn75,78, 185n86, 187n115; *Administración de Impuestos Internos* decision, 48; *Aerolineas Argentinas* decision, 46–47, 64; *Aramayo* decision, 49; *Arlandini* decision, 48; *Avellaneda Huergo* decision, 48; *Balbín* decision, 45; *Budano* decision, 49; *Calvete* decision, 43; *Chiaparrone* decision, 43; Chief Justices, 38; *Colella* decision, 68, 190n45; Constitutional provisions for, 30, 41; and de facto doctrine, 32, 48–49, 50, 178n1, 179n4; *Dufourq* decision, 49; *Egidio Ziella* decision, 48–49; and emergency powers of government, 32, 46, 70; *Godoy* decision of 1990, 49; impeachment of justices, 36, 40–41; *La Prensa* decision, 45; and line-item veto, 68, 190n45; *Lockman* decision, 49; vs. lower courts, 39, 42, 46, 47, 64; under military governments, 31–32, 44, 45, 48–49, 50, 58–59; *Municipalidad de la Capital* decision, 43; and Olivos Pact, 30, 35, 40; *Peralta* decision, 46, 70–71, 185n92; under Perón, 28, 31, 44–45, 48–49; per saltum used by, 47, 64, 92; *Radio Nacional* decision, 186n96; *Ríos* decision, 43, 184n75; *Rolón Zappa* decision, 45, 46, 70; *Sejean* decision, 45; Senate approval of nominees, 30, 34, 35–36, 62, 71; size of, 25, 27, 33, 34, 40, 41–42, 50, 58, 59, 62, 139, 150; *Soengas* decision, 186n96; *Sojo* decision, 44; *Timerman* decision, 45; *Unión Ferroviaria* decision, 186n96. *See also* appointment process for judges; Attorney General's Office; judicial review; salary protection, judges'; tenure protection, judges'
Supreme Court of Mendoza, 98, 120, 128–29, 154, 195n28; *Campoy* decision, 92; *Merga* decision, 92; vs. San Luis, 81, 89, 92–93, 95
Supreme Court of San Luis, 80, 82, 87–88, 90, 141, 152, 207n26; vs. Mendoza, 81, 89, 92–93, 95; per saltum used by, 92
Suriani, Osvaldo, 87, 97, 102

Taiwan, 20
television, relation to reform coalition, 150, 152, 153–54
tenure protection: for Accounting Tribunal (Argentina), 77; for Accounting Tribunal (Mendoza), 131; for Accounting Tribunal (San Luis), 113; for Attorney General's Office (Argentina), 74–75; for Federal Prosecutor of Administrative Investigations (FNIA), 46, 54
tenure protection, judges,' 30, 38–41, 180n16, 195n28; under Alfonsín, 39–40, 50, 182n53; under Cámpora, 38–39, 40; in Constitution of Argentina, 30; in Constitution of Mendoza, 80; in Constitution of San Luis, 80; under Frondizi, 39, 40, 58; in Mendoza, 120, 129; under Menem, 39–41, 50, 74–75; under military governments, 38–39, 50; under Perón, 38, 39, 40, 50, 56; relationship to judicial autonomy, 24–25, 27, 36, 38–41, 50, 80; in San Luis vs. Mendoza, 81, 82, 87–89, 95, 128, 195n20
Timerman, Jacobo, 45, 185n85
Tocqueville, Alexis de: on democracy, 18; on distribution of economic resources, 19; on newspapers and civil society, 22; on primogeniture, 19
Transparency International, 212n98
Tres Puntos, 153
Trocella, María Gloria, 142
TVC Puntana, 152

UCeDé. *See* Unión del Centro Democrático
UCR. *See* Unión Cívica Radical (UCR)
UCRI. *See* Unión Cívica Radical Intransigente
UCRP. *See* Unión Cívica Radical del Pueblo
Ueltschi, Ernesto, 117, 118
UNDP. *See* United Nations Development Program
unified government, 7–8, 16, 31, 52, 61–64, 157, 163, 190n43; vs. divided government, 41, 53–54, 55, 56, 57, 58, 64, 70–71, 72, 73–74, 76, 77, 78, 79, 158, 159–60, 161, 167–69; relationship to number of political parties, 65–66. *See also* monolithic party control
Unión Cívica Radical del Pueblo (UCRP), 58, 188n14
Unión Cívica Radical Intransigente (UCRI), 58, 86, 117, 188n14
Unión Cívica Radical (UCR): and Concordancia, 56, 57; in Córdoba, 159–60; and Impeachment Jury, 73–74, 75; in Mendoza, 86, 89, 117–33, 124, 204n28; and Olivos Pact of 1993, 30, 35; origin of, 55; party discipline in, 55, 65–67, 159–60; relations with Frepaso, 65–66; relations with PJ, 30, 59, 61, 65, 100–102, 106; in San Luis, 100–104, 106, 142, 198n5; and Supreme Court nominees, 32, 34, 36, 37, 41, 59. *See also* Alfonsín, Raúl
Unión del Centro Democrático (UCeDé), 62, 64, 65, 118
United Nations Development Program (UNDP), 143–44
United States: vs. Argentina, 39, 41, 66, 161; vs. Chile, 161; Constitution of, 13, 30, 42; Democratic Party, 162, 163, 215n18; distribution of economic resources in, 19; divided government in, 161, 162; Jim Crow laws in, 173n3; judicial autonomy in, 161–62, 165, 178nn62,63; Line-item Veto Act, 190n45; party competition in, 157, 159, 161–62; party discipline in, 163; Republican Party, 162, 163; Roosevelt administration, 41, 162; rule of law in, 1–2, 161–62; state of Louisiana, 157, 159, 162–64, 165; unified government in, 162
United States Agency for International Development (USAID), 143, 176nn40,43
United States Supreme Court, 24, 161, 177n54, 179n10; *Bowers v. Hardwick* decision, 177n55; *California v. Bakke* decision, 177n55; Justice Harry Blackmun, 177n55; and Line-item Veto Act, 190n45; relations with Franklin Roosevelt, 41, 162, 178n62; *Roe v. Wade* decision, 177n55
Universidad Nacional de San Luis, 142
Uriburu, José, 39, 48, 56, 57
Urquiza, Justo José de, 31
Uruguay: vs. Argentina, 23; distribution of economic resources in, 18, 19; informal practices vs. formal rules in, 23
USAID. *See* United States Agency for International Development

Vacca, Domingo, 110–11, 114
Valenzuela, Arturo, 160
Vanossi, Jorge, 48, 51, 63, 70, 191n54
Vázquez, Adolfo, 35, 36, 37, 181n36
Venezuela, 1, 12, 18, 23
Ventura, Adrián, 149, 192n66
Verbitsky, Horacio, 59, 135, 149
Victorica, Benjamín, 38

Weingast, Barry, 162; on asymmetric equilibrium, 11, 183n59; on rule of law, 11–12
Williamson, Oliver E., 11
Wiñazki, Miguel, 97, 137–38, 148, 151–52, 153

Yrigoyen, Hipólito, 55, 57

Zaffaroni, Eugenio Raúl, 45, 94, 109, 110, 153, 184n84, 198n4, 201n41
Zapata Mercader, Jorge, 121, 129, 202n4